Rural Communities

Rural Communities

LEGACY AND CHANGE
Second Edition

Cornelia Butler Flora
Jan L. Flora
With Susan Fey

Westview
PRESS

A Member of the Perseus Books Group

Copyright © 2004 by Westview Press, A Member of the Perseus Books Group

Published in 2003 in the United States of America by Westview Press, 5500 Central Avenue, Boulder, Colorado 80301–2877, and in the United Kingdom by Westview Press, 12 Hid's Copse Road, Cumnor Hill, Oxford OX2 9JJ.

Find us on the world wide web at www.westviewpress.com

Westview Press books are available at special discounts for bulk purchases in the United States by corporations, institutions, and other organizations. For more information, please contact the Special Markets Department at the Perseus Books Group, 11 Cambridge Center, Cambridge, MA 02142, or call (617) 252-5298, (800) 255-1514 or email j.mccrary@ perseusbooks.com.

Library of Congress Cataloging-in-Publication Data

Flora, Cornelia Butler, 1943-
   Rural communities : legacy and change.—2nd ed. / Cornelia Butler Flora, Jan L. Flora, with Susan Fey.
      p.   cm.
   Rev. ed. of : Rural communities / Cornelia Butler Flora ... [et al]. 1992.
   Includes bibliographical references and index.
   ISBN 0-8133-9769-3 (pbk. : alk. paper)—ISBN 0-8133-4051-9 (hardcover : alk. paper)
   1. United States—Rural conditions.   2. Sociolgy, Rural.   I. Flora, Jan L., 1941-   II. Fey, Susan.   III. Rural communities.   IV. Title
HN65R85 2003
307.72'0973—dc21

2003006400

The paper used in this publication meets the requirements of the American National Standard for Permanence of Paper for Printed Library Materials Z39.48–1984.

Designed by Reginald Thompson
Typeface used in this text: Bembo

10   9   8   7   6   5   4   3   2   1

Contents

Tables and Illustrations

Boxes

1

The Rural Landscape

Christine Walden grew up in paradise. Christine, the daughter of schoolteachers, spent her childhood in Mammoth Lakes, California, surrounded by the majestic peaks, lush forests, and crystal-clear lakes of the Sierra Nevada range. The town, population 2,000, provided a nurturing environment. Changes began occurring in 1954 when an all-weather road and a double chair lift opened, beckoning skiers to the north face of Mammoth Mountain. By 2000, the town's population was more than three times what it had been in 1970, the year Christine was born. Golf courses replaced horse pastures, as befit a major tourism destination. Christine now teaches in the same school district that her parents did, but she no longer lives in Mammoth Lakes. Land development and speculation have driven housing costs beyond what a local teacher's salary can support. So Christine lives in Bishop and commutes forty miles each way to work.

Wade Skidmore grew up working in the mines. Part of the fifth generation of Skidmores to live in McDowell County, West Virginia, Wade's childhood was shaped by what was underground rather than by the slopes of the rugged Appalachian Mountains. He attended school only through the tenth grade; working in the mines did not require a high level of education and offered him a chance to work at his own pace. For a time, the work was steady and the pay was good. Then coal-loading machines came along—machines that could do the work of fifty men. Then some veins started giving out. The coal company changed first to long-wall and then to open-pit mining, cutting of the tops of mountains with huge machines. Wade was laid off, and the company left the town where he lived, which it had built. The company no longer maintained the water system, and the house was expensive to maintain. Wade's children were confronted with substandard housing, water pollution from mine runoff, raw sewage in the streams, poor schools, and few opportunities to use the knowledge and skills they had. McDowell County, which lost more than 22 percent of its population between 1990 and 2000, and Wade Skidmore represent a region and a people trapped in persistent poverty. To make things worse, devastating floods swept the county in 2002, seriously damaging the

Skidmore home built along the banks of the Tug Fork of the Big Sandy River—
the only flat land around. Most of the communities in McDowell County were destroyed, and it is projected that the recovery effort will continue until 2012.

Maurice and Mae Campbell face a life-changing decision. Their farm near
Irwin, Iowa, inherited from Mae's parents, may lead them deep into debt because
they need new equipment to replace their combination harvester and planters,
which are nearly forty years old and constantly breaking down. When hog prices
were low in the late 1990s, they regretfully closed their hog-raising operation.
They fed their hogs on corn and soybeans that they raised themselves and sold the
finished pigs to the stockyard in Sioux City, Iowa. But that stockyard has since
closed, and the Campbells are raising only corn and soybeans. Unfortunately, the
amount of land they own is not enough to convince the local banker to lend
them money to buy new equipment. To get the loan, they would have to buy or
rent land from their neighbors.

The Campbells have a few other options to consider as well. Some of the
Campbells' neighbors have contracts with Murphy Farms, a large conglomerate,
to raise feeder pigs, which also require a large investment in hog houses and manure pits. However, the bank readily lends them money because they have ten-
year contracts with the conglomerate. Such a contract would relieve the Campbells of the risks of the fluctuating hog prices but would carry alternate risks,
involving possible manure spills or increasing energy costs. Additionally, with such
a contract, they would no longer purchase their feed additives, seed, fertilizers, and
herbicides at the Farm Services Cooperative in Irwin; Murphy Farms would deliver their feed on a regular basis. If they decided to expand their farm operation,
they would buy their new equipment from Robinson Implement, Inc., in Irwin.

Another alternative was presented to them by a friend they met through Practical Farmers of Iowa, a group interested in sustainable agriculture. Their friend raises
hogs in hoop houses and sells them to Neiman Farms, which markets to high-end
restaurants and mail-order consumers. This takes less capital, but it requires a lot of
skill and learning—and if the hogs are not the right quality, they will not be purchased. This kind of contract also has its risks. Mae holds a job in the office of the
local consolidated school, which gives her summers off and, most important, health
insurance. Maurice feels as if he "just has to farm." All of these options leave the
Campbells with more questions: Should they go into debt to get more land and
equipment or to construct the infrastructure to raise contract hogs? Should they
risk an innovative way of producing "happy hogs" for a specialty market? Or should
they rent out their land or find a farm management company so that someone else
will farm it and sell their equipment? (Mae's siblings would never agree to sell the
land.) In any of those cases, the new operators would probably not buy locally. Or
should they replace aging machinery, rent land from retired farmers, and cut back
their paid employment during planting and harvest seasons?

Billie Jo Davis Williams and her husband, Clayton Williams, are moving to Atlanta. Raised in Eatonton, Georgia, they grew up enjoying the gentle hills and dense stands of loblolly pine in Putnam County. Eatonton is home—both the Williams and Davis families go back to plantation days. But Billie Jo cannot find a job. She just finished a degree in business administration at Fort Valley State College, and Putnam County is growing rapidly—it grew by more than 33 percent between 1990 and 2000. But there are few jobs for African American women in Eatonton, other than in the textile factory or as domestic workers for the rich families who have built retirement homes on the lake. And the textile factories are moving to other countries in order to employ cheaper labor. Clayton settled into a factory job right out of high school, but he figures he can find work in Atlanta. It seems strange. Eatonton has been more successful than most communities in adapting to change—shifting from cotton to dairying to manufacturing and now to recreation/retirement economies. However, most African Americans have a hard time finding jobs offering more than minimum-wages.

★ ★ ★

Which is the *real* rural America: ski slopes of California, mines of West Virginia, farms in Iowa, or exurban resort and manufacturing communities in Georgia? Family farms and small farming communities dominate our images of rural America, in part because politicians, lobbyists, and the media cultivate those rural icons, supporting the myth that agricultural policy is rural policy. In fact, rural areas embrace ski slopes, mines, manufacturing, farms, retirement communities, American Indian reservations, bedroom communities, and much, much more. On average, in the twenty-first century, rural communities differ more from each other than they do from urban areas.

The diversity found among rural communities extends to the issues that emerge as each responds to the social and economic changes underway. Some communities, which are rural and remote, share the concerns of Irwin, wondering if their population will become too small to support a *community*. The *amenity-based community* of Mammoth Lakes faces *rapid growth*. Its citizens are grappling with how to protect both the environment and the small-town character they value. In Eatonton, Georgia, which is a long commute from several large urban centers, the growth has been substantial because of the expansion of the resort economy and manufacturing, but Eatonton's black citizens have not shared equally in its success. Eatonton's population is highly transient, and its poverty rate remains higher than that of the state of Georgia as a whole. Those living in McDowell County face poverty and high out migration, despite the wealth that the mines produced. Nearly one-third of the population falls below the poverty level, and median income is nearly $13,000 less than in the rest of West Virginia.

Despite the stereotype that life in the country is simpler, rural people face many of the same issues and concerns urban residents do, plus issues related to dispersion and distance. Indeed, rural and urban areas are linked. The garbage produced in New York City may find its way into landfills in West Virginia. Italian sausage served in Chicago could be made from hogs fattened on Iowa corn, grown with fertilizers that increase productivity but that may endanger rural water supplies. A housing boom in San Francisco creates jobs in the lumber industry in Oregon. However, the jobs last only as long as the forests. Air-quality concerns in Boston could shut down coal mines in West Virginia.

This book examines the diversity of rural America: its communities, the social issues they face as the twenty-first century begins, and the histories that explain those issues. It also addresses ways that different rural communities use their history and their increasing connectedness to creatively address those issues.

Defining Rural

Giving a place a particular characteristic by thus "naming" it suggests how people and institutions act toward it. Government-established labels for places are generally for administrative purposes: determining which places are eligible for specific government programs. Box 1.1 shows different governmental definitions of "rural" and provides a Web site address that shows the most recent nonmetropolitan county designations.

When scholars establish labels, it is generally for analytic purposes, but because governments collect data, scholars often use government-established categories. Media and advertisers use place labels such as "rural" to evoke particular images. In the past, small size and isolation combined to produce relatively homogeneous rural cultures, economies based on natural resources, and a strong sense of local identity. But globalization, connectivity, and lifestyle changes accompanying shifting income distributions have altered the character of rural communities. They are neither as isolated nor as homogeneous as they once were.

Isolation

Isolation is part of the rural image. There is a belief that rural people live out their entire lives in the town in which they were born, with some people going no further than a regional trade center or the state capital throughout their lifetime, but in actuality this was never true. Loggers, miners, farmers, and a host of others routinely moved to wherever they could find work or land. Other rural people were, in fact, isolated. In parts of McDowell County, mountain men and women lived in

---

BOX 1.1 Designations of Rural

County Designations

Metropolitan counties: Those with more than 50,000 people within a county, mostly in an urban core

Nonmetropolitan counties: Those with less than 50,000 people and/or no urban core

Micropolitan: Those with 10,000 to 49,999 people with an urban core.

Place Designations

Rural (U.S. Census): Open countryside or towns of less than 2,500 outside urbanized areas.

Rural (Statistics Canada): Nonurban; not continuously built-up areas with populations of 1,000 people or more and a density of less than 400 people per square kilometer.

Eligibility Designations

Sample population size cutoffs for qualifying for rural programs (definitions fixed by statute made by Congress or regulation made by the administration).

- *Rural housing:* 20,000 or less
- *Telecom loans:* 5,000 or less
- *Water and waste grants:* 10,000 or less
- *Intermediary relending loans:* 25,000 or less
- *Rural business Programs:* 50,000 or less outside a metropolitan area
- *Electric:* Prior to 2000: 1,500 or less in 1993
- *As of 2000:* 2,500 or less

"hollows" in the hills, living on wild game and part-time construction work or cutting and selling wood. They created a rich culture of self-sufficiency. Canals, railroads, highways, and airways have altered much of rural isolation. Improved road systems have also changed the occupations and spending patterns of rural people. Those living near urban areas often commute to work, living in one town and working in another. They purchase many of their material goods in suburban malls.

Communication technologies have had an even greater effect in reducing isolation. Electronic chat rooms link rural residents with people from around the world who share their interests. Rural people now watch opera from New York, football games from San Francisco, ballet from Houston, and congressional deliberations from Washington, D.C. over satellite dishes. Rural people have become as literate, informed, and enriched as their urban counterparts. There is still a rural-urban connectivity divide, however. Many residents on reservations in the Great Plains do not have phone service, much less broadband Internet connectivity. Wireless strategies based on satellites still present problems in mountainous areas. Although the isolation that distance imposes is much less than it once was, communities that are *rural and remote* and those that are *persistently poor* are much more isolated than rural residents in areas of urban sprawl and high rural amenities.

Ethnicity and Change in Rural America

Ioway Sioux Indians were some of the original settlers along the rich river bottoms of the Nishnabotna River in Shelby County, Iowa. In Mono County, California, the Northern and Owens Valley Paiute walked through what is now Mammoth Lakes as part of their sacred rituals to ensure success in their hunting and gathering. Shawnee and Delaware occasionally hunted in what is now McDowell County, West Virginia. Creek Indians occupied mid-Georgia, including Putnam County, prior to being forced west, first by the Cherokee and then by the Europeans. The U.S. government then forcibly removed the Cherokee to Oklahoma, where many lost their lives on the Trail of Tears *(Nunna daul Tsuny)*.

First commercial and then industrial interests brought Europeans, Africans, and Asians to rural America; national interests encouraged Europeans, in particular, to settle land. Fur trappers for British, Spanish, French, and then American trading companies, spurred by the Lewis and Clark expedition, pushed westward across Canada and the United States. Fur trading was only a prelude to the development of settled agriculture.

African Americans were critical to the land-extensive, labor-intensive agricultural system of the South. Prior to the Civil War, African Americans escaping slavery from Missouri and Arkansas crossed over Shelby County on their way to freedom. African Americans who had worked in the coal mines in Birmingham, Alabama, moved to McDowell County to open those mines, even though their children attended segregated schools until the late 1950s. Asians, particularly Chinese, who helped build the western half of the intercontinental railroad, participated in the mining boom in Mammoth Lakes in the 1880s and 1890s. When they were barred from mining, they provided essential services, such as cooking and washing, to the miners.

Spanish and Native American cultures occupied much of the West long before U.S. expansion. The abolition of slavery left African American families scattered throughout a rural South extending from the Atlantic Ocean to central Texas and as far north as Kansas and Missouri. Migrant workers from the Deep South and Mexico followed the harvest as far north as Maine in the East and Washington State in the West. More recently, as a result of the war in Southeast Asia, refugees from Vietnam, Laos, and Cambodia, including very distinct cultures such as the Hmong, have moved to rural areas. Like the Mexicans, they also took jobs that U.S.-born rural residents were unwilling to fill, such as in meat-packing plants in rural areas. Immigrants saved money by having many workers per household and by keeping their consumption low. Although some stayed in the rural Midwest, other Asian refugees used their modest savings to move to urban or coastal areas, excelling in both fishing on the Gulf of Mexico and in raising vegetables around large cities.

As other international conflicts create refugees, migrants from the Sudan, Bosnia, and now Afghanistan settle in rural communities as well as in large cities. This changes the religious as well as the racial composition of areas that were once extremely homogeneous.

Defining Community

Thus far, all definitions and descriptions of rural areas have focused on counties, as the smallest geographic unit for which data are readily available and comparable. Yet people typically act through communities. As of the 2000 census, nearly 5 million rural people lived in communities of fewer than 2,500 residents. Demographers can count communities, but sociologists have a much harder time defining just what a community is. In this section, we look at the concept of community, the definition used in this book, and the extent to which our study of rural communities relates to urban communities.

The Concept of Community

Sociologists use the term "community" in several different ways, all of which focus on groups of people. In one use of the term, "community" refers to a place, a location in which members of a group interact with one another. A second use of the term looks at the social system itself, the organization or set of organizations through which a group of people meet their needs. Finally, sociologists also use the word "community" to describe a shared sense of identity held by a group of people who may or may not share the same geographic space.

The concept of community is often based on a shared sense of place. This sense of place involves relationships with the people, cultures, and environments, both natural and built, associated with a particular area. For many rural residents, the area associated with a particular place may be very different from any area defined by the political boundaries of town or even county. Stereotypes of rural communities conjure up images of isolated, relatively self-sufficient, sometimes backward or unsophisticated cultures. The stereotype may never have been entirely accurate, but there was a time when rural people turned to their communities for nearly everything. People lived, worked, worshipped, shopped, banked, sent their children to school, and socialized all in the same place. When the community's economy rested on a single resource, such as mining or farming, people even had a shared sense of what it took to make a living and run a household.

These three elements of community—location, social system, and common identity—are increasingly separate. In the past, a community offered a place that housed a set of social institutions (schools, churches, governments, businesses) through which people's needs could be met, and a place where people could share a sense of identity. However, improved transportation has made us more mobile, and telecommunications now put us in touch with a wider circle of acquaintances. Some people feel a sense of community from those who do similar things or share common values, not from those living in the same town. Thus, we consider both communities of place and communities of interest. A group of high-energy physicists, for example, might be a community of interest. These people share a common identity—they interact through meetings, journals, e-mail, or telephone—yet they are dispersed throughout the world.

The rural landscape may not have changed as much over the past century as has the social organization of rural communities. Cars enable people to live in one town, work in another, and shop in yet a third. Better roads have allowed schools to consolidate, which has led to social institutions that may be less attached to their communities, both physically and socially. As rural communities broaden their economic activity, people's work roles become very different from one another and much less publicly visible. Thus, rural people, like urbanites, are known less by what they do than by what they consume.

Our definition of "community" applies to both rural and urban areas. Communities may have political boundaries, or they may simply have social ones. Communities may be recognized politically, through local governments and the power to tax their residents. They may also be informal groupings of households—neighborhoods—within the larger city. Issues can cause neighborhoods to band together to demand better services from the city just as they inspire rural communities to take control over their economic future. Although the focus in this book is on rural communities, many of the topics are immediately relevant to communities within urban settings as well.

In this book, we talk primarily about communities of place, although they are crosscut by communities of interest. A geographic community may or may not provide the social system through which its members' needs are met. It may or may not provide a sense of identity for its members. What a geographic community does provide is what some sociologists now call "locality," a geographically defined place where people interact. How people interact shapes the structures and institutions of the locality. Those structures and institutions in turn shape the activities of the people who interact. Consider your sense of community. Where do you go to college? Where did you grow up? Where does your family live? Or where do you vacation? These communities of place relate you to people and the environment, both natural and built. Or is your main community one of interest? Your sports team, your fraternity or sorority, or your political party may provide you with a sense of belonging and of purpose.

Communities and Resources

Every community, however rural, isolated, or poor, has resources within it. When those resources, or assets, are invested to create new resources, they become *capital.* We have found it useful when looking at communities to focus on six types of capital: cultural, human, social, financial/built, natural, and political. These resources can either enhance or detract from one other. Furthermore, resources can be transformed from one form of capital to another. When one type of capital is emphasized over all others, the other resources are *decapitalized,* and the economy, environment, or social equity can be thus compromised.

Cultural capital includes values and approaches to life that have both economic and noneconomic implications. Cultural capital can be thought of as the filter through which people live their lives, the daily or seasonal rituals they observe, and the way they regard the world around them. The socialization process serves to transmit values and cultural capital from a group to its members. Cultural capital is used by elites to gain strategic class-based ties for their children, thereby excluding the children of others who lack those resources and the necessary strategic vision to move their children up the social ladder (Bourdieu 1986).

Human capital is the skills and abilities of each individual within a community. It includes potentials, like a good ear for music, and acquired skills, such as playing the trumpet. Formal and informal education contribute to human capital. One's health and leadership skills are also part of human capital.

Social capital includes the networks, norms of reciprocity, and mutual trust that exist among and within groups and communities. It contributes to a sense of a common identity and shared future. Community social capital facilitates groups' working together. Both bonding (multiple linkages to enforce norms and encourage trust) and bridging (single-purpose linkages) forms of social capital are important for community prosperity and sustainability.

Financial capital consists of money that is used for investment rather than consumption. *Investment* means using a purchase or a financial instrument to create additional value. Financial capital is important for communities and individuals within them because it can be transformed into *built capital:* factories, schools, roads, restored habitat, community centers, and the like, all of which contribute to building other capitals for communities.

Natural capital is the landscape, air, water, soil, and biodiversity of both plants and animals. It can be consumed or extracted for immediate profit, or it can be a continuing resource for communities of place.

Political capital is the ability of a group to influence the distribution of resources within a social unit, including helping set the agenda for what resources are available and who is eligible to receive them. Political capital includes organization, connections, voice and power. Rural communities have relatively little political capital. The ability of *commodity organizations*, such as the National Corn Growers or National Pork Producers, to channel government funds to large producers is not the same as political capital for rural communities.

Rural Communities and Change

Rural communities have never been insulated from the social and economic change under way in the broader society. The interstate highway system, started by President Dwight D. Eisenhower in the 1950s as a national security measure, had a profound effect on rural communities. For example, people can live in Eatonton and work in Atlanta.

Telecommunications have broken the isolation experienced in remote regions. Irwin has several *e-based businesses.* Increased competition with foreign products led manufacturers to abandon urban labor markets for rural ones during the 1970s, only to abandon those for even cheaper labor overseas a decade later. With the North American Free Trade Agreement (NAFTA) and the World Trade Organization (WTO), the twenty-first century is seeing even greater movement of low-wage manufacturing to less developed countries. Mexico, the low-wage country in NAFTA, is today experiencing an exodus of jobs to China, where wages are considerably lower than in Mexico. Thus, for example, nothing easily replaces mining in McDowell County. Increasing affluence has led to more decisions on where to live being based on lifestyle than on jobs alone. As the affluent choose their lifestyle, the less affluent move in behind them to support that lifestyle, as in the case of Mammoth Lakes.

The rural profiles that opened this chapter illustrate some of these differences among rural communities and the impact of those differences on people's lives. The problems Christine Walden faces arise from the rapid growth occurring in Mammoth Lakes. Growth in the exurban town of Eatonton has not greatly benefited African American citizens such as Billie Jo Williams. Wade Skidmore, the miner from McDowell County, finds his family trapped in poverty. Maurice and Mae Campbell see their options to farm decreased through farm concentration and international competition. These four patterns—rapid growth based on natural amenities, rapid growth based on nearness to urban areas, persistent poverty, and rural and remote location—provide a useful structure with which to compare communities, the capitals they have, and impact that changes in market, state, and civil society have on them.

Amenity-Based Rapid Growth

Mammoth Lakes has always revolved around its natural capital, though its population varied as the economic activity of the region shifted from mining to timber to hiking and fishing and finally to skiing. Today, Mammoth Lakes is one of many rural communities in high-amenity areas struggling with the problems of rapid growth: high in-migration, high housing costs, increasing taxes that force long-term residents out of the community, and a growing migrant population attracted by jobs in the service economy.

Rapid development affects natural capital as well. Water used for commercial development lowers lakes and decreases the flow of area streams, threatening the very wildlife that beckons hunters and fishers each summer. Forests and meadows are disappearing under condominiums and parking lots, and sewage has become a serious problem. Increased use of the land also contributes to soil erosion and to a general degradation of nearby wilderness areas.

Depending on the specific character of the amenities, such areas may attract younger adults interested in active sports, as is the case of Mammoth Lakes, or they may primarily attract retirees. The two patterns sometimes shade into one another when people regularly visit a particular place for recreation and decide to retire these. Communities such as Mammoth Lakes are growing because of the natural amenities they provide. Box 1.2 provides a map that shows the natural amenities areas of the country.

Persistent Poverty Communities

McDowell County is one of many rural counties struggling with low incomes and the problems of persistent poverty. As the mining companies pulled out, they left families who had known nothing but mining for generations. Illiteracy is high, as is infant mortality. Doctors, dentists, and other professionals are hard to find. Young people see little reason to invest effort in school because there are no jobs to prepare for. Communities find it hard to attract businesses; there is no tax base with which to build the needed roads, bridges, and schools. Those who can leave do. Those who can't leave simply make do.

BOX 1.2   Natural Amenities Areas of the Country

Natural amenities scale

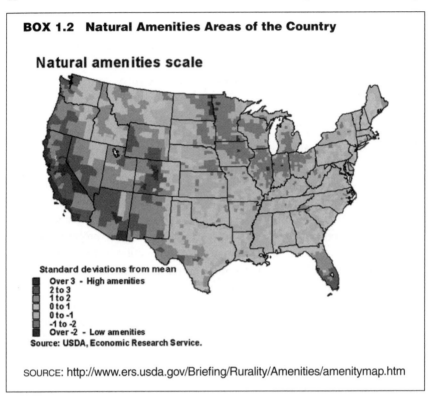

Standard deviations from mean
- ■ Over 3 - High amenities
- 2 to 3
- 1 to 2
- 0 to 1
- 0 to -1
- -1 to -2
- ■ Over -2 - Low amenities

Source: USDA, Economic Research Service.

SOURCE: http://www.ers.usda.gov/Briefing/Rurality/Amenities/amenitymap.htm

McDowell County is among the 363 *nonmetropolitan counties* classified as persistently poor counties. Ninety percent of these counties are found in the sixteen states shown on the map in Box 1.3. Nearly 13.4 percent of rural people in these counties had income levels below the 2000 poverty level, established as $20,550 for a family of three. Many of these counties have been successful in attracting and creating jobs. In some cases, they have experienced population increases. Although poverty decreased in these counties, particularly in Appalachia and the Mississippi Delta during the 1990s, there are still substantial proportions of the population with low incomes.

Rural and Remote

The term "rural and remote" refers to counties that have small populations and are far from metropolitan centers. Often they are losing population. The map in Box 1.4 shows that most of these counties are located in the upper Great Plains. They are home to a little more than one-fourth of the nation's nonmetropolitan population. For the most part, these populations are well educated and have enjoyed

BOX 1.3 Persistently Poor Counties

Nonmetro persistent poverty counties, 1990*

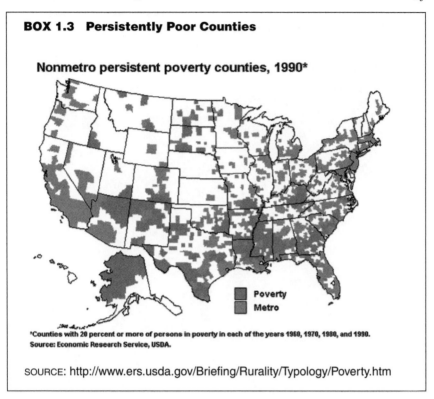

*Counties with 20 percent or more of persons in poverty in each of the years 1960, 1970, 1980, and 1990.
Source: Economic Research Service, USDA.

SOURCE: http://www.ers.usda.gov/Briefing/Rurality/Typology/Poverty.htm

relatively high average incomes in the past. Jobs have not grown fast enough, however, to replace those lost. Some ask whether the residents of this region will become the new poor.

Rapid Growth Exurban

Communities within commuting distance of large metropolitan areas, such as Eatonton, face a different set of problems. Urban sprawl threatens their natural, financial, and social capital. A map showing commuting areas is provided in Box 1.5. As farmland gives way to development, new services are required. The tax base does not expand as fast as the needs of the growing population. Although developers make money, local governments struggle to keep basic services in place for community residents. There is often disagreement among residents as to what constitutes adequate services. Newcomers and long-term residents often have different expectations for schools, the role of local government, and appropriate neighborly behavior and different tolerances for barnyard or feedlot smells, slow-moving vehicles on the roads, and the accumulation of old vehicles and machinery around rural farmsteads.

BOX 1.4   Rural and Remote Communities

Nonmetro net migration, 1990-99

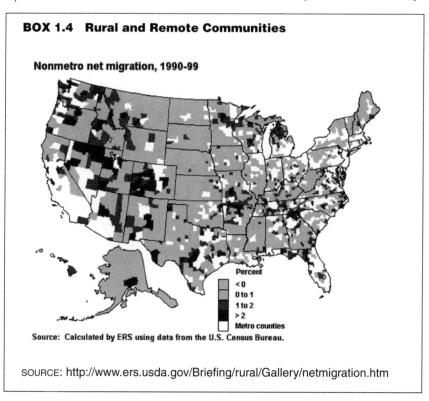

Percent
- < 0
- 0 to 1
- 1 to 2
- > 2
- Metro counties

Source: Calculated by ERS using data from the U.S. Census Bureau.

SOURCE: http://www.ers.usda.gov/Briefing/rural/Gallery/netmigration.htm

About This Book

The four patterns just described give rise to many of the social problems felt by people living in rural communities. Rapid growth characterizes counties in eighteen states and affects about 25 percent of the nation's nonmetropolitan population. But the way those problems emerge and are dealt with vary as to whether that growth is generated by high natural amenities or proximity to metropolitan centers. Persistently poor rural counties are found in twenty-five states and involve almost 7 million rural people. Counties in thirteen states are rural and remote. These states include 27 percent of the U.S. nonmetropolitan population.

Social problems have both objective and subjective features. Although the four patterns describe an objective portrait of some rural conditions, many people could argue that these conditions are not a social problem. What the people of Irwin see as a problem, people in Chicago may regard as inevitable. What the environmentalists in Mammoth Lakes see as a danger, outside investors and local developers see as the price of growth. What the white population in Eatonton sees as acceptable, the African American population may find to be intolerable. Some see

BOX 1.5   Commuting Areas

Commuting zones for the United States, 1990

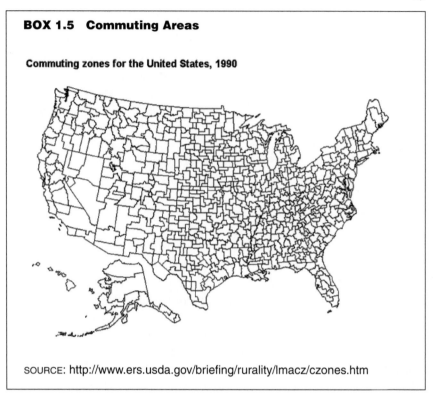

SOURCE: http://www.ers.usda.gov/briefing/rurality/lmacz/czones.htm

the poverty in McDowell County as the responsibility of society, whereas others see it as the responsibility of the individuals living there. Thus, definitions of social problems depend on what people feel they can control, what they think is fair, and what they value. All these, in turn, are a part of cultural capital.

Assumptions

Perhaps the most basic assumption we make here is that the rural perspective is worth exploring. Our society has become so deeply urbanized that we almost assume urbanization to be a natural law. Urbanization was important to industrialization, but many people now argue that the economic reasons for urbanization are no longer as compelling as they once were. Others point to the limits of growth, arguing that the social costs of overcrowding have now exceeded whatever economies of scale made urbanization preferable. Still others point to the contributions rural areas make to the nation: (1) food security, (2) a sense of land stewardship that protects natural resources, (3) a value system connected to both the land and human relationships, and (4) protection of diversity.

The reality is that more than one-fourth of the nation's people have chosen to live in rural areas. As we make the transition to the information age, it seems appropriate to reexamine rural areas—asking why people have stayed, how federal and state policies have contributed to current conditions in rural areas, and what role individual choice can play in dealing with current social issues.

Given the choice to focus on rural communities, these assumptions guided the selection of topics and organization used for this book. First, we have assumed that trends are not destiny. Individuals, groups, and communities can modify trends through appropriate actions. Our understanding of the drivers of those trends becomes part of the reality in which we live, affecting the choices we make as individuals and as a society.

Second, we have assumed that what occurs in rural areas is the result of history, especially the changing relationship between urban and rural society. Although it is simpler to think about rural and urban communities as separate worlds, in reality they are connected. Georgia was established as a colony because of London's problems with debtors. Much of the rural West was settled to provide the resources needed to fuel industrial growth in the East. Timber in Washington State was cleared to build the houses in Los Angeles. McDowell County was populated because industry needed coal to operate its factories. Irwin was settled because the railroads needed grain to haul and eastern cities needed a dependable food supply. The connections continue today. In order to understand what is occurring in rural areas, we must continually look to both past and present rural-urban linkages.

Social issues involve human relationships and thus social capital, but much of what leads to these problems are related to access and control over the other capitals. A 4-H leader in the Florida Panhandle points out that he cannot separate the problems of child abuse from the problems of persistent poverty. Efforts to build an economy capable of alleviating poverty are as important to him as programs on effective parenting. Our third assumption is that it is necessary to look at the six capitals as highly interrelated. Increasing only one capital without attention to the others can lead to many unintended—and unpleasant—consequences.

The fourth and fifth assumptions simply describe the tension between public policy and individual choice. The fourth assumption states that political decisions at the state and national level influence where and how economic and social change takes place. Problems of rural poverty, ethnic conflicts, or natural-resource extraction can be understood partly in terms of public policy, that is, in terms of the political choices, made by *state*, *market*, and *civil society* actors. Thus, the differential availability of political capital influences rural realities.

The fifth assumption adds that the rural experience is the sum of group responses to both political constraints and individual choice. People can make a difference, either by influencing the broader policy agenda that constrains them or by making choices within the policy framework. We are not just victims of society or passive consumers of broader national change. The choices rural people make affect the direction change takes in their communities.

Simply stated, these assumptions argue that rural issues can be examined in terms of change. Change can be explained in terms of history and in terms of the interplay among the different types of capital in the context of global trends and local condition. Change involves both individual and institutional choices.

Organization of This Book

We first introduce the six capitals, separating financial and built capitals. Each chapter opens with one or more rural profiles. These profiles are fictional in the sense that they are not descriptions of actual individuals. The circumstances are real, however. Historical documents, site visits, research journals, taped telephone and video interviews, newspaper articles, and a variety of other sources were used to collect information about real rural communities. The issues identified are also real, expressed by people living in rural communities throughout the country.

Individual experiences often have causes embedded in the institutions and conventions of society. Understanding how this happens is a part of what sociologists undertake as they study human society and social behavior. Each chapter is structured to help the reader move from an issue voiced by rural people to the sociological issue suggested by the concepts and theories of the social sciences. Seen from this broader perspective, social problems experienced by rural people become societal problems capable of being solved through collective action.

Part 1 looks at cultural capital (Chapter 2), social capital (Chapter 3), human capital (Chapter 4), and political capital (Chapter 5): those resources that we think of as primarily related to humans and their interactions with each other. Part 2 looks at natural capital (Chapter 6), financial capital (Chapter 7), and built capital (Chapter 8): those resources we think of as physical. Part 3 examines how the community capitals interact with and are transformed by globalization (Chapter 9), consumption (Chapter 10), and government (Chapter 11).

Part 4 looks at mobilizing capitals for social change. Chapter 12 describes models for effective community change and describes situations when those models have been successful. The focus is on how rural communities can identify and combine community capitals for change that addresses the triple bottom line: equity, economics, and environment.

Chapter Summary

Many people imagine a rural America characterized by farming, homogeneous cultures, and close-knit communities. In reality, rural communities differ more among themselves than they do, on average, from urban areas. Four major circumstances predominate in rural America: sprawl in areas near cities, rapid growth near natural amenities, persistent poverty, and rural and remote areas.

What is defined to be a rural community has changed over time. In general, definitions of "rural" include descriptions of both size and location. Some current definitions use the distinction between nonmetropolitan and metropolitan counties, equating "nonmetropolitan" with "rural." Definitions of community have also changed. This text defines "community" as a place or location in which people interact for mutual benefit. The community need not provide all the services individuals require and may not necessarily offer community members a common sense of identity.

Rural communities differ in terms of ethnicity and in terms of the realities that most affect their alternatives. Rural communities are among the most ethnically diverse as well as the most ethnically homogeneous, depending on the region of the country in which they are located.

This book assumes that social issues can be explained in terms of a community's history and the resulting capitals that are available to that community. Economic and policy choices made at the state and federal level and individual choices made by the communities themselves mean that, even for poor, remote rural communities, trend is not destiny.

Key Terms

Amenity-based communities are those located near natural resources that are viewed as a source of beauty and recreation by the larger population. They include counties by bodies of water and mountains.

Built capital is capital that is transformed from financial capital and includes factories, schools, roads, habitat restoration, community centers, all of which contribute to building other capitals for communities.

Capital is a resource invested to create new resources.

Civil society is made of groups of people organized around beliefs or interests that do not seek to make a profit through those groups. Civil society is made up of both formal associations and informal groups.

A *commodity organization* is a group with market interest in commodities (general categories of goods). Its constituents join together to achieve political and market goals.

A *community* is a place or location where groups of people interact for mutual support.

Decapitalized resources lose value when one type of capital is emphasized over all others, and the economy, environment, or social equity is thus compromised.

E-based businesses conduct business via the Internet.

Financial capital consists of money that is used for investment rather than for consumption.

Human capital consists of the skills and abilities of each individual within a community.

The *market* is made of profit-oriented firms and individuals when they buy or sell goods or services.

Metropolitan areas consist of one or more adjacent counties containing at least one city of 50,000 inhabitants or more.

Natural capital is the landscape, air, water, soil, and biodiversity of both plants and animals.

Nonmetropolitan counties are those counties that lie outside a standard metropolitan area and do not include a city of 50,000 or more inhabitants.

Persistently poor counties are those whose per capita family income was in the lowest 20 percent in 1960, 1970, 1980, 1990, and 2000.

Political capital is the ability of a group to influence the distribution of resources within a social unit, including helping to determine what resources are available and who is eligible to receive them.

The term *rapid growth* applies to rural counties that experienced population increases greater than the national average. Rapid growth exurban counties owe their growth to the adjacent metropolitan areas.

Rural and remote counties are those that are not adjacent to urban areas and that themselves have no town of substantial size.

Social capital includes the networks, norms of reciprocity, and mutual trust that exist among and within groups and communities.

The term *state* refers to all governments at all levels: local, county, state, national, and international. These governments have specific territorial responsibilities that may overlap with those of other state entities.

References

Bourdieu, Pierre. 1986. "The Forms of Capital." In *Handbook of Theory and Research for the Sociology of Education*, ed. John C. Richardson, 241–258. New York: Greenwood Press.

Lobao, Linda M. 1990. *Locality and Inequality: Farm and Industry Structure and Socioeconomic Conditions*. Albany: State University of New York Press.

Luloff, A.E., and R.S. Krannich. 2003. *Persistence and Change in Rural Communities: A Fifty Year Follow-Up to Six Classic Studies*. Oxon, UK: CABI Press.

Salamon, Sonya. 2003. *Newcomers to Old Towns: Suburbanization of the Heartland*. Chapel Hill: University of North Carolina Press.

Wilkinson, Kenneth P. 1991. *The Community in Rural America*. New York: Greenwood Press.

Part 1

The Human
Factors in Communities

2

Cultural Capital and Legacy

Dave and Rosemary glared at each other. There had been some heated discussions around the dinner table recently. Dave opposes the local school bond. He is trying to save money in order to buy more land, so he doesn't want property taxes to increase. Rosemary believes that the quality of the school must be maintained, so she wants the school bond to pass.

Dave Stitz and Rosemary Turner met while attending college. He majored in general agriculture, and she majored in botany. Dave was a fourth-generation farmer, the first in his family to go to college. Rosemary's father was a county extension agent and her mother was a schoolteacher. Dave and Rosemary married soon after graduation and moved to the Stitz family farm. Dave works the fields with his father, and Rosemary runs the heirloom seed business they started with Dave's mother, an avid gardener. In order to understand their different positions on the school bond issue, it helps to know something about each of their personal histories.

Ever since Dave Stitz could remember, he knew he was going to be a farmer. He had a long lineage of farmers in his family. His great-great-grandparents came to western Kansas in the 1890s by covered wagon. Their granddaughter, his grandmother, married the son of a local farmer, and they began farming as soon as they were married. Over time, his grandparents expanded their farm and acquired enough land for their four children. Upon their death, they left an equal part of their land to each of their children. Dave's father was left with one-fourth of the family farm, which would not be enough land to pass on to his future children. Therefore, once Dave's parents were married, acquiring more land became a high priority.

Dave's parents bought more land during the expansive times of the 1970s, even though the land was priced higher than it could ever yield in crops. Because they anticipated having a family, they knew they needed more land. They postponed their family when land prices suddenly dropped, and they struggled to make their loan payments. Dave's father got a job driving a truck across country while he continued to farm and negotiate with local bankers to refinance the farm. With sacrifices, they were able to keep the farm and start their family, and they had one son, Dave. Land payments absorbed much of their income, although Dave's father was able to give up cross-country trucking. Dave came home from school each day to help with the farming, leaving no time for extracurricular activities outside of church. Dinner conversations were subdued, for everyone was exhausted and the television was on. Once Dave graduated from high school, he chose to go to college, paying his own way. He attended only in the spring semester so that he could be home during winter wheat planting and milo harvesting. Once he started farming, first with his father and later on his own, his parents' friends were impressed. At first they asked him to custom plant or custom harvest their wheat, and he brought his machinery to the land they indicated just for that particular operation. Once he had proven the quality of his work on their land, they asked him to rent their land or work it for a share of the crop.

Despite their struggle, the effort was worth it to Dave's parents. The farm was their legacy to their child, and they believed they provided him with an excellent set of tools for a happy and productive life: access to land and the willingness to work hard at making that land productive.

Rosemary was the daughter of a county extension agent and a town librarian, so she was no stranger to farming. Her parents did not make a large income, but it was secure. From the day Rosemary was born, however, they regularly put aside money for her college fund. Her parents felt that a college education was the most important thing they could give their daughter. They encouraged her to get into organizations in the community and in school, and they constantly encouraged her to talk to the professionals in the county about how they chose their careers. Dinner table conversations were structured around current events. Rosemary's parents, too, were thinking of legacy. A college education and knowing people and politics would enable Rosemary to support herself and maintain a comfortable lifestyle.

Given this background, it is less surprising that Dave and Rosemary are on different sides of the school bond issue. Dave's parents saw how education, particularly vocational agriculture, could be useful on the farm. When hard choices had to be made, however, they emphasized the need to acquire land. By contrast, Rosemary's parents put a college education and cultivating skills for her future career above everything else. In their reactions to the school bond issue, Dave and Rosemary are simply reflecting and continuing the legacies bequeathed them.

Both Dave's and Rosemary's parents gave them what they valued most: land and education. Like most parents, they were concerned that their children be able to earn a good living and live a good life. As the example illustrates, however, what parents believe they should pass on varies from one family to another. This chapter examines legacy, the social and economic factors that contribute to the legacy young people receive from their family and community, and how that legacy is affected by gender, race, and ethnicity.

★   ★   ★

What Is Legacy?

We normally think of legacy as the money or property bequeathed to someone through a will, typically what parents leave their children. But parents leave more than just material goods to their children. They pass on an understanding of society and their role in it, speech, dress, and ways of being—cultural capital—that in turn affect the choices their children make. *Legacy* is what families, communities, groups, and nations pass on to the next generation.

There are many cultural capitals even within North America, although one cultural capital is more highly valued than others and is thought to be the right way to know, act, and understand. Cultural capital determines what constitutes "knowledge," how knowledge is to be achieved, and how knowledge is validated. Those with power are able to define these key issues according to their own values, and they provide their children with cultural advantages that are translated into social and economic advantages.

Cultural capital includes the values and symbols reflected in clothing, books, machines, art, language, and customs. Cultural capital can be thought of as the filter through which people live their lives, the daily or seasonal rituals they observe, and the way they regard the world around them. The socialization process serves to transmit values via various forms of communication, both verbal and nonverbal. Whether people learn to share money or save it, whether they trust people in authority or fear them, what career they choose to pursue, or simply what they think is important are all products of cultural capital.

From the parents' perspective, legacy provides the tools needed for survival. Dave's parents saw land ownership as a key to his future. Consequently, they were willing to risk nearly everything to ensure that Dave had that tool for survival. Rosemary's parents had never owned land—at least not beyond their house and the property on which it was located—and both had made a living based on their college degrees. Rosemary's parents scrimped and saved in order to ensure that she left home equipped with the tool that had been most valuable to them, education.

Communities also impart legacies in terms of aspirations. In the dominant U.S. society, the norm is to succeed educationally and to achieve a higher status than one's parents. For middle-class, suburban, European Americans, this is normal. These shared aspirations of parents and children unite them during the end of their high school years in order to make preparations for leaving the community and entering college life. These aspirations tie them more closely to their parents and their parents' lifestyle. But in Appalachia, on American Indian reservations, and in the Mississippi Delta, as well as in many inner-city neighborhoods, educational aspirations separate young persons from their community and their parents. It is obvious to all in the community, to peers and to parents, that some young people are "learning to leave." Local folks no longer want to have much to do with them, figuring that they already feel superior to their community. The community, observing that such young persons are "opting out" by spending time studying instead of reinforcing local ties, may even become hostile toward them.

Conflicting Cultural Capitals and Cultural Domination

What happens when one group is technologically and militarily superior and attempts to impose its cultural capital on another group with a very different legacy? This is illustrated by the cultural clash between Native American and European American cultures. For the Owens Valley Paiute People of California, their language was critical, for its words conveyed important meaning about survival techniques: how to find food in different places in different seasons of the year, how to find and process material for baskets, what ceremonies to perform in order to ensure that food and materials were available, and how to watch the weather to decide when to plant and when to hunt. Their cultural capital allowed them to live in a wide territory during different seasons of the year and through both dry and wet years. Social advantage was determined by the degree to which one shared what one had and how one adhered to the religious rituals and rules. Children were carefully taught what their elders thought was critical for survival, and they learned through watching and practicing.

The Dawes Act of 1887 was specifically aimed at substituting the cultural capital of the dominant U.S. society for the "unproductive" cultural capital of Native Americans. The goal was to make the Native Americans become like white people—and also to take their land. Congressman Henry Dawes, author of the act, once expressed his faith in the civilizing power of private property with the claim that to be civilized was to "wear civilized clothes . . . cultivate the ground, live in houses, ride in Studebaker wagons, send children to school, drink whiskey [and] own property" (quoted by Marcus et al. 1998). The act allotted 160 acres of land to individual tribal members, giving the "excess" land to the U.S. government to dispose of to white settlers. The reduction of land area was supposed to force Native Americans to become farmers. The privatized land was, in many cases, quickly lost to European Americans, taking advantage of the fact that private land ownership was an absolutely foreign concept to most Native American bands and tribes. The cultural capital of those in control completely negated the ability of Native Americans to use their local cultural capital to maintain their social and economic well-being.

However, land loss was not enough to convince many Native Americans to give up their own cultural capital to adopt "the white man's ways." Other mechanisms to remove Native American cultural capital (assuming that it would then automatically be replaced by the dominant cultural capital, making the hearts and minds of Native Americans identical with those of European Americans, even if their skin color was not) included forced attandance at boarding schools, where European hairstyles and dress were enforced, despite the religious significance of long hair for many Native American males. Native Americans' names were changed to "sound" English. These names were often similar to the names of those allocating the land, who then slipped the names of their own European relatives into the roles, making them owners of Native American land. Native American children were punished for speaking their native language. The Native Americans' religion was seen as the basis for their unwillingness to adopt a more materialist approach to life that would allow them to properly conform to the values of the European Americans, so the U.S. government supported Christian missionaries from different denominations (specifically excluding Catholics and Mormons), putting them in charge of different parts of Indian Country. And since religion was tied to specific sacred places, many tribes were moved long distances to more barren lands, which conveniently left their fertile lands and forests to European Americans.

Paiutes throughout the West sought to maintain and re-create cultural capital in many ways. A Paiute Indian, Wavoka (who had been given the English name Jack Wilson), had a revelation during a total eclipse of the sun. This revelation was the genesis of a religious movement, the Ghost Dance. To participate in the dance, Native Americans of different tribes gave up alcohol, farming, and other practices of the European Americans in order to restore the past. The movement spread eastward from tribe to tribe. Desperate Native Americans began dancing and singing the songs that would cause the world to open up and swallow all other people, leaving the Native Americans and their friends on the land, which would return to its beautiful and natural state. The unity and fervor that the Ghost Dance movement inspired among different tribes, however, only spurred fear and hysteria among white settlers, which ultimately contributed to the events ending in the massacre of Lakota women and children by the U.S. Army at Wounded Knee, South Dakota, in 1890. Violence was a final tool used to eliminate a conflicting cultural capital.

Although the Dawes Act was repealed by the Indian Reorganization Act in 1934, Native American land loss continued. The 1934 act had a number of provisions that would seemingly benefit Native Americans; however, they were never funded or put into place. Additionally, this act ended traditional tribal government, and the system that replaced it took the form of the federal government, with constitutions, elections, short-term offices, and governmental branches. Systems that were far more integrated and beneficial to the health and well-being of the tribe were uprooted and replaced. The idea of lifetime service and leadership within a tribe was eradicated when this new governmental system was implemented. Consequently, Native Americans lost their form of tribal leadership and their land. The natural, political, and financial capitals that these represented had dramatic impacts on cultural capital.

Relocating Native Americans in the United States continued well into the twentieth century. Relocation of Native Americans to urban areas of the United States was introduced in 1952. By 2003, two-thirds of the Native American population resided in urban areas. The relocation effort was presented as a way to find jobs, make money, and attain affordable housing. Many of the relocatees were single Native American men who, after much convincing, "voluntarily" moved into cities. These relocation efforts appeared to benefit Native Americans by providing them with jobs and housing; however, their cultural ties diminished. Additionally, in the cities, Native Americans were treated as outsiders and were alienated through obvious forms of discrimination. People did not understand Native American culture, and Native Americans did not easily embrace big-city culture. Consequently, many Native Americans felt as if they did not fit in anywhere, and living in the city was overwhelming and uncomfortable. In some instances, returning to the reservation was an option; however, their cultural and spiritual connections to their tribes had been compromised by living in the city. When men returned to their tribes from the city and became tribal leaders, their commitment to preserving some of the very fundamental parts of cultural capital leadership, language, and religion was decreased. Thus, cultural capital was diminished because of their urban experience.

By 2003, few Paiute language speakers were left among the Owens Valley Paiutes, despite attempts on the part of elders to teach young people to "talk Indian." Their young people have lost their traditional cultural capital. And they have not received the cultural capital of working- and middle-class European Americans. Their access to the natural resources they traditionally used for survival was lost, with the U.S. government substituting Treaty Rights, which stated that the U.S. government would take care of them since they were giving up their ability to care for themselves. Removal and denigration of cultural capital combined with economic dependence on the federal government left a legacy of lack of identity and many social problems, including substance abuse on the reservation. Many tribal leaders are working hard to re-instill tribal cultural capital as a basis for improving the other capitals on the reservations.

Social Class, Stratification, and Domination

Societies and most social groups, including communities, rank households and its members hierarchically. Some individuals and families have more prestige, power, or wealth than others. Sociologists disagree on how this ranking takes place. Some sociologists argue that it occurs because of differences in functional importance: What some people do is more important to society than what other people do. Thus, they argue, it makes perfect sense for the chief executive officer (CEO) of a corporation to receive a salary more than five hundred times that of the average worker in the firm. (This ratio does not take into consideration stock options—relatively worthless in 2003—year-end bonuses, and loans forgiven that are part of CEO privileges not available to ordinary workers.) Other sociologists argue that it is not functional importance that gives some people more resources than others but differential power. They say that certain groups have more power than others and use that power to maintain a higher position in a group or society. Both sets of sociologists agree that in American society, those on top tend to have more income, wealth, power, and prestige. Other characteristics, such as age, sex, ethnicity, race, and religion are associated with different positions in the hierarchy. Furthermore, there is a strong relationship between the position of parents and the position their children achieve in that hierarchy.

Sociologists have explored inequality and social class from a variety of perspectives. Marxist approaches focus on material relations; Weberian approaches focus on social groups; and Bourdieu and his followers look at the intersection of financial and cultural capital.

Marxian Perspectives

Writing during the industrial revolution of the nineteenth century, Karl Marx defined social class in terms of the economy. In order to understand his perspective, however, we need to first look at how a business functions and how individuals within that business accumulate wealth.

The goal of any business is to make money. Profit essentially represents the difference between the price of the product sold and the cost of producing it, including the costs of materials, labor, land, and capital (interest paid on debt). Business owners receive the profits, either directly as proprietors or indirectly through dividends paid to them as investors. Those who own the business, then, accumulate wealth through business profits over which they have some control and through the increase in the value of their business, as indicated by the daily value of its stock.

Those who sell their labor to the company, who work for the company, receive a wage in return. Only rarely do they receive part of the profits, as in a cooperative or in an employee stock ownership plan (ESOP). Consequently, they accumulate wealth through their labor and any saving that can be generated from their wages after paying for the costs of maintaining themselves and their families. Their bargaining power with business owners is based on their ability to make their labor scarce. They either acquire skills and knowledge that are in demand or collectively threaten to withhold their labor through labor unions or employee associations.

Given this difference in the capacity to accumulate wealth, Marx identified two social classes: capitalists and proletarians. Those who own the means of production, the factories or offices, make up the *capitalist class.* Those who sell their labor for wages form the working class, or *proletarians.* Marx also identified a part of the capitalist class that he called the *petty bourgeoisie,* which included small shopkeepers and farmers. These were individuals who owned the means of production, managed the firms themselves, and often used family labor alone or combined with hired labor. Marx saw the petty bourgeoisie as a remnant of the preindustrial economy. Consequently, he expected it to disappear entirely once the transition to the industrial age was complete.

We have now moved through the industrial age and beyond, leading some sociologists to revise Marx's early theory. As corporations grew increasingly larger, sociologists saw a class of people emerge that fit somewhere between the capitalist and proletariat classes, the *managerial and professional class.* This group includes managers or professionals within businesses or who serve businesses as well as public-sector managers. These individuals do not own the means of production, yet they enjoy more autonomy and control over the work environment than do members of the proletariat.

A second modification is needed because the petty bourgeoisie class has not disappeared. Although there was a substantial decline of small-business owners and farmers in most industrialized nations, the numbers of self-employed people (now reported as "proprietors") has increased since the 1960s. In the United States, for example, self-employment fell from nearly 42 percent of the workforce in 1880 to 13 percent in 1969. By 1998 proprietors had increased modestly to 16.6 percent of the total workforce. They represent an even higher proportion of the labor force in rural areas. This is in part because people are adding new sources of income as real wage rates decline, thus increasing the number of jobs and the number of business endeavors. More important is the changing structure of the labor market. As industrial firms downsize, they subcontract work out to smaller businesses, and employment shifts to the service sector of the economy, a sector that consists primarily of smaller businesses. Thus, sociologists have concluded that the petty bourgeoisie (made up of small-business owners) is an integral part of the class system in this postindustrial age. Many governmental and private-sector programs are aimed at encouraging entrepreneurship.

Weberian Perspectives

Whereas Marx defined class in terms of material relationships, including the intergenerational transfer of wealth and property, sociologists have argued that other factors are equally important in defining social class. Writing during the late nine-

teenth and early twentieth centuries, Max Weber argued that people are also stratified by prestige and power, which combine in a hierarchy of status groups. These
groups have their own status culture, which controls access to rewards and privileges. Stratification is based on cultural capital as well as on financial and built capital. *Socialization,* the process of learning the cultural expectations of one's group,
and association (social capital) reinforce it.

From the Weberian perspective, then, *social stratification* describes the hierarchy
of status groups. Social stratification seems to be a feature of all societies. What differs is the extent to which the stratification system is open or closed. Closed systems are those in which members are not free to move from one class to another.
Open systems allow individuals and families to move across layers. *Social mobility* is
the term used to describe the movement of an individual from one status group to
another, either up or down.

Bourdieu and Social Domination

Pierre Bourdieu linked Marx's materialism and Weber's notion of society composed of status groups to examine the social and mental structures of domination
of some people and groups by others. Families, through kinship ties, and communities, through their educational systems, contribute to inequality. These are major
mechanisms through which cultural capital is transmitted. Like other capitals, cultural capital can be thought of as what Bourdieu called "congealed and convert-
ible social energy." Cultural capital determines how we see the world, what we
take for granted, what we value, and what things we think are possible to change.
Hegemony allows one social group to impose its symbols and reward system on
other groups.

Bourdieu, observing the rigid class structure in France, saw that the wealthy
provided personal and symbolic connections for their children. They "automatically" knew how to behave in formal situations and could chat easily with others
of their class. That shared behavior and knowledge of symbols gave the children of
the upper classes power beyond their material situation when dealing with those
in authority, from government bureaucracies to corporations to civic organizations. Richard Sennet and Jonathan Cobb (1972) saw different kinds of cultural
capital contributing to the "hidden injuries of class." The discomfort powerless
people feel in the presence of the powerful is partially due to their failure to comprehend all the symbols that give meaning to the situation. People in positions of
power feel uncomfortable and threatened upon entering communities composed
of excluded groups because the excluded groups may be resentful of power symbols they do not have, such as cars, dress, and language. And powerful people in
such situations do not comprehend the symbols that define the situation.

Class and ethnic cultures—and the cultural capital they represent—develop out of each group's experience with the social world. Cultural capital that is helpful in one setting is often a disadvantage in another, as was shown when a streetwise city boy from Chicago, Emmett Till, came to a small Mississippi town. His inability to judge correctly the dominant symbolic signals—and the violent power they implied—was fatal. Till was an African American teenager who, in August 1955, on a dare, spoke to a southern white woman in Mississippi as he would to white women he knew in Chicago, leaving her store saying, "Bye, baby." In response, the outraged husband and a white male friend beat, mutilated, and murdered Emmett Till. Despite their clear responsibility for the crime, the all-white jury acquitted them. The defense attorney for the two men called upon the importance of defending southern white symbols in the face northern pressure in his closing statement: "Your fathers will turn over in their graves if [J. W. Milam and Roy Bryant are found guilty] and I'm sure that every last Anglo-Saxon one of you has the courage to free these men in the face of that [outside] pressure" (Williams 1987).

Legacy and the Family

In preparing for their children's future, parents typically work toward three goals: enabling their children to have a place to live, a means by which to earn a living (sometimes viewed as standard of living), and personal fulfillment (sometimes viewed as quality of life). In one sense, legacy stands at the intersection between what parents have achieved in their own lives relative to these goals and what parents see as possible and desirable for their children to achieve.

Survey researchers have shown that middle-class parents have very different values and childrearing styles than do working-class and poor parents. (Michèle Lamont [2000] points out that steadily employed men in what scholars refer to as working-class occupations refer to themselves as "lower-middle-class.") Parents' behaviors in socializing their children are strongly influenced by their awareness of the traits they consider necessary for survival and success. Because environmental and economic risk increases as social class position declines, working-class and, in particular, poor parents focus more on survival than on success. Middle-class parents value creativity, reasoning, and autonomy, whereas working-class parents favor obedience and conformity. Middle-class parents tend to encourage exploration, whereas poor parents focus on limit setting. These are rational responses to different levels of experienced environmental risk. This is then related to the job rewards that young people seek. Young people concerned with having a predictable, secure future including not moving from place to place, are less likely to continue in school. They are also more likely to come from poor or working-class homes. Those interested in intrinsic rewards (interesting jobs that use all of one's skills and abilities, the learning of new skills, the chance to be creative) and in influence (participating in challenging work and decisionmaking) are more likely to continue their education and to have middle-class backgrounds. Thus, initial cultural capital that came from socialization is increased through acquiring the dominant cultural capital through formal schooling.

Annette Lareau has done systematic ethnographic work to show how parental values are translated into cultural capital. Middle-class parents engage in *concerted cultivation* of their children. They feel that what they do will have an enormous impact on their children's future. Thus, they actively assess and foster each child's talents, options, and skills. To do this, they actively organize their children's lives, ensuring participation in leisure activities orchestrated by adults. This requires that the parents own work generates a high enough income to pay for their child's participation (from sporting gear to music lessons) and has enough flexibility to allow them to provide transportation and to attend school programs when needed. Middle-class parents are particularly concerned about language use. They use reasoning, even when offering directives: "Put on your cap and coat before we go out. It is very cold today and you know how unhappy you are when your ears are cold." Children are allowed, even encouraged, to contest adult statements: "It's not really that cold, can't I wear a sweater?" which may result in extended negotiations between parent and child: "Let's look at the thermometer outside your room to see what the temperature is. Is the wind blowing? You know that makes it feel even colder. Let's look at the trees to see if we can tell." Middle-class families have weak extended family ties. Because of their low concern for roots and security within the extended family, they are likely to live apart from relatives. And when they do live near relatives, scheduled children's events (such as starring in the school play) take precedence over family events (such as Grandma's birthday). Middle-class children are therefore more likely to spend time in homogeneous age groupings, for that is the way most of their activities are organized.

Middle-class parents feel comfortable intervening when their children experience problems, and they encourage their children to do the same: "You got a 'C' on the math test. Did you talk to your teacher to help you understand long division better?" That pattern of concerted cultivation encourages an emerging sense of entitlement in the children.

Poor and working-class parents, in contrast, believe that as long as they provide love, food, and safety, their children will grow and thrive. Lareau calls this the *accomplishment of natural growth* approach to childrearing. These parents do not have the resources or do not believe it necessary to engage their children in a multitude of free time activities to encourage their particular talents. These children have more leisure time and hang out a lot, particularly with kin. Parent-child interactions are often in terms of directives: "Put on your jacket and cap." A child who responds that it doesn't seem that cold out is admonished to "Put on your jacket and cap NOW." If the child resists, physical punishment is more likely to result. However, it is rare for young poor or working-class children to question or directly challenge adults (although they may not actually wear the cap and jacket to school). There are strong extended-family ties, and most older adults feel very comfortable giving directives to their younger relatives. Children spend much of their time in mixed-age groups.

Working class and poor adults feel much less comfortable around authority figures. Their experience with police, teachers, doctors and social workers has generally resulted in having things taken away—including having their children taken away from them. Thus, they are hesitant to share information with authority figures, for they are unsure how the information might be used against them. Working-class and poor adults and children are deferential and outwardly accepting in their interactions with professionals, but they are very distrustful of them. Lareau found that the accomplishment of natural growth encourages an emerging sense of constraints. (Table 2.1 summarizes the differences between these two approaches.)

Differences in family life lie not only in the advantages parents obtain for their children but also in the skills they transmit to children for negotiating their own life paths (Lareau 2002).

Independent Entrepreneurs

People who expected to run their own business, what we now call independent entrepreneurs, settled many rural communities, particularly in the Northeast and the Midwest. These businesses are often family businesses, and self-employed businesspeople make up a higher percentage of the workforce in rural communities than in metropolitan areas.

Independent entrepreneurs are the backbone of the Jeffersonian view of the ideal society, which the Dawes Act sought to promote among Native Americans by taking away most of their access to land. That ideology promotes attitudes of industriousness, self-improvement, and optimism. Following slavery, African Americans became independent farmers and entrepreneurs, generally in their own towns or on the "black" side of the tracks. Unfortunately, after Reconstruction, their successes were reversed by illegal and violent actions against them, and they lost their land and businesses to European Americans.

The rural myth, best expressed in *Small Town in Mass Society* (Vidich and Bensman 1968), describes the ideal rural entrepreneur. That individual has the right attitudes and thus works hard. As a result of good attitudes and hard work, that individual accumulates wealth over his or her lifetime. Thus, those who do not accumulate wealth are viewed as lazy ("They don't work hard") and as having the wrong attitudes ("They don't value what we value"). Work is pursued with great

TABLE 2.1   Summary of Differences in Childrearing Approaches

Dimensions Observed	Childrearing Approaches	
	Concerted Cultivation	Accomplishment of Natural Growth
Key elements of each approach	Parent actively fosters and assesses child's talents, opinions, and skills.	Parent cares for child and allows child to grow.
Organization of daily life	Multiple leisure activities are orchestrated by adults for child.	Child "hangs out," particularly with kin.
Language use	Reasoning/directives Child contestation of adult statements Extended negotiations between parents and child	Directives Rare questioning or challenging of adults by child General acceptance by child of directives
Social connections	Weak extended-family ties Child often in homogeneous age groupings	Strong extended-family ties Child often in heterogeneous age groupings
Interventions in institutions	Criticisms and interventions on behalf of child Training of child to intervene on his or her own behalf	Dependence on institutions Sense of powerlessness and frustration Conflict between childrearing practices at home and at school
Consequences	Emerging sense of entitlement on the part of the child	Emerging sense of constraint on the part of the child

NOTE: this is taken directly from the article Annette Lareau. 2002. "Invisible Inequality: Social Class and Childrearing in Black Families and White Families." *American Sociological Review* 67: p. 753.

personal sacrifice and is oriented to the improvement of self and family and to the accumulation of wealth. Wealth, however, is generally not sought for its own sake or for the consumption of luxury goods and services. Instead, wealth is needed to acquire or develop an independent business. Thus, attitudes of industriousness, self-improvement, and optimism lead to behavior oriented to economic activity, which in turn generates wealth.

The legacy such parents have for their children is influenced directly by the resources they have accumulated. Parents work hard to invest in farms or businesses. These investments, in turn, provide employment and housing for their children as well as a source of social status within the community. All of this hard work is considered an investment in their children's future as well as their own. Since Dave Stitz's father had acquired land for his son, it seems only natural that Dave is now acquiring land for a son yet to be born.

For those who farm or operate small businesses in rural communities, the three legacy goals are combined in a single place. A place to live is often part of the means by which a family makes its living. Consequently, houses are valued for their use, and they are worth maintaining for long-term use by the family and community. Personal fulfillment comes from the family business and involvement in the local community, which makes the connection between legacy and place enormously strong. When that legacy is blocked, as it was for many farm families during the farm crisis of the 1980s, the loss can be especially difficult to accept.

Values such as industriousness, self-improvement, and optimism are certainly important to any business. But so are social connections. Legacy for this social class is thus place-specific. Parents develop a set of skills crucial to running their business and being accepted within a community. While some of the knowledge needed to run a successful business may transfer from one community to another, understanding how to run a business in any particular town may be specific to that town's culture. Consequently, knowledge and connections important to economic survival in a given community are transferred from parent to child. For David Stitz, the connections he inherited from his parents that gave him access to more farmland than he owned allowed him to continue farming.

Managers and Professionals

The managerial and professional class includes those who sell their labor but retain some autonomy in their work. Rural communities have always collectively purchased the labor of certain professionals, such as ministers and teachers. Although these individuals do not necessarily earn a big income, they enjoy the respect of the community and are critical in reproducing the community's cultural capital. Manufacturing plants and service industries now require managers and administrators to regulate the labor of workers and clerks. For the most part, these managers are relatively well paid.

These salaried managers and professionals share some characteristics with those who own the means of production. They have a high degree of autonomy on the job. In addition to determining the schedule and content of their own work, they often make decisions that affect others. Conversely, this autonomy reinforces self-esteem and enhances the value of independence and decisionmaking ability. Consequently, the most important legacy that middle-class parents impart to their chil-

dren is the ability to command a high price for their labor, based on the creden-
tials they earn through formal education.

For Rosemary Turner's parents, who are themselves salaried professionals, education substitutes for the transmission of material wealth. Like many others in this
social class, they encouraged Rosemary and her siblings to do well in school, helping them with their homework and challenging them to question and discuss issues with teachers. Independent thought is valued as part of the education process,
and it is a trait that is important in making management decisions. Like many of
their counterparts, the Turners believe that their success is in direct relation to
their education; likewise, they believe that their children's hope for satisfaction is
linked to their higher education. These families struggle to save money for their
children to attend college.

Families like the Turners expect that their children will become part of a regional or national labor force. To an extent, this legacy is location-free. Parents will
be committed to and actively involved in the local school system in order to assure
their children the preparation needed for college. Buying a home becomes an investment made for its exchange value. In contrast to the independent entrepreneur, however, the three legacy goals are not linked together by a place.

Working Class

Mining, timber, manufacturing, and service industries in rural areas all create a
working class, those who sell their labor but have little autonomy or control over
their work. Throughout history in the United States, Textile mills in the South,
garment and shoe factories in New England, lumber camps in the Northwest and
the upper Great Lakes, and the mines in various parts of the country have all employed large numbers of workers. Many went to work in these industries with the
hope of saving enough to open their own business. Some eventually succeeded.
Others, however, found that the low wages and high expenses involved in living in
mill towns, mining towns, or lumber camps made saving difficult. A strong labor
movement later increased wages in some of these industries, especially mining and
timber. Wages rose to the point that workers could not afford to quit and start
their own business. Many settled into depending on wages for their livelihood.
Their children have continued that tradition. But as these sectors of the economy
are restructured due both to technologies that substitute capital for labor and to
globalization, which moves labor-intensive production to nations where labor is
cheaper, the options of the rural working class become more limited.

In most cases, working-class jobs require skills that are learned on the job
rather than through formal education. In some industries, such as mining or logging, workers receive substantially higher wages than do some with jobs requiring

a college education, such as teachers. Consequently, there is little incentive to invest in education. This was the case in mining areas, such as McDowell County, West Virginia. Anxious to earn money for personal use or to help the family with debts, young people go to work at an early age. Homes are not purchased for their resale value but as a secure place to live. Seasonal layoffs or changing patterns in national and international markets often make employment unstable, so families seek security through home ownership.

For workers whose jobs depend on natural resources, legacy is often tied to a sense of place. In the early days, those in logging or fishing simply moved on when they tired of a particular job. Other jobs were always waiting, sometimes for better wages. The introduction of unions substantially increased the wages paid in these jobs, but at a cost to worker mobility. Those in McDowell County have become second- or third-generation mineworkers. Their investments, in homes for example, are tied to a place. When the local economy declines, the value of their homes decline, making it impossible to recover the cash needed to relocate. Consequently, most workers try to weather periodic economic downturns and layoffs. Like independent entrepreneurs, those in the rural working class often see legacy and place as strongly connected. The loss of an industry can mean the loss of all three legacy goals.

The Poor

Some working-class jobs in rural areas pay very poorly, and their employers, whose cultural capital prevails, describe these jobs as requiring few skills. These jobs are unstable, low paying, part-time, or seasonal, and they sometimes require migration. The wage earned depends not on a worker's skills but, rather, on the supply of workers willing to take jobs and on the cultural assessment of what the work is worth. Since the supply of workers almost always exceeds demand, the state's minimum wage becomes the maximum wage for this group. In many cases, these individuals see little chance of accumulating enough money to buy their own business or home. These individuals move often, because they live in low-quality housing or in undesirable areas or cannot pay that month's rent. A few months with relatives or friends, a few months of independent living, moving to a new town hoping to find better work, or even sleeping in the car means that children attend school irregularly and often change schools during a school year.

Poor parents' aspirations for their children focus around physical safety and physical nurturing. Those in authority are viewed as threatening, as are the everyday conditions of life. Parents see inner discipline as less important, since keeping a job depends more on the labor supply or an employer's whim than on an individual's behavior. Those who are poor often feel that they have little control over their environment. They perceive, often correctly, that hard work does not lead to wealth or high self-esteem. People are often pessimistic about their children's prospects for the future, and they may feel unable to influence them positively. The legacies they desire to give to their children are modest: stay safe, find steady work, and stay out of trouble.

In contradiction to the stereotype that poor people are lazy and do not want to work, a substantial number of the rural poor are among the working poor. More than two-thirds of the rural poor who were not ill, disabled, or retired work all or part of the year. The legacy passed on by the working poor is, in many respects, an accurate representation of the society they have experienced.

Transmitting Legacy Through the Community

Like culture, legacy is transmitted from one generation to another through social institutions. Institutions that control the means of production, provide education, reinforce values, or support personal connections all influence the legacy that is handed down. This section looks briefly at two of the institutions, the family and the schools.

Family Influence on Legacy

Families are, of course, the primary means by which legacies are transmitted. Parents exert a great deal of influence over the values their children adopt, the sense of self-esteem and self-worth with which children face the tasks of growing to adulthood, and the opportunities available to them. As described earlier, these legacies are a link between what parents have achieved and what they see as possible for their children. To some extent, however, these legacies also depend on whether parents expect their children to remain in the community.

Rural families are deeply affected by the opportunity structure present in their community. If parents expect or want their children to stay in the local community, then they are very much aware of the job opportunities and class structures within the community. The legacies they pass on to their children often perpetuate existing class structures and certainly reflect parents' experience in the workplace.

If parents expect their children to leave, then the legacy passed on may be very different. Middle-class parents, who are managers or professionals, emphasize education. Working-class families who are anxious to see their children achieve a better life also emphasize education, realizing that job opportunities, class structures, or both will require that their children leave the community in order to achieve more. Those in declining farm communities or in manufacturing communities such as Eatonton, Georgia, often encourage their children to leave. Different families in expanding communities, such as Mammoth Lakes, California, may see vastly different opportunities. Latinos migrating to the town for seasonal work see the chance to make ends meet. Middle-class families see the opportunity for entrepreneurial activity.

Role of the School

The family is not the only institution that transmits legacy. Funded and staffed by community members, schools play an important role in orienting children to their future position in society. In turn, the legacies parents have for their children influence the character of the school.

In the rural Midwest, where small businesses are still somewhat prevalent, legacies reflect the sense of social equality that existed during the settlement period when everyone aspired to the same goal, owning a business. Class differences are often ignored. Parents expect their children to manage a business or become a salaried professional, so they want their children to develop independence and the work habits needed to make such a living. They also understand that both businesses and professions depend on connections with people who have power and authority, so they try to help their children feel comfortable around people with power in their community through informal interactions. Schools generally encourage participation by all students, regardless of class. Smaller schools in the Midwest and Northeast have higher rates of participation in extracurricular activities, a part of "concerted cultivation" on the part of the school. Education may also be oriented toward out-migration as parents acknowledge that few jobs are available locally. This, in turn, leads to disinvestments in community by both parents and children.

In communities in other parts of the country, particularly in low-income areas in the South and Appalachia, parents see limited job opportunities for their children. As discussed earlier, they also see little connection between hard work and success. Consequently, their investment in education is not nearly as great. Dropout rates are high. Problems such as teenage pregnancy are also more prevalent. Parents and young people do not see any immediate advantage to remaining in school. Consequently, the sense of independence created by going to work, even at a low-paying job, is not offset by what seems to be the remote chance that education will lead to higher earnings. Unfortunately, high school dropouts experience higher rates of unemployment. Between October 2000 and October 2001, more than half a million youths dropped out of high school, and 35.9 percent were unemployed (U.S. Bureau of Labor Statistics 2002).

August Hollingshead's (1949) study of "Elmtown" (pseudonym for a midwestern town) looked at the extent to which social class, and thus legacy, was passed from parent to child through community institutions such as the school. In socially stratified rural communities, schools are also stratified. Hollingshead identified three mechanisms by which the social structure of the community was reproduced in the school: First, through cliques and recreational activities, the young people replicated the social structure of the adult world. Second, those adults who had a direct impact on the children, including teachers, school administrators, and community leaders, systematically discriminated against children from lower classes. Finally, children from the lower class learned patterns both at home and in school that hampered them in educational and occupational attainment.

As social institutions that transmit legacy and culture, schools are an enigma. Rural communities have fought long and hard to maintain local control of schools, in part to ensure that the values and attitudes of the local community are respected and transmitted through education. Tribal schools and tribal colleges were established by tribal governments in order to make sure that Native American cultural capital related to that tribe and that place are transmitted as well as the dominant cultural capital. State and federal courts informed by congressional and state civil rights legislation, however, see education as a social equalizer, enabling anyone willing to apply him- or herself in school to move into the middle and upper middle classes. Research like that conducted by Hollingshead demonstrates the extent to which schools can block this mobility, replicating the social class structure in place in the community, so that those in the lower classes see no way to advance. Some rural communities are now looking very carefully at who succeeds and does not succeed in school, asking themselves to what extent the school serves all students fairly.

Impact of Gender, Race, and Ethnicity

Although class and social status are important in shaping legacy, their impact differs depending on gender, race, and ethnicity. Parental aspirations vary greatly for their children, depending on the sex of the child and the family's race or ethnic heritage.

Any discussion of these issues carries some of the same risks as discussions of the relationship between social class and legacy: It is extremely difficult to generalize across populations without seeming to stereotype. Differences in legacy based on gender, race, and ethnicity do exist, although they are complex. This discussion reflects some of the current thinking as to how these differences occur. By no means, however, does it capture the full complexity of the issues involved or the diversity found across any given population.

Gender and Legacy

Traditionally, parents, schools, and communities expected different things of girls and boys. Through the 1950s, men and women assumed distinct roles in society, so parents expected male and female children to need different skills and values. Parents expected that male children had to be able to earn a living capable of supporting themselves and their families. Men were socialized to be independent, able to compete, and competent in some skill or profession. Women were socialized to make the best marriage possible, relying on men for financial security. Maintaining an attractive appearance and developing homemaking and social skills were the values and skills considered important to that future. To some extent, the social and homemaking skills women needed depended on their parents' assessment of the kind of men they would marry. Thus, a farm girl would learn a variety of production skills, such as gardening, home canning, and sewing. A town girl, whose parents felt her future rested on marrying a middle-class professional, would learn music, arts, and leisure sports as well as homemaking skills.

The Turners' commitment to Rosemary's education demonstrates how dramatically these expectations have changed since the 1970s. Women are now entering the labor force in increasing numbers, partly to achieve self-sufficiency and self-satisfaction. Economic conditions also require that many women work to help support their families, sometimes because they are single parents. In 2002, women represented 57.5 percent of employed persons ages sixteen and above.

Women's increased presence in the workforce has affected childrearing patterns. Increasingly, women choose to or are forced to return to the labor force soon after the birth of their children. They are no longer willing, or in some cases able, to stay out of the workforce to raise a family. Between 1999 and 2000, more than 55 percent of women ages fifteen to forty-four returned to work or actively sought a job within one year of having a baby, compared to the record high of 59 percent set in 1998 (U.S. Census 2000).

Legacy and Race

Despite advances in civil rights made during the past three decades, race continues to exert a dramatic impact on legacy. African Americans made up the largest portion of the minorities in the United States until 2002, constituting nearly 13 percent of the population. Their history, shaped by periods of slavery, segregation, and the Civil Rights movement of the 1950s and 1960s, has left a variety of legacies, some positive and others negative.

Because of their roots in slavery and the persecution that followed emancipation, generations of blacks in the United States were not able to pass on significant material wealth to their children. Instead, many focused on providing children with a social and cultural heritage that allowed them to survive in an often-hostile environment. Legacy for rural blacks meant stressing the linkages within the family and to the larger black community, as well as the mutual obligations and supports such linkages provided. Black parents, regardless of class, stressed family relations, the value of family, and family links to the community and to church. Because of segregation, African Americans lived in multiclass communities, and thus children of sharecroppers were able to see schoolteachers, doctors, and preachers who looked like they did. In the face of segregated school systems, many African American communities in the South started, supported, and staffed their own schools, providing mobility within the community for youth with promise.

As it has become possible for African American professionals to move into areas from which they were once excluded, poor African American children in both rural and urban areas are less likely to interact with professionals whom they know socially. When schools were integrated, European Americans usually got the teaching positions. That means that the cultural capital once present in rural African American towns has shifted away from the cultural values that stress and demonstrate the importance of education and the possibilities of social mobility.

Dignity in the face of continued racism is an important part of legacy for blacks. Ways of responding to racism without resorting to violence or being the object of attack are important components of the skills parents foster in their children.

Legacy and Ethnicity

In addition to gender and racial differences, parents are influenced by their ethnic heritage in identifying suitable legacies for their children. An ethnic group is a population that shares an identity based on distinctive cultural patterns and shared ancestry. The United States is often referred to as a "melting pot," implying that the diverse ethnic origins of migrants are blended. In reality, distinct ethnic subcultures continue to exist.

For example, there are about 2.4 million Native Americans now living in the United States. Almost 22 percent live in rural areas or on reservations, mostly west of the Mississippi River. They represent the poorest ethnic minority in the country. Despite the rich history and culture of the various tribes, Native Americans today offer their children one of the bleakest of legacies. In 2000, 26 percent of Native Americans lived below the poverty line, more than twice the national rate of 11.8 percent. The average length of schooling is only eight years, and the high school dropout rate is twice the national average. Alcoholism is a pervasive and persistent problem. The rate of alcoholism among Native Americans is nearly five times that of the nation as a whole. Tribal elders stress the necessity to build and use tribal cultural capital to confront these forms of dependency, which mirror the dependency established by Treaty Rights, through which Native Americans gave up their ways of supporting themselves in response to a promise that the U.S. government would take care of them, directly and explicitly creating dependency.

Even in the face of such devastating statistics, Native Americans strive to maintain and convey pride in their heritage. Schools on some reservations, once used as a tool to eliminate the Native American cultures, now incorporate native and the dominant culture in their curricula. Efforts to stimulate economic development on native lands are also beginning to reflect native values and orientations toward the land. Increasingly, Native Americans seek to transfer a legacy that respects their own culture but equips young people to function more effectively in the white world.

"Latino" is used to refer to people of Spanish-speaking ancestry, but this is clearly not a homogeneous group. Of the approximately 15 million Latinos living in the United States, about 9 million are Mexican American, 2 million are Puerto Rican, close to 1 million are Cuban, and the 3 million remaining are drawn from many countries of Central and Latin America. Latinos are the fastest-growing ethnic minority in the United States and officially surpassed blacks as the dominant minority in 2002.

Although many Latinos in the West and Midwest can trace their residence in the United States back for generations, their ancestors having arrived earlier than those of immigrants from Northern Europe, the vast majority of Latinos in the rural West and Midwest arrived during the period following World War II. Significant migration continues today, particularly from Mexico and such countries of Central America as El Salvador, Honduras, and Guatemala. As other newly arrived immigrants did in the past, Latinos tend to reside in national enclaves, to an extent resisting assimilation into the wider culture. For many, there are few job opportunities, a function in part of inadequate English-language skills. Many are drawn into low-paying manufacturing and service occupations in rapidly expanding rural communities. These typically offer few opportunities for advancement. Like the black community, Latinos value family loyalty, respect, obligation, and commitment to mutual support.

Asian migration began on a large scale during the late nineteenth century as Chinese were recruited to serve as cheap labor for the developing industries of the West, such as mining and construction. Although Chinese immigration was legally suspended in 1882, a diminished but continuous stream of Asians made their way to the United States. Many settled in California or in large cities such as New York and Chicago. Changes in immigration laws in 1965 resulted in increased flows once again, particularly from war-torn areas of Vietnam, Laos, and Cambodia. Today, many Asian Americans reside in rural areas, settling in small towns in states such as Kansas, Minnesota, and Massachusetts.

Although the different nationalities represented among Asian Americans value different characteristics and behaviors, there is a general appreciation for education, industriousness, and family cohesion. Until such time as material success is widely available to these ethnic groups, these qualities will define the principal legacy bequeathed to Asian American children by their parents.

Inequality: Whose Legacy?

Rosemary and Dave Stitz received different legacies from their parents, legacies that contributed to their different stands on the school bond issue. Heated discussions aside, both inherited a legacy capable of helping them maintain a stable lifestyle and contribute to the community.

Cultural capital gives individuals their sense of identity and their range of alternatives in a changing society. Throughout our history, dominant groups have tried to impose their cultural capital on others—including values that reinforce the current hierarchies and inequalities. At times the imposition of the values of cultural capital has been violent, as the dominant society sought to eliminate those who did not seem to incorporate the dominant values. Education once was aimed at getting every child to accept the dominant cultural values, to learn to advance if they had the ability, or to accept their place in life if they did not. However, now scholars understand that it is not that simple. Cultural capitals can coexist. The self-confidence to act positively toward oneself and others requires a pride in legacy rather than a complete rejection of it. Individual and social problems arise when cultural capital is given up, yet it is impossible to completely appropriate the cultural capital of the dominant group. Individuals who do try to replace their own cultural capital with that of the dominant group are vulnerable, marginal to both their group of origin and the dominant group.

Chapter Summary

Legacy is that which parents seek to pass on to their children, including both material possessions and values and norms. Legacy depends, to some extent, on current economic opportunities. Parents' social class also affects legacy. Sociologists define *social class* either in terms of how individuals relate to the means of production or in terms of their social status within the community. When social status differences are large, a community or society is said to be highly stratified.

Membership in a given social class often affects the legacy passed on to children. Parents who are small-business owners or entrepreneurs often pass on land or a business to their children. Legacy is thus strongly linked to place. Although desiring that their children take over the business or farm, other small-business owners or farmers realize that such a legacy may not be realistic in the current economy. Therefore, they encourage their children to get a good education.

Those in the middle class, particularly managers and professionals, typically invest in their children's education and value independent thinking and the capacity to make decisions. Limited to the manufacturing or natural-resource jobs available in the local rural community, working-class parents value discipline and want to ensure that their children can adapt to externally imposed rules. Some working-class parents find that their salary is not sufficient to keep the family out of poverty. Those who are persistently poor often feel they have little control over what happens to themselves and their family. Consequently, they see little connection between hard work or education and a better future. Thus, even when they have high levels of ability recognized by themselves and others, they "underinvest" in acquiring the dominant symbols and values and maintain local cultural capital.

Legacy is transferred from one generation to another through social institutions. Of course, the family serves as the primary social group through which legacy is transferred. Schools can either reinforce existing class structures or offer opportunities that increase social mobility.

Issues of gender, race, and ethnicity often modify the relationship between legacy and social class. In earlier times, men and women had distinct roles that affected the legacy bequeathed to each. Racial discrimination often blocks black parents from passing acquired social mobility on to their children. Native American people struggle with the legacy left by decades of oppression. Social inequalities continue to exist, inequalities that limit communities as well as individuals.

Key Terms

Accomplishment of natural growth describes a situation where parents do not intervene in their children's activities or associations, but provide for their basic needs, including love, food, and physical safety.

The *capitalist class* includes those who own the means of production.

Concerted cultivation describes a situation where parents work hard to determine how their children spend their time, how they think and speak, and with whom they associate.

Legacy is that which parents seek to pass on to their children, including material possessions, values, and behavioral patterns.

The *managerial and professional class* includes managers, professionals, and government officials, individuals who sell their labor but maintain considerable job autonomy.

The *petty bourgeoisie* includes those who own the means of production but rely primarily on their own labor rather than on the labor of others.

Proletarians include those who sell their labor for wages.

Social class has two distinct meanings. It describes people with similar relationships to the means of production. Alternately, it refers to a particular layer, or stratum, in a social stratification system.

Social mobility is the process through which people move from one position in a stratification system to another.

Social stratification is the division of people into layers, or strata, based on a series of attributes related to social status.

Socialization is the process through which people learn to think, feel, evaluate, and behave as individuals in relation to others and to social systems.

References

Bourdieu, Pierre. 1986. "The Forms of Capital." In *Handbook of Theory and Research for the Sociology of Education,* ed. John C. Richardson, 241–258. New York: Greenwood Press.

Hollingshead, August B. 1949. *Elmtown's Youth: The Impact of Social Classes on Adolescents.* New York: John Wiley and Sons.

Johnson, Monica Kirkpatrick, and Glen H. Elder Jr. 2002. "Educational Pathways and Work Value Trajectories." *Sociological Perspectives* 45:113–138.

Kohn, Melvin L. 1963. "Social Class and Parent-Child Relationships: An Interpretation." *American Journal of Sociology* 68:471–480.

Kohn, Melvin L., and Carmi Sholler, eds. 1983. *Work and Personality: An Inquiry into the Impact of Social Stratification.* Norwood, N.J.: Ablex.

Lamont, Michèle. 2000. *The Dignity of Working Men: Morality and the Boundaries of Race, Class, and Immigration.* Cambridge, Mass.: Harvard University Press.

Lareau, Annette. 2002. "Invisible Inequality: Social Class and Childrearing in Black Families and White Families." *American Sociological Review* 67:747–776.

McElhaney, Kathleen Boykin, and Joseph P. Allen. 2001. "Autonomy and Adolescent Social Functioning: The Moderating Effect of Risk." *Child Development* 72:220–235.

Marcus, Jonathan, Tara Ruotolo, Michael Masters, and Cathy Slater. 1998. A Study and Timeline of the Lakota Nation. University of Michigan. Online; available: http://www-personal.umich.edu/~jamarcus/dawes.html; accessed April 17, 2003.

Pevar, Stephen L. 2002. *The Rights of Indian Tribes.* 3rd ed. Carbondale: Southern Illinois University Press.

Sennett, Richard, and Jonathan Cobb. 1972. *The Hidden Injuries of Class.* New York: Vintage Books.

Steelman, Lala Carr, and Brian Powell. 1991. "Sponsoring the Next Generation: Parental Willingness to Pay for Higher Education." *American Journal of Sociology* 96:1505–1529.

U.S. Bureau of Labor Statistics. 2002. "College Enrollment and Work Activity of Year 2001 High School Graduates." Online; available: www.bls.gov/news.release/hsgec.nr0.htm; accessed January 24, 2003.

U.S. Census 2000. Online; available: www.census.gov; accessed January 24, 2003.

Vidich, Arthur, and Joseph Bensman. 1968. *Small Town in Mass Society.* Princeton: Princeton University Press.

Williams, Juan. 1987. *Eyes on the Prize: America's Civil Rights Years, 1954–1965.* New York: Penguin, Inc.

3

Social
Capital and Community

*At the present time the liberty of association has become a necessary
guarantee against the tyranny of the majority.*
　　　　　　　—Alexis de Toqueville, Democracy in America

The farming community of Solidale (a pseudonym) is located in the rich bottom-
land of the Platte River about five miles off Interstate 80. This town of more than
4,200 inhabitants boasts a first-class library and community center, a hands-on science center, and a farm museum. It has a lively industrial park, a farmers' cooperative and cooperative gasohol plant, and a thriving locally owned telecommunications firm. Unlike most farming communities of comparable or smaller size, it has
grown (from 3,700 persons in 1980)—even gaining population during the farm
crisis of the 1980s. It has also gained big business. In 1998, a large software company
moved into town, with no plans of leaving the area; the town continues to grow.

When researching Solidale in 1996, we (Jan L. Flora and Jeff S. Sharp) interviewed Stan Logan (a pseudonym), a crusty, sometimes cantankerous, always de-
cisive, and by and large benevolent leader. He moved to Solidale in 1948 and
became the Ford automobile dealer. He did well for himself, as he pointed out:

> I came in this town with nothing and I mean truly nothing. (I'm going to offend
> surely my brothers and sisters.) We pooled the family resources to get me started,
> see. I had about $10,000 that I saved in the military and my years with Boeing and
> the family came up with another $15,000. . . . The only thing that I've done is get
> involved in so many things real estate and so forth. In the old days had a hell of a
> time getting mortgage payments but I always kept right on going and inflation
> keep bailing me out, you know.

Through his real estate dealings and the dealership, which he has managed with his daughter in recent years, he has made a good living for himself and his wife. As his career as a car dealer began to wind down, he began buying modest-sized old homes and either fixing them up or, if they were eyesores, tearing them down and replacing them with attractive brick one- and two-story row houses and apartments for retired persons and young working families. He also built an attractive and modestly priced nonfranchise motel behind his Ford dealership "so visitors would have a nice place to stay."

It seemed obvious that Stan could have made a lot more money than he did, and when asked about it, Stan agreed emphatically.

When asked, "Why did you choose to do it this way?" he avoided the philosophical question of why he chose the path of generosity rather than greed and replied simply, "You can't take it with you."

Logan, along with being a businessman, has served on several boards in his hometown, in the local area, and statewide, including the hospital board and the local community college board. In fact, he founded the hospital board in 1960, serving on it as president from 1968 until 2001, when he retired from business. He continues to serve as an active member of the hospital board, and on March 7, 2002, Logan received the Trustee of the Year award from the Nebraska Hospital Association. Along with this accomplishment, Logan received another special honor in 2001, his high school diploma, which was something he had "always wanted . . . but [he] never had the opportunity to finish high school" (Letheby 2001). In 2002, at age eighty-two, Logan's dedication to Solidale was as strong as ever. He continues to serve as a member of the chamber of commerce, and he owns approximately 125 rental homes in the area.

Over the years, Stan has played a facilitating role in strengthening community leadership. He was a founder of the Solidale Development Authority (SDA), which brings together virtually all the movers and shakers in the community. He cajoled and maneuvered to make sure that individuals representing all major local economic interests were at the table, and with others he devised a mechanism for bringing promising young men (few women have been groomed for leadership in the town) into an outer circle of leadership in the SDA. Once they were trained or schooled in how to operate in Solidale, they were invited into the inner circle.

Stan Logan is not the only leader in Solidale. In fact, one is impressed with how many there are. Bill Johnson (a pseudonym) transformed the local telephone company into Solidale Telecommunications. Citizens, out of habit or out of affection for this successful locally owned business, still call it "the telephone company." This misnomer frustrates Bill because he has worked vigorously to make it much more than *just* a telephone company, and he corrects them to no avail. Solidale Telecommunications was a key factor in attracting a large software company in 1998 that was originally based in Denver, Colorado; the software company's president affirmed that the telecommunications company provided more options and better transmission power than was available in Denver. Solidale Telecommunications provides sophisticated electronic communication for its customer base and has the contract with the state for a "translation" center for deaf and hearing-impaired telephone customers throughout the state (required by the Americans with Disabilities Act). The firm has trained and now employs forty-five skilled translators. The company also runs a telemarketing firm that employs two hundred, but at very modest wages. The company also acts as a model community citizen, recognizing that the well-being of the community and of "the telephone company" are intertwined. The public relations person for the company was one of the young newcomers to the community who was recognized and mentored by Stan Logan and the SDA and is now a semiofficial spokesperson for the community to the outside.

★   ★   ★

It is the actions of people that transmit culture and legacy. It is people who must determine a community's development options, make decisions, and take action. Furthermore, this action is often most effective through groups. Ultimately, it is the quality of community social capital that affects the extent to which people expand their scope of concern beyond self-interest and beyond their family to include the community as a whole.

Solidale clearly has a good deal of social capital, but how a community develops this *social capital* is a much more elusive consideration. Does it help to have financial and human resources? Can it be explained by the presence of one or a small group of dedicated and visionary leaders? Does it help if the community is ethnically homogeneous (as is Solidale)? Or is the essence of social capital something much more intangible? In Solidale, two childless bankers, upon their death, left their estate to trusts that focused on building and maintaining key public buildings that became important venues for building social capital. The trusts and the establishment of a community foundation eventually led financial advisers to ask their clients when making their will to consider—along with providing for their families—a bequest to a local trust or foundation. Thus, an ethic of generosity, rather than of scarcity, has been created. Having a comfortable but utilitarian community center (which houses basketball courts, a weight room, and the like for organized recreational sports for youth and adults) has undoubtedly contributed to greater civicness. Formal and informal luncheons are arranged regularly; it is around these meals that much of the community's business is completed. Private but collective decisions are then ratified and, where appropriate, implemented by city government.

Although the answer to all the questions asked in the preceding paragraph is "yes" (except perhaps the one regarding ethnic homogeneity), no factor by itself explains how community social capital is built. Precisely how social capital is constructed depends on the history and character of the individual community. In this chapter we will explore the elements of social capital in order to provide clues for building this particular form of capital that contributes to civic engagement and community betterment. We will also examine what Robert Putnam (2000) calls the "dark side" of social capital. For example, when does (or what configurations of) social capital have a negative effect on community well-being? Can social capital be used to exclude certain categories of community members? We will also introduce the concept of *entrepreneurial social infrastructure (ESI)* as a means of using social capital for community betterment. Finally, we will mention the interaction of social capital with other kinds of capital.

What Is Social Capital?

Human interaction is the foundation of all communities. People may inhabit the same place for extended periods of time and never interact; conversely, people are increasingly interacting with others who live outside of their geographic community. Interactions in human communities are based not solely on proximity but also on history. Understanding the configuration of interactions, along with the inequalities, power differentials, and *social exclusion* that structure interactions, requires an understanding of the historical context as well as of current processes.

Social Capital Defined

Social capital is interactive. It is a group-level phenomenon. Individuals do not by themselves build social capital. Sociologists often explain social capital in terms of norms of reciprocity and mutual trust (Coleman 1988). Norms can be reinforced through a variety of processes: forming groups, collaborating within and among groups, developing a united view of a shared future, and engaging in collective action. Putnam describes social capital as referring to "features of social organization, such as networks, norms, and trust, that facilitate coordination and cooperation for mutual benefit. Social capital enhances the benefits of investment in physical and human capital" (Putnam 1993b: 35–36).

Communities can build sustainable social capital by strengthening relationships and communication on a community-wide basis and encouraging community initiative, responsibility, and adaptability. Clearly it takes time for these processes to unfold and for social capital to develop. Stronger relationships and communications can result from fostering increased interactions among unlikely groups inside and outside of the community and increased availability of information and knowledge among community members. Community initiative, responsibility, and adaptability are enhanced by developing a shared vision, building on internal resources, looking for alternative ways to respond to constant changes, and discarding the victim mentality, which only causes the community to focus on past wrongs rather than future possibilities. To understand social capital, it is useful to look at the concept historically.

Is Social Capital Something New?
From a Nation of Associations to Bowling Alone

Social capital is as old as human society. Emile Durkheim, a great nineteenth-century French sociologist/anthropologist, introduced the concept of *collective representations* or *social solidarity.* He drew his conclusions from the works of ethnologists who studied native North American and Australian aboriginal peoples, suggesting that all simple societies (that is, those with a noncomplex *social structure,* the order that shapes daily, weekly, and yearly interaction between and among people) engaged in sacred ritualistic behavior (Durkheim [1912] 2001). He concluded that such groups merged the mundane (day-to-day activities) and sacred realms: All activities were infused with religious meaning. He then applied the framework to modern people in terms of the development of a *civil religion,* that is, patriotic beliefs and related "sacred" rituals that unite a people. Examples of violation of sacred symbols include the burning of the American flag or publicly imputing crass business or political motives to a leader during time of war. Neither act of protest is against the law, but those engaging in either act have, at different times in our history, been subjected to informal or extrajudicial punishment. Such in-group solidarity generally results in the drawing of sharp boundaries between insiders and outsiders and may even result in persecution of those who do not share (or who are perceived as not sharing) the values of the in-group. These distinctions between those who do and do not share the in-group's values are strongest when the non-in-group values are perceived as outside threats. Examples of such persecution include the internment of Japanese Americans during World War II and the adamant refusal of the U.S. government to release the names of more than 1,200 suspects arrested after the September 11, 2001, terrorist acts and the war in Afghanistan or to indicate where they were incarcerated. One year after the September 11 attack, none had been charged with terrorism, although it was believed that many had been deported.

Pierre Bourdieu defined social capital as actual or potential resources that derive from "a durable network of more or less institutionalized relationships of mutual acquaintance and recognition—or in other words, to membership in a group—which provides each of its members with the backing of the collectivity-owned capital" (1986: 248–249). He said that to the individual member, social capital is a form of credit that allows him or her to claim certain elements of those resources when they are needed. Much as Durkheim did, he argued that these networks—and one's place in them—must be constantly rebuilt through the giving of gifts (real or symbolic) that instill emotions of gratitude, friendship, respect: "a continuous series of exchanges in which recognition is endlessly affirmed and reaffirmed" (1986: 250). From the individual's point of view, these exchanges are "investment strategies," a claim on short- and long-term profit, symbolic or real. We might call these norms of reciprocity that foster commitment to the group and at the same time strengthen the group itself.

But, Bourdieu said there is a negative side of social capital, which is the obligation of each group member to be "a custodian" of group limits or boundaries. In other words, someone needs to keep out the "riffraff," that is, those who might change the essential nature of the group. This has important implications for geographic communities, since residents are—or should be—citizens of the community. But if they are excluded from community networks that provide credit or access to collective resources, how can they be full community citizens? Groups are excluded from key community networks for a variety of reasons: because of certain unconscious beliefs held by men regarding hierarchy of the sexes (women: "It's the women who really run this place—through their husbands"), because a group is seen as being permanently "in training" for full community citizenship (young people: "We tried that before you were born; it didn't work"), because they are undeserving (poor people: "They are too lazy to come to meetings; why else would they be poor?"), or because they are outsiders (newcomers and immigrants: "They don't know how we do things here").

A much earlier observer who viewed social capital (although he did not use the term) more positively was Alexis de Toqueville, an aristocratic Frenchman who traveled at length in the United States and who in 1835 and 1840 published the two volumes of *Democracy in America* ([1835 and 1840] 1956). He feared the "tyranny of the majority." He was generally suspicious of the motives and lack of formal education of the lower and working classes. However, upon observing the workings of communities of all sizes in the United States, he concluded that a fundamental bulwark against that tyranny was the degree to which Americans organized themselves into what we would today call *civil society*. The development of civic associations to accomplish different collective purposes involves building social capital: promoting interaction that strengthens members' commitment to particular values and goals and, in seeking to carry out those goals, forging a common identity. By and large, Toqueville's observations about the United States are still valid, although Putnam has documented that civic engagement has declined very significantly in the past quarter century. Putnam uses the metaphor of bowling alone to represent the decline in civic engagement: Following World War II, bowling leagues regularly brought neighbors and colleagues together on weeknights in a relaxed atmosphere where they often discussed family and community topics. Now, although the number of lines bowled in the United States has remained more or less constant, most people are bowling alone rather than in leagues. He does note, however, that although civic involvement of all kinds has declined, voluntary organization membership in the United States still remains higher than in many other developed countries. (See Box 3.1 for a synopsis of Putnam's findings and interpretations.) He attributes the high levels of civic activity in the first two-thirds of the twentieth century to, first, the effects of the Progressive era and, second, to the mobilization of all U.S. citizens during World War II.

BOX 3.1   The Strange Disappearance of Civic America

For the last year or so, I have been wrestling with a difficult mystery. . . . The mystery concerns the strange disappearance of social capital and civic engagement in America. . . . I use the term "civic engagement" to refer to people's connections with the life of their communities, not only with politics. . . .

Evidence for the decline of social capital and civic engagement comes from a number of independent sources. Surveys of average Americans in 1965, 1975, and 1985, in which they recorded every single activity during a day—so-called "time-budget" studies—indicate that since 1965 time spent on informal socializing and visiting is down (perhaps by one-quarter) and time devoted to clubs and organizations is down even more sharply (by roughly half). Membership records of such diverse organizations as the PTA, the Elks Club, the League of Women Voters, the Red Cross, labor unions, and even bowling leagues show that participation in many conventional voluntary associations has declined by roughly 25 percent to 50 percent over the last two to three decades. Surveys show sharp declines in many measures of collective political participation, including attending a rally or speech (off 36 percent between 1973 and 1993), attending a meeting on town or school affairs (off 39 percent), or working for a political party (off 56 percent).

Some of the most reliable evidence about trends comes from the General Social Survey (GSS), conducted nearly every year for more than two decades. The GSS demonstrates, at all levels of education and among both men and women, . . . a drop of roughly one-third in social trust since 1972. (Trust in political authorities, indeed in many social institutions, has also declined sharply over the last three decades, but that is conceptually a distinct trend.) Slumping membership has afflicted all sorts of groups, from sports clubs and professional

Continued on next page

associations to literary discussion groups and labor unions. Only nationality groups, hobby and garden clubs, and the catch-all category of "other" seem to have resisted the ebbing tide. Gallup polls report that church attendance fell by roughly 15 percent during the 1960s and has remained at that lower level ever since, while data from the National Opinion Research Center suggest that the decline continued during the 1970s and 1980s and by now amounts to roughly 30 percent. A more complete audit of American social capital would need to account for apparent countertrends. Some observers believe, for example, that support groups and neighborhood watch groups are proliferating, and few deny that the last several decades have witnessed explosive growth in interest groups represented in Washington. . . . With due regard to various kinds of counterevidence, I believe that the weight of available evidence confirms that Americans today are significantly less engaged with their communities than was true a generation ago. Of course, American civil society is not moribund. Many good people across the land work hard every day to keep their communities vital. Indeed, evidence suggests that America still outranks many other countries in the degree of our community involvement and social trust. But if we examine our lives, not our aspirations, and if we compare ourselves not with other countries but with our parents, the best available evidence suggests that we are less connected with one another.

Reversing this trend depends, at least in part, on understanding the causes of the strange malady afflicting American civic life. This is the mystery I seek to unravel here: Why, beginning in the 1960s and accelerating in the 1970s and 1980s, did the fabric of American community life begin to fray? Why are more Americans bowling alone? (Putnam 1996)

In his book *Bowling Alone,* published four years later, Putnam refines his assessment of the plausible explanations of that decline. He concludes that the decline in civic engagement is not due in any great degree to the usual suspects: entry of women into the workforce in greater numbers and the alleged lengthening of the workweek, geographic mobility of households (which is not greater than in earlier decades) or suburbanization (suburbanites participate at higher rates than do residents of the central city, the main source of new suburbanites).

Increased viewing of television is the only expected reason for the decline of civicness for which he finds substantial supporting evidence. How-

Continued on next page

ever, he finds that a greater impact is the replacement of more-civic-minded cohorts by less-civic-minded ones in those age groups that are most civically involved. That only leads to another question: Why are younger adults today less likely to be engaged civically than were their grandparents during and prior to World War II? Putnam argues that people's lifetime trajectory of civic engagement is set in the events of their formative youthful years. Although the patterns are somewhat varied for different indicators of civic engagement, there is a dip in people's civic participation if they were born after the 1930s. "As we continue along the line to the boomers and then to the X'ers, the downward trend in joining, trusting, voting, newspaper reading, church attending, volunteering and being interested in politics continues almost uninterruptedly for nearly 40 years" (Putnam 2000: 254). However, Putnam suggests that civic engagement is cyclical, having expanded and peaked during the Populist and Progressive eras and again during the 1930s and 1940s. The former period corresponds to the period of greatest expansion of industrial capitalism in the United States (and of abuses resulting from that expansion), and the latter combines a period of social upheaval and ferment (the Great Depression) with a period of war, in which people in all walks of life were called upon to do all they could for the war effort, wherever they were.

There is a lag in the statistics of involvement, since it takes time for the younger groups to replace the previous cohorts as the numerically dominant group in the age categories in which participation is greatest, which generally corresponds to the ages in which people are in the workforce. If one looks at the major national membership organizations, an amazingly large proportion were founded in the two decades surrounding the turn from the nineteenth to the twentieth centuries—and many of the same organizations began losing membership precipitously in the 1960s, although for others the loss happened a decade or so earlier. Putnam argues that, more in the sense of the Progressive era than in the sense of sacrifice exhibited in World War II, the time is ripe for a new period of reform and civic involvement. This may be overly optimistic, since there are not yet many signs of an impending turnaround. What do you think?

REFERENCES: Robert D. Putnam. 1996. "The Strange Disappearance of Civic America." *The American Prospect* 7, no. 24 (1 December). An abbreviated version is online; available: http://www.prospect.org/print/V7/24/putnam-r.html; accessed April 2003.

_____. 2000. *Bowling Alone. The Collapse and Revival of American Community.* New York: Simon and Schuster.

Toqueville rightly pointed out that in the first half of the nineteenth century, European societies were too stratified to be able to develop strong associations throughout the society: The wealthy did not often need them, for they had the resources to act alone. When they did need to work through an association, they were quite capable of forming one, accomplishing the objective, and then disbanding it. The working and lower classes, because they possessed so few cultural, financial, or human resources, were effectively barred from building associations; thus, great inequalities made it difficult for the lower classes to get organized. It is not surprising that in 1848, eight years after Toqueville published the second volume of *Democracy in America,* revolutions broke out in many parts of Europe as the subordinate classes perceived no other alternative for redressing grievances.

What Toqueville did not capture—and it was more than half a century later that Durkheim provided the conceptual and empirical tools to do so—was the fact that strong associations did not necessarily add up to a collective will. Certainly, what we now call a strong civil society made it more difficult for one leader or one group to capture political power and turn it to parochial and antidemocratic ends. The Civil War, which Toqueville foresaw because of the inequalities generated by slavery, was a case in point. Although the marketplace of ideas where American associations hawked their wares of values and desired futures was bustling, a large and important group—African Americans—was prohibited from entering that marketplace. Once blacks were emancipated and the secession of the southern states from the Union was ended, the process of removing this greatest bottleneck to the achievement of democracy—the subjugation of black people— had begun, although it would take a century more for African Americans to fully gain their political and legal liberation.

But still the cacophony of voices that resulted from having many associations in U.S. communities did not assure an improvement in well-being, happiness, or domestic or community tranquillity. More than half a century after Durkheim completed his *Elementary Forms of Religious Life* (1912), Harold Kaufman and his student Ken Wilkinson, rural sociologists from Mississippi, examined this all-too-frequent contradiction between a flurry of activities by community-based organizations and a lack of improvement at the level of the community itself. Using an interactional approach, they proposed that it was important to distinguish the *social field* from the community field. According to Wilkinson, a social field is "a process of interaction through time, with direction toward some more or less distinctive outcome" (1972: 317). There are numerous social fields in a community. Each field consists of individuals and organizations working toward a particular goal. A good example in Solidale was the group of organizations and individuals that worked to establish a cooperative/joint venture for making grain ethanol as an additive to gasoline (commonly known as "gasohol"). The ethanol plant benefited the community secondarily, but its main beneficiaries were the farmer members from various communities in the central part of the state, who had a guaranteed market for their irrigated corn at a modest premium, and the regional energy company, which provided additional capital in return for equity in the plant through a joint venture with the farmers' ethanol cooperative (see Box 3.2).

BOX 3.2   An Example of a Social Field: Organizing for the Ethanol Plant in Solidale

Solidale's ethanol project is an example of how the dense organizational core [see Figure 3.1] can be tapped and the support of the local power elite can be utilized to facilitate a project. The Solidale Farmer Co-op and its local manager initiated the project. A number of state and federal subsidies made the venture attractive. To raise $20 million in equity capital for a 25 million gallon capacity plant, priced at $40 million, a limited liability corporation was created among three partners: a regional energy company, a national agriculture co-op, and a newly constituted closed member Farmer Cooperative. The Solidale co-op manager coordinated a regional effort, which raised $5.7 million from 215 area farmers and 15 area co-ops. The national agriculture co-op invested a couple million and the regional energy company invested the remaining balance. Farmers in the new co-op committed to a minimum initial investment of 5,000 bushels of corn at $2.50 a bushel ($12,500). The farmer cooperative serves as a shell, receiving its share of the profit from the limited liability corporation and distributing the profit to the farmers in the form of patronage dividends. As an obligation of membership, farmer members are obligated to sell a certain minimum number of bushels each year to the cooperative.

While the project did not require an outpouring of local resident support, a number of actions by local government and community organizations made the activity possible. Land for the plant was made available by the Solidale Development Corporation. Extending water to the plant was paid for cooperatively by the City of Solidale, the ethanol plant and the Development Corporation. Paving of the access road to the plant was paid for by county government. A favorable agreement was achieved between the City of Solidale and the ethanol plant for making necessary upgrades to Solidale's sewer treatment facility. Perhaps one of the more interesting types of support was provided by the local Chamber, which utilized promotional funds to charter two planes to transport area farmers to an ethanol

Continued on next page

An Example of a Social Field: Organizing for the Ethanol Plant in Solidale (continued)

facility in a neighboring state to generate additional farmer support of the farmer cooperative. The local newspaper provided extensive coverage of the trip as a further promotion.

Although local civic organizations were not engaged in the project and there was no out-pouring of resident support of the project, there also was no opposition to the activities necessary for the project to succeed. As the co-op manager and project leader explained, "had it not been for a very positive community that I knew would support the project, I probably wouldn't have tried any of this." The necessary support was generated within the organizational core and the two generalized community leaders, Sumner and Sorenson [pseudonyms], were instrumental. According to the co-op manager, Sorenson "put the glue together in the community between the city, the county and [the ethanol plant]."

The ethanol project benefited from the capacity of local leadership and the organizational structure to quickly achieve a consensus among the elites and build support for the project. The co-op manager had access to the central individuals and core organizations through his involvement in several core organizations and as a member of the densest consultation clique. Acquisition of local governmental support was not problematic with the support of the key elites. Resources necessary for final promotion of the project were easily acquired from the Chamber of Commerce, and the newspaper (whose editor is a member of the Development Corporation's advisory board) provided favorable coverage.

The project also illustrates the importance of extra-local ties and the capacity to access these extra-local resources. Funding for the limited liability corporation coupled with the state and federal subsidies were important resources that made project start-up viable. . . . [S]ome of the outside connections of the co-op manager were important for the project's success.

SOURCE: Excerpted from Jeffrey S. Sharp. 1998. "The Interactional Community: A Structural Network Analysis of Community Action in Three Midwestern Towns." Ph.D. diss., Iowa State University, 146–148.

If a set of interrelated actions associated with a social field is focused on the whole community, we may talk of a *community field*. A set of actions within a community field serves a general community interest rather than specific private interests. Examples of social fields are groups of associations—as discussed by de

Toqueville—that interact with one another for a common purpose. A community field, then, is the pattern of interaction that focuses on the entire community. It can be a single organization that looks out for the interests of the community— the Solidale Development Authority might qualify—or, more likely, it may be a web of associations, firms, and even governmental entities that collaborate for a common purpose. Figure 3.1 shows the interaction patterns of the core organizations in Solidale. Included among those organizations and arguably the organizing force for the web of core organizations is the Solidale Development Authority.

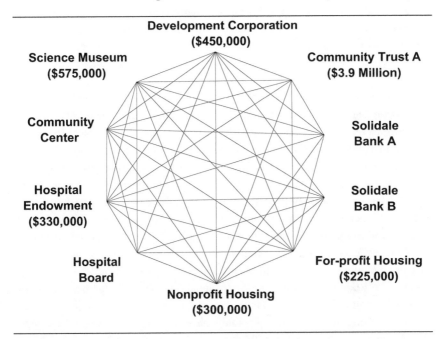

FIGURE 3.1   Core Clique of the Solidale Organizational Structure

Bonding and Bridging Social Capital: Homogeneity or Inclusion?

Social capital can be divided into two parts:[1] *Bonding social capital* consists of connections among individuals and groups with similar backgrounds. They may be based principally on class, ethnicity, kinship, gender, or similar social characteristics. Members of a group with high bonding capital know one another in multiple settings or roles. *Bridging social capital* connects diverse groups within the community to each other and to groups outside the community. The ties that make up bridging social capital are usually single purpose or instrumental, whereas bonding ties are affective or emotionally charged. Bridging social capital fosters diversity of ideas and brings together diverse people.

Deepa Narayan incorporates the notion of power into the bonding-bridging relationship. Regarding bonding social capital, she said,

> While primary groups and networks undoubtedly provide opportunities to those who belong, they also reinforce pre-existing social stratification, prevent mobility of excluded groups, minorities or poor people, and become the bases of corruption and co-optation of power by the dominant social groups. Cross-cutting ties which are dense and voluntary, though not necessarily strong . . . help connect people with access to different information, resources and opportunities. (Narayan 1999: 13)

Thus, Narayan suggested that the development of *weak* or *crosscutting ties* is important for breaking down inequalities of power and access. For instance, a contributing factor to racial inequality is the lack of information available to African American youth about where they can find "good" jobs. Furthermore, a lack of parental connections to smooth the way for African American children to gain access to those jobs contributes to inequality. These notions of exclusion are complementary to those presented by Bourdieu (1986), who proposed that elite French families and upwardly mobile middle-class families use family economic and cultural capital to gain strategic class-based ties (social capital) for their children, thereby excluding the children of parents who lack resources and the necessary strategic impulses for moving their children up the social ladder.

How do bridging and bonding social capital interact at the (geographic) community level in order to determine the extent of collective action that takes place in those communities? A simple fourfold table is used in an effort to predict levels of collective action (see Figure 3.2).

Bridging and bonding social capital can reinforce one another: When both are high, we get effective community action, or entrepreneurial social infrastructure (ESI), discussed later in this chapter. When both are low, extreme individualism dominates, which is reflected at the community level in social disorganization. Community action is low when residents predominantly relate apathetically to their community. When bridging social capital is high but bonding social capital is low, there is *clientelism,* and the relationships formed within and outside the community are predominantly vertical. When bonding social capital is high but bridging social capital is low, there is often conflict. The community may be organized against an outside entity or against itself. In the latter case, bonding social capital occurs within homogeneous groups within the community, and these groups oppose one another.

Four characteristics of networks build bridging social capital. First, networks include a *horizontal* dimension. Lateral learning is critical in networks; communi-

FIGURE 3.2 Community Social Capital Typology

ties learn best from each other. Such social capital is built in the course of lateral learning, both between communities and within communities. Second, networks include a *vertical* dimension. It is critical that communities be linked to regional, state, and national resources and organizations; however, it is also critical that there not be just one gatekeeper who makes that linkage. Elected officials and members of organizations need to attend regional, state, and national meetings so that one person cannot say to other members of the community, "Well, the rules won't let us." Other points of view that are still within the rules can uncover alternatives. Third, networks are *flexible;* being part of a network should not be a lifetime commitment. Participation increases and burnout decreases when people are asked to participate in a network that has a finite life span or a regular rotation of leadership. People are willing to participate where they can make a difference and when they are asked to participate primarily in things in which they have a genuine interest, although care must be taken that the larger vision is shared. Flexibility means that more people have the opportunity to become leaders. Fourth, networks have *permeable boundaries;* the community of interest is expanded and the community of place grows larger as new partnerships and collaborations are formed. On the other hand, when very local action is required, the boundaries can become temporarily narrowed. For instance, it is appropriate to involve multiple communities in an effort at industrial development, since an industrial firm will draw workers from various communities around the one in which it is ultimately located. On the other hand, a bond issue for expanding a wastewater treatment plant will appropriately involve a single community and perhaps its hinterland. Permeable and flexible networks are critical for community sustainability.

Exploring how the two dimensions of social capital relate to community change is a vital component in this discussion (see Figure 3.3).

FIGURE 3.3 Community Social Capital Typology and Change

Absence of Social Capital (Bridging, Low; Bonding, Low)

Communities lacking bonding or bridging social capital also lack the capacity for change. Individuals in these types of communities view themselves as self-reliant—or as totally adrift. In the absence of social capital, some people can succeed by substituting financial capital for social capital. For communities without financial capital, the absence of social capital can be fatal, as health studies are increasingly showing. People in communities that lack social capital are more likely to experience stress, hypertension, and mental health problems, among other difficulties. Crime rates are high where there is an absence of social capital; personal security is a major problem. The wealthy can protect themselves with expensive security systems. They install alarms and even hire their own police, but no protection is available in the poor communities.

Conflict with the Outside/Internal Factionalism (Bonding High; Bridging Low)

When bonding is high and bridging is low, communities resist change. This may occur in two ways. The community may organize in opposition to the outside in a kind of reactive solidarity; newcomers are viewed with suspicion in such communities. This reduces access to information from the outside. Alternatively, different homogeneous groups or factions within the community may have varying perspectives on the kinds of change that might benefit their community. The groups do not trust each other and therefore are unwilling to cooperate with one another. Conflict is internal and becomes the dominant community-level attribute. Although collective action may occur within groups in the geographic community, it is difficult to organize and carry out action at the community level if internal conflict persists. Social fields overcome the community field.

External Influence via Local Elites
(Bridging High; Bonding Low)

Where bridging social capital is high but bonding capital is low, some degree of control from outside the community is exercised through community elites or, in the most extreme form, local "bosses." This arrangement does not preclude collective action on the part of community residents, but that action is more apt to benefit outsiders or their local surrogates. Although this pattern of social capital is also built on norms of reciprocity and mutual trust (or at least mutual obligation), those relationships are vertical rather than horizontal. Power is clearly concentrated. Traditional patron-client relationships, typical of urban gangs or boss-run political machines, are created. Those at the bottom of the hierarchy—who are obviously beholden to the few at the top—are the majority of the population in such communities. As a result, recipients of favors owe substantial loyalty to their patron when it is time to vote for public office, to collect from a loser in the numbers racket, or to settle a score with a rival gang. As a result, horizontal networks are actively discouraged, particularly outside the sphere of influence of the patron, godfather, or elite clique. Such systems create dependency.

This type of social capital is prevalent in some persistently impoverished communities. For instance, the Appalachian coal-mining community of Blackwell (a pseudonym) studied by Cynthia Duncan (1999) involved control of most of the resources, businesses, and services by absentee-owned coal companies. When employment in the coal mines declined, jobs were in short supply. An elite group of families controlled many public-sector and private-sector jobs through their control of local government and the school system and through exclusive ties to state government. Gaining employment depended on whether one came from a "good" or a "bad" family. A more "modern" version of this hierarchical social capital is the power elite community model, in which social and economic inequalities are generally substantial. There is clearly a ruling clique that maintains its social distance from the rest of the community, but it preserves political influence either directly or through pliable middle- or working-class officeholders.

Entrepreneurial Social Infrastructure
(Bridging and Bonding Both High)

Horizontal social capital implies egalitarian forms of reciprocity without necessarily implying equal wealth, education, or talents. Community resources or capital are broadly defined. Not only is each member of the community expected to give, earning status and pleasure from doing so, but each is expected to receive as well. Each person in the community is deemed capable of sharing something valuable with all members of the community, including contributions to collective projects, from parades to the volunteer fire department to Girl Scouts. Norms of reciprocity are reinforced, but payback to the donor is not required or even expected.

Such communities also have diverse contacts with the outside, which provide needed information to the community, information that can often be used to generate outside resources without exercising control over the community. Solidale is a good example of a community with both high bridging and high bonding social capital. Over the past few decades, the community has had impressive economic growth, resulting in substantial population growth. The leadership has followed a few simple rules. First, they are not afraid to use local resources if a potential economic enterprise or amenity looks like a good risk; local funds beget outside investments and industries in part because local investments send the message that the community is willing to partner with others. Second, there is a conscious effort to recruit young males and newcomers into community leadership, particularly through the private Development Corporation. Third, it is an attractive place to live, with amenities such as attractive and affordable housing, an excellent library, a community center, and a science museum. All were financed largely through trusts endowed (at least initially) by bankers without progeny, a community foundation, two housing corporations and a Development Authority organized by local elites. Clearly, Solidale has high bonding *and* bridging social capital.

Entrepreneurial Social Infrastructure

Communities that are high on both bridging and bonding social capital are poised for action, able to engage the community field. We use the term "entrepreneurial social infrastructure (ESI)" to indicate the structures and impacts that occur when both bridging and bonding social capital are high. ESI is a measurable form of community action, conceptually distinct from social capital. We hypothesize that it is a consequence of high bridging and bonding social capital.

Two main characteristics distinguish ESI from social capital: First, ESI can readily be changed through an explicit collective effort; it links social capital to *agency*. A community with a well-developed social infrastructure tends to engage in collective action for community betterment, which is why we call this phenomenon *entrepreneurial social infrastructure*.[2] ESI is a less abstract concept than the concept of social capital. For example, it is difficult to directly change levels of community trust, but it may be possible to encourage previously combative groups to cooperate through conflict management or by redefining issues.

Second, whereas *diversity,* the presence of different perspectives regarding means and ends, and social inclusion, assuring that those groups usually without voice are empowered, are central to bridging social capital, ESI focuses on the outcomes of the inclusion of diversity—the willingness to consider and accept alternatives. In a community-planning process, diverse types of information are sought from individuals and groups with different values, backgrounds, and perspectives from both inside and outside the community. The flow of information is not channeled exclusively to or from a particular group but is dispersed widely throughout the community. Furthermore, the inclusion of all citizens in the decisionmaking process itself ensures greater commitment to carrying out those decisions. Decisions, once made, are more generally accepted.

We have identified certain basic features within a community with high ESI, including legitimation of alternatives, inclusiveness and diversity of networks, and widespread resource mobilization.

Legitimation of Alternatives

Some communities seek a silver bullet to solve problems, whereas in others, various perspectives are discussed and combined. These latter communities recognize that there are alternative ways of reaching shared goals. As with continuous improvement in industry, definitive solutions are not sought. Instead, countermeasures are implemented as progress is monitored, and alternative ways of achieving goals are examined.

This leads to the acceptance of controversy, which contrasts with conflict. Acceptance of controversy means that people can disagree and still maintain mutual respect. In contrast, in a conflict situation, lines are drawn and labels are assigned according to one's stance on a particular issue. Conflict-prone communities may tacitly agree to not deal with issues around which disagreement exists, thereby suppressing controversy. New issues are not brought forward, visions of the future are not shared, and alternative ways of achieving goals are not developed. In this situation, conflict often lies right beneath the surface.

In communities that accept controversy, politics are depersonalized. Ordinary citizens are willing to run for public office and feel able to implement measures to resolve community issues without being castigated by their constituents. There is awareness that the public sector is vital to provoking change at the local level; consequently, participation increases in both civic and governmental organizations. Furthermore, ESI is strengthened when market actors are involved. In the city of Marshalltown, Iowa, a community with a meatpacking plant and a growing immigrant population as the primary workforce in the plant, the addition of business leaders (market actors) and local government actors to a diversity group allowed it to succeed where it previously had failed in ameliorating the situation of immigrants.

In such communities, great attention is given to process. That meetings are conducted in a civil fashion and that all are given the opportunity to present their viewpoints is given great importance. When controversy begins to spill over into conflict, specific conflict-management mechanisms are put in place, often with the assistance of an outsider trained in conflict management. On the positive side, individual and collective successes are celebrated. In communities where it is not legitimate to look at alternatives, the notion of a "limited good" is strong. One person's success is considered to have occurred at the expense of another. These are communities where controversy does not occur because people are unwilling to risk expressing contrasting viewpoints.

The local newspaper can play an important role in conveying or failing to convey the information needed to make informed decisions. It can also set the tone of community dialogue on an issue. If it seeks to provide information and to suggest that controversy is legitimate, it will help prevent the conversion of disagreements into rancorous conflict with the potential to split the community. In a nationwide study of nonmetropolitan communities conducted by the authors, one of the strongest predictors of whether a community had carried out a successful economic development project was the presence of a newspaper that not only reported community issues but reported them fairly.

Unfortunately, in some small communities, the newspaper, often a weekly, tends to be long on ads and social announcements but short on news. The biggest zucchini of the season and the scores of the high school basketball games are highlighted, but there is seldom a reporter at the school board or town council meetings. Often, no hint of any bad news is allowed to appear in print. In only a minority of communities is the editor willing to take on controversial issues or address emerging community problems and thereby risk offending people. Communities, where controversy is openly aired and accessible factual information drives out rumors, are best able to process information from a variety of sources and make choices that have the potential to enhance community well-being.

Focusing on process allows for the assessment of progress toward goals. When progress does not meet expectations, a discussion of countermeasures for advancement occurs. There is less concern about "Whose crummy idea was that?" or "Why didn't you listen to me? I had a better idea" and more consideration of "What did we learn from this last effort?" and "What will we try now?"

Inclusive and Diverse Networks

Several qualities of *social networks*—webs of relationships within a community—allow communities to gain control of their social and economic development effectively and to become entrepreneurial communities. They include depersonalization of politics, development of extracommunity linkages, diverse community leadership, and approaches to involving excluded groups. Each of these is discussed in turn.

Discussion of politics in many rural communities involves personalities, not issues. The quality of social networks is much higher in communities that accept and confront reasoned disagreement and do not turn a public stand on a controversy into a symbol of either moral rectitude or degeneracy. Those who disagree on one issue may be allies on another in a coalition that facilitates collective resolution of a problem. Furthermore, disagreements can surface early rather than being suppressed until they explode and divide the community. Political depersonalization requires the acceptance of controversy as a normal feature of community life.

Through the development of linkages with the outside, a community gains access to information it needs to make choices about its future. Entrepreneurial communities foster extracommunity links and actively seek resources from other communities and from state and federal sources. They participate in regional planning groups, confer with the cooperative extension service, and apply for federal grants. They also engage in lateral learning from other communities. For instance, citizens of Decatur County, Kansas (its county seat, Oberlin, is another community with considerable entrepreneurial social infrastructure) decided to develop their own community carnival rather than relying on "sleazy" and "unreliable" itinerant carnivals to come to their 4-H fair. They inquired about communities that had built their own carnivals and dispatched a delegation to Hydro, Oklahoma, to learn from that town's successful effort. The delegation reported back to the community, adapted Hydro's experience to their situation, and built their own carnival, run entirely by volunteers. Civic groups from across the county are responsible for a particular ride or game each year. That gives every organization a concrete project and strengthens social capital among groups as they work together to plan the event each year. The proceeds from the carnival support new enterprises throughout the county.

By emphasizing flexible, dispersed community leadership, communities avoid becoming dependent on a single broker who has contacts or charisma. In entrepreneurial communities, members rotate through public offices and share informal leadership roles. Often newcomers to the community are active in leadership positions. Newcomers often bring with them a convert's appreciation of the community and an awareness of outside forces acting upon it. The Solidale Development Authority does not leave to chance the integration of newcomers into the leadership structure. However, the incorporation of members of new ethnic groups, youth, and even women into leadership positions seems to present a challenge to many rural communities, including Solidale, that are perfectly willing to include white male newcomers.

Being inclusive does not simply mean having people at the table. Some youth programs intended to teach leadership skills, which the youth can then share with their community, have discovered this: A common response to the presence of these youths is, "Wonderful, here is someone to sell the donuts and do the cleanup." The youths may be willing to do these tasks, but they are also eagerly prepared to help plan the development activities. But when they try to participate in the planning, the response of the established leaders is, "Well, we don't do it that way here" or "We tried that twenty years ago and it didn't work." The mere presence of the youth does not equal inclusiveness.

The best approach to diversity is not to ask, "Are we being politically correct?" A more appropriate question is "Whose viewpoint is necessary as we move forward toward our goals?" For example, if a community development project's goal is to create more jobs, local people who take those jobs need to be part of the process so that there can be a better link between human capital and the built capital that offers employment opportunities.

Promoting diversity involves directly asking nonparticipants why they are not involved: Is it the time of day? Is the place too expensive for lunch? Is it the location? Meeting at lunch on workdays is impossible for people who work in factories or in hourly wage employment. In addition, people who are poor or have mobility problems may find some meeting places difficult to access because of the lack of transportation.

Blanket invitations do not promote inclusiveness. Personal invitations are preferred over advertisements in newspapers. People who do not receive personal invitations and who are not part of the planning team generally only attend meetings if they are really incensed and want to protest. Personal invitations should explain how that person's or institution's special capabilities are critical to the effort.

When excluded groups are not organized, it is difficult to get effective participation from members of that group—or it is only the more educated or wealthy members of the group who participate. We have concluded in our work with rural Hispanics that encouraging them to form their own interest group is an important prerequisite to their effective participation in community-wide organizations that represent the community field. Inclusiveness and diversity must go together, but inclusiveness sometimes means encouraging unorganized or excluded groups to form their own organizations in order to become more effective community participants.

Resource Mobilization

Resource mobilization is the last critical piece of structured community action, or ESI. First, resources in the community must be fully accessible. This applies to private resources, such as access to credit, as well as to public resources, such as high-quality schooling, recreational opportunities, and other opportunities. This does not mean there cannot be criteria for access, but the criteria should be publicized, and there should be opportunities for people to increase their chance for access.

When mobilizing private resources, financial institutions need to decide how to disperse appropriate loan amounts, with the appropriate terms, to all levels of entrepreneurs and citizens. In communities that successfully mobilize their resources, private citizens of all levels contribute financial aid when there is a need, and opportunities are available for individuals to contribute their time and goods to worthwhile causes. The ability to mobilize private resources is an important element of community action and gives everyone a chance to contribute.

Social capital building for development, or ESI, includes communities of interest and place. We also find that ESI is enhanced by forming advocacy and action coalitions among institutional actors of the different sectors (for example, market, state, and civil society) and at different levels (such as international, national, regional, provincial, and local levels). Civil society is key to adding sustainability to the policy mix, and governments (the state) are uniquely able to provide rewards for market actors who conserve and protect natural and human resources and punishments for those who do not. Although market firms initially resist regulation of their treatment of employees or pollution, in the longer term many firms discover that pollution and not valuing workers are forms of waste; profits can be enhanced through environmental cost accounting and by building employee commitment.

Interactions of Different Forms of Capital

Favoring only one form of capital can deplete all capital within a community for the future; however, each form of capital has the potential to enhance the productivity of the others. For instance, increasing social capital greatly reduces transaction costs, making other resource uses more efficient. Social capital has an independent effect on the functioning of economic systems. Transaction cost economics suggest the importance of social capital in increasing competitiveness, whether among firms or among nations.

James Coleman (1988) found that private religious schools had lower dropout rates than either public schools or secular private schools. He explained the difference in terms of what he calls "closure." In the parochial schools, parents of children who were friends knew both their children's friends and the parents of those friends. Coupled with the close contact that parents had with teachers, this assured a good deal of social control by parents over children's behavior both in and out of school. That parents had similar values also contributed to both social control and a sense of belonging on the part of the children. Therefore, they were not likely to drop out of school. The U.S. Department of Education published *The Condition of Education 2002,* a report showing that private schools rated higher than public schools in student achievement. Private school students took more classes than public school students, especially more college-preparatory classes, and had a higher graduation rate, 98.4 percent. The graduation rate for public schools was 91.4 percent. Additionally, more private school students than public school students attended college after high school. Does this mean we should privatize public schools or use vouchers?

Differences among public schools are as great or greater than the differences between public and private schools. A study of Missouri public school districts showed that schools with high levels of social capital—measured by such indicators as high attendance at intervarsity sports events, a perceived safe and drug-free school and community environment, and low student-teacher ratio—have fewer dropouts than comparable schools with low levels of social capital (Buckley 1997). The challenge is to maintain and strengthen social capital in order to enhance other forms of capital.

Additionally, overemphasis on generating financial and built capital without regard to the pollutants emitted in the process can reduce the value of human capital through negative impacts on health. Destroying soil and water quality can negatively affect natural capital, and if local networks are bypassed and replaced with impersonal bureaucratic structures with top-down mandates, social capital can be damaged. Attention solely to natural capital can lead to a wasting of human capital and a decline in financial and built capital as natural capital preservation is pursued.

Conclusions

As suggested by Putnam's research in Italy (1993a), research done by the World Bank (2001), and other studies, development is enhanced when social capital exists. But when bonding social capital is not tempered by bridging social capital, it creates barriers to change. When bridging and bonding social capital reinforce one another, development can occur; local resources are innovatively combined with and augmented by outside resources. Situations must be established so that all community members have a chance to contribute to the collective endeavor—and have their contributions appreciated.

Although a balance of bridging and bonding social capital is needed at all levels of society, building bridging social capital of excluded groups is key. Unless there is a certain amount of social capital within excluded groups, it is difficult for a community to build its social infrastructure. And unless there is a certain degree of community bridging social capital—an inclusive orientation by the dominant community groups—increased social capital on the part of excluded groups may lead to reactive solidarity on the part of the dominant group within the community, further distancing a now well-organized excluded group. Attention to the components of entrepreneurial social infrastructure—legitimation of alternatives; building inclusive and diverse networks of those likely to be affected by the particular project, policy, or objective; and fostering widespread resource mobilization—can lead to community betterment.

Chapter Summary

Building social capital, which includes norms of reciprocity and mutual trust, is vitally important if small communities are to thrive. Communities can foster lasting social capital by improving communication within and outside the community. This phenomenon is not new; it is as old as human society and involves bonding and bridging social capital. Bonding social capital includes making multiple connections with individuals and groups from similar backgrounds. Bridging social capital ties different groups together within and outside a community. When both bridging social capital and bonding social capital are high, entrepreneurial social infrastructure (ESI) is enhanced. If bridging social capital and bonding social capital are low, individual solutions to collective problems are sought. There are several combinations of bridging and bonding social capital that can have positive and negative results on community development.

Accepting controversy in communities can have positive results if people can disagree while still maintaining mutual respect. If a community's local news media only reflect positive occurrences, then progress cannot be made because existing conditions are not being evaluated sufficiently. Social networks within and outside a community allow economic growth. These networks need to be inclusive and diverse. Diverse groups must not only be invited to sit at the table but may have to be encouraged to organize among themselves before participating in community-wide coalitions.

Resources within a community must be accessible and mobilized effectively. Favoring only one form of capital can have negative results; each form of capital has the potential to enhance the productivity of others. Sustaining success in a community requires building synergy among forms of capital. All forms of capital can be utilized effectively if their relationships to one another are regularly considered.

Key Terms

Agency is the capacity to change social structure through the will of an individual or group to do so.

Bonding social capital involves ties among persons (or organizations made up of persons) who are located similarly in the socioeconomic system. Such individuals generally know one another well, having multiple ties that can be characterized as emotional ties.

Bridging social capital involves singular ties between individuals or organizations. Those ties are generally instrumental—that is, single purpose—and therefore do not involve an exchange of emotion or affect. Bridging social capital may be horizontal (between equals) or vertical/hierarchical.

Civic engagement refers to people's involvement in their communities and in the civic life of their nation. It includes involvement in political life, but it generally relates to participation in civil society.

Civil religion is a set of cultural ideas, symbols, and practices oriented to the direct worship of society (or the nation-state) by its members. Generally, if certain members do not show sufficient deference or patriotism, they will be sanctioned negatively, either by state authorities or by other members of the society.

Civil society is the organized sector of a society that imparts or seeks to impart values to the society as a whole. Civil society consists of associations that are separate from government (state) and from market- or profit-oriented firms.

Clientelism is a system by which persons subordinate in the social structure are beholden to and do things for a *patron*. The patron, in exchange for loyalty from the client(s), provides certain largesse, but the patron is always in the more powerful position.

Collective representations or *social solidarity* are the common tightly held or "sacred" symbols deriving from shared practices (ritual) and strong networks. They are similar to bonding social capital and contribute to a strong sense of collective identity or bonding.

A *community field* is a social field that focuses on the whole community; that is, it consists of structured interactions among individuals, families, organizations, firms, and/or government agencies for the purpose of changing the community.

Diversity, as the term is used here, refers to the presence of different perspectives regarding means and ends and the recognition that individuals with different backgrounds and experiences will view an issue differently and therefore may contribute fresh ideas to the solution of a particular problem.

Entrepreneurial social infrastructure (ESI) is both the social capacity and the collective will of local communities to provide for their social, economic, and environmental well-being.

Flexible networks are those that expand, contract, or shift their composition in response to differing circumstances. People can readily move into and out of leadership.

Horizontal networks are those that link persons or organizations that are at the same or similar level in a system of authority.

Permeable boundaries are characteristic of communities or organizations that are not rigid in distinguishing members from outsiders and allow their boundaries to expand or contract according to the issue at hand. Such communities tend to be inclusive rather than exclusive.

Social capital includes norms of reciprocity and mutual trust. Norms can be reinforced through a variety of processes: forming groups, collaborating within and among groups, developing a united view of a shared future, and engaging in collective action.

Social exclusion is the shunning or leaving out of decisionmaking discussions and resource allocation of certain members of a community or group.

A *social field* is a process of interaction of individuals and organizations with specific interests through time, with direction toward some more or less distinctive outcome.

Social networks are webs of relationships that link individuals or organizations within a community or with the outside.

Social structure is the institutional framework that shapes order in daily, weekly, and yearly interaction between and among people.

Vertical networks involve ties between individuals, organizations, or communities that are in a hierarchical relationship to one another.

Weak ties are links with persons with values and experiences different from one's own. They are usually single-purpose links. A similar term is *crosscutting ties.*

References

American Civil Liberties Union. 2002. "Civil Liberties after 9-11: The ACLU Defends Freedom" (September 20, 32 pp.). Online; available: http://www.aclu.org/SafeandFree/SafeandFree.cfm?ID=10898&c=207; accessed April 2003.

Bourdieu, Pierre. 1986. "The Forms of Capital." In *Handbook of Theory and Research for the Sociology of Education,* ed. John C. Richardson, 241–258. New York: Greenwood Press.

Buckley, Barbara Ann. 1997. "High School Dropout Rates and Social Capital Influences in Missouri's School Districts." Master's thesis, Iowa State University.

Coleman, James C. 1988. "Social Capital in the Creation of Human Capital." *American Journal of Sociology* 94 (Supplement S95–S120):95–119.

Duncan, Cynthia M. 1999. *Worlds Apart: Why Poverty Persists in Rural America.* New Haven: Yale University Press.

Durkheim, Emile. [1893] 1984. *The Division of Labor in Society.* New York: Free Press.

_____. [1912] 2001. *Elementary Forms of Religious Life.* Trans. Carol Cosman. Abridged by Mark S. Cladis. Oxford: Oxford University Press.

Flora, Cornelia B., and Jan L. Flora. 1993. "Entrepreneurial Social Infrastructure: A Necessary Ingredient." *The Annals of the American Academy of Political and Social Science* 529 (September):48–58.

Flora, Cornelia B., Jan L. Flora, and Reuben J. Tapp. 2000. "Meat, Meth, and Mexicans: Community Responses to Increasing Ethnic Diversity." *Journal of the Community Development Society* 31:277–299.

Flora, Cornelia B., Michael Kinsley, Vicki Luther, Milan Wall, Susan Odell, Shanna Ratner, and Janet Topolsky. 1999. "Measuring Community Success and Sustainability: An Interactive Workbook" (August). Online; available: http://www.ncrcrd.iastate.edu/Community_Success/about.html; accessed September 2002.

Flora, Jan L. 1998. "Social Capital and Communities of Place." *Rural Sociology* 63, no. 4 (December):481–506.

Flora, Jan L., Jeff Sharp, Cornelia Flora, and Bonnie Newlon. 1997. "Entrepreneurial Social Infrastructure and Locally-Initiated Economic Development." *Sociological Quarterly* 38, no. 4 (Fall):623–645.

Granovetter, Mark S. 1973. "The Strength of Weak Ties." *American Journal of Sociology* 78, no. 6:1360–1380.

Kaufman, Harold F. 1959. "Toward an Interactional Conception of Community." *Social Forces* 38 (October):9–17.

Letheby, Pete. 2001. "Vets Finally Getting their Due . . . and Diplomas" (September 21). Online; available: www.theindependent.com/stories/092101/opi_letheby21.html; accessed January 8, 2003.

Narayan, Deepa. 1999. "Bonds and Bridges: Social Capital and Poverty" (August). Policy Research Working Paper 2167, Poverty Division, Poverty Reduction and Economic Management Network, The World Bank. Online; available: http://www.worldbank.org/poverty/scapital/library/narayan.pdf; accessed January 5, 2003.

Putnam, Robert D. 1993a. *Making Democracy Work: Civic Traditions in Modern Italy.* Princeton: Princeton University Press.

———. 1993b. "The Prosperous Community: Social Capital and Public Life." *The American Prospect* 13:35–42.

———. 1996. "The Strange Disappearance of Civic America." *The American Prospect* 7, no. 24 (1 December). An abbreviated version is online; available: http://www.prospect.org/print/V7/24/putnam-r.html; accessed April 2003.

———. 2000. *Bowling Alone. The Collapse and Revival of American Community.* New York: Simon and Schuster.

Sharp, Jeffrey S. 2001. "Locating the Community Field: A Study of Interorganizational Network Structure and Capacity for Community Action." *Rural Sociology* 66, no. 3:403–424.

Töennies, Ferdinand. [1887] 1957. *Community and Society.* Trans. and ed. Charles P. Loomis. East Lansing: Michigan State University Press.

Toqueville, Alexis de. [1835 and 1840] 1956. *Democracy in America.* Specially ed. and abridged by Richard D. Heffner. New York: New American Library Mentor Books.

U.S. Department of Education. 2002. National Center for Education Statistics. *The Condition of Education 2002*. NCES 2002-025. Washington, D.C.: U.S. Government Printing Office. Online; available: http://nces.ed.gov/pubs2002/ 2002025.pdf; accessed April 2003.

Wilkinson, Kenneth P. 1972. "A Field Theory Perspective for Community Development Research." *Rural Sociology* 37, no. 1:43–52.

_____. 1991. *The Community in Rural America*. New York: Greenwood Press.

World Bank. 2000. *World Development Report, 2000–2001: Attacking Poverty*. New York: Oxford University Press. Also online; available: http://www.worldbank. org/poverty/wdrpoverty/; accessed September 2002.

Young, Frank W. 1970. "Reactive Subsystems." *American Sociological Review* 35:297–307.

1. This dichotomy is similar to the classical formulations by Ferdinand Töennies (gemeinschaft versus gesellschaft) and Durkheim (organic versus mechanical solidarity) and to Mark Granovetter's more recent (1973) strong versus weak ties.

2. The term "social infrastructure" was chosen because the name suggests that it operates in a parallel way to physical infrastructure (which we include under the term "built capital") in community development.

4

Human Capital

The Tennessee Overhill Heritage Association was at a critical stage in bringing together its ecotourism plan. Although the maps of its trails were good, the association needed more knowledge of the plants and animals that could be seen at various points on the trails. They had brought in a wildlife specialist from the Tennessee Department of Environment and Conservation, but she had gotten her Ph.D. based on research in another part of the state. She had general information to share based on her formal education and fieldwork in western Tennessee, but she could not give them the local details they needed to put their plan in action.

The eight members of the ecotourism committee were stymied. Should they just go with something general? Or should they follow their principle of developing a unique cultural and environmental experience? Andrew Finney, one member of the committee, suddenly realized something. He turned to another member, Jean Littlefox. "Your husband, Thad, grew up in these woods. His grandmother taught him all about the plants and animals. He can whistle more birdsongs than anyone I know. Would he help with the ecotourism committee as we put our map together?"

Jean was embarrassed. She knew how uncomfortable Thad felt around groups, especially college-educated people who tended to write everything down on flip charts. She said, "You know, Thad doesn't know how to read. He just never took to it, somehow."

Andrew stopped for a moment. Then he replied, "We have eight people on this committee who know how to read. We don't have anyone who knows as much as Thad does about nature around here."

Thad joined the committee. The project not only served tourists, who were impressed by the uniqueness of the different places on the trail, but also schoolchildren, who were thrilled to accompany their custodian on hikes and learn the birdcalls from him.

★　　★　　★

Human capital consists of the assets that each person possesses: health, formal education, skills, knowledge, leadership, and talents. Although the dominant cultural capital tends to define human capital in terms of formal learning, human capital is far more than educational attainment.

What Is Human Capital?

Gary Becker and his colleague Theodore Schultz, both Nobel Prize laureates, have done the most to assure that human capital is a core concept in economics, and indeed, in social sciences in general. Here is how Becker describes human capital:

> To most people capital means a bank account, a hundred shares of IBM stock, assembly lines, or steel plants in the Chicago area. These are all forms of capital in the sense that they are assets that yield income and other useful outputs over long periods of time.
>
> But these tangible forms of capital are not the only ones. Schooling, a computer training course, expenditures on medical care, and lectures on the virtues of punctuality and honesty also are capital. That is because they raise earnings, improve health, or add to a person's good habits over much of his lifetime. Therefore, economists regard expenditures on education, training, medical care, and so on as investments in human capital. They are called "human capital" because people cannot be separated from their knowledge, skills, health, or values in the way they can be separated from their financial and physical assets. (Becker 2002)

Human capital includes those attributes of individuals that contribute to their ability to earn a living, strengthen community, and otherwise contribute to community organizations, to their families, and to self-improvement. Thad Littlefox strengthened his community by using skills and knowledge he already had, like birdcalling and knowledge of nature. Although Becker defines human capital rather broadly, he categorically states that education and training are the most important forms of human capital. But one also suspects that economists and sociologists have focused on formal education because level of education is easy to measure and the data are accessible. But equally important are learning skills and gaining knowledge through experience, as demonstrated by Thad Littlefox.

As Becker suggests, investment in the healthcare of persons in the labor force and of the citizenry in general is an investment in human capital. In a rich country such as the United States, health is not often thought of as being an important component of human capital, but in poorer countries, illness and impoverishment limit the contributions of large parts of the population as members of the workforce, as community members, as contributing family members, and as citizens.

Communicable diseases associated with poverty may also spread to those who are not poor, reducing the effectiveness of their human capital. If poor people are not vaccinated or treated for communicable diseases, others in the society may be at risk as well. To the degree that inequalities breed crime against property or person, victims may find their own human capital diminished. The fact that in the United States mental illness is not covered by insurance at the same level as are physical illnesses may substantially reduce the effect of other investments in human capital.

Interpersonal skills, values, and leadership capacity are part of human capital. What values individuals hold and how they exercise leadership may determine whether they make a greater or lesser contribution to production, family, and community. If an individual's values, interpersonal relations, and leadership styles are not appropriate for an occasion or for the organization or community of which he or she is a part, these components of human capital can actually have a negative effect on productive or other collective enterprises.

During an earlier era, human capital was also related to strength and tenacity in carrying out physical work. Strength and physical labor, although still important in many occupations, are not well rewarded. Frequently, employers turn to immigrants to supply the labor for jobs that require physical strength or that are dangerous, dirty, or otherwise unpleasant. The settlement of rural areas of the United States by Europeans (voluntarily), Africans (involuntary until recently), and Asians and Mexicans and other Latin Americans (voluntarily but welcome only when there was a labor shortage) is largely a story of people with very little formal education but with an ability to innovate and the willingness to engage in hard physical labor.

Historic Settlement Patterns and Human Capital

Governments and owners of land who had the means to transform and transport raw materials employed different regional strategies for recruiting and utilizing human capital to transform natural capital into financial capital. For governments, increasing their legitimacy (political capital) and their territory (natural capital) was part of their human capital strategy. As we understand these differences in access to resources, we can also understand the current regional differences in human capital.

Max Pfeffer (1983) argues that labor availability or scarcity was a major factor in explaining the development of the three main systems of farm production after the Civil War. All developed from highly concentrated landownership patterns. The three systems are sharecropping in the southern Cotton Belt, large-scale corporate farming in California (and later, parts of Arizona, Texas, and Florida), and family farming in the Midwest and interior West, following the pattern earlier developed in the Northeast.

Transformation of the
Plantation System in the Old South

Cotton and tobacco, both indigenous to the Americas, and rice, originating in Asia, were grown in the American South, where large grants of land to individuals created a landowning class. The government-sanctioned presence of slavery allowed landowners to plant labor-intensive, land-depleting *cropping systems*. Rice and cotton were cultivated in malarial areas. The Native American populations generally avoided those areas. Africans, whose sickle-cell gene gave them a higher level of immunity to malaria than other population groups, were brought in in large numbers to provide the labor in the plantation economy. Both cotton and tobacco were exported from the South, and both depended on slave labor and abundant land. For African Americans, the end of slavery was the most important legacy of the Civil War. The second most important legacy of the Civil War for African Americans was notable for its absence: the failure to institute land reform. Plantation owners were allowed to keep their land. But they faced a problem: a shortage of human capital to do the work on the land. They devised a *sharecropping* system as a more palatable way of enticing African Americans to raise cotton for the owners than hiring them outright as wageworkers under direct supervision of their former masters. The sharecropping system gave the sharecroppers a degree of autonomy but had the advantage (for the landowners) of shared risk. If there was a crop failure, the cost was borne by both parties. This transformed labor force was further controlled through *Jim Crow segregation laws,* reinforced by vigilantism with the collusion of local and state governments. Only with the push-and-pull factors of the boll weevil epidemic at the end of the 1920s and of World War II, both of which caused the exodus of many African Americans from the South, was the back of Jim Crow broken. The Civil Rights movement of the 1950s and 1960s sealed its fate. This history of perceiving human capital as "cheap" is reflected in the low educational levels and poor health status of many African Americans in the rural South today, particularly in the old plantation areas where their ancestors toiled as slaves.

Great Plains Family Labor Farms

The "filling in" of the Great Plains and the West, to which European Americans turned their attention after the Civil War, involved removing Native Americans. Military incursions and wars (up to the presidency of Ulysses S. Grant), movement to reservations (from 1870 to the 1930s), and assimilation (attempted through boarding schools, which were aimed to "get the red out," and through movement to urban areas) were the means of removal.

Although skeletal evidence from the 1600s on both continents suggests that Native Americans on the Great Plains and northern woodlands of North America were probably healthier than their European counterparts, the health status of Native Americans declined rapidly with European settlement as disease and removal from their food supply decimated their populations.

Railroads were key in European settlement of the Great Plains and the interior West of the United States from the 1860s to the 1890s. Government land grants to railroads and cheap government land prices for speculators with available cash led initially to large private landholdings. Labor scarcity and high risk, due mainly to unpredictable weather, came to define the production systems that developed. There was a shortage of human capital to work in agriculture. The rapid industrial growth and expanding demand for labor in the cities, the difficulty of recruiting a laboring "underclass" to the countryside, and a scattered and scarce population meant that more than wages was required to attract the people necessary to get agricultural work done. The promise of landownership brought yeoman farmers to the central and western grasslands and forests to raise grains and livestock, with their large families providing substantial but inexpensive labor.

The need for more settlers to generate railroad freight in the form of grain and livestock, the spectacular failure of a large-scale corporate grain farm experiment (called Bonanza Farms) on the western plains, and higher rates of return in urban economic activities led corporate landowners to divide and sell this land in the great midwestern part of the nation to smallholders, that is, farmers who relied on family labor. U.S. railroads advertised widely in northern Europe and the eastern United States to sell land to people who wanted to improve their lot in life. The growing cities, such as New York, Chicago, and Boston, needed cheap food to feed the workers that fueled their industrial revolutions.

Although these new family farmers were diverse ethnically, they were homogeneous racially. The only groups or individuals with adequate capital to purchase land—or to buy passage from overseas—were Europeans or Americans of European descent. For example, in 1872 Emil Flushe began selling railroad land west of Irwin, Iowa, recruiting Catholics from Germany to come to a town he named Westphalia (just as he had named Westphalia, Minnesota, and would name Westphalia, Kansas) as he followed the railroad west. Westphalia, Iowa, maintains its street signs in German and still has a strong collective orientation centered on the culture of its German Catholicism. A Norwegian American farmer who recently moved to the community worried about fitting in. He did, for with time and two world wars, the ethnic differences between and within most midwestern and western communities were covered by a durable varnish of U.S. culture. Today, the fact that grandparents or great-grandparents of the "native" (European) residents of those communities were immigrants who maintained their own language for several generations does not appear to contribute to rural acceptance of new waves of immigrants from Latin America, Asia, and Africa to certain communities of the Midwest. Iowa, for example, made English the official language in 2002.

Labor-Intensive Corporate Agriculture in the West

The history of the West is a history of large landholdings, beginning with the Spanish (later Mexican) land grants. After the 1848 defeat of Mexico in the Mexican-American War, one-third of Mexico's territory was ceded to the United States. Long-term residents found it more difficult to access natural capital, such as land, water, and timber. Some land grants were sold intact to Anglos (non-Hispanic whites). In other cases, U.S. courts did not recognize legal ownership of the land grants. In northern New Mexico, Spanish communities settled in the 1600s lost their right to graze the common lands. This was in spite of the fact that they had title to land grants consisting of homesteads and of common grazing lands. Community common lands had been eliminated in England with the enclosure acts of the eighteenth century in order to "free" labor for industry, and the new nation of the United States did not recognize commonly held land. Common lands were not compatible with the U.S. approach to property rights. The community common lands were ceded to the states or sold to entrepreneurs and logging companies, or they became federal lands. The Hispanic inhabitants, called *españoles,* or Spaniards, lacked adequate land for grazing their sheep and other livestock.

The need for labor—in mining, in building the transcontinental railroad, and in agriculture—brought waves of immigrants to rural areas of the West. First came the Chinese, then the Filipinos, Japanese, and Mexicans, to which have recently been added other Latin American peoples. Asian groups, often pushed by difficult economic or political conditions in the sending country, were welcomed as a new source of cheap labor when there was a particular job to be done. Chinese workers cleared 88,000 acres of rich swampland in California in the San Joaquin–Sacramento delta area and built the western end of the transcontinental railroad that joined in Ogden, Utah, in 1869.

When a project was finished or when the economy contracted in the United States, these Asian immigrants were then excluded. The Chinese were prohibited from immigrating to the United States in 1882, the Japanese in 1908, and the Filipinos in 1934 (when Congress legislated the independence of the Philippines, although independence was actually granted in 1946). Asians in general were excluded from citizenship in 1924. California's Alien Land Law of 1913 forbade persons not eligible for citizenship to lease or own land.

Japanese Americans were the most productive truck farmers in California in 1941, producing half of the vegetables in the state. Their strong social capital and the credit system that it spawned helped them acquire property where other immigrant groups were not so successful. Following the bombing of Pearl Harbor, they were evacuated to concentration camps, even though there was scant evidence that they would be anything other than loyal to the United States. Most lost access to land and most other possessions. Only in 1965 did the United States eliminate the anti-Asian bias in its immigration law. Given the greater opportunities in urban areas, it is not surprising that in 2000, 96 percent of Asian Americans lived in metropolitan areas.

Human Capital as Labor Force

A job meets several human needs. It provides income, regulates daily activity, establishes a sense of identity, and offers opportunities for social interactions and meaningful life experiences. Thus, the kinds of jobs available and the opportunities for creating jobs within communities have enormous implications for the individuals who live or come to work there.

Character of the Local Labor Force

Human capital attributes of the labor force include both the skills and training acquired and the level of schooling completed by people in a community. Despite the lower status often accorded to natural-resource-based industries, most such industries required workers to develop skills for which they were then relatively well paid. Those skills were generally acquired from experience on the job and from family and friends.

Despite the importance of skills acquired through on-the-job training, level of schooling is becoming an important asset to a community. The industries that are currently growing, such as computer and information-processing activities, require more highly educated workers. Manufacturing plants planning to convert to new technology look carefully at the educational level of current workers. If current workers cannot be trained to handle the new equipment, companies will relocate. Math skills are critical to training success. Historically, rural areas have lagged behind urban areas in terms of the educational level of the labor force. This is one reason that routine manufacturing plants are more likely to locate in rural areas than in metropolitan areas.

The growth of high-tech firms and the decline of routine manufacturing in the United States is reflected in wage rates. Becker points out that, nationwide, the salary premium for completion of college had by the 1980s grown to its highest in history, whereas the average wage of persons without a high school diploma has dropped by 25 percent since the early 1970s (Becker 2002). Unfortunately, in many parts of the rural Midwest and South, in response to the farm crisis and the recession of the early and middle 1980s, rural communities recruited low-wage firms in the belief that "any job is better than no job." Since the early 1990s, there has been much greater awareness of the importance of generating high-quality jobs, but it is not easy for a community to change an existing low-wage industrial profile.

The age structure of the community is another important aspect of the labor market. Is there an abundant labor force at the entry level? In many urban areas, a lack of young people willing to work for minimum wage and no benefits has driven up wages for jobs such as fast-food counter worker. In the Midwest, declining populations often result from the exodus of young people. The average age of rural farming communities is increasing, which leaves few workers at the entry level. Consequently, these communities are at a relative disadvantage in attracting manufacturing plants. A high proportion of elderly residents in a community influences both the types of jobs available and the types of workers available to fill them. Although recreation counties and counties that attract retirees are growing faster than any other category of rural counties, the jobs that are generated tend to be in the lower register of the service sector and are often seasonal.

One of the most significant changes in the nature of rural labor forces is the increasing participation of women. Rural women have traditionally participated less in the formal labor market than have urban women. This has been partly because of the importance of women's unpaid economic activities, including caring for livestock, helping with crops, or maintaining the financial records. Changes in the economy have made these traditional activities less effective. Financial pressures have also increased the need for women to seek cash income. Many of the industries that have located in rural areas, including the textile, electronics, and pharmaceutical industries, now employ mainly women. The urban-rural differential in female participation in the labor force has narrowed substantially.

Finally, increased mobility makes the description of a rural labor force somewhat complex. Improved transportation has increased the likelihood that a person can live in one town yet commute to work in another. Any description of a labor force often has to be regional rather than local. To capture this activity, economists have introduced the concept of *labor market areas (LMAs)*, which include both the residence and work destinations of local people. These areas are multicounty regions that encompass those places where relatively large numbers of people routinely move back and forth from home to work. Approximately half the nation's LMAs are rural. Most are very large, particularly those in the West. Rural people are very mobile in their pursuit of work.

The Dual Labor Market

The *labor force* consists of all employed persons plus all persons seeking employment. The labor market can be divided into two segments: the primary labor market, which seeks specific skills, and the secondary labor market, which seeks unskilled workers. Peripheral firms hire mostly from the secondary labor market. Core industries increasingly hire from both segments of the labor market (Parcel and Sickmeier 1988).

People are recruited into the primary labor market because of their educational and skill levels. Jobs in the primary labor market provide good wages, safe working conditions, opportunities for advancement within the firm, stability of employment, and due process in the enforcement of work rules. Jobs in the primary labor market can be either managerial/professional or craft/skilled worker.

Jobs in the *secondary labor market* generally have low status, low pay, poor benefits, and little or no chance for advancement. Working conditions can sometimes be less clean and safe. Job security is often low. There is little movement from the secondary to the primary labor market, but much movement by an individual from one secondary labor market job to another. In addition, there is little correlation between education and income. For example, people with certain characteristics may be hired preferentially for the secondary labor market. Thus, in certain firms or industries, women may be hired into lower-wage positions with less opportunity for advancement than men are hired into, regardless of formal qualifications such as education. Organizing job ladders within communities or regions that allow workers to advance from secondary to primary labor markets is a new rural-development strategy.

In 1999, more than one-fourth of the rural wage and salaried workforce twenty-five years old and older earned low wages. Somewhat fewer than half of these workers, 43 percent, were the sole or principal wage earners in their households. Rural low-wage workers are more likely to be employed in service and retail trade industries, part of the secondary labor market. In a given industry, low-wage workers tend to work in less-skilled occupations requiring less education. Although the share of white men in low-wage jobs has grown since 1979, low-wage rural workers continue to be overwhelmingly women and minorities. The average weekly earnings for rural wage and salary workers rose nearly 11 percent (adjusted for inflation) between 1990 and 1999 (reaching an average of $11.25 per hour), but rural low-wage workers earned a median hourly wage of only $6.50 (ERS 2001).

In the secondary labor market, *ascribed characteristics* related to human capital, such as race and gender, are much more important than *achieved characteristics,* such as education.

Most firms generate jobs that are regulated by laws specifying limits on number of hours worked, safety regulations, dismissal procedures, and so on. Records are kept that can document the exchange of work for wages and thus the number of individuals employed in a given industry. Firms that provide such employment and receive governmental oversight make up the *formal economy.* The *informal economy* includes firms unregulated by societal institutions. A handshake rather than a contractual relation between employer and employee is the basis for hiring in the informal economy. Individuals hired to do informal activities generally represent the lower part of the secondary labor force. They lack social benefits, are often paid less than minimum wage (often in cash), are subject to arbitrary dismissal, and often work under unapproved safety and health conditions.

The informal sector has existed for a long time. As Manuel Castells and Alejandro Portes point out, what is new is that it is growing at the expense of previously formalized positions, particularly in urban areas. In rural areas, one kind of informal activity is substituted for another. Informal relations are shifting from agriculture and natural-resource sectors to manufacturing, construction, and particularly to service sectors, such as tourism.

How a community's human capital is divided between the primary and secondary labor markets or between formal and informal activities affects the stability and well-being of a community. For the most part, employment in rural areas is more likely to be in the secondary labor market. Hanes Textiles is the second-largest employer in Eatonton, Georgia, but nearly all its local employees are in the secondary labor market. Those working at Hanes are paid minimum wage and see limited opportunities for advancement. Most are women; African American women are overrepresented.

Ultimately, a dual labor market benefits firms more than the local community. Labor costs are kept low. However, those employed are working at jobs that may not fully use their skills, let alone their potential talents. Incomes are limited, which makes it difficult for the local economy to flourish. The community suffers because much of its human capital is underutilized. Companies that rely heavily on the secondary labor market often make a relatively small contribution to the community.

Opportunity Structure and Human Capital

Just as the educational and skill levels of a community help determine the types of industries that locate in an area or the businesses that can be initiated, the types of jobs available in turn influence the educational level of the community. When coal mining and logging were profitable, young men often dropped out of high school to go to work in the mines or forests, assuming that within a relatively short time, they would be making more money than their teachers. Thus, any further investment in education seemed foolish and unnecessary. Regions such as McDowell County, West Virginia, characteristically developed low commitments to schools.

Towns such as Irwin and Eatonton face a different dilemma. Much of the agricultural Midwest has historically had a strong commitment to education, and well-supported local schools enable most young people to pursue some type of postsecondary education. Once they finish college, however, Irwin's young people go elsewhere. Few local jobs require the skills or knowledge they have developed.

In Eatonton, African American women work either for the textile factory or as domestics. When Billie Jo Williams finished her degree in business administration, she found she could not use her education in Eatonton (see Chapter 1).

The interaction between educational level and type of jobs available has become a vicious circle for many rural communities. The *opportunity structure* of the community—the types of jobs and investment opportunities available—affects the character of the local labor force. The local labor force in turn affects the community's success in attracting or supporting new business enterprises. Communities that invest heavily in education see the more educated young people leave because of the lack of opportunity unless community leaders and citizens work collectively to generate jobs that they would like their own children to take. Those that do not invest in education rely on assembly plants for jobs—industries that depend upon the less educated workers who are willing to accept lower wages. These jobs offer young people little motivation to invest in education. Communities, in their efforts to promote local economic development, need to focus both on creating high-quality jobs and on developing and sustaining a strong educational system.

Building Human Capital

Rural Schools

One of the most dramatic changes in rural areas has been the decline in the number of public school districts since World War II. In 1942, there were about 108,000 school districts in the United States. By 1962, that number was down to just under 35,000. As of 1987, there were 14,721 school districts, and in 2002, the numbers show a decrease again, with 13,522 school districts remaining. Kieran Killeen and John Sipple mark the period of most intense consolidation as being between 1939 and 1973. Current shortfalls in state revenues are leading many states to push for further consolidation of school districts.

School consolidation illustrates the tension that often exists between local and state governments. Professional education groups and state departments of education pushed school district mergers in the 1950s. Because professional educators were concerned about the quality of education in extremely small districts, they pushed for consolidation in an effort to standardize schools. States were beginning to assume more responsibility in funding education and were eager to increase the fiscal efficiency of school systems. Small schools were said to be inefficient; thus, most of the decrease in the number of school districts resulted from the consolidation of rural districts. Efficiency, in terms of return to social and human capital, was ignored.

Before the move toward consolidation, each of the small, one-room elementary schools scattered throughout the country formed a single district. When students graduated from the elementary schools, they changed districts to attend high school in town. During the first phase of consolidation, these one-school districts were unified into districts of kindergarten through twelfth grade (K–12) based in villages and cities. Initially, these new school districts had multiple attendance centers, but gradually the centers in the countryside were closed, and all children attended school in town. A second wave of consolidation occurred in more sparsely populated areas. In that phase, some villages or towns lost their schools entirely. Often, when two or more towns could not reach agreement as to which one would have the new school, new high schools were built in wheat or cornfields, equidistant from all of them.

The consolidation of rural school districts has been accompanied by increased state control of education. The state of Vermont, for example, maintains firm control over nearly every aspect of the educational system, including the following matters:

- The licensing and qualification of all public school personnel
- Attendance and records of attendance of all pupils
- Standards for student performance
- Adult basic education programs
- Approval of independent schools
- Disbursement of funds
- Equal access by all Vermont students to a high-quality education

As the educational system has become more standardized, some critics argue that it has become less responsive to local needs and resources. Given the extent to which state funds are now being used to support local schools, however, states may feel that they have little choice.

Losing schools in rural areas has a significant impact on the welfare of the community as a whole, as Thomas Lyson (2002) points out in his research on the loss of schools in rural communities. Lyson collected data from all 352 villages and towns with populations under 2,500 in New York State. He divided them into two groups based on the population size and made comparisons within groups. For the smaller group (population 500 or less), he found that only 46 percent of the communities without schools grew in population between the years 1990 and 2000, whereas 60 percent of those with schools saw population growth. (For the larger communities, the difference was only four percentage points, but in the same direction.) Communities with schools have higher home values and somewhat higher wages and per capita income. Lyson also established that communities with schools have more professional, managerial, and executive workers, along with more self-employed residents and fewer residents who commute outside the community to work. Lyson recognized that keeping schools close to the community should be a significant part of every state's rural development strategy.

Beyond research establishing that students have better attitudes and more involvement in extracurricular activities in smaller schools, the U.S. Department of Education report *Violence and Discipline Problems in the U.S. Public Schools: 1996–97* revealed that larger schools (1,000 students or more) have 825 percent more violent crime, 270 percent more vandalism, 378 percent more theft and larceny, 394 percent more physical fights or attacks, 3,200 percent more robberies, and 1,000 percent more weapons incidents. Fifty-two percent of principals of small schools (fewer than 300 students) report that they have either no or only minor discipline problems, and small schools' dropout rates are substantially lower. The report revealed that virtually none of the large-school problems were evident in the smaller schools. School consolidation, although a popular economic solution, may not always be the best one for a community's welfare (see Box 4.1 for a study of Nebraska schools that uses smaller school-size gradations and shows that smaller is better with respect to high school graduation rates and subsequent college attendance).

BOX 4.1 Small Schools, Big Results in Nebraska

It is widely believed that smaller schools are "inefficient" because they tend to have above average costs per pupil. Current school finance policy rests on the premise that higher costs due to small size should not be subsidized by state funds unless there is no consolidation alternative. As a result, taxpayers in small school districts may be faced with a decision to override the school levy limits, or jeopardize school quality by severely cutting expenditures, or look for a consolidation option. . . .

Findings

High school completion and postsecondary enrollment rates increase as school size decreases.

- The proportion of Nebraska students who graduate from high school without dropping out averages 97 percent in districts with less than 100 high school students, compared to the statewide average of 85 percent.
- High school completion rates are lowest for school districts with 600–999 high school students, averaging 80 percent. [The completion rate is only a little higher—84 percent—for districts with more than 1,000 high school students. Eds.]

Continued on next page

Small Schools, Big Results in Nebraska (continued)

- Nebraska postsecondary institution enrollment rates are 73 percent for counties that average less than 70 high school students per district, compared to 64 percent for counties that average 600 to 999 high school students per district.
- The percent of students who complete high school and enroll in a Nebraska college is 25 percent higher for counties with the smallest schools compared to those with the largest schools.

Annual cost differences between the smallest schools and the most "efficient" size school are cut in half when measured as cost per graduate rather than as the traditional cost per pupil.

- Nebraska schools with less than 70 high school students average only 25 percent higher cost-per-graduate amounts than those with 600–999 students, compared to 50 percent higher on cost-per-pupil measures.

Any higher school finance costs associated with small schools virtually disappear when the substantial social costs of non-graduates and the positive societal impact of college educated citizens are considered.

Compared to high school graduates without any college education, high school dropouts

- are one-third less likely to be in the labor force and are 3 times as likely to be unemployed
- average only 62 percent of annual income
- are 2.5 times as likely to receive some form of means-tested public assistance
- are 3.6 times as likely to be in state prison.

Conclusions

. . . Currently, the state aid to education distribution formula penalizes most small schools for any above average per pupil costs, placing their excellent quality in jeopardy. A more equitable approach would be to reinstate a system of cost groups based on size. It is essential that we not discriminate against small schools when the student outcomes for most of these schools are so positive. The state aid formula should offer incentives for schools to

---

Small Schools, Big Results in Nebraska (continued)

maintain a high quality education at a fair cost to the public, rather than penalize small, high quality schools for any higher per pupil costs.

SOURCE: Patricia E. Funk and Jon Bailey. 1999. "Small Schools, Big Results: Nebraska High School Completion and Postsecondary Enrollment Rates by Size of School District" (September). Nebraska Alliance for Rural Education. Online; available: http://www.cfra.org/resources/Publications/small_schools_big_results.htm; accessed February 19, 2003.

Investing in the Rural Poor

The Welfare Reform Act of 1996 has as its primary goal getting poor people off welfare and into the workforce. In that objective it has succeeded magnificently, although there is evidence that with the recent recession and slow recovery, use of food pantries, food stamps, and other welfare services is on the rise. However, has human capital investment in low-income people been sufficient to ensure that they can both be productive members of society and provide for their own needs? In 2000, the poverty rates in nonmetropolitan areas of the United States was as low as it had been in the mid-1970s: 13.4 percent (see Figure 4.1). By 2001, it had risen somewhat to 14.2 percent, in response to the recession of that year (see Table 4.1). That was nearly 30 percent higher than the overall metropolitan poverty rate (11.1 percent) but still lower than the rate for central cities (16.5 percent) (U.S. Bureau of the Census CPS 2002). After a steady decline in the post–World War II era, poverty—both rural and urban—leveled off in the 1970s and grew noticeably in the 1980s. After 1979, the gap between rural and urban poverty, which into the early 1970s had steadily narrowed, began to widen once again. By 1985, the gap exceeded 6 percent. By 2000, the difference was less than half that amount.

Poverty grew in rural areas in the 1980s for a variety of reasons. Most important was the fact that beginning in that decade, the quality of industrial jobs declined even faster in rural areas than in urban areas. In the 1970s, rural industrialization grew substantially, and urban industrial employment stagnated. Employment of educated and skilled persons grew, as did employment of unskilled workers in rural areas. In contrast, the 1980s were a period of unusually high out-migration of skilled and educated persons from rural areas, reflecting the increasingly peripheral nature of the rural economy. The 1990s encompassed a long stretch of economic expansion, which accounts for the improvement shown

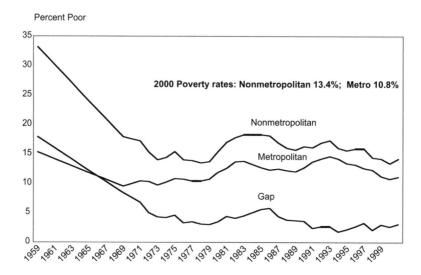

Percent Poor

NOTE: Data imputed for years 1960–1969,1970, and 1984.
Metropolitan– Nonmetropolitan area definitions typically
change in fourth year of the decade

FIGURE 4.1   Poverty Rates by Residence, 1959–2000

in rural poverty. There were record rates of job creation and the lowest rate of unemployment in more than thirty years (ERS 2001). However, even with this economic growth, poverty rates continued to be significantly higher in rural areas
than in urban areas, especially in the South and West.

Although the rural poor are more likely than the urban poor to be in the labor
force, many of the employment opportunities in rural areas are with companies so
small or in jobs so marginal that benefit and minimum-wage legislation does not
cover them. The service sector, which tends to be a low-wage sector, especially in
rural areas, has replaced manufacturing as the rural growth sector. Furthermore, in
rural areas there is a strong ideology against labor legislation and few labor unions
to bargain collectively for higher wages.

Rural communities are noted for their ability to respond to extraordinary
tragedies that lead to temporary poverty, such as a fire or, more recently, at least in
some communities, the farm crisis. But rural communities are much less able to
respond to conditions of chronic poverty. As discussed in Chapter 3, rural people
tend to feel that proper attitudes lead to hard work, and hard work should lead to
material success. Thus, lack of material success—such as an inadequate income or
the lack of a decent home (preferably owned)—is viewed as a moral failing. The
dominant view is that rewarding such moral failings by providing "handouts" to
those out of work or with low incomes should be avoided.

TABLE 4.1 Poverty Status of People in 2001: Residence and Region by Household Relationship, Race, and Hispanic Origin (both sexes)

	% Below poverty level							
	All Races		Black		Hispanic (all races)		Non-Hispanic White	
	Metropolitan	Non-metropolitan	Metropolitan	Non-metropolitan	Metropolitan	Non-metropolitan	Metropolitan	Non-metropolitan
All ages	11.1	14.2	21.4	31.4	21.1	25.4	6.9	11.2
Under 18 years	15.4	20.3	28.7	40.5	27.5	32.3	7.9	15.3
18 to 24 years	16.0	17.6	25.9	34.5	20.9	21.7	11.8	14.1
5- and 10-year age groups from 25 to 64 (range)	6.6–10.5	9.2–13.7	14.2–19.0	22.2–27.4	12.4–20.5	15.5–25.4	4.6–7.3	7.5–10.9
65 and over	9.5	12.2	19.8	33.0	21.8	21.8	7.3	10.4
In married couple families	5.2	7.6	7.2	15.5	14.7	21.6	2.9	5.9
Related children, < 6	8.4	12.9	10.9	20.4	19.6	28.8	4.5	10.0
Related children, 6–17	6.8	10.3	8.2	16.1	18.2	25.2	3.3	7.9
In families with female householder or no spouse present	27.3	35.0	36.2	45.3	37.6	40.8	17.4	29.0
Related children, < 6	47.3	55.6	53.3	61.8	54.6	—a	36.5	48.9
Related children, 6–17	33.7	42.8	41.0	54.7	46.1	46.4	21.6	36.0

a— not enough cases to be reliable.

SOURCE: U.S. Bureau of the Census, Current Population Survey (CPS). 2002. "Detailed Poverty (P60 Package), 2001" (September 23). *Annual Demographic Survey: March Supplement. P-60 Package.* A joint project between the Bureau of Labor Statistics and the Bureau of the Census. Online; available: http://ferret.bls.census.gov/macro/032002/pov/toc.htm.

The dominant cultural capital plays an important role in deciding whom people view as the worthy poor and the unworthy poor. The worthy poor are usually seen as being in poverty as a result of experiencing a catastrophe or as a result of inexorable forces, such as the aging process. The unworthy poor are often defined as able-bodied adults with no job or working only part-time.

According to dominant rural values, a higher proportion of the rural poor than urban poor are "worthy." Rural families are more likely than urban (metropolitan) to be employed and still poor. In 1998, two-thirds of rural poor families had at least one member working at some time during the year; 29 percent of such families had one or more full-time, year-round worker, and 16 percent had two or more full-time year-round workers! The culprit is exceedingly low rural wages, particularly for workers with a high school education or less: In 1999, 27 percent of rural workers over age twenty-five received wages that if earned full-time, full year, would not lift a family of four above the official poverty line (so-called low-wage workers) (Fluharty 2002).

High poverty among young adults—who are often parents—means high poverty among children, who are part of the worthy poor. Table 4.1 shows that among rural or nonmetropolitan African Americans and non-Hispanic whites, the age group with the second-highest poverty rate is persons eighteen to twenty-four years of age. Among rural Hispanics, this age group actually has lower poverty rates than all older age groups but one. In all cases, nonmetropolitan young people are more likely to be in poverty than are metropolitan youth. For all racial and ethnic groups, children have the highest poverty rate, particularly those under six years of age. Increasing poverty among rural children is one of the best-kept secrets in this country. In 2001, one out of every four nonmetropolitan children was in poverty. For the period between 1996 and 1999, child poverty rates declined in both rural and urban areas, but the decline was greater in urban areas. The largest gap between rural and urban poverty rates in 2001 was for children under eighteen years of age.

The collective view that able-bodied persons in poverty are undeserving has an impact on the behavior of the rural poor. Because of the shame involved in admitting one needs help, many rural poor do not seek the help available to them. The rural poor are less likely than urban poor to take advantage of the means-tested resources available to them.

Although a smaller proportion of the population than in urban areas, single parents in rural areas face particularly severe problems. Poverty rates of children under six in families headed by single mothers are astronomical; 56, 62, and 49 percent of young children of all races, African American, and Anglo (non-Hispanic white), respectively, are below the poverty line (Table 4.1). Furthermore, daycare is generally not available at an affordable price. Single parents who are in a family network often rely on female relatives to care for children, but increasingly, those female relatives have had to join the labor force and are no longer available as baby-sitters. Thus, the single parent is faced with low wages and lack of daycare. There are some communities, such as Harlan, Iowa, that have instituted a community-supported day care system with a sliding fee scale that enables single parents and two-parent families in which both spouses work to find reasonable, reliable, high quality childcare. However, this kind of community action is the exception rather than the rule.

Another problem of poverty in rural areas is the fact that to gain better-paying jobs, workers need to travel great distances. The cost of transportation and the lack of public transportation often force families to depend on old and unreliable automobiles. Not only is getting to work difficult, but it is challenging and costly to get to places to purchase groceries and other necessities at a reasonable price. The declining availability of intercity public transportation as bus and train routes have vanished makes the rural poor even more vulnerable.

The one comparative advantage of living in rural areas for the rural poor is cheap housing. However, the high inflation in urban housing prices means that the rural poor who have housing are basically trapped. They are unlikely to be able to move to a place that pays better wages because they cannot afford the housing costs involved. To a degree, the cheaper housing reflects the fact that housing stock is older and more likely to be dilapidated. The rural poor are much more likely to live in mobile homes than are their urban counterparts. One of the strategies poor people have developed in rural areas is to send one member of the family to live temporarily in a higher-wage area, often with relatives, while the rest of the family remains at home. Often remaining at home means having no vehicle and very little money. In turn, lack of transportation and money limits the family members' ability to participate in community activities, which further isolates the rural poor.

Because of the moral connotations associated with poverty, integrating people who are poor into the rural community is often more difficult than integrating people who are elderly or who have developmental disabilities. Enabling the poor to participate involves providing basic necessities, such as healthcare, that often must be underwritten, at least partially, on a local basis. Local governments are increasingly challenged to provide healthcare and other welfare programs because of the sharp curtailment of federal funding of social programs in the 1980s and 1990s, and which has continued until the present.

In some communities, the farm crisis helped reduce the stigma of poverty and made the needs it represents more legitimate. Many communities responded to the consumption needs of the hardworking poor by such poverty-reducing mechanisms as winter coat trades, in which members of the community collected the clothing their children had outgrown, sorted it by size, and then made it available to everyone. Other mechanisms involve such seemingly trivial matters as exchanges of prom dresses; such solutions allow individuals to acquire some of the symbols of normal community participation at minimal investment and therefore to participate in mainstream community activities. These kinds of activities do not solve the economic problems of poverty, but they do reduce the social isolation of the rural poor and can eventually lead to the inclusion of similar efforts as part of community-level programs.

The central cause of poverty among the rural able-bodied poor (the able-bodied poor make up about one-third of all poor people, both rural and urban) is a lack of employment and low wages when employed. Rural areas would benefit significantly from increases in the minimum wage because of the large share of low-wage workers (Whitener and Parker 1999). Economic development efforts that seek to expand high-quality employment in both urban and rural areas will be the most effective long-term antipoverty program. Such efforts must be coupled with educational reform involving substantial investment in upgrading the capabilities of young people, particularly in areas of persistent poverty. Unfortunately, the 1996 Welfare Reform Act allows for only two years of education during the time one receives temporary assistance to needy families (TANF). Realistically, that is not enough time even to get an associate of arts degree from a community college if one is a single parent. The welfare reform law was written more to get welfare recipients off welfare and into the job market than to encourage them to obtain the assets that would keep them permanently out of poverty.

Given the present antiwelfare mood, political support can be gained only for the worthy poor. Children are the most obvious target group. Expansion of the Women, Infants, and Children (WIC) program and other programs benefiting children (and the families of which they are a part) are likely to be much more effective than the current spate of so-called workfare programs. The Earned Income Tax Credit, by which low-income working families receive a tax benefit, is a form of bonus for performing low-wage work. Yet few rural low-income workers know of its existence or how to access it. Getting women off welfare (more than 80 percent of adults on welfare are women) is likely to be more effective if coalitions are made between advocacy organizations and urban and rural poor people. Only if the welfare of children becomes defined as a strategic interest of the United States is there a chance of making substantial inroads against poverty.

Health and Human Capital

Rural healthcare issues have both individual and social aspects. Many rural hospitals, clinics, and nursing homes are experiencing a fiscal crisis. The changing structure of medical care is one of the contributing factors. First and foremost, the fiscal crisis of rural healthcare is related to federal health policies. Because many rural communities have a very high proportion of elderly among their population, a higher proportion of patients in rural hospitals are on Medicare. In nonmetropolitan and metropolitan areas, respectively, 47 percent versus 39 percent of hospital costs are for Medicare patients (*RUPRI* 1999). Medicare reimbursements for particular procedures are lower than the rate hospitals charge patients with private insurance. Similar issues arise with Medicaid, which, unlike Medicare—a federally financed program—operates with shared financing between the states and the federal government. With the current fiscal crisis, states are cutting back on Medicaid appropriations. Furthermore, nonmetropolitan hospitals are reimbursed at a lower rate for the same procedures than are hospitals in metropolitan areas. Members of Congress from more-rural states and districts are seeking to change that inequity, but urban representatives have dug in their heels on this issue, since it would involve either the shifting of large amounts of funds from urban to rural areas or the appropriation of substantial amounts of new money. Furthermore, because rural people are more likely to be small-business owners or to be employed by small firms, they are less likely to have employer-provided insurance (although there is little difference in the proportion of workers who are totally uninsured in rural and urban areas). Those without employer-provided insurance will either pay higher premiums or have more-limited coverage, since they are less likely to get group rates. Of urban nonelderly workers, 55.1 percent have employer-provided insurance, compared to 52.6 percent of rural workers (Pol 2000).

Increased specialization of medicine and the expensive technology that accompanies that specialization means that rural people go more frequently to major medical centers for treatment of complex illnesses. Rural hospitals and clinics are left doing routine medicine, which has lower profit margins. Many rural hospitals host specialists from regional medical centers or metropolitan areas who come once a week or once a month to see patients with illnesses related to their specialty. In other cases, aggressive regional medical centers have purchased clinics, and the doctors who practice in those clinics become their employees. Telemedicine holds promise in linking rural patients to urban expertise. There is also a shortage of rural doctors. Only 10 percent of medical doctors practice in nonmetropolitan areas, although 20 percent of the population resides there (Moody 2002). Many rural doctors are from other countries, but in a post–September 11 move, the U.S. Department of Agriculture halted administration of the J-1 visa waiver program for foreign doctors in rural underserved areas, citing homeland security concerns—even though most of the doctors in question had been practicing in rural parts of the United States for three years (Mueller 2002).

Poverty is highly related to *health status.* Poorer and less educated elderly women enrolled in Medicare+Choice plans reported poorer health, experienced more chronic illness, and reported that they felt depressed or sad more of the time in the preceding year than their more affluent and better-educated counterparts, according to an analysis of data from the Medicare Health Outcomes Survey. The survey provided the opportunity to examine the health and functional status of 91,314 elderly women enrolled in Medicare managed-care programs in 1999. Race and ethnicity also influenced elderly women's health status (Bierman, Haffer, and Hwang 2001).

Bierman and colleagues found that women with annual household incomes of less than $10,000 were more than twice as likely to report fair or poor health compared with women whose incomes were more than $50,000 (40 percent versus 15 percent). Nearly half of those with an eighth-grade education or less said they were in fair or poor health. They were nearly three times more likely to report fair or poor health than college graduates (47 percent versus 16 percent). Women with some high school education were more likely to report fair or poor health than high school graduates (38 percent versus 26 percent). About one-fifth (21 percent) of women with annual incomes of less than $10,000 reported depressed mood compared with 8 percent of women who had incomes of more than $50,000.

More than half of black, Hispanic/Spanish, and American Indian/Alaska Native elderly women had household incomes less than $20,000, and more than half of these women had less than a high school education. More than one-third of Hispanic/Spanish women had an eighth-grade education or less. Elderly black women were most likely to report fair or poor health (46 percent), followed by Hispanic women (42 percent) and American Indian/Alaska Native women (36 percent). White and Asian/Pacific Islander women were least likely to report fair or poor health (27 percent and 28 percent, respectively). One in every seven women overall—but one in five black, Hispanic/Spanish, and American Indian/Alaska Native women—reported they had been depressed or sad in the preceding year.

Rural residents are more likely than people in urban areas to engage in behavior that can harm their health because their level of self efficacy is often low. For example, smoking among people twelve to seventeen years of age was highest in the more remote rural areas and generally lower in central cities. Nationwide, in 1999, about 15 percent of adolescents reported having smoked in the preceding month. In the West and the South, they were much more likely to smoke if they were in rural areas, although those adolescents in the West in general were less likely to smoke than adolescents in the South and Midwest. Only in the Midwest did adolescents in the urban fringe smoke more than either central-city or rural adolescents. Except in the Midwest, cigarette smoking among those over eighteen years of age was higher in the rural areas than in metropolitan areas. People smoked less in the West than in other regions. Those most likely to smoke were rural residents in the South (Eberhardt et al. 2001). Smoking has obvious implications for health, as does obesity, which is higher in rural areas than in urban areas (see Chapter 10, "Consumption in Rural America"). However, if people see no reason to improve their lifestyle, they are more likely to engage in harmful behaviors. Accidental death rates are also higher in rural areas.

What do these differences in health status mean for rural America? First, it is harder to work one's way out of poverty when one's health is poor; the ability to show up for work on time on a regular basis is severely limited. Second, it is more difficult to get access to healthcare—preventative or curative—in rural America. Third, for children, poor health is associated with poor school performance, exacerbating the disadvantages that come from living in a home where the educational attainment of the adults is low. Increasing availability of healthcare would be an excellent investment for rural human capital, an investment that could be translated into higher levels of financial and social capital.

Chapter Summary

Gary Becker and other economists argue that education and training are the most important forms of human capital. Human capital also includes the personal attributes of individuals that contribute to their ability to earn a living, strengthen community, and otherwise contribute to community organizations, family, and self-improvement.

The attraction of human capital in the settlement period, and subsequent opportunities for different categories of farmers and laborers to realize their individual potential, depended greatly on the patterns of settlement across the country. In the settlement period, attributes of human labor that were needed included physical strength, endurance, and, in some cases, innovativeness. Education was often denied to those who were expected to do only manual work all their lives. Where settlement was accompanied by relatively widespread access to property, education was more highly valued and more universally available, although rural schools were still segregated well into the 1970s in some places.

The employment opportunities in rural areas both determine the kind of education available and the degree to which students are motivated to take advantage of them. Workforce opportunities can be divided into two segments: the primary and secondary labor markets. The primary labor market recruits people based on educational and skill levels. Jobs in the primary labor market can be either managerial/professional or craft/skilled worker. Jobs in the secondary labor market generally have low status, low pay, poor benefits, and little or no chance for advancement.

In the past, miners and loggers, and often farmers as well, did not have high educational levels because they left school for work. However, this has changed. The interaction between educational level and type of jobs available has become a vicious cycle for many rural communities. Communities that invest heavily in education see the more educated young people leave because of the lack of opportunity—unless such communities work collectively to generate jobs they would like their children to take. Rural areas are now losing their local schools to consolidation, which has hurt local economies without improving school effectiveness.

Rural poverty continues to be higher than urban poverty in the United States. People living in rural areas have fewer opportunities and may have less education, both of which contribute to rural poverty. Human capital thus suffers. Poverty is related to poor health status. People in rural areas are somewhat more likely than those in urban areas to engage in personal and occupational behaviors detrimental to their health. Rural areas are less likely to have the resources to invest in increasing human capital.

Key Terms

Achieved characteristics are those gained through education, training, experience, "hard work, connections, or "native" intelligence.

Ascribed characteristics are social characteristics assigned by society to individuals and are based on physical (gender, race), cultural (ethnicity, religion), economic (social-class), or demographic (young person, elderly) characteristics that were not chosen by those individuals. Ascription can readily lead to stereotyping or even scapegoating.

A *cropping system* is the set of crops grown on a particular farm in which the farm operator takes into account the interrelations among the crops, usually through an understanding of the biological interactions and the social and economic relations implicit in growing that set of crops in a particular way.

The *formal economy* includes economic activities that are regulated by laws and monitored through routine data collection.

Health status refers to physical and mental conditions that may be acute (temporary) or chronic (long term).

The *informal economy* includes economic activities that are not regulated by laws, such as noncontractual exchange of labor or goods. Such activity is generally not monitored through the use of invoices, paychecks, or formal accounting procedures.

Jim Crow segregation laws, named after a popular nineteenth-century minstrel song that stereotyped African Americans, were a set of local and state laws upholding oppression and segregation, initiated after the end of Reconstruction in 1877 and accepted by the U.S. government. The end of Jim Crow is generally marked by the beginning of a strong Civil Rights movement in the 1950s and the *Brown v. Board of Education* ruling by the U.S. Supreme Court (1954) that overturned the "separate but equal" doctrine in schools throughout the nation.

The *labor force* includes all working-age persons within a community, local area, state, region, or nation who are able-bodied and who hold a paid job or are seeking one or who are self-employed in providing goods or services to the market. In most countries, including the United States, the decision was made early on not to include unpaid family members engaging in household or other economic activities as part of the labor force. The *workforce* is that part of the labor force that receives wages or salaries; that is, it excludes those who are self-employed.

Labor market areas (LMAs) encompass both place of residence and place of work of a local population. It is a local region (often a cluster of counties), centered on a trade center or urban city, within which a pool of workers make their homes and can readily commute to work.

Opportunity structure describes the types of jobs and investment opportunities available in a community.

The *primary labor market* consists of jobs that provide good wages, safe working conditions, opportunities for advancement, reasonably stable employment, and due process in the enforcement of work rules.

The *secondary labor market* consists of jobs that do not require specific skills, are relatively low-paying, have few chances for advancement, and have a high turnover.

Sharecropping is an arrangement between a landowner and tenant farmer to split the crop or the profit from its sale, actually *sharing the crop*. In southern sharecropping, which replaced slavery as a mechanism for ensuring a labor force for growing cotton and other field crops following the end of Reconstruction (1877), the balance of power was shifted sharply toward the landowner through local enforcement of "vagrancy" laws and through the *furnishing* system, which kept the sharecropper permanently in debt to the landowner.

References

Becker, Gary S. 2002. "Human Capital." In *The Concise Encyclopedia of Economics.* Online; available: http://www.econlib.org/library/Enc/HumanCapital.html; accessed April 16, 2003.

Bierman, Samuel, C. Haffer, and Yi-Ting Hwang. 2001. "Health Disparities among Older Women Enrolled in Medicare Managed Care." *Health Care Financing Review* 22:187–198.

Castells, Manuel, and Alejandro Portes. 1989. "World Underneath: The Origins, Dynamics, and Effects of the Informal Economy." In *The Informal Economy: Studies in Advanced and Less Developed Countries,* ed. Alejandro Portes, Manuel Castells, and Lauren A. Benton, 11–37. Baltimore: Johns Hopkins University Press.

Eberhardt, Mark S., Deborah D. Ingram, Diane M. Makuc, Elsie R. Pamuk, Virginia M. Field, Sam B. Harper, Charlotte A. Schoenborn, and Henry Xia. 2001. *Urban and Rural Health Chartbook.* Hyattsville, Md.: National Center for Health Statistics.

Economic Research Service (ERS). 2001. "Rural Low-Wage Employment" (updated April 27, 2001). Rural Labor and Education Briefing Room. Washington, D.C.: ERS/U.S. Department of Agriculture. Also online; available: http://www.ers.usda.gov/Briefing/LaborAndEducation/lwemployment/; accessed April 16, 2003.

Fitchen, Janet M. 1991. *Endangered Spaces, Enduring Places: Change, Identity, and Survival in Rural America.* Boulder, Colo.: Westview Press.

Flora, Jan L., and Cornelia B. Flora. 1999. "Race, Gender, and Class in Rural America." In *Introduction to Sociology: A Race, Gender, and Class Perspective,* ed. Jean Ait Belkhir and Bernice McNair Barnett, with Anna Karpathakis, 369–383. Race, Gender, and Class Book Series. New Orleans, La.: Southern University.

Fluharty, Chuck. 2002. "Toward a Community Based National Rural Policy: The Importance of the Rural Health Care Sector." Presentation at the National Rural Health Association 25th Annual Conference in Kansas City, Missouri, May 17. Online; available: http://www.rupri.org/presentations/; accessed May 13, 2003.

Killeen, Kieran, and John Sipple. 2000. "School Consolidation and Transportation Policy: An Empirical and Institutional Analysis" (April). A Working Paper for the Rural School and Community Trust Policy Program. Online; available: http://ruraledu.org/docs/killeen_sipple.pdf; accessed February 23, 2003.

Lyson, Thomas A. 2002. "What Does a School Mean to a Community? Assessing the Social and Economic Benefits of Schools to Rural Villages in New York." *Journal of Research in Rural Education* 17:131–137.

Moody, Robin. 2002. "Rural Health Care Faces Crisis." *The Business Journal* (Portland), December 30. Online; available: http://portland.bizjournals.com/portland/stories/2002/12/30/daily6.html; accessed April 16, 2003.

Mueller, Keith J. 2002. "The Immediate and Future Role of the J-1 Visa Waiver Program for Physicians: The Consequences of Change for Rural Health Care Service Delivery," Policy Paper P2002-3. Rural Policy Research Institute, April. Also online; available: http://www.rupri.org/pubs/archive/reports/P2002-3/index.html; accessed April 17, 2003.

Parcel, Toby L., and Marie B. Sickmeier. 1988. "One Firm, Two Labor Markets: The Case of McDonald's in the Fast-Food Industry." *Sociological Quarterly* 29, no. 1:29–46.

Pfeffer, Max. 1983. "Social Origins of Three Systems of Farm Production in the United States." *Rural Sociology* 48, no. 4 (Winter):540–562.

Pol, Louis. 2000. "Health Insurance in Rural America." RUPRI Rural Policy Brief 5, no. 11 (PB2000–11), August.

The Rural Policy Research Institute (RUPRI). 1999. "Implementation of the Provisions of the Balanced Budget Act of 1997: Critical Issues for Rural Health Care Delivery" (July 29). P99–5 RUPRI Rural Health Panel. Online; available: http://www.rupri.org/pubs/archive/reports/1999/P99-5/index.html; accessed April 16, 2003.

Schultz, Theodore. 1961 "Investment in Human Capital." *American Economic Review* 51:1–17.

U.S. Bureau of the Census, Current Population Survey (CPS). 2002. "Detailed Poverty (P60 Package), 2001" (September 23). Annual Demographic Survey:

March Supplement. P-60 Package. A joint project between the Bureau of Labor Statistics and the Bureau of the Census. Online; available: http://ferret.bls.census.gov/macro/032002/pov/toc.htm; accessed April 16, 2003.

U.S. Department of Education. 1998. *Violence and Discipline Problems in the U.S. Public Schools*: 1996–97. National Center for Education Statistics. Also online; available: http://nces.ed.gov/pubs98/98030.pdf; accessed April 16, 2003.

Whitener, Leslie A., and Timothy S. Parker. 1999. "Increasing the Minimum Wage: Implications for Rural Poverty." *Rural Development Perspectives* 14:1–8.

5

Political Capital

Joe and Ellen McDougal had grown up in Small Lake, in the boot heel of Missouri, a persistently poor area, and thought they knew the town well. As adults, they had decided to stay and raise a family in their hometown. Joe was employed in a small manufacturing plant. Ellen made crafts at home and worked part-time as a waitress at the Down Home Café, the social hub in town.

As their children grew older, Joe and Ellen realized there were few recreational facilities available to them. What was available was in poor condition. In particular, they believed that lights should be installed at the city park's baseball diamond so that more games could be scheduled for the children's softball leagues.

For several years, they went to the city council with signed petitions, but there was no result. Their elected officials explained that funding was not available for "recreational luxuries" and that nothing could be done. Finally one of Ellen's regular customers at the cafe said, "Oh, if you want something done in this town, you really need to talk to Hank Jones." Ellen knew Hank, the owner of the local feed and farm supply store, because he drank coffee almost every day in the Down Home Café, but she was unaware that he was influential in town politics; he had never been elected to public office. Hank just seemed like "one of the boys."

Hank arrived the following day, and Ellen poured his coffee and chatted with him about the need for lights at the city park and about how athletics played a vital role in keeping youngsters out of trouble. Within a week, the item was brought before the city council again. It was easily passed and was funded through a small property assessment. Why had Ellen's casual conversation with Hank Jones been more productive than two years' work with the elected town officials?

★   ★   ★

In this chapter, we look at political capital in rural communities. We examine different theories and ways of measuring community power, different sources of power or vested interests, and the importance of outside linkages to community power. Finally, we examine some of the implications that various power structures have for community development and change.

Political Capital

Political capital consists of organization, connections, voice, and power. Political capital is the ability of a group to influence the distribution of resources within a social unit, including helping set the agenda of what resources are available. Generally, political capital reflects the dominant cultural capital: There is a tendency to support the status quo. In many rural communities, high levels of bonding social capital reinforce the current situation and discourage groups with different ideas and agendas from coming forward to offer alternatives. Very often, those that control political capital are not in elected positions but are regularly consulted by elected officials. Sometimes they are not consulted, but elected officials, in giving reasons for not acting on new ideas, anticipate their response, as was the case in Small Lake when the McDougals were told funding was not available for "recreational luxuries." The city council, knowing that Hank was opposed to anything that might increase property taxes, automatically rejected any suggestion that might incur expenditures.

Our attention to political capital is to understand not only who runs things in rural communities but also how excluded groups whose issues are not on the agenda when resources are allocated can increase their voice and influence. Under what circumstances can excluded people organize and work together, know and feel comfortable around powerful people, and bring their issues forward for action?

Rural communities are greatly affected by outside forces; even the smallest places feel the repercussions of national and international events (see Chapter 9). Yet even very small communities have the power to generate and distribute resources (see Chapter 11).

Manhattan, Kansas, "the little apple," population 44,831, was greatly affected by the September 11 tragedy in New York City. Sharing the name "Manhattan" with victims of the terrorist attack made residents of the Kansas town reflective about the events, as did the fact that several Islamic students attend Kansas State University. There are three hundred Muslims in Manhattan, Kansas, and one mosque. Instead of distancing themselves from the Muslim population, other residents reached out, sending flowers and cards of support and accompanying the Muslim women and children to playgrounds to ensure their safety. The residents also reached out to New York by raising $500,000 for the victims. A huge banner signed by schoolchildren was sent to New York, and during a football halftime ceremony, a New York City policeman was honored for his service. Friendships across ethnic boundaries were formed because of the tragedy, and residents of this small community generated resources that were distributed to victims of the tragedy as well as to people in their own town who may have felt alienated because of the events of September 11. Even though Manhattan is a "small college town in mid-America, where hot issues are rezoning so Wal-Mart can expand, declining grade-school enrollment, a proposed half-cent sales tax hike for economic development, and a recycling fee," this town realized the power they have as a community to make an impact locally and nationally (Knickerbocker 2002).

Defining and Exercising Power

Power is the ability to create a situation that otherwise would not happen or to prevent an event from occurring that others wish to make happen. Hence, the ability to affect the distribution of both public and private resources within the community is called *community power*. It is possession of political capital in the community realm. Often community power can be augmented by connections with the outside. Who possesses power and the degree to which it is widely available can greatly affect the quality of life for community residents and the future existence of the community itself.

An important dimension of power is the means by which it is exercised, including physical force, institutionalized force or authority, and influence. In totalitarian regimes, power is often based on the threat of exercising physical force. Institutional power—power that derives from occupying a position of authority in an institution—requires subordinates to follow orders or regulations if they want to remain part of that institution. Only when superiors go beyond institutional rules is it acceptable for subordinates to refuse to carry out an order. Even then, refusal can jeopardize one's longevity with the organization. "Influence" refers to power derived from more informal relationships, such as friendship or social status. Whistle-blowers, such as Coleen Rowley in the FBI, Cynthia Cooper at WorldCom, and Sherron Watkins at Enron, are examples of individuals who withstand the cultural and political capital of their organization. Rowley, Cooper, and Watkins first went through the appropriate hierarchy to report discrepancies and, when corrective action was not taken by those with authority, then went outside the chain of command to try to correct the situation in the organizations in which they worked.

If excluded voices are to be heard, it is important to find out who really runs an organization or a community. Individuals who hold formal positions of authority may or may not actually set the agenda. People like the McDougals can live in a place all their life without knowing who really makes things happen—or stops them from happening—in their community.

Patterns in the exercise of community power are called *community power structure*. In a community, we can map local power to determine the degree to which it is widely participatory or more concentrated. For instance, in Small Lake there is a hidden power structure that has a great impact on town politics and decisions; the elected officials are not always the people running the town. In some communities, an influential network of individuals who never face public election or accountability greatly affect what does or does not happen.

Competing Theories

Social scientists disagree about the way power is exercised in North American communities and about how to determine the way community power is structured. In part the disagreements arise from the fact that all communities do not have the same power structures. But researchers also bring diverse assumptions to their study of community power. This chapter describes four approaches to the study of community power: pluralism, elitism, class-based analysis, and "the growth machine," a variant of the class-based approach. Although most of the initial studies of community power were carried out in urban places, later elaboration and testing of the different theories occurred in rural communities (Humphrey and Krannich 1980; Ramsey 1996; Sharp and Flora 1999). Consequently, we use these theories to explore power in rural communities.

Social scientists have devised several ways of determining who has power. Each of these measurement techniques is related to a supportable theory of power, and each tends to give somewhat varied answers to the question "Who is running this town?" After each theory of power is discussed, the method of measuring community power most closely related to that theory is described.

Pluralism Versus Elitism

Early studies of community power were conducted from a pluralist perspective and focused mainly on who held formal positions in community government. After a more in-depth investigation into how communities worked, sociologists began to notice patterns of inequality in the exercise of power and distribution of resources. In many cases, small groups of individuals controlled the community by virtue of their economic and social position, leading to a competing view of power: elitism. This section explores these two models and the strategies used by each in measuring power.

Pluralism and the Event Analysis Technique

The pluralist approach to power—whether in the community or on the regional, state, or national level—is based on fundamental assumptions about the way democracies work. Adherents of the *pluralism* theory of power assume that there is no dominant source of power. They assume that the capacity for acquiring power is widely distributed within the population unless analysis shows otherwise. Moreover, they

TABLE 5.1 — Structure of Influence in Community Decisionmaking

Method	Elitist	Pluralist
Positional Basic assumption: Those in official positions have predominant influence.	A small, close-knit group of officials has power, and they agree on major issues and hang together against opposition.	A number of different officials wield power, and they disagree on a number of major issues and have different bases of support and opposition in the community.
Reputational Basic assumption: People throughout the community are aware of who has power.	People perceive that a small number of individuals wield influence over all areas of community decisionmaking, and this group makes decisions in its own interest.	People perceive that many different individuals are involved in decisionmaking and that only a few are involved in more than one area of community decisionmaking.
Event/Decision Analysis Basic assumption: Different people are influential in different decision areas.	A small, close-knit group of individuals dominate all major areas of public decisionmaking, and they agree on major issues and hang together against opposition.	Different sets of individuals are influential in different areas of public decision-making. There is little overlap in membership between the groups, and members either tend to restrict their activities to their specialty area, disagree on a number of major issues, or have different bases of support and opposition in the community.
Growth Machine Basic assumption: Landed interests—owners, developers, real estate, and banking control local decisionmaking.	A small close-knit group of landowners, developers, real estate, and banking interests are influential in all major issue areas, and they agree on major issues and hang together against opposition.	Landowners, developers, real estate, and banking interests have an interest in and promote local economic growth; they tend to permeate the growth-related areas but not all major areas of local decisionmaking, and they are restrained by other interests and can be defeated on many issues by organized groups of citizens.

SOURCE: Hyman, Higdon, and Martin, 2002, p. 219

hold, power is dispersed among competing interests. Although one particular group may prevail on one issue, it may not be influential on the next issue. Furthermore, without studying the situation, one cannot determine what the interest of any particular group is (Polsby 1960).

Community theorists who take a pluralist perspective see citizens in a democracy deciding on political issues in the same way they make decisions vis-à-vis the market: as unattached individuals with perfect access to information. Thus, the individual is the basic building block of politics. Individual citizens exercise their political influence principally through voting. The concept of one person, one vote is essential for pluralism to work. That vote may be exercised directly, as in the case of the New England town meeting. Much more frequently, however, votes are cast for someone who represents a group of constituents. Under this system of representative democracy, citizens are not directly involved in making all public decisions. Instead, the chosen representatives are periodically subjected to electoral validation. It is assumed that this periodic validation is a means by which representatives (be they school board members, town councilpersons, county supervisors, state officials, or presidents or prime ministers) generally reflect the desires of their constituents. Although individual voters may see their objectives deferred in the short term (particularly if they voted for the losing candidate), decisions should benefit the greatest number of people in the long term.

From the pluralist perspective, the U.S. democratic system is grounded in a legal system that prohibits power being used arbitrarily. One such mechanism introduced in the U.S. Constitution is a system of checks and balances among the different branches of government: The legislative body makes the laws, the administration implements them, and the judiciary arbitrates when there are disputes. This is different from other forms of government, like in England and in France, where the legislative arm of government also acts as the administrator of the policies it enacts. The Bill of Rights and other laws guarantee that minorities have freedom of expression and equality of opportunity. This equality includes the electoral system itself, in which those elected have only temporary power gained through periodic election and challengers have a reasonable opportunity of gaining office. All citizens share the civil right of participation in government through the election process, including the right to run for office themselves.

According to community theorists who take a pluralist perspective, representative democracy does not mean that all citizens exercise equal influence in politics. Some may choose not to participate in voting, in party caucuses, or in contributing funds to a particular candidate. However, if they do participate and have the innate ability, their influence can roughly equal that of any other active citizen. Differences in influence among different classes or ethnic groups can be explained by the statistical tendency of certain groups or classes not to participate as actively in the political process as do others. It is an individual's decision to participate or not, and individuals who fail to participate have made the choice of noninvolvement.

The dispersion of economic, political, and social power that is assumed by community theorists who take a pluralist perspective also applies to the decision-making process. They believe that the best way to assess how and by whom decisions are made is to look at overt activity; in other words, decisions are made by those in positions of formal power. Community theorists who take a pluralist perspective are suspicious of analyses based on assumptions of behind-the-scenes influence. In fact, they reject the idea that certain groups have certain a priori interests. They do not subscribe to the notion that different classes have contradictory political interests. The degree to which class interest involve conflicting policies is a matter for investigation. Hence, lack of controversy on a particular issue is, for the community theorists who take a pluralist perspective, an indication that there is basic agreement among the citizenry on a publicly articulated position.

Those who study community power from a pluralist perspective use what is called the *event analysis technique*. This research methodology involves identifying and using controversial public issues to reveal the decisionmaking process. Newspaper coverage, observation, and interviews are used to determine which decisions were important and who made them. The information gathered through these sources generally shows a diversity of sources of inputs to public decisions; this diversity lends support to the pluralist perspective.

The classic pluralist study *Who Governs? Democracy and Power in an American City* (1961) was conducted by Robert Dahl in New Haven, Connecticut. Dahl examined three issues: political nominations, urban renewal, and public education. He found that no single group dominated the decisionmaking process in all three arenas; different groups and individuals were active in each. Only the appointed bureaucracy and the elected mayor were common to more than one issue area (see Box 5.1). Thus, Dahl concluded, his results supported the pluralist perspective.

BOX 5.1 New Haven: Support for the Pluralist, Elitist, or Growth Machine Theories?

New Haven, Connecticut, is a small metropolitan city. With the advent of the railroads, its port declined, and the automobile caused its carriage-manufacturing enterprises to go out of business; consequently, New Haven had stopped growing by 1920. Yale University began growing in the 1930s and soon became the city's primary engine of growth (Domhoff 1983: 188–189).

Using event analysis methodology, Robert Dahl and a group of other political scientists from Yale University were the first to study New Haven. The city's population was approaching 170,000 in the late 1950s when

Continued on next page

New Haven: Support for the Pluralist, Elitist, or Growth Machine Theories? (continued)

Dahl studied it. Dahl selected three issue areas "because they cut across a wide variety of interests and participants" (Dahl 1961: 333) and because they had prima facie importance to the community. They were (1) nominations to public office by each of the two main parties; (2) the New Haven Redevelopment Program, which received more federal funds per capita than any other urban renewal program in the country; and (3) public education, the largest item in the city's budget. Using newspaper accounts, documents, records, and extended interviews with participants, Dahl selected and analyzed eight major decisions taken over the decade of the 1950s in the areas of education and redevelopment. Decisions about who should be nominated by each party for mayor from 1941 to 1959 were also examined.

The "economic notables" included chief executive officers and chairmen of the boards of the major corporations operating in New Haven, major local property holders, all bank directors, and those sitting on the boards of directors of three or more firms operating in New Haven. Only 24 percent of those involved in exercising power—defined as successfully initiating or vetoing a policy proposal—were economic notables. (The percentage rises to nearly 40 percent if redevelopment issues are considered alone, excluding public educational issues and political nominations.) Only 16 percent of "social notables"—those whose families attended the annual debutante balls of the exclusive New Haven Lawn Club—were found to have exercised power in the three issue areas. There was only about a 5 percent overlap between economic and social notables. Dahl concluded that the economic and social notables were no more involved in making important community decisions than were a half dozen other groups and that there was minimal involvement of the same people across issue areas.

Urban renewal in New Haven was initiated by Mayor Richard Lee, who took office in 1954, was reelected three times, and retired in 1970. During his tenure, he transformed the center of the city by replacing slums with high-rise student apartments and laboratories for Yale University and with commercial buildings in an expanded downtown. In fact, during that time New Haven received the highest per capita federal funding for urban renewal of any city in the country. Dahl attributed this success to the extraordinary capacity and determination of the Democratic mayor and his aides. He pointed out that Lee's predecessor, a Republican, had been unable to

Continued on next page

New Haven: Support for the Pluralist, Elitist, or Growth Machine Theories? (continued)

galvanize the business community for such an effort and that Yale University played a passive role in the urban renewal process.

A decade and a half later, G. William Domhoff, a psychologist and sociologist who had chosen national power structure as his primary research activity, did a restudy of New Haven. Domhoff (1983) looked not only at Dahl's data, including transcripts of his interviews, but also at minutes of the chamber of commerce and in-house memos of key economic and governmental elites who had not been previously available. He came out with a very different picture:

1. Using an interlocking-directorate approach for identification of the top economic elites and using membership in any of three elite social clubs in New Haven for identification of the top social elites, Domhoff found a more significant overlap between the economic and social elites or notables.
2. In reexamining the three issue areas, Domhoff found good reason why the elites would not be heavily involved in school and nomination issues. Dahl had pointed out that because most of the social and economic notables sent their children to private schools, they would have little interest in public educational policy. Domhoff argued that they did have one interest with respect to public schools: keeping their taxes low. Indeed, he found that members of the Board of Finance, which makes recommendations on tax rates to the Board of Aldermen (the city council), were overwhelmingly from the business community. With respect to political nominations, Domhoff argued that who gets elected is not of great concern to the elites unless they can be shown that it makes a difference to their interests. In fact, urban renewal—which was definitely of concern to the economic elites—was implemented by a Democratic mayor in cooperation with economic elites who were predominately Republican.
3. Urban renewal occurred through the close cooperation of Yale University, the economic notables, a powerful Republican senator, and the Democratic mayor.

Critical to the success of the program were changes in federal laws beginning in 1954—the same year Mayor Lee took office—under the Eisenhower administration. These changes transformed the slum-clearance provisions of the 1937 Housing Act into a massive program to redevelop the central cities,

Continued on next page

New Haven: Support for the Pluralist, Elitist, or Growth Machine Theories? (continued)

with concern for the former residents of the "redeveloped" areas occupying a secondary position at best. (Organized neighborhood opposition to urban renewal emerged in New Haven only after Dahl's study was completed, and it was not successful in stopping or ameliorating the effects of the program.)

Yale University began planning for expansion in the 1940s. In 1947, the Yale trustees appointed a committee to investigate the university's future needs. Headed by New York investment banker, Prescott Bush, who also was a trustee, the committee produced a report released in 1950 that called for an $80 million development program over the next ten years, with one-fourth of the funds going to a building program. Federal urban renewal laws required that after the local government had cleared the land, a private entity had to purchase the land. Yale became that entity. Yale's president appointed a close friend and graduate of Yale Law School, Morris Tyler, as the university's liaison to the New Haven Redevelopment Agency, and he effectively served as its legal counsel. Tyler was also a partner in the New Haven law firm that was most central in the city's business networks (as determined by Domhoff's interlocking-directorate study).

Yale's importance to the urban renewal effort was strengthened even more by the election of Prescott Bush to the U.S. Senate in 1952. (Bush was the father of President George Herbert Walker Bush and the grandfather of President George Walker Bush, also Yale graduates.) He promptly obtained an assignment to the committee that oversaw the urban renewal program. During his tenure in the Senate, not only did New Haven receive more per capita funds for urban renewal than did any other city, but Connecticut also ranked first among states in its per capita receipt of such funds. After the functions of Mayor Lee's redevelopment agency became routine, which was when Dahl did his study, urban renewal was largely controlled by the mayor, but in the crucial period of initiation, Yale University and the business elite were critical to the success of New Haven's urban renewal effort.

The New Haven case studies demonstrate that a researcher's perspective and methodology can affect the results and interpretations. Which of the two approaches did you find more convincing?

REFERENCES: Robert Dahl. 1961. *Who Governs? Democracy and Power in an American City*. New Haven: Yale University Press.

G. William Domhoff. 1983. *Who Rules America Now? A View for the '80s*. Englewood Cliffs, N.J.: Prentice-Hall.

G. William Domhoff (1983) reexamined the urban renewal issue, exploring what went on behind the scenes as well as during the decisionmaking process itself. He found that urban renewal in New Haven was predominately the product of economic interests in New Haven that benefited handsomely from the program. The politicians were merely the implementers, not the decisionmakers. Dahl had looked at the decisionmaking process only after it became public, thus examining only the pluralist veneer. Thus, if one is using the event analysis technique to determine who has power in the community, it is important to study the period that preceded public airing of an issue to see whose agenda originally included the issue, the behind-the-scenes machinations that determined how the issue would be presented to the public, and which interests stood to gain when the decision was implemented.

Elitism and What Happens Behind the Scenes

The elitist school of thought received its methodological orientation from Floyd Hunter (1953) in his study of Atlanta, Georgia. However, the perspective obtained its name from the work of sociologist C. Wright Mills, who wrote *The Power Elite* (1956). Mills argued that "a power elite"—a coalition of government officials, business executives, and military leaders—controlled the nation and that the political and economic interests shared among individuals in the coalition were reinforced by their social similarities. Members of the elite had attended the same schools and universities, belonged to the same clubs, and relaxed at the same resorts. In addition, the branches of the elite interlocked professionally. Business executives became politicians, politicians had business interests, and retired military leaders sat on corporate boards; all of these connections further ensured and strengthened mutual interests. Domhoff's book *Who Rules America?* (1967) elaborated on and modified Mills's analysis at the national level, as did the work of Domhoff's followers.

Elitism is a perspective based on the assumption that power conforms to the stratification system. Community theorists who take a power elite perspective argue that power is distributed hierarchically. The premise is that sources of power (control over means of coercion, authoritative position, command of wealth or information, and prestige or other personal traits) can be accumulated. For instance, wealthy persons are often viewed as having exceptional talents; otherwise, it is commonly believed, they would not be wealthy. Possession of wealth can then lead to prestige, control over information, and authoritative position. The pluralistic theory of power sees the community as having a series of factional coalitions: Group boundaries are fairly fluid, members disagree on specific issues over time, and no coalition dominates for any extended period. The community theorists who take a power elite perspective, on the other hand, see a pyramidal structure of power: A few individuals representing key economic institutions with like interests have the largest influence in what happens in towns, large and small.

Floyd Hunter, in one of the most significant works on community power, *Community Power Structure* (1953; a study of Atlanta, Georgia), developed the *reputational technique* for determining power in a community. Hunter collected lists of community leaders and activists from local newspapers and organizational membership rolls. He came up with a list of 175 names and then sought the aid of knowledgeable people in the community, who presumably knew about power and politics, to cull the original list, eliminating those who did not actually exercise much power. The forty people who remained on the list were then personally interviewed. Each individual was asked a number of questions, including "If a project went before the community that required decisions by a group of leaders, leaders that nearly everyone would accept, which ten on this list of forty would you choose?" The responses gave him a list of top reputational leaders.

As a result of using this reputational technique, which has been modified by multiple researchers studying different cities, Hunter found an elitist power structure in the form of a pyramid. At the top was a small group of business leaders, an elite upper class who dominated the city's economy through a web of interlocking directorships. They lived in the same exclusive neighborhoods, belonged to the same expensive clubs, and entertained each other in their homes. The elites rarely held office and were not visible to the general public. In fact, only four of the forty top elites were public officials. The rest were bankers, manufacturers, and other business leaders. Their power was informal. Elected officials were subordinate to them, doing their bidding but not seeing them socially.

Hunter found this small policymaking group, largely from the business class, to be in overall agreement on most major issues. He noted that "controversy is avoided, partly by the policy-making group's not allowing a proposal to get too far along if it meets stiff criticism at any point in decision making" (Hunter, 1953: 111). Thus, Hunter did not conclude that this small group had absolute control over major issues, but he did propose that it played a major role in setting the public agenda.

Community theorists who take a power elite perspective criticize the event analysis approach on the grounds that it often focuses on controversial issues, defining power in terms of who makes decisions politically. They argue that most decisions are not controversial and are never debated publicly. Many of these decisions systematically support one set of interests in the community over another. Viewed from this perspective, power is held by those who control the public agenda but who may not be visible players in the political process. It becomes important, then, to look at what issues in the community are never publicly decided: the nondecisions that happen abruptly. Matthew Crenson, in a study conducted when pollution became an issue in urban communities, concluded that the problem of dirty air became a "key political issue" in those communities where "industry's reputation for power was relatively puny," suggesting that the critical stage is not at the point of public decision but when "a community sifts out subjects that will not be given political attention and so will never become key political issues" (1971: 131, 90).

Power and Economic Interests

Class-based theories of community power focus attention on the economic roots of power. This theory and its variations assume that those who control the corporate economic system control the wider society. It is often in their economic interest to influence or to control political decision-making so as to achieve their economic goals. This section explores the class-based theory of community power and one of its more recent variations, the growth machine.

Class-Based Theory of Power

According to the *class-based analysis* of power, it makes little difference to the economic elites which person or group actually makes decisions as long as those policy and allocation decisions facilitate profit making. Those in official decisionmaking positions may not be the economic elites themselves, but the decisionmakers tend to represent the interests of the economic elites. This appeared to be the case in Small Lake, where Hank Jones, a local businessman, had a good deal of informal control over the city council.

The influential study undertaken in the 1930s by Helen and Robert Lynd (1937) found that economic institutions were key to understanding power and the distribution of resources in "Middletown," the name they gave to Muncie, Indiana. Now a metropolitan city, in the 1930s, Muncie was a fast-growing nonmetropolitan community, increasing from fewer than 39,000 inhabitants in 1925 to more than 47,000 ten years later.

The locally based Ball family owned and operated the Ball Jar Company, the largest producer of home-canning equipment in the world. The Lynds found that after the "bank holiday" in 1933, the family controlled or had a major interest in all surviving local financial institutions. The Balls were also heavily involved in local real estate and shaped the city's growth. Through philanthropy they influenced the growth of the local college (now Ball State University), the hospital, the community fund, and the YMCA and YWCA. Although family members only occasionally held local public office, they controlled the Republican Party and had influence in the Democratic Party and thus were able to bring about or prevent change in many arenas. In short, the Ball family exercised political power in Muncie.

The Muncie studies questioned the independence of those holding political office. According to the Lynds, elected officials were of meager caliber: people the Ball family and the rest of the inner business group ignored economically and socially yet used politically. Those who controlled the economic institutions (the Balls were among these elites) did not want to bother with direct political involvement, but they did need to limit government interference in their concerns. Elected officials were thus considered a necessary evil.

A case study of business-class control and citizen mobilization in a small Kansas town by Eugene Hynes and Verna Mauney (1990) offers insight into the reasons that the elites, particularly specific business interests, are concerned about city government and want to control decisions.

Many rural communities own their own utilities; this was the case in the town studied by Hynes and Mauney. Utility pricing policies and rate structures in this Kansas town were such that domestic households paid higher rates than did commercial and industrial enterprises. The business group that almost invariably owned these enterprises was from the same town as the officials. By charging high domestic utility rates, officials made it possible to keep property taxes low. This was to the advantage of those who owned a lot of property. Zoning decisions also were systematically made in favor of those with direct influence on the city council. Special-interest groups also influenced the public financing of business projects that might otherwise have been funded through private sources. People with these vested interests had tangible reasons for controlling both the community government and the nongovernmental institutions involved in distributing resources. Generally, they were very accomplished at doing so.

Working-class people in rural communities have a set of interests different from the interest groups just described. Of primary importance to them are wage levels, benefits, and actions that would increase the prevailing wage. Local governments influence wage levels by how much they pay their own employees, by whether they consciously recruit high- or low-wage firms, and by other such actions. Yet a number of structures in small communities prevent working-class citizens from influencing these decisions: They rarely sit on the public boards, and even when elected to office, they often find it difficult to attend the informal and sometimes the formal meetings called during daytime working hours. Hynes and Mauney document well the case of the working-class mayor in the town they studied. He was publicly ridiculed in the press because of his irregular attendance at city council meetings. His job kept him from the impromptu meetings called by the city council, which was composed of small-business operators who had flexible schedules.

Hynes and Mauney also clearly demonstrated the chilling nature of a local elite's tight control that was preventing people from running for office or publicly addressing issues they knew were negatively affecting them. People were often reluctant to act because of their perceived vulnerability. For example, Hynes and Mauney reported that one prominent member of the concerned citizens group became inactive when she came to fear that her cousin, a schoolteacher, would lose his job if her activities continued. When individual members of a power elite occupy economic, political, and civic roles almost interchangeably, one can expect little participation in decisionmaking. The more widely dispersed economic, political, and civic roles are within the community, the more likely it is that various citizen voices will be heard.

The Growth Machine

With the publication of "The City as a Growth Machine" in 1976, Harvey Molotch introduced a variation of the class-based theory of community power. Studies in a number of urban areas had identified the importance of a group, which later came to be called the "growth machine." The *growth machine* is a coalition of groups that perceive economic gain in community growth. The growth machine, led by certain groups within the business class, works to encourage growth and to capture its benefits. These groups tend to include a combination of interests of developers, construction companies, real estate agents, and owners of commercial buildings and rental units, banks, and other businesses dependent on an increase of aggregate rent levels through the intensification of land use (Logan, Whaley, and Crowder 1997). The ability to increase aggregate rent levels (income from land or other real property) is heavily dependent on increases in the community's population. These growth machines compete with growth machines in other communities to attract capital that, in turn, will attract residents to increase return on land, buildings, merchandise, and services.

The most active elites in the local power structure are generally members of the *rentier class,* those who receive their income from property. Members of this class promote population growth (and thus constant construction and city expansion in order to office and house the new population), usually in the name of increasing jobs. These modern rentiers have financial interests in the use of local land and buildings and include developers, commercial and residential landlords, and those who speculate in real property. The rentier class does not produce goods or services but, rather, makes money by preparing the foundation for manufacturing, service, or retail firms by providing them with desirable sites. Profits for the rentier class depend primarily on population growth but secondarily on their degree of political capital with local governments. Local government in the United States has unique powers to regulate land use (see Chapter 11), and it is land use that provides potential profit to this class of people. Thus the rentier class works very hard to make sure that the people with formal decisionmaking power have the rentier class's interests at heart. They are big political contributors at the national level, assuring tax deductions for interest paid on mortgages and federal government disaster funding to help them continue to profit when building on flood plains. On the local level, this class is generally well organized to explain why they need an exception to zoning, the extension of a sewer or expansion of a sewage treatment plant, the paving of a road, or tax relief.

The growth machine ideology sees economic growth as being value-free. Thus, the growth machine and the rentier class are eager to attract industry because it generates commercial and residential construction and results in increased land values. That may explain why, despite the large number of studies that universally show that the incentives given to attract industry do not repay the local area, such incentives continue to be offered, jeopardizing the quality of life that other uses of that money would bring, such as schools, parks, and libraries. Therefore, there is minimal discussion about what is produced, the wage levels paid by new employers, or the impact of new industrial or service firms on the quality of life. Industry is often put in the low-income part of town, even in rural communities. Thus, people in the wealthy part of town gain the profits, and costs of development are borne by the poor, often in terms of decreased quality of life because of polluted air, overcrowded schools, and traffic congestion. Or, in some rural areas, the rural area gets the pollution and the investors, who definitely do not live there, get the profits. When this occurs in predominately African American, Native American, or Hispanic communities, it is referred to as "environmental racism." Those who are poor and further excluded because of race or ethnicity have little political capital with which to counter that of industrial investors seeking profit. Those communities are often chosen because they have few environmental laws and little means to enforce those that exist.

Thus, the central conflict in many communities is between the growth machine and neighborhoods. This conflict can be understood in terms of a conflict between use value and exchange value—two terms that are almost self-explanatory. Something that has *use value* is valued because of its use, instead of its monetary value. *Exchange value* is realized only when the commodity is sold.

For example, an apartment building has little use value to the owner. It has exchange value in terms of the income generated either from its rental units or from its sale. On the other hand, one's ancestral home has only use value because there is no intention of selling it. It may be sold when the individual dies, giving it exchange value, but the owner, now deceased, did not realize any exchange value from it—only use value. Properties have values that lie between these two extremes. For example, the home of a professional who expects to move several times has use value while the person lives in it, but maintaining its market value is of concern because of the expectation of selling it at some time in the not-too-distant future. Thus, any improvement the owner makes must be made with dual concerns: First, does it increase the owner's enjoyment of the house (use value)? Second, does it increase the salability of the house (exchange value)?

In the case of urban renewal, use value and exchange value come into direct conflict. Those who live in the affected neighborhood embrace use values. They first seek to preserve their homes (the longer they have lived in them, the greater their use value compared with their exchange value). Second, neighborhood people have an interest in keeping the value of land low because it means lower property taxes. Those who are part of the growth machine thrive on profit derived from increasing land values and thus support efforts at urban renewal.

In rural communities, the growth machine has a similar composition to that in the cities. David McGranahan points out that "locally owned banks, utilities, law firms, and other firms operating largely within local trade areas," for which "income and wealth depend on the volume of business, especially to the extent that there are economies of scale," are likely to be part of the growth machine (1990: 160). The growth machine also includes those in construction, real estate sales, apartment and housing rentals, abstracting, and home insurance. Because growth is in itself supposed to be a good thing, everything should be done to promote it. The dominant cultural capital provides the values that undergird the activities, justify public and private investment, and support the regulatory setting that makes growth profitable for at least some of the community. Although outside interests, such as multinational firms seeking to locate a branch plant, may mobilize the political capital of the local growth machine to get special tax benefits or environmental exceptions, the core of the growth machine is made of local firms and individuals.

There are other groups in small towns that might be characterized as a no-growth coalition, though that coalition differs somewhat from its urban counterpart. Unlike in the cities, the rural no-growth coalition tends to dominate, especially in the smaller, non–trade center communities, though its precise nature depends on the principal source of the community's wealth.

The no-growth coalition in small communities includes manufacturers, processors, commercial farmers, and others who produce for an export market ("export" here means that the product is sold outside the community). Their interest is in having low-cost labor, not in generating a larger local market. Bringing in new employers, particularly branch plants that have paid higher wages in metropolitan areas, is not in the interest of this group. For instance, the peanut processors who dominated politics in Early County, Georgia, until the 1980s not only opposed higher wages but also were against spending on public schools because they feared that educating the largely black population would result in higher wages. In the 1970s, affluent whites often attended a white private academy, thus keeping down public school expenditures. Lower school funding was doubly in the interest of the powerful group because (1) it helped keep wages down by keeping the bulk of the labor force unskilled and (2) it resulted in low taxes. Another example is in midwestern farm communities, where farmers (often retired) usually dominate the board of county commissioners or supervisors. They favor a limited government, no-growth approach because they do not depend on the local population to buy their products and because they have an interest in low real estate taxes. Their interest in improved roads and bridges in order to get their products to market more efficiently is an exception to their low-expenditure perspective.

Retired persons, whose concern lies more with the use value of their homes than with their exchange value, also are part of the no-growth coalition. This group makes up a substantial part of the population of rural communities that are experiencing out-migration. Although retirees may not participate actively in community affairs, they tend to vote in large numbers and can sometimes defeat industrial revenue bonds, as well as school and other infrastructure bonds.

The small village of "Springdale" in upstate New York studied by Arthur Vidich and Joseph Bensman (1968) is an example of a community where the no-growth mentality dominated. After a long period of decline, Springdale became a low-rent bedroom community for industrial workers from nearby Binghamton, New York. The business elite controlled village politics through an "invisible government" that consisted of the three members of the village Republican committee: a feed and seed dealer, the editor of the weekly newspaper, and a lawyer who was the clerk (counsel) to the village board. This group determined the nominees for village offices and manipulated voting behavior so that their candidates always won. (Because the Democrats who voted were a distinct minority in the village, nomination on the Republican ticket was tantamount to election.) The hours that the polls were open were not convenient for the industrial workers, and "safe" voters could be recruited as soon as it appeared that too many of the "wrong" kinds of people were voting during a local election.

Vidich and Bensman found the following informal requirements for being on the village board: (1) being a resident of the community for at least ten years, though lifelong residency was preferable; (2) either being economically vulnerable, and hence amenable to being manipulated by those holding real power, or having a kinship connection with one of the dominant figures of machine politics; (3) having little knowledge about the way government works; and (4) subscribing to a low-tax, low-expenditure ideology. The authors summed it up accordingly: "It thus happens that the incompetent, the economically vulnerable, and the appropriately kinship-connected individuals are elected with regularized consistency . . . to a village board on which they find they have nothing to do because, in their own perspective, the routine affairs of government are automatic" (Vidich and Bensman 1968: 116).

Vidich and Bensman indicated that another characteristic united the members of the village board as well as the invisible government: They all owned rental property. As owners of real estate, they should logically have been part of the growth machine. However, decline was so deeply imprinted in their experience that they had developed a low-tax approach to making money in real estate: keeping their expenses low and seeking to make money on rentals rather than on sale of real estate. The modest influx of commuter residents allowed them to reap some benefits of growth without having to spend their own or others' money to bring it about. Making sure that the "right" kind of people were elected to the village board was imperative. Restricting the vote and ensuring that individuals believing in limited—very limited—government were elected to the village council made this happen.

In somewhat larger rural communities, influence over city government is more commonly exercised through such semigovernmental units as the chamber of commerce. (Chambers of commerce often channel government funds, but without much public accountability, for such things as tourism and economic development.) Both no-growth and growth machine business interests choose to be active in the local chamber of commerce or similar civic organizations in order to seek to impose their view of local development.

Unlike urban communities, where the growth machine typically dominates, rural communities vary substantially in terms of whether they project a no-growth or pro-growth orientation. The ability of the no-growth group, as in Springdale, to make the routine affairs of government automatic is sufficient in some communities to defeat the growth machine and to keep new economic activity out. Pro-growth groups dominate other nonmetropolitan communities, which are often regional trade centers. In other instances, as has occurred during times of crisis and population decline, the rentier class and those who benefit individually from low taxes may join together to save their rural community by seeking to attract or generate capital to increase employment in the community. Rural communities that elect to do nothing when faced with decline are much more numerous.

Local Versus Absentee Ownership

In a modern capitalist system, ownership is separated from management. Those that provide the capital or have inherited it are not assumed to possess the managerial knowledge and talents necessary to enhance capital accumulation (profits and corporate growth). Furthermore, modern businesses require huge amounts of capital, often more than a single individual or family can readily save or borrow. Thus, the limited liability corporation allows for the sale of stock in order to raise capital, in exchange for a vote on who will sit on the board of directors, which sets policy for the company. When a business or corporation sells shares of itself in public offerings on a stock exchange, it is known as a "publicly held corporation." When a family or only a few people hold those stocks, it is known as a "privately held corporation." Does who owns community businesses matter in terms of what happens to the people and the place? Does it matter if the parent corporation is based in the community, the same state, the United States, or overseas? If a parent corporation is not locally based, does the company have the same kind of local political capital and does it utilize what local political capital it does have in the same way as a locally based company does? Is it more likely to threaten to leave if a community does something it does not like? Or is it more likely to let other voices be heard?

Both the San Jose study discussed later (Trounstine and Christensen 1982) and the growth machine literature suggest that the increasing international ownership of firms will result in less involvement in day-to-day community issues by industry and business and more involvement by an increasingly diverse group of players. Furthermore, the awareness citizens have of nonlocal ownership encourages them to mobilize collectively as insiders against outsiders to address serious issues such as environmental pollution. At the other extreme, an outside firm may threaten to leave a community if it does not win concessions on issues that directly affect its profitability (see the discussion in Chapter 8, "Built Capital").

Increased nonlocal ownership could lead to a bias favoring the growth machine. Nonlocal firms tend to have managers who are geographically mobile and who thus exert less long-term influence in the community. Managers of absentee companies generally do not invest their human, social, financial, or political capital in community affairs or charitable activities. In contrast, local industrialists are often active in all civic realms and are often linked to the rentier group through co-ownership of speculative property. Local industrialists are often local philanthropists providing a trickle-down of local wealth through community-based foundations with a local range of giving.

Furthermore, nonlocal firms are usually linked to national or international supply networks; local entrepreneurs do not benefit from such commercial links. There are smaller multiplier effects from absentee-owned firms than from those locally owned. When local businesses are aligned with the growth machine, these benefits, both tangible and symbolic, can be exploited to foster the growth mentality and to generate support for policies that benefit local firms.

The concentration that is occurring in manufacturing firms is also occurring in the media. Daily newspapers are less likely to be locally owned than they used to be. Chain newspapers, with limited links to individual communities, are less likely than locally owned newspapers to be active promoters of the local growth machine and therefore are more likely to take an independent editorial stand. Domhoff (1983) points out that local newspaper publishers are committed not to a particular faction of the growth machine but to the growth machine in general: The newspaper's interest is in selling more newspapers and, in particular, more advertising. Thus, the local publisher often serves as an arbiter among different groups within the growth machine, acting as a spokesperson for the growth machine as a whole. Hence, when the newspaper is no longer locally owned, the growth machine loses an important integrative element.

Similarly, banking is becoming more concentrated in fewer interstate firms that have less interest in controlling the uniquely local resources of tax rates and land use. Unlike its locally owned predecessor, the consolidated bank is not usually allied with the local growth machine. It may also be less interested in investing in the local community.

Absentee-owned enterprises have a contradictory impact on the community by creating space for greater community pluralism through their lack of interest in local politics. That lack of interest will mean less commitment to the interests of the dominant community elites, and the lack of political coordination among economic elites provides a greater opportunity for nonelites to organize in their own interest. Alternatively, when an issue arises that affects the absentee-owned firm directly, it may threaten to leave the community if the issue is not resolved in a way favorable to it. That threat may carry considerable weight if the firm makes a large contribution to the economy of the community.

Power Structure and Community Change

With the decline of branch manufacturing plants in rural areas as they move to areas with even cheaper labor and no environmental controls (see Chapter 9, "The Global Economy") and with the expanded growth of service-sector activities, the growth machine—whether local or national—has found it more difficult to manage community symbols to its own benefit. Because industrialization was generally seen as the solution to all communities' problems, the local growth machine could convince local governments to offer tax breaks to new industries. Such offers were made, even though people on fixed incomes found that they lost more than they gained from the presence of such plants, and unemployed persons often did not benefit because more-educated commuters took the new jobs. Now the service sector has replaced manufacturing as the growth sector. This has created new problems for nonelites and for some elites in rural communities. Even in small cities, downtown malls built through urban renewal have uprooted people from poorer neighborhoods, and suburban malls have replaced locally owned stores with chains and franchises within the mall. Merchants in small communities have been "Wal-Marted" by the general-merchandise chain store in the nearby larger community (see Chapter 10, "Consumption in Rural America").

Environmental awareness has increased as people have become more concerned about urban garbage filling rural landfills or about nuclear waste dumps and missile sites replacing farmland and ranchland. In some cases, the interests of the entire community coalesce if such facilities do little to generate wealth for local elites. Just as frequently, such issues split communities that are desperate for jobs and income (see Box 5.2).

In rapid-growth communities, the new in-migrants are often professionals with a strong commitment to the residential value of the community, organizational skills, and a willingness to participate in community affairs. Their commitment includes concern for the environment, often coupled with an unwillingness to pay the fiscal and social costs of development. They have political capital outside the local community that allows them to counteract the power of the growth machine.

BOX 5.2 Caliente, Nevada, and the Political Capital of Nuclear Waste Storage

Meeting over coffee to discuss nuclear waste may not be an attractive idea to most people, but for two county leaders, it is of utmost importance. In Caliente, Nevada, an economic depression was evident in 1998, and the mayor, Kevin Phillips, was hard-pressed to find a way to help the community. However, his answer to the town's financial struggle was not one that most Nevada residents agree with. He volunteered the town to become part of the Yucca Mountain Project, meaning that it would be a transfer point for nuclear waste. The railroad that once provided the community with financial security now passes through Caliente without stopping. If nuclear waste was put on the trains, Caliente, in Lincoln County, Nevada, could be a point where the waste would be off-loaded and then moved to a storage facility at Yucca Mountain. Phillips is not alone in his ideas about financial gain through this process either; County Commission Chairman Taguchi from Nye County is also interested, even though his constituents may not be. The two community leaders met in 2002 to discuss the possibility of working together on the project to improve the financial situation in both places. Nye County has worked with the Department of Energy for years, gaining grant money to collect data on water-testing wells.

The state of Nevada does not want to see the Yucca Mountain Project happen and is frustrated that these counties are working against the state. Many citizens and environmentalists, characterized as Not In My Backyard (NIMBY), are upset as well. State officials in Nevada see the project scaring off tourists and residents because of the possible health risks associated with nuclear waste. Since the counties are political subdivisions of the state, there is not a lot state officials or environmental activists can do. Nye County officials do not view themselves as helping out the Department of Energy; instead, they see themselves as helping out their own county by bringing in needed funds. Taguchi does not regard the county or himself as "pro–Yucca project," but he does see an opportunity for the county to gain economic stability if the project is enacted.

Thus far, the project has been tied up in court. Nevada opposes the project and is fighting the Department of Energy to have it stopped. President George W. Bush signed the approval to the project in 2002, but state attorneys filed an appeal, and three judges on the U.S. Court of Appeals are to hear the case and make a decision in 2003 or the beginning of 2004. There are many questions surrounding the protection of Nevada's

Continued on next page

Caliente, Nevada, and the Political Capital of Nuclear Waste Storage (continued)

water, and whether the Department of Energy has shown enough proof that it is protecting the water sufficiently. State attorneys feel confident that the decision to use Yucca Mountain as a waste dump will be thrown out because the DOE cannot prove it is following all the federal laws regarding environmental protection. Many Nevada residents are relieved to hear that the Yucca project will not happen, but for Miller and Taguchi, it may mean disappointment. If the appeal is rejected and the project continues, the Yucca Mountain storage facility could hold 77,000 tons of nuclear waste.

SOURCES: Fialka, John J. 1998. "Tiny Nevada Town Vies to Be Site for Nuclear Waste." *Wall Street Journal,* March 19.

Ryan, Cy. 2003. "State Confident in Victory of Nuke Waste War." *Las Vegas Sun,* February 7.

Tetreault, Steve. 2002. "Nye County Seeks Role in Nuclear Waste Project." *Las Vegas Review Journal,* August 11.

National economic elites are mobilizing anew to have an effect at the local level. Management-level personnel in branch firms are required to become active in local organizations, form their own associations to lobby local governments, support political candidates, and publicize their views on zoning, land use, and the free enterprise system. As the interests of national and local elites diverge, the national elites and national power structure seek to convince local elites that the ideology of the national growth machine should also be their ideology. Thus, local chambers of commerce may come up with programs that seem antithetical to local development needs but that match the U.S. Chamber of Commerce's political and ideological agenda—which is that of the national growth machine.

Communities vary enormously in the degree to which power is concentrated and in the degree to which it is wielded by local or absentee individuals, firms, and institutions. It is important to assess the structure of local power in analyzing how change takes place within a community and what kinds of tactics are needed in order to institute grassroots change. Challenging the power elite is an empowering experience because disenfranchised groups can learn to be successful through their mobilization. However, it is also risky because of the ability power elites often have to control information and symbols (cultural capital) and thus, to totally discredit people who are in opposition to them, not by systematically attacking their position on issues but by casting doubt on their personality and character.

Understanding Power Structure and Increasing the Political Capital of Excluded Groups

Selecting one technique for use in a community study would bias the results in favor of that perspective. More recent studies have introduced new analytic techniques (such as network analysis) and combined research methodologies in order to create a more complete picture of community power structures. For excluded groups, understanding the power structure is key to gaining political capital.

Jeff Sharp and Jan Flora (1999) found out vital information about power structure in communities by asking four key questions: "Who can best represent this town to the outside?" "Whose support do you need to get things done?" "Whom do you need to implement a project?" "Who can stop a project in the community?" From the answers, it was evident that "old guard," middle-aged males were more likely to be project stoppers.

Drew Hyman, Francis Higdon, and Kenneth Martin (2001) combined positional, reputational, and event analysis in order to see what differences in power structure identification emerged in a town that contained a major university. They found that who had influence depended on the specific issue area under consideration; no one group influenced everything that went on in the community, suggesting that people felt the power structure may be different for different issues or aspects of community affairs. They found that the positional method and the reputational method did not identify the same individuals, although there was overlap. They concluded that both methodologies were necessary to achieve an understanding of who exercises political capital. They also determined that if they had used only these methodologies, they would have concluded that the community had an elitist power structure. But when they looked at the public record and key informant interviews using event analysis of issues important for growth machine interests (zoning of public lands, whether or not to build a new school building, and local government consolidation), they found a different set of individuals influential in each event. But almost all of the individuals found influential in each event were on the positional list, the reputational lists, or both. They found that on each issue, the local growth machine was a player, and each time it was defeated by organized citizen interests. Political capital was relatively dispersed and had countervailing influences.

They conclude that although growth machine proponents have an advantage over local citizens in that they have careers that depend on pursuing growth (and are thus paid to make sure that growth happens through developing political capital with key decision makers), "if citizens are willing to maintain some continuity and even 'infiltrate' local government, boards, and commissions, there can be very pluralistic outcomes" (Hyman, Higdon, and Martin 2001: 218). The key to building and maintaining political capital for disadvantaged groups is persistence and permanence. It is critical to organize, stay active, and form coalitions. It is also critical to know about other groups organizing with opposing views. Often, a group may organize to stop something (such as a large shopping center) and then disband, only to have something equally disadvantageous to the area's social and natural capital put in its place.

Both community theorists who take a power elite perspective and the class-based theorists of community power use network analysis of the key positions in major institutions in a community. Class theorists use it to determine the corporate structure and to identify the top corporate leaders.

Network analysis involves obtaining the names of the members of the boards of directors or officers of all the important firms or organizations in town, determining linkages between organizations or individuals, and assessing patterns of linkages. Network analysis in various circumstances shows a single power elite or different power factions. The people are then ranked according to their number of connections and their centrality in the networks. Networks of interlocking firms can be examined to determine the kind of resources they bring together and whether they represent a growth machine or other type of resource network (see Box 5.3).

BOX 5.3 Measuring the Growth Machine

Community power structure can be measured by networks of communication. An important means of communication among corporations is through a common member of their boards of directors. If two corporations are willing to have one or more individuals know the inner workings of both firms, it suggests a certain level of trust, perhaps even commonality of goals, between the two companies. Thus, one approach to analysis of community power is to discover resource networks of corporations with interlocking directorates. By looking at the functions of the component corporations, the researcher can determine the purpose of those resource networks. This approach was used in a study of interlocking corporate directorates in Manhattan, Kansas. That study showed the existence of a tightly interlocked growth machine.

The two most important industries in Manhattan, Kansas, are Kansas State University and Fort Riley. Fort Riley, a U.S. Army base and home of the First Infantry Division, is located fifteen miles to the west of the city. Manhattan had a population of about 30,000 permanent residents and 15,000 students at the time of the study. The steady growth of the university and expansion of Fort Riley during the two decades preceding the study resulted in a 45 percent growth in the city's population between 1950 and

Continued on next page

Measuring the Growth Machine (continued)

1970. Thus, the principal private economic activity within the community during that period centered on land development and construction, both residential and commercial.

Annual corporate reports from the Kansas secretary of state's office provided the names of the members of the boards of directors of all Manhattan-based corporations with more than $100,000 in assets. The names were entered into a database, and a computer program was developed that identified the most tightly interlocked corporate clusters or cliques. Three large cliques emerged; each was based on one of the three major banks in the community. The Union National Bank clique was the largest and the most densely interlocked of the three.

As can be seen from Figure 5.1, nearly all of the core corporations in the Union National Bank network were related directly or indirectly to the growth machine. Of the fifteen core companies in the Union National Bank clique, eight were involved in construction, construction supplies, land investment, and real estate. Four were financial institutions, providers of capital for residential and commercial development. The abstract company—the only one in the city—was important in providing members of the growth machine with knowledge of real estate movement because all property transactions within the city and county had to be registered with the company. The principal partner in the abstract company was on the boards of five of the development companies and of the Union National Bank. The clique also contained the only radio station in town; it was linked to the only newspaper through common ownership. Among the core firms, the only one that was not part of the growth machine was the ice company, which had been started in another era by the two brothers who had historically dominated the Union National Bank and were the preeminent leaders in the community for a couple of decades.

The cliques centered on the other two banks also showed a growth machine orientation, but they were less complete in their control of resources. (The only important growth machine industry absent from the Union National Bank clique was the city's structural steel and pipe supply firm; it was part of the second-largest clique, that of the First National Bank.) The three major cliques were linked with one another principally through members of local law firms, several of whom were present or past elected officials at the local and state level. Thus, lawyers served not only as gatekeepers to the larger political system but also as the glue that held the various cliques together.

Continued on next page

Measuring the Growth Machine (continued)

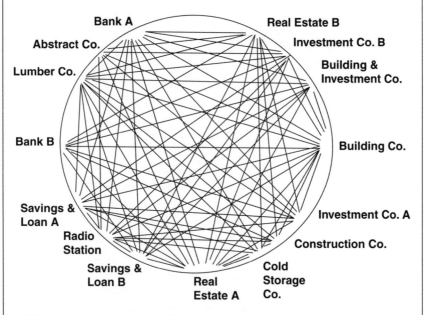

FIGURE 5.1   Union National Bank Clique

A similar network analysis was conducted for the voluntary-organization sector of the community, and the impact of the corporate sector on the voluntary sector was determined. Persons employed by the firms that were in the corporate cliques were overrepresented (compared with their proportion of the adult population of the city) by a factor of twenty-five to one in the largest and most densely interlocked voluntary clique, which centered on the chamber of commerce. Other businesspeople were overrepresented by a factor of nine to one. Independent professionals and university and government officials were represented at approximately the same rate as they were in the community as a whole. Finally, the 59 percent of the population that was lower middle class (clerical and sales workers), working class, and service workers had no representatives on the boards of directors of those voluntary organizations.

This study illustrates how network analysis can be used to assess the presence of a growth machine and to determine the extent to which economic

Continued on next page

Measuring the Growth Machine (continued)

notables are involved in a community's key voluntary organizations. The initial analysis was also used by excluded groups within the community to develop a plan to get their representatives onto key boards to present alternative views.

SOURCE: Jeff S. Sharp, Jan L. Flora, and Jim Killacky. Forthcoming. "The Growth Machine and Voluntary Sector: Analysis of Business Elite Involvement in Civic Organizations of a Nonmetropolitan City." *Journal of the Community Development Society.*

Balanced studies of power structure often combine a number of these mechanisms to limit the theoretical bias of the studies. An example of a study that combines methods is *Movers and Shakers,* a study of community power in San Jose, California, by Philip J. Trounstine and Terry Christensen (1982). They did a reputational study, conducted a network analysis, and, finally, looked at actual decisions using a historicojournalistic approach. (Trounstine, now director of the Survey and Policy Research Institute at San Jose State University, was a journalist. A political scientist, Trounstine has written the political history of San Jose.) The historical analysis helped identify which issues were important. The most important ones included annexation and land use policies, urban renewal, and district versus at-large elections. Research on how decisions were made went beyond examination of the formal decisionmaking to include examination of agenda setting and manipulation of symbols. The authors found that there was indeed a pro-growth power structure. However, the power structure changed over time. Mechanisms evolved to increase democratic participation and flow of information and hence the degree of pluralism. These included changes in ownership of the newspaper from local to absentee and the change from at-large to district election of public officials. As pluralism increased, the strength of the pro-growth faction declined.

Furthermore, Trounstine and Christensen found that as ownership of major firms in the area shifted from local to multinational firms, pluralism increased. The multinational firms were very interested in specific decisions directly affecting their operations but less interested in other decisions within the community. Thus, their strategy was to decrease the range of their power but to keep it relatively strong in areas directly affecting their immediate financial interests.

There are a number of ways to identify which groups and individuals have power. Important vested interests in local communities need to be identified and linked to the exercise of community power. Participating groups will mainly define specific arenas in which power is sought and exercised.

Who Gains?

Joe and Ellen McDougal were able to enlist Hank Jones's influence in getting lights for the city park's baseball diamond. Had the issue been more sensitive, however, they might not have been so successful. Issues that directly affected Hank's feed and farm supply store, for example, might have had a different outcome. Sociology has long been concerned about power in modern society. A major sociological problem has been to determine which segments of the population gain from what kind of activities.

Studies of community power structures have shown that in different circumstances, different power actors are important. For example, upper-middle-class environmentalists have been able to confront the growth machine in certain U.S. cities (Molotch 1976). Other sociological studies show different winners. For example, a study by Clarence Lo (1990) suggests that the tax revolt in California began in working-class communities because working-class citizens were hard-pressed financially and felt that taxes were the reason they had little discretionary income (money to spend once basic expenses were paid). Furthermore, they felt that government was inefficient and uncaring. However, business interests joined that group in order to have an impact. Ultimately, the tax revolt favored real estate developers.

From early studies that concentrated on a power elite that exercised monolithic control (Mills 1956), the focus has shifted to particular issues to reveal a range of who controls what and profits from it. Even rural communities like Small Lake can have complex power structures. Political capital is key in determining not only how issues get resolved but also which situations become issues.

Chapter Summary

Political capital can be transformed into built capital, social capital, cultural capital, and financial capital. That transformation is the exercise of power. Community power is the ability to affect the distribution of both public and private resources within the community. Power can be exercised by physical force, economic force, institutionalized force, and influence. The patterns in the exercise of community power are the community power structure. That structure affects communities and how they function.

Social scientists do not agree about how power is exercised, nor do they agree about how to measure it. Pluralism assumes that the capacity for acquiring power is widely distributed within the population. This model relies on the event analysis technique to detect and measure power. Researchers identify controversial public issues and then use the decisionmaking process employed to resolve those issues as a device to measure power. The elitist perspective of power assumes that power conforms to the way a community is stratified. Power is not widely dispersed; instead, it is held by just a few. Researchers who use an elitist model of power rely on the reputational technique to measure power. Knowledgeable persons in the community are asked to identify those who have the greatest reputation for power.

The class-based theory of community power assumes that those who control the economic system control the community. A more recent variation of this model is the growth machine model. The growth machine is a coalition of groups that perceive economic gain in community growth. This coalition exercises power in order to promote economic growth. The model has been applied successfully to urban areas. Rural communities differ more in terms of whether they project a growth or no-growth orientation.

In order to make power structures more pluralistic, broad participation in setting the community agenda is important. Once issues are made public, they need to be discussed and debated adequately. However, without the first two steps of community empowerment and broad participation in agenda setting, the final decisionmaking process of discussion, debate, and compromise is relatively meaningless.

Key Terms

Class-based analysis as a theory of power assumes that those who control the economic system control the community.

Community power is the ability to affect the distribution of both public and private resources within the community.

Community power structure is the patterns identified in the exercise of community power.

Elitism as a perspective of power assumes that power generally conforms to the social stratification system; wealth, prestige, and power tend to be associated with one another.

Event analysis is a research methodology that involves identifying and using controversial public issues to reveal the decisionmaking process.

Event analysis technique is the preferred strategy for measuring power from a pluralist perspective. Researchers identify controversial public issues and then look at the decisionmaking process used to resolve those issues. Those who make the decisions are deemed to have power in that issue area. Frequently, different issues are examined to determine if the same or different people exercise power across issues.

The *exchange value* of an object, such as a house, is its value to the owner insofar as it can be exchanged for money.

Growth machine is a coalition of groups that set about to use power to encourage growth and capture its benefits.

Network analysis is a way to measure power by looking at the patterns of linkages between organizations and individuals considered to be important in the community.

Pluralism as a theory of power assumes power is an attribute of individuals and that the capacity for acquiring power is widely distributed within the population.

Power is the ability to make something happen that otherwise would not happen or to prevent something from happening that others wish to make happen.

The *rentier class* is made up of those whose principal income derives from rent or an increase in the value of property. It includes landlords of residential, commercial, and industrial establishments and of agricultural land as well as speculators in land and buildings.

Reputational technique measures power by asking knowledgeable members of a community whom they think has power.

The *use value* of an object, such as a house, is its value to the owner for her own uses. Factors taken into consideration include comfort, sentimental value, prestige imparted by the object to the owner, pleasure in possessing or using the object, and so on.

References

Crenson, Matthew A. 1971. *The Un-Politics of Air Pollution: A Study of Non-Decisionmaking in the Cities.* Baltimore: Johns Hopkins University Press.

Dahl, Robert. 1961. *Who Governs? Democracy and Power in an American City.* New Haven: Yale University Press.

Domhoff, G. William. 1967. *Who Rules America?* Englewood Cliffs, N.J.: Prentice-Hall.

_____. 1983. *Who Rules America Now? A View for the '80s.* Englewood Cliffs, N.J.: Prentice-Hall.

Humphrey, Craig R., and Richard S. Krannich. 1980. "The Promotion of Growth in Small Urban Places and Its Impact on Population Change, 1975–78." *Social Science Quarterly* 61, no. 314:581–594.

Hunter, Floyd. 1953. *Community Power Structure.* Chapel Hill: University of North Carolina Press.

Hyman, Drew, Francis X. Higdon, and Kenneth E. Martin. 2001. "Reevaluating Community Power Structures in Modern Communities." *Journal of the Community Development Society* 32:251–270.

Hynes, Eugene, and Verna Mauney. 1990. "Elite Control and Citizen Mobilization in a Small Midwestern Town." *Critical Sociology* 17 (Spring):81–98.

Knickerbocker, Brad. 2002. "In 'Little Apple,' Change Etches Hearts" (March 11). *Christian Science Monitor.* Online; available: http://www.csmonitor.com/2002/0311/p01s02-ussc.html; accessed September 27, 2002.

Lo, Clarence. 1990. *Small Property versus Big Government: Social Origins of the Property Tax Revolt.* Berkeley and Los Angeles: University of California Press.

Logan, John R., Rachel Bridges Whaley, and Kyle Crowder. 1997. "The Character and Consequences of Growth Regimes: An Assessment of 20 Years of Research." *Urban Affairs Review* 32 (May):603–630.

Lynd, Robert S., and Helen Merrell Lynd. 1937. *Middletown in Transition: A Study in Cultural Conflicts.* New York: Harcourt, Brace, and World.

McGranahan, David A. 1990. "Entrepreneurial Climate in Small Towns." *Regional Science Review* 17:53–64.

Mills, C. Wright. 1956. *The Power Elite.* New York: Oxford University Press.

Molotch, Harvey. 1976. "The City as a Growth Machine." *American Journal of Sociology* 82, no. 2:309–330.

Polsby, Nelson W. 1960. "How to Study Community Power: The Pluralist Alternative." *Journal of Politics* 22 (August):474–484.

Ramsey, Meredith. 1996. *Community, Culture, and Economic Development: The Social Roots of Local Action.* New York: State University of New York Press.

Sharp, Jeff S., and Jan L. Flora. 1999. "Entrepreneurial Social Infrastructure and Growth Machine Characteristics Associated with Industrial-Recruitment and Self-Development Strategies in Nonmetropolitan Communities." *Journal of the Community Development Society* 30, no. 2:131–153.

Sharp, Jeff S., Jan L. Flora, and Jim Killacky. Forthcoming. "The Growth Machine and Voluntary Sector: Analysis of Business Elite Involvement in Civic Organizations of a Nonmetropolitan City." *Journal of the Community Development Society.*

Trounstine, Philip J., and Terry Christensen. 1982. *Movers and Shakers: The Study of Community Power.* New York: St. Martin's Press.

Vidich, Arthur, and Joseph Bensman. 1968. *Small Town in Mass Society.* Princeton: Princeton University Press.

Part 2

The Material
Factors in Communities

6

Natural Capital

Eric Ritter was frustrated. It was the third time he had called the Colorado Division of Wildlife (DOW) about the elk tearing down his fences. He just wanted to organize a group of guys to shoot the herds of elk that were competing with his cattle for grass and ruining his fences. But the laws were clear. Instead, he requested financial assistance to fix his fences. He always got the money, but he still had to rebuild the fence. Something had to change.

About a month later, Eric got a call from the Colorado Cattlemen's Association to meet with the DOW and others to come up with alternatives. The meeting included hunters, outfitters who took people on hunting trips in the mountains where Eric ranched, and people from various environmental organizations. Eric felt uncomfortable with the last group, folks he viewed as "tree huggers." Especially Sue Graves, who was always stopping everything in the name of environmental protection. He privately called her "Mother Earth." But he stuck with the new program, called the Habitat Partnership Program. He learned that similar groups were meeting in other districts in Colorado—all with the same concern about the conflicting use of natural capital in the mountain valleys.

After getting together for meals and field visits, the environmentalists and the livestock producers realized they shared some common concerns. Since fires had been suppressed, trees were invading the meadows and pastures, limiting the grass available for both the game animals and the cattle. If there was more grass available higher up, the deer and elk might not come down to the cattle areas. And if more grass grew in the valleys, the occasional presence of the deer and elk would not be such a problem. Furthermore, as they talked, he learned about a new kind of fencing that had a shiny white strip along the top wire. When the deer and elk saw it, they just jumped over it, but it still served as a barrier that kept the cattle in their proper location. Working together, they wrote a plan for burning and restoring pastures and meadows, and they even had a good time putting the plan into action. Now, Eric knew the environmentalists by name—and he even drops in for coffee with Sue Graves. He learned that she used to call him "That Redneck."

And as he enters her shop in town, he shouts out, "Mother Earth, do you have the coffee on? This Redneck is mighty thirsty."

★   ★   ★

When the Europeans came to North America, the landscape was already managed by Native Americans in ways to ensure animal production (making grass more available for wild ruminants, such as buffalo, deer, elk, and moose) and crop production (identification and protection of areas where there grew berries, edible roots, reeds, and trees for constructing tools and homes, and irrigation in more arid regions of the continent). That management favored some species over others, changing the biodiversity of the area over time. However, to European eyes, the land looked wild and untamed. In Europe, most land had been privatized, fenced, and cultivated. The natural capital of the New World, plants, animals, soil, and water, seemed abundant. All that was needed was to "tame" the wild lands in order to produce financial and built capital.

Whereas most Native American tribes used the land to develop a subsistence economy, with a strong focus on converting natural capital to social and cultural capital, most Europeans came to the Americas to transform natural capital to financial capital. Fur trappers, timber companies, and miners used the resources until they were depleted and then moved on. European governments often financed explorations of the New World and expected new wealth in return. A number of English companies actually sold stock to finance early settlements. Once established, these settlements were expected to become self-sufficient and then to begin exporting products to pay off their debts.

The notion of the conversion of natural capital to financial capital motivated the U.S. government to finance such expeditions as Meriwether Lewis and William Clark's Corps of Discovery and other westward exploration. The explorers and those that accompanied them expected to receive land as a result of their work, which would then be translated into financial wealth (Ambrose 1996). Although the expeditions generated cultural capital in terms of new knowledge about the people and the lands, their goal was to beat the English, French, and Spanish to claim the territory and the wealth of its natural resources.

Understanding the intersection of natural and political capital is increasingly called "political ecology."

Land Use

Land-settlement policies played an important role in the economic character of early rural communities. In New England, the English Crown gave land to trading companies that, in turn, gave land to groups of settlers. These groups established central villages surrounded by farmland. Farmers worked their fields by day but returned to the village at night. A village-style settlement created an environment capable of eventually supporting other economic functions, such as manufacturing and domestic crafts.

In the South, however, the English Crown gave land directly to individuals. The landowners then settled large, relatively self-sufficient plantations that depended upon slave labor. Few villages or towns were created.

Although a few hardy adventurers were always willing to push westward, efforts to settle land west of the Appalachian Mountains were slow to develop. Once forests in the Northeast had been exhausted in the 1840s, logging companies pushed into the Great Lakes region in search of new timber. The discovery of gold and silver in the late 1840s brought waves of prospectors westward.

Despite these early migrations, it was not until Abraham Lincoln signed the Homestead Act in 1862 that substantial settlement of the West by European Americans began. The Homestead Act gave settlers 160 acres of land each if they would establish a home on the land and work to increase its productivity for at least five years. Railroads also received land grants. They then sold tracts of land to raise funds for the construction of the rail lines. Because the Homestead Act required settlers to live on the land, people remained dispersed across the countryside.

In some states, such as West Virginia and Kentucky, mining companies bought up huge tracts of land. When they did not own the land itself, they bought the mineral rights, which allowed them to mine underneath homes and farms, an activity that was often followed by the collapse of the land itself and the destruction of homes and livelihoods. Mining companies also sought timber rights, for timbers cut from nearby hillsides shored up the mines. Control over natural resources by those companies, generally incorporated in urban areas, meant that the transformation of natural capital to financial capital drained both capitals from rural communities.

Urban sprawl and the development of remote areas is often a result of the use of political capital (see the discussion of the growth machine in Chapter 5). The resulting paving over of farmland and filling in of natural areas such as wetlands have led to declines in water quality, increased tendencies toward flooding, loss of biodiversity and the habitat that supports it, loss of open space, and increased traffic congestion, which is accompanied by a decline in air quality with serious health impacts. More and more communities are seeing these outcomes as undesirable. A variety of mechanisms is available for local governments to address these issues (see Chapter 11 on the powers some local governments have over land use through zoning, property taxes, and tax abatements). Using bridging and bonding social capital for coalitions to design and implement alternative solutions is increasingly used for management of these disputes (see Box 6.1).

BOX 6.1 Working Together to Combat Sprawl

In Steamboat Springs, Colorado, "progress" is a loaded term. This small community, located in Routt County, has a popular ski resort, great shopping, beautiful mountainous views, and many, many tourists. Steamboat Ski and Resort Corporation, the third-largest ski resort in Colorado, has more than a million skier-days annually in good years, contributing half a million dollars to the community by way of fees, services, and cash and donations. Although the community welcomed the financial revenue, some residents felt that the growth in this resort area was spiraling out of control. In the early 1990s, when another new ski resort wanted to move in six miles from the existing one, people responded. Ranchers in nearby small communities began to see their access to land for grazing cut off, and they did not like it. Other residents were concerned about more traffic congestion and increasing real estate prices. Still others were concerned about land conservation and pollution. Bumper stickers appeared saying "Stop the Brutal Marketing of Steamboat." There were many groups that wanted the growth to slow down or cease altogether, but they were somewhat unaware of each other. That would soon change.

When Dean Rossi, head of the local cattleman's association, met with Holly Richter, a scientist from the Nature Conservancy, they may not have known what mutual goals they shared. However, it was not long before they realized they had made an important and necessary connection. Richter's goal was to build a sustainable plant community; Rossi wanted to make sure this did not impinge upon his land, but he felt that more plant growth could help his cattle. These sorts of coalitions have helped save more than 10,000 acres around Steamboat for ranching; needless to say, the new ski resort was not built in Routt County. A project named Vision 2020, which included a diverse group of citizens, encouraged discussions about what residents wanted to protect and enhance around Steamboat. What everyone began to realize was that being confrontational and shrill did not work. Everyone had to collaborate to improve the community; offering rational alternatives made the difference. This sort of mentality spread as a group called Environment 2000 began sponsoring annual "nonconfrontational" conferences to discuss topics surrounding community development. People began to listen to others' ideas, and respect between groups became apparent.

A strong connection was formed among ranchers, conservationists, and local government officials. Saving ranching in the area was something that all groups agreed upon. They all wanted to protect their water and air

Continued on next page

Working Together to Combat Sprawl (continued)

from pollution caused by high-density resort development, particularly in places like the Yampa Valley, a lush and unique landscape. Instead of fighting the land-preservation mentality, Gary Mielke, the president of Steamboat Ski and Resort Corporation, got on board, recognizing the heritage of the area: "We're committed to preserving the area's open lands and developing only where it's appropriate. . . . Our ranching heritage is as important to this company as snow" ("Routt County . . ." 1997).

In 1996, a project entitled the Yampa River System Legacy Project was invited to submit a grant proposal to Great Outdoor Colorado, a foundation with a lottery coffer of $10 million to $20 million per year. Representatives from all parts of Steamboat, including private business and landowners, educators, government officials, and others, came together to form a committee. They wrote a 150-page proposal that included forty-three letters of support from the region's most important leaders. The project's theme, "to protect and enhance the ecological health of the Yampa River and the productive agricultural lands it supports while providing for appropriate recreational opportunities," was coupled with five goals. The overriding goal was to protect and conserve the river and the area surrounding it. It was soon apparent that the project was well received. Great Outdoors Colorado awarded the project $6 million, its second-largest grant ever in the state and its largest per capita.

Coalition-forming between diverse community leaders and residents is unique and vital to community development, but as Routt County Commissioner Ben Beall pointed out, it takes learning and listening to people who live and work on the land: "My advice to other county officials is to look at your culture and figure out how that fits in with your vision and how the preservation of land fits with your culture. If it doesn't, then it's not going to work" ("Routt County . . ." 1997). Remarkable things can happen when people work together toward a common goal, which is evident in and around Steamboat, but it takes shared passion and mutual respect among all players.

SOURCE: "Routt County, CO: Holding the Reins." 1997. Washington, D.C.: Joint Center for Sustainable Communities.

There are increased conflicts over land use and local governments' attempt to protect the natural capital in their area and thus their human capital. For example, in Iowa, those who stand to benefit from large *confined-animal feeding operations* have frequently sued rural counties that have attempted to limit confinement operations.

Those companies have very deep pockets (that is, abundant financial capital) compared to cash-strapped county governments. Investment in lawyers and court fees is a legitimate capital investment (that is, it is tax deductible), whereas for rural governments, defense against lawsuits requires drawing on already limited resources.

Although some say that changes in land use are a natural result of market forces, others point to the role that political capital and government subsidies play in the creation of urban sprawl and the exploitation of natural resources on public lands. Ultimately, negotiation of alternative uses of natural capital that is sustainable depends on such groups as the Habitat Partnership Program to establish places of common ground and sustainable alternatives.

In the course of American history, land has been viewed as valuable in terms of

- Provision of natural resources to be turned into financial capital (logging, mining, trapping)
- Production of natural resources to be transformed into financial capital (farming and some timber production)
- Consumption to enhance cultural, built, and social capital (those with wealth purchasing land on which to build elegant homes and large estates to entertain their friends)
- Speculation to directly increase financial capital (land bought on the assumption that its price would increase)
- The foundation for built capital (housing developments, shopping malls, factories)
- Provision of important *ecosystem services* (clean water, air, biodiversity, carbon sequestration)
- Cultural capital (land valued for its spiritual meaning)

These differing values given to land have led to struggles over its access and control. Does it matter that what I do on my land to produce financial capital (building a mall or a mine) affects what happens on your land (flooding, decreased air quality, or landslides)? How are different values for land negotiated in the market and in public policy? And how do our decisions about land use affect natural capital in general?

Water

The availability of clean, potable water has been called the number one challenge facing the world and its people today. In the western United States, water has always been a scarce commodity. The first men and women recognized it as one of the fundamental elements of the universe, and husbanded it accordingly. The control of water literally shaped the history of the West. . . . [F]or years, Albuquerque's approach to managing water resources was simple and relatively inexpensive. The city just extracted all the water it needed from its underground aquifer, assuming the river was replacing it. We carved Midwestern landscapes into the desert, and were among the highest water users in the southwest—with about the lowest water rates. However, times have changed. (City of Albuquerque, Albuquerque Municipal Utilities, Water Resources Division 2000)

Water—its quantity and quality—is an increasingly scarce natural resource as one moves from east to west across the North American continent. Whereas in the East, the current water issues in rural communities revolve around water quality, in the West, they involve access to water. The old western adage "Whiskey is for drinking, water is for fighting" holds true now as much as it did during the settlement period.

To grow, communities must acquire new sources of water. Los Angeles, for example, could not have grown to its present size had it not been able to divert water from the north down into the arid southern California lands (see Box 6.2). The land was initially so dry that land values were determined by the quantity and certainty of the water supply. "Sell the water and throw the land in free" became the slogan of real estate brokers subdividing the rolling hills of southern California. Recognizing the tremendous importance of water for all phases of residential and industrial development, public officials and private entrepreneurs struggled over whether it should be public or private. The classic movie *Chinatown* presents a somewhat fictionalized account of the intrigues involved in that fight.

BOX 6.2   Water and Urban-Rural Connections?

Imagine a valley that is empty, where shade trees dot the landscape where houses once stood. A dusty basin where dust and toxic pollutants are kicked up when the wind blows is the only remaining part of the lake that once occupied the valley. This is an image of an Owens Valley, California, that has lost not only its vitality but its water supply.

Drought in the 1890s made Los Angeles aware of its vulnerability and the need to locate new sources of water. Two officials, Mayor Fred Eaton and water engineer Bill Mulholland, identified a potential source of water near Mammoth Lakes, California: the Owens River and Owens Lake. The river supported lush agriculture in the valleys on the eastern side of the Sierra Nevada. Farmers in those valleys controlled the river privately and

Continued on next page

Water and Urban-Rural Connections? (continued)

were using the water to such an extent that the water level of Owens Lake was diminishing. The lake itself was becoming salty.

To gain access to the water, Los Angeles had to do two things: First, it had to buy the water rights from the local farmers, the right of way for an aqueduct, and land for a reservoir. Initial visits to Owens Valley by representatives of the city of Los Angeles were disguised as tourism. By disguising their true goals, city officials avoided skyrocketing land prices. Then officials had to change the uses approved for that water. That change involved a major public choice: Should water from Owens Lake be used to support residential use in Los Angeles or agricultural use in the Sierra Nevada?

The second step was figuring out how to get the water from Owens Lake down to Los Angeles. Eaton conferred with investors, who envisioned large profits in building the aqueduct and controlling the water rights. Mulholland sought public funds to develop the infrastructure as a public trust and pressured Eaton to give up a private role in the Owens Valley project, from which Eaton would have gained financially. Los Angeles was well on its way to gaining control of the Owens Valley aqueduct project.

Los Angeles quickly won the right to have the water system in public hands, in part because of the high construction costs. There was pressure from the privately held Pacific Light and Power Company to use the flow of the water to generate electricity. At this point, the city had to decide whether to become a public utility and provide energy. Officials decided to diversify into a related monopoly for the generation and distribution of electrical power.

Many utilities in communities across the nation are privately held. Others are local government enterprises. A number of communities, from the city of Los Angeles to the county seat of Harlan, Iowa, generate their own electricity and collect the revenues from it. The decision to function as a utility is based on assumptions about equity, efficiency, and the proper role of government in providing built capital.

Construction of the aqueduct led to the development of other built capital by Los Angeles. For example, a great deal of cement was required for construction of the aqueduct. Rather than buy it from private contractors, Los Angeles constructed its own cement plant at Monolith, California. The city invested public funds in an element of built capital that is private in most parts of the United States.

Continued on next page

Water and Urban-Rural Connections? (continued)

Once Owens Valley residents realized what Los Angeles planned to do with the water, the battle over who would control the water began—a battle that is still in the courts today. Owens Valley newspapers defended local water rights while Los Angeles newspapers declared that the well-being of Owens Valley communities must be sacrificed for the greater good and the greater profit of Los Angeles. To this day, decisions by the Los Angeles Department of Water and Power, whose board members are nonpartisan but highly political, have a huge impact on communities all along the eastern side of the Sierra Nevada. In 1997, a Los Angeles Water Agreement and Memorandum of Understanding between the city of Los Angeles, Inyo County (where Owens Lake is located), the Owens Valley Committee, and other groups led joint projects to revegetate land and rewater the Owens River. However, the Los Angeles Department of Water and Power has missed several deadlines, and the city continues to pump groundwater from Owens Valley at a harmful rate. Disputes over the size of the pumpback station to return water from the lower Owens River to the Los Angeles aqueduct are ongoing. There is also speculation that the Los Angeles Department of Water and Power is eyeing water sources beneath the Mojave Desert.

The fight to stop construction of the aqueduct illustrates the role that different levels of government play in providing built capital. The aqueduct, ultimately paid for by the taxpayers of Los Angeles, had to pass over public land. The people of Owens Valley tried to block the city's access to public land as one means of stopping the project. Not only was the aqueduct allowed to cross public lands, but the U.S. Forest Service, by presidential proclamation, claimed the Owens Valley as part of the Sierra Forest Reserve, thus eliminating private claims on the land.

Despite the investment by Los Angeles and the diverse support for the project, Owens Valley residents continued to fight against it. In 1913, the first water from Owens Valley arrived in Los Angeles. The aqueduct went into operation in the late 1920s and was not fully completed until 1941. During those twenty years, resistance to the aqueduct included physical attacks on it. Explosions would rock the valley as people, angry as they watched lush vegetation and agricultural production wither for lack of water, attempted to blow holes in the aqueduct. The growth of Los Angeles was accompanied by the decline of the towns, ranches, and farms along the river valley. The communities and ranchers of Owens Valley had little chance to prevail when pitted against the financial and political power of the city of Los Angeles.

Providing water to one community can mean depriving another. Thus, conflicts and public debates have emerged over who gets water from where and who pays for it. Although these issues are important throughout the country, they are gaining increasing attention in the Southwest and on the western plains. For example, the people of Caliente, Nevada, a remote rural community, became concerned about the efforts of Las Vegas to buy up water rights. Under the appropriation doctrine, Las Vegas can purchase the rights to water and divert it to support its own rapidly growing population, even if this usage diminishes the water available to the people of Caliente. Denver is seeking access to the aquifer in the San Luis Valley in south-central Colorado, much to the dismay of rural communities and landowners. This situation has caused much discord between urban dwellers and rural farmers. Urban dwellers and lobbyists believe that they are the engine that keeps the state running and that they deserve access to the water. Rural farmers who do not want to give up any of the water supply have been targeted as being "selfish." However, it is the farmers' position that people living in the city do not understand their reliance on the water supply for farming their land. The water crisis in the West is real, and decisions regarding the use of rural water supplies are difficult and multifaceted.

Large-scale agricultural users have also been drawn into conflict with traditional dryland farmers. The withdrawal of water from the Ogallala aquifer to irrigate fields and support feedlots and packing plants in Garden City, Kansas, is lowering the water table. Dryland farmers and rural communities in the area are finding it necessary to dig deeper wells simply to continue to use water for livestock and for residential and commercial use. Because the Ogallala aquifer is essentially not replenishable, residents fear that the future of any economic activity is being compromised.

Water for human use comes from two sources: surface water (lakes, streams, and in some cases—such as in Tampa, Florida, with its desalinization plant—oceans) and groundwater, which is pumped from underground aquifers. Water's mobility and its relatively tenuous relation to land has resulted in the need to set rules around access and control of water. In the United States, these laws are primarily state laws. However, the federal government has heavily subsidized the provision of water, particularly in the West. During the Era of Reclamation, from about 1880 to 1980, the American people, through their legislative leaders, saw augmenting the water supply for multiple users as an appropriate role for governments. There is no longer a strong constituency (political capital) for subsidized federal water projects. Environmental concerns about irrigation-induced water and soil quality problems have also united political and natural capital.

As water supplies become more erratic due to climate change, the laws that govern access to and control of water become points of hot contention. We have now moved to an era of reallocation and improved management (National Research Council 1992). The current conflict involves not only the market transfer of water (based on who will pay the most) but also the third-party effects—who will suffer or benefit from water loss or gain. Because urban areas generally have more market power, there is concern that such water transfers will disadvantage rural areas in terms of water quantity. How the rural lands are managed also has an enormous impact on water quality. Recognition of what is needed if rural land managers are to manage lands to enhance water quality has resulted in new rural-urban partnerships (see Box 6.3).

BOX 6.3   Rural-Urban Collaborations for Safe Drinking Water: New York City and the Catskills

Nine million residents of New York City and surrounding suburbs rely for the source of their drinking water on a series of reservoirs located many miles away in the Catskill and Delaware watersheds in upstate New York. New York City owns less than 10 percent of the watershed, which covers roughly 1,900 square miles. The Catskill/Delaware watershed has a year-round population of around 77,000, as well as a significant number of summer residents. Dairy farms comprise a majority of the 350 farms there.

For many decades, relations between New York City and the watershed areas have been marked by controversy and conflict, focusing on the City's past acquisitions of reservoir lands and the use of regulatory and management authority in the watershed. In 1989, the EPA's Surface Water Treatment Rule (SWTR), issued under the federal Safe Drinking Water Act, required filtration of all surface water supplies (rivers and lakes) to protect against microbial contamination of drinking water. This requirement can be waived if a water system's treatment processes and natural conditions provide safe water and if the watershed is actively protected to ensure that safety in the future. For New York City, the new regulation meant they had to get cooperation from those who managed the land in these two watersheds if they were not to spend tens of billions of dollars building complex filtration systems.

The Stresses

Although New York City residents have enjoyed superior drinking water for 150 years because of its high quality upland supplies, the potential for microbial contamination has become an increasing concern as evidenced by a series of boil water alerts since 1993. Wastewater discharges from treatment plants (some operated by New York City) and runoff from urban

Continued on next page

Rural-Urban Collaborations for Safe Drinking Water: New York City and the Catskills (continued)

and agricultural sources, which contribute both microbial pathogens as well as phosphorus, are the primary pollution sources.

The Strategy

In 1993, the EPA issued New York City a waiver of the filtration requirement on condition that the City would take numerous steps to maintain and protect the Catskill/Delaware's drinking water quality. The EPA then urged the Governor to convene a group representing New York City, New York State, watershed communities, the U.S. EPA, and environmental groups to negotiate an effective and equitable watershed program. It was hoped that such a program would enable the City to meet the waiver conditions, protect the City's water supply while avoiding the multi-billion dollar cost of a filtration plant for Catskill/Delaware water supplies, and address the concerns and goals of residents in the upstate counties.

The negotiations produced a landmark agreement that successfully resolved long-standing controversies and set forth responsibilities and benefits for all major parties. The City finalized its regulations for watershed land uses, acquired sensitive lands to protect key reservoirs and waterways, conducts more extensive water quality testing in the watershed, and supports upstate/downstate partnership programs (including major investments in wastewater treatment facility upgrades, a fund for compatible economic development in the watershed, and a regional watershed partnership council). . . . [U]pstate community representatives participate in the regional watershed partnership council, which includes representatives of the State, City, and downstate consumers.

[In reviewing the implementation, which began in 1997, the National Research Council stressed the intersection between technical solutions and community involvement and priority setting. Without urban investment in sustainable rural development, rural areas could not invest in decreasing non–point source pollution for urban water consumers.]

SOURCE: EPA. 1996. "Watershed Progress: New York City Watershed Agreement." EPA840-F-96-005. December. Online; available: http://www.epa.gov/owow/watershed/ny/nycityfi.html; accessed April 14, 2003.

Who has rights to use water and who has the responsibility of improving poor water quality remain contentious issues. The role of rural people in resolving these issues nationwide is increasingly recognized. Because water is seasonally and geographically limited in the West, encouraging the productive use of water has always been a key policy objective, from the days of the Ancestral Pueblo People (referred to by some as the Anasazi) to the present.

In the Middle Rio Grande Valley (MRG), where Albuquerque, New Mexico, is located, there are many claimants to the water. First, the Pueblo Indians of the MRG have the longest historic claim to water. Because they were practicing irrigated farming when the Spanish arrived, the king of Spain granted them *Mercedes del Aqua* (water rights) as part of the treaty following the Pueblo uprising in the late 1600s. The Mexican and then the U.S. governments have each in its turn honored those rights. The Pueblo rights, spelled out in treaties, involve water quality as well as quantity. Rituals, key to maintaining cultural capital, demand very high quality water.

The second claim is by farmers, who claim historic water rights dating back to the Spanish era under the collective *acequia* system. *Acequia*s are ditch canals that are operated and managed locally but that operate under a deed from the government that guarantees them rights to a given amount of water from the general system. The term is also used to mean a collectivity of irrigation farmers who live along the ditch network and distribute water among themselves. The *acequia*s are, in turn, under the management and distribution authority of the elected, regional conservancy district, which monitors water distribution for a fee. Landowners with holdings along the irrigation ditch network, whether or not they are farmers, have voting rights in conservancy district elections.

The most recent holders of water rights are the various municipalities, which have purchased or been granted water rights over time. Specifically, Albuquerque will soon lay claim to the Rio Grande's water for drinking water, though they will divert the San Juan River upstream into the Rio Grande, using the newly constructed San Juan/Chama Diversion to do this. All of these claims do not factor in the downstream rights of the state of Texas and the nation of Mexico. Texas has guaranteed its claims to Rio Grande water through the Rio Grande Compact, signed by Texas, New Mexico, and Colorado in 1957 to guarantee access to water for each state. Mexico maintains some rights to Rio Grande waters under the "First in time, first in rights" laws that were applied under Spanish rule and then adopted by Mexico and codified in the treaty between the United States and Mexico following the Mexican-American War.

Water Rights

There are legal doctrines that govern appropriate or fair use of surface water. The *riparian doctrine* governs water use primarily in states east of the Mississippi River. Water rights are given to those whose lands are adjacent to streams. Landowners do not own the water, but they can make reasonable use of the water flowing over their lands, as long as such use does not severely diminish the flow of streams or levels in lakes. The *appropriation doctrine,* sometimes called the California Doctrine, is used throughout the more arid states of the West. This policy allows users to divert water from its original channel as long as the water is used for beneficial purposes and the amount of water withdrawn does not exceed what the user is entitled to under the permit. As originally implemented, the appropriation doctrine honored the rights of those who first used the water. Definitions of "beneficial use" have undergone change, and more recently, societal needs as well as individual uses of water are recognized. Such definitions have two components, the nature or purpose of use and efficient, nonwasteful use of water. State constitutions, statutes, or case law (legal precedent) may define uses of water that are "beneficial," and this may be different in each state. The definition of "beneficial use" itself may change over time. The right to use water established under state law may be lost if beneficial use is discontinued for a prescribed period of time.

Laws governing groundwater are even more complex. Early in this century, laws allowed landowners to use groundwater on their own land even if it depleted the groundwater available to adjacent landowners; but these same landowners could not deplete groundwater resources by removing water from their land and using it elsewhere. More recently, some states have modified this doctrine to protect neighboring landowners and waterways that are supplied by the groundwater. Landowners are allowed to withdraw groundwater, but they may not exceed their fair share of water resources or harm neighboring uses of groundwater.

Both the appropriation and the riparian doctrines saw water as a private good to be used to promote individual financial capital. Increasingly, however, states are defining water as a public good. More and more states are establishing permitting authorities. Those laws recognize all water occurring in the state as "public water and public wealth of the people of the state and subject to use," and they establish one central state agency to provide permits for the use of water. Landowners are restricted in making alternations to waterways on their land that would affect the quality of the water or its availability to other users. Most states now require permits to use both surface water and groundwater.

With increasing population and development of the West, less unappropriated water is reliably available. Consequently, the acquisition and transfer of already established water rights frequently satisfy new water demands. For example, the city of Las Vegas, Nevada, has acquired the water rights of many of the surrounding valleys, which has definite implications for the future of those areas.

Cultural Capital and Natural Capital

A part of the problem of water scarcity is a result of cultural capital. Immigrants from the East and the Midwest, where rain was abundant, sought to re-create the green lawns and colorful gardens that had been brought to the North American continent from England. Thus, the expectation of water abundance was implicit in the planning of cities. Yet as many western cities built in deserts rose to be important urban centers—Las Vegas, Los Angeles, San Diego, Albuquerque, and Denver, among others—the water had to come from somewhere. That "somewhere" was rural areas, often hundreds of miles away.

Rural citizens west of the Sierra Nevadas in California, who settled the land to farm, were astounded when they found that Los Angeles had acquired rights to their water and was building an aqueduct to ship it to the ever-expanding city to the south at the beginning of the twentieth century. The Los Angeles Department of Water and Power (LADWP) took water first from the once-verdant Owens Valley, in spite of legal fights and sabotage of the aqueduct by local community groups (see Box 6.1). By 1941, Los Angeles growth meant expanding the water supply. The LADWP diverted Mono Lake's tributary streams 350 miles south to meet the growing water demands of Los Angeles. Deprived of its freshwater sources, the volume of Mono Lake halved while its salinity doubled. Unable to adapt to these changing conditions within such a short period of time, the ecosystem began to collapse.

Islands in the lake, previously important nesting sites, became peninsulas where birds were vulnerable to mammalian and reptilian predation, reducing biodiversity. Photosynthetic rates of algae, the base of the food chain, were reduced, and the reproductive abilities of brine shrimp became impaired. Stream ecosystems unraveled due to lack of water. Air quality grew poor as the exposed lake bed became the source of air-borne particulate matter, violating the Clean Air Act. If something was not done, Mono Lake was certain to become a lifeless chemical sump. In 1978, the citizens of Mono County and others from across California formed the Mono Lake Committee (MLC) and began talking to conservation clubs, schools, service organizations, legislators, lawyers, and anyone who would listen about the value of this high-desert lake. The MLC grew to 20,000 members and gained legal and legislative recognition for Mono Lake. They organized around seeking a solution that would "meet the real water needs of Los Angeles and leave our children a living, healthy, and beautiful lake" (Mono Lake Committee 1978).

In 1979, the MLC and the National Audubon Society (NAS) argued in the Mono County Superior Court that water diversions to Los Angeles did not comply with the public trust doctrine. This legal doctrine, which came to California law from ancient Roman codes, states that the government has the duty to protect navigable bodies of water for the use and benefit of all the people. In a 1983 precedent-setting decision, the California Supreme Court agreed with the MLC, ruling that the state has an obligation to protect places like Mono Lake "as far as [is] feasible," even if this means a reconsideration of past water allocation decisions.

In 1984, California Trout, MLC, and NAS brought suit against the city of Los Angeles, charging that the city's water diversions did not comply with California's fish and game codes. These codes require that enough water always be allowed to flow below a dam to keep fisheries in good condition. Eventually, the *Public Trust* suit and the *Fish and Game* suits were combined into one case before the State Water Resources Control Board (SWRCB), the agency that allocates water in California.

In 1994, the SWRCB issued Decision 1631, which set minimum flows for the streams, set limits on water exports based on the level of Mono Lake—designed to raise and stabilize the lake at a level twenty feet above its lowest level—and ordered LADWP to restore the streams and waterfowl habitat.

The MLC, mobilizing around natural capital, created alliances (political capital) with organizations that shared their cultural capital regarding appropriate biodiversity, water quality, and air quality. Although the MLC was not obligated to meet the water needs of Los Angeles, it has found ways of doing so through cooperative solutions, without transferring environmental problems to other areas.

Biodiversity

Biodiversity is defined as the variety of life in all its forms, levels, and combinations. It includes ecosystem diversity, species diversity, and genetic diversity. Maintaining biodiversity at all three levels allows for greater resilience in the face of change. Those concerned about biodiversity generally understand that ecosystem diversity is necessary for species diversity.

All species alter the ecosystem, humans more than most. By focusing on only one linear relationship, we ignore collateral changes that have an even greater impact than intended changes. Ecologists make clear that our problem has never been insufficient data; rather, the problem is insufficient understanding of that data and, specifically, of the relationship between the parts and the whole in living systems (Lewontin 2000).

For example, rural interests have been greatly conflicted over the definition and function of wetlands and thus over the degree to which they should be protected. To some, protecting the prairie potholes in rural, remote areas of North Dakota, which only held water part of the year, seemed like a foolish waste of perfectly good farmland; they thought the potholes should just be leveled to maximize productivity. Their political capital was manifested through a variety of traditional farm groups, such as the Farm Bureau. For others in the rural communities and their urban allies, the prairie potholes, with water in the spring, were critical habitats for migrating waterfowl, bringing hunters and bird-watchers who helped diversify the local economy and maintain worldwide biodiversity. Local chapters of the Audubon Society worked with their national organization to mobilize political capital to negotiate with the farm groups. The 2002 Farm Bill (Farm Security and Rural Investment Act) contains language that would allow farmers to be paid to protect biodiversity (and water quality, for wetlands also filter chemicals from water) at the same time they are give a variety of supports (loan deficiency payments, counter cyclical payments, and direct payments) for the agricultural commodities they produce (which decreases biodiversity). Like many programs, the 2002 Farm Bill contains both perverse and positive incentives regarding protection of natural capital in rural areas.

Rural areas have suffered in the past from lack of genetic diversity in the crops and animals they produce. Although genetic similarity can yield a standard crop or animal, it can also make that crop or animal extremely vulnerable to disease and pests. Pathogens spread more easily and epidemics are more severe when hosts (corn plants, hogs, or chickens) are more uniform and abundant. Outbreaks of avian flu (a fatal chicken disease) occur regularly in the Chesapeake Bay area, where large numbers of chickens of the same genetic stock are raised in close confinement. In Hong Kong in 1998, an outbreak of a new avian flu strain to which humans seemed susceptible led to the death or destruction of hundreds of millions of chickens. The Great Potato Famine of 1845–1849 in Ireland and the southern corn leaf blight in 1970 in the United States, which totally wiped out the corn crop, were both caused by insufficient biodiversity in the affected crops (CAST 1999).

Invasive Species

Another threat to biodiversity is *invasive species.* These are species of plants and animals (including insects) that are introduced, either accidentally or on purpose, from another area of the country or the world and that, removed from their natural enemies, out-compete native species and become a monoculture. For example, in order to control soil erosion in "cottoned out" areas in the South, the Soil Conservation Service introduced kudzu from Japan. Although the soil has been stabilized, kudzu covers everything in its path, crowding out native plants that were habitats for many indigenous species of wildlife.

Cheat grass was first identified in the United States in the late 1800s. This noxious Eurasian weed was introduced through packing materials and spread along the rail lines. Grazing animals spread the weed further, and it now thrives in all fifty states, covering more than 100 million acres.

"Cheat grass out-competes sage and bunch grasses and Nevada's Great Basin is the area most impacted," ecologist Jennifer Vollmer said. "The arms of the seeds are long and sharp. They can puncture the mouths and throats of cattle and when the cattle have sores, they stop eating" (Vasquez 2002).

In addition to affecting sheep and cattle, this weed seriously hurts the ecosystems of the Great Basin, crowding out native plants like sage and bunch grasses.

"Cheat grass is nutritionally good only three to four weeks, yet in Nevada, it can be the only winter range for bighorn sheep, elk and mule deer," Vollmer explained. "When they come down from the mountains into the flatlands in the winter, all they're finding is cheat grass. It has no nutritional value and the animals can starve to death" (Vasquez 2002). By contrast, native bunch grasses provide nutritional forage for three to four months out of the year and can produce twelve times more forage during drought years.

Fire is a natural phenomenon that can rejuvenate rangelands, but with the advent of cheat grass, those fires burn faster and hotter. Furthermore, cheat grass recovers faster after fire than native species, further decreasing biodiversity. About 1.6 million acres burned in Nevada in 1999 and 1.3 million in 2000, a five- to tenfold increase over the turn of the century. Cheat grass has increased the negative impact of fires wherever it is present.

Plateau™, a chemical herbicide made up of organic elements and approved for use by the Environmental Protection Agency (EPA) in December 2001, affects an enzyme needed for plant growth, which selectively impedes the growth of cheat grass. But application on individual plots of land will not serve to suppress cheat grass permanently. Scientists, environmentalists, and landowners and operators need to work closely together to control cheat grass, given its negative impact on natural and financial capital. Attention to the systems impacts of unintended consequences is critical to contain the damage of invasive species on biodiversity.

Coordinated efforts among agencies and communities can reduce the area a destructive invasive species affects, as in the case of crop-strangling African parasitic witch-weed in North Carolina, which was initially sold as an ornamental plant. One agency sprays weeds with pesticides, while another has just released biocontrol insects on the weeds in an adjacent field each negating the others efforts (Kaiser 1999).

Climate Change

Global climate change will have major impacts on human capital through health threats brought about by changes in food production, access to freshwater, exposure to vector- and water-borne diseases, sea-level rise and coastal flooding, and extreme weather events. Extreme weather events mean longer and more severe droughts and more intense rain and snow. Those weather events have implications for soil erosion and thus water quality.

Scientists argue that our ability to respond is limited not by lack of knowledge but by our failure to synthesize and distribute what we know (Pimm et al. 2001). Rural areas will both be affected by climate change and able to act to reduce it.

Although we know of actions that can slow global warming, such as decreasing greenhouse gases and increasing the amount of carbon sequestered, few have acted on that knowledge. The fact that climate is a free access good (see the discussion in

Chapter 11) and that those who act to reduce global warming do not receive any immediate personal benefit (except perhaps in enhancing social or cultural capital) make it difficult to justify the transaction costs of moving to new ways of doing things. In the United States, we have made decreasing pollution a market good by creating a market for pollution trading as a way to comply with U.S. environmental laws. But, the reluctance of the U.S. government to acknowledge human agency as a cause of climate change has kept the United States from making carbon sequestration a similar tradable good. Although some farm groups want the federal government to pay them for sequestering carbon through such things as no-till agriculture, they are unwilling to tax carbon emissions as a way of supporting the carbon sequestration payments. They are encouraged in this stand by oil companies and some industries that are also hesitant to change the way they do business.

Energy

What can communities do? Some communities have moved to reduce carbon emissions through a variety of measures that also reduce their expenditures. For example, a number of small communities have purchased hybrid cars (powered by both batteries and internal combustion engines), such as the Toyota Prius and Honda Civic Hybrid, for city employees, including police on routine business. Others put their police on bicycles in good weather. Small cities use "smart growth" strategies to encourage use of public transportation, recycling, and dense neighborhoods where stores and housing are in walking distance of each other. Yet others have moved to renewable energy sources, combining with private-sector firms to generate wind power. The Blackfeet Nation (located in the state of Montana) is working with SeaWest WindPower, Inc., of San Diego, California, to develop a wind-power project. The project will generate financial capital for the tribe and reduce the need to use fossil fuels in other areas of the Northwest. However, it is not just the increasing price of oil that helps make wind energy competitive. The Wind Energy Production Tax Credit, extended in 2000, gives a credit of 1.5 cent per kilowatt-hour to users of wind energy, thus effectively cutting its price.

Not only can the energy choices made by communities save money, but they can help ensure a healthy planet for their children's children.

Natural and Political Capital: Rural Environmentalism

Shifts in rural population and economic growth patterns may help explain rising levels of support for environmental values in many rural areas. Some scholars present a model of "green migration," which assumes that domestic in-migration, with its impacts on the character and composition of rural communities, is one of the reasons environmental values may be gaining support in rural America. A study by Robert Jones and colleagues (2003) found that a majority of the in-migrants to the Appalachian region came because of its environment, and protecting environmental values remained a high priority. Amenities-seeking in-migrants are a bit more knowledgeable about environmental issues, are more concerned about the environment, place higher priority on environmental protection, and are more engaged in activities that promote environmental values than are nonmigrants.

Furthermore, old-time rural residents who state proudly that they would shoot a spotted owl if they saw one are finding that they share many values with environmentalists about habitat protection. Old-timers do not like stupid laws that seem to be imposed arbitrarily, and they do not like being told what to do, but they do understand systems. When groups can be brought together to consider alternatives in the use of natural capital, other forms of capital can be enhanced. However, there is still a caution. Solutions worked out by local groups can be undone by the political capital of groups outside the community who view these decisions as having a potentially negative influence on their broader agenda. Thus, management of conflicts over natural capital must keep in mind the lessons of political capital.

Chapter Summary

Humans have often sought to use natural capital to build other forms of capital. Native Americans used—and continue to use—natural capital in the strengthening of cultural and social capital; European settlers converted it into financial capital, moving westward when natural capital was depleted in settled areas. Today, urban sprawl places stress on natural capital in ways that more compact settlement patterns would not do. Land and water are forms of natural capital central in European Americans' closing of the frontier. Village-centered settlement stimulated industrial and commercial development in nonmetropolitan parts of the Northeast, whereas plantation settlement retarded such developments in the South. In the arid West, human-directed organization of water gave value to the land during the settlement period and today. Property law regarding water developed differently west of the Mississippi from east of it. In the West, where one did not have to own the land through which a watercourse ran, water was overappropriated by the time the frontier closed. This overappropriation of a scarce commodity generated conflict, which continues to this day. As cities grow, rural-urban conflicts grow as well. Agricultural, environmental, and urban interests vie to control water for purposes each values highly. As water is increasingly recognized as a public good, legal patterns change and negotiated solutions such as that between residents of the Adirondacks region and New York City can occasionally generate a win-win situation. Too often, parties still view the situation as a zero-sum game.

As globalization proceeds apace, interdependence among different groups, regions, and nations becomes more evident. Global warming, introduction of exotic species, and other issues related to natural capital will increasingly require greater recognition that it is in the long-term interest of the well-to-do (whether individuals or nations) to provide monetary and other incentives to those that are less well-off to "do the right thing" by the environment. This presupposes that the wealthy themselves are concerned about the environment. If greed can be curbed and creativity given its head with the objective of lightening the footprint of humans on the earth, perhaps we can pass a planet on to our children that is indeed better than what we inherited.

Key Terms

Appropriation doctrine allows water rights to be established by the first claimant even if that user does not own land adjacent to the watercourse. The user is limited to a specified amount of water that can be withdrawn.

Biodiversity is the variety of life in all its forms, levels, and combinations.

Confined-animal feeding operations involve raising livestock and poultry in an industrial fashion. The animals are confined in large buildings where the conditions are controlled so as to produce a uniform product. A huge amount of manure is a by-product. To the degree possible, the production system is "rationalized" to increase output per unit of labor, much as occurs on the industrial assembly line. Also, holding the animals in a confined space promotes efficient conversion of feed to meat or eggs, since the animals expend very little energy in exercise.

Ecosytem services, critical services like water purification, biodiversity maintenance, and climate stabilization, are spontaneously generated by healthy ecosystems. Because these services are chronically undervalued in the marketplace, they are highly vulnerable to degradation.

An *invasive species* is one (1) that is nonnative (or alien) to the ecosystem under consideration and (2) whose introduction causes or is likely to cause economic or environmental harm or harm to human health.

Riparian doctrine limits water rights to landowners whose lands are contiguous to streams. They can make reasonable use of the water but cannot severely diminish its flow.

References

Ambrose, Stephen E. 1996. *Undaunted Courage: Meriwether Lewis, Thomas Jefferson, and the Opening of the American West.* New York: Simon and Schuster.

City of Albuquerque Public Works Department. Water Resources Division. 2000. 2000 in Water and Our Future, advertising supplement, *Albuquerque Journal,* December 10.

Council of Agricultural Sciences and Technology (CAST). 1999. "Benefits of Bio-diversity." Task Force Report No. 133.

Jones, Robert Emmet, J. Mark Fly, James Talley, and H. Ken Cordell. 2003. "Green Migration into Rural America: The New Frontier of Environmentalism?" *Society and Natural Resources* 16:221–238.

Kahrl, William L. 1982. *Water and Power.* Berkeley and Los Angeles: University of California Press.

Kaiser, Pauline. 1999. "Stemming the Tide of Invasive Species." *Science* 285:1836–1841.

Lapping Mark B., Thomas D. Daniels, and John W. Keller. 1989. *Rural Planning and Development in the United States.* New York: Guilford.

Lewontin, Richard C. 2000. *The Triple Helix: Gene, Organism, and Environment.* Cambridge, Mass.: Harvard University Press.

Mono Lake Committee. 1978. Online; available: http://www.monolake.org/committee/history.htm; accessed April 16, 2003.

National Research Council. 1992. *Water Transfers in the West: Efficiency, Equity, and the Environment.* Washington, D.C.: National Academies Press.

———. 2000. *Watershed Management for Potable Water Supply: Assessing the New York City Strategy.* Washington, D.C.: National Academies Press.

Pimm, Stuart L., Mácia Ayres, Andrew Balmford, George Branch, Katrina Brandon, Thomas Brooks, Rodrigo Bustamante, Robert Costanza, Richard Cowling, Lisa M. Curran, Andrew Dobson, Stephen Farber, Gustavo A.B. da Fonseca, Claude Gascon, Roger Kitching, Jeffrey McNeely, Thomas Lovejoy, Russell A. Mittermeier, Norman Myer, Jonathan A. Patz, Bradley Raffle, David Rappaport, Peter Raven, Callum Roberts, Jon Paul Rodriguez, Anthony B. Rylands, Compton Tucker, Carl Safina, Christián Samper, Melanie L.J. Stiassny, Jatna Supriatna, Diana H. Wall, and David Wilcove. 2001. "Can We Defy Nature's End?" *Science* 293:2207–2208. Online; available: http://www.all-species.org/content/reference/2207.pdf, accessed May 14, 2003.

Reisner, Marc P. 1986. *Cadillac Desert: The American West and Its Disappearing Water.* New York: Viking.

Vasquez, Susie. 2002. "New Herbicide Could Be First Major Step Toward Cheat Grass Eradication." *Nevada Appeal* (October 7). Also online; available: http://www.nevadaappeal.com/apps/pbcs.dll/article?AID=2002210070104.

7

Financial Capital

Tina Fernandez wanted to be the first person in her family to go to college. A daughter of migrant farm workers in the Rio Grande valley, a persistently poor region in Texas, she had started working in the fields when she was six years old. She was accustomed to hard work. Her parents could not afford to send her to college, so she decided to forgo her dream and marry her high school sweetheart. Unfortunately, the marriage only lasted three years, and Tina was left alone to raise a son. They moved back to the *colonia* to her parents' home, where she had someone she trusted to help care for her son and someone she loved to help put food on the table.

The economic downturn of the early 1990s made it difficult for her to find work, even with a high school degree. She finally found a part-time job waiting tables at a locally owned restaurant in McAllen, a fifty-minute drive in her unreliable car, for less than minimum wage. Fortunately, her mother provided childcare and her father was a skilled mechanic who kept many of the *colonia*'s cars running by swapping parts on the junkers he kept in his yard.

Her excellent service and friendly manner resulted in good tips, and the owner liked Tina's work ethic. She showed up regularly on time, followed directions—and even anticipated what the owner might ask next—and got along well with the cook and the other waitresses, for whom she served as peacemaker when tension arose in the restaurant. The owner began to depend on Tina to do some of the administrative tasks for the restaurant and recognized her knack for business; soon Tina was promoted to assistant manager, a full-time position with benefits. Encouraged by her parents, Tina took a night course in bookkeeping at the local community college. Tina felt that she was earning the degree she had always wanted as she began to learn the inner workings of the restaurant business. The owner acquired another restaurant in McAllen and put Tina as the manager.

Tina was making good money, but she knew that she wanted to be a restaurant owner, an entrepreneur. However, she only had $7,000 start-up capital of her own to use, even after her parents and cousins loaned her what they could. She decided to look at low-cost resources to help her start a restaurant business of her own. She

turned to a small-business development center for women to help her do her research and develop a successful marketing plan. The center informed her about alternative credit resources that she could tap into for her start-up costs. Tina soon
found out about a few restaurant-supply companies that provided equipment for
start-up businesses; the interest rates were favorable, and the equipment itself would
become *collateral*. She would need many commercial appliances for her new restaurant, and the expenses would be well above $7,000. She joined the Latino chapter
of the chamber of commerce in McAllen, despite the time away from her business
and family to drive to meetings. There she began networking with local businesspeople who offered their expertise, including a few investment bankers, who offered more advice about alternative forms of credit, including private placement
deals where investment banks get *minority ownership* in exchange for capital to begin the business. Within a few months, the plans were drawn up, and she had built
up enough capital, both social and financial, to begin her entrepreneurial career.
Finding sources of alternative capital had been a key factor in her success.

Her restaurant, with its Latino flare, was a local hit. She hired dependable wait-
staff and trained them well. Her chef was new but extremely creative and talented.
After three years, Tina had opened two more restaurants in the valley, and she had
a great start on her son's college fund. She now lives across the street from her parents and has added rooms, plumbing, and a sewage connection to both dwellings,
working with the barrio organization.

★   ★   ★

Financial capital is important because it can be transformed into more productive
labor as it is invested to increase human capital and built capital. Tina Fernandez
needed financial and bridging social capital in order to convert her idea into a
profitable business. Yet for rural communities and businesses alike, there is a crisis
of capital availability. Lured by higher profits outside the local area and facilitated
by new laws making it easier to move from one place to another, financial capital
is becoming more and more mobile.

As capital becomes more mobile, rural communities lose control. Tina Fernandez had to go outside of the *colonia* to build social capital that helped her learn
how to access and invest financial capital. Her restaurant is one of the few in the
colonia, and it is doing very well, attracting people from as far away as McAllen.

This chapter examines financial capital in its various forms. The extent to
which communities depend on financial capital is explored, as are the various institutions created to provide loans to businesses. Traditional sources of financial
capital are contrasted with the new sources rural communities must develop to
adapt to the changing rules of the financial playing field.

The Concept of Financial Capital

The term "financial capital" often translates to money: the money needed to start a new business or the money used to *speculate* in the currency market. But money is not always financial capital, nor is financial capital simply money. This section explores the definition of "financial capital," the various forms financial capital can take, and both the public and private character of financial capital.

Defining Financial Capital

Capital is any resource capable of producing other resources (See Chapter 1). Financial capital represents resources that are translated into monetary instruments that makes them highly liquid, that is, able to be converted into other assets. This definition forces us to distinguish between consumption and investment. If you buy a car for personal enjoyment, the car is not considered a form of capital. But if you buy a car in order to run a shuttle service, the car becomes a means for generating income. A resource (the car) is capable of producing other resources (your income).

Although financial capital is more than just money, some examples based on money are helpful in building a definition of financial capital. Money can be used for a variety of purposes. We use it to buy things, such as a new stereo or food for dinner (both goods), or a ticket to a movie or trash-collection services (both services). These uses of money are part of *consumption* (see Chapter 10). Money can also be used to make more money. Money invested in a savings bond, for example, generates more money in the form of interest. People invest money in a business because they expect to receive part of the profits in addition to the money they originally invested. Money is a form of financial capital when it is used to make more money.

Keeping Track of Financial Capital

Sociologists have been intrigued with the interaction between social organization and economic organization. Some theorists (Weber 1978) have suggested that the way money was accounted for can be linked to the emergence of capitalism. In earlier days, the most common form of accounting was cash accounting, keeping track of the money coming in and going out in a business. There was no way to keep track of exchanges in which money was converted to capital goods, as happens when a business invests in a new plant or accumulates an inventory. When accountants began keeping track of assets rather than simply of cash, capitalism as a form of economic organization began to emerge.

The scandals of the early twenty-first century around accounting practices—what was counted where for what—demonstrate the importance of having clear, standard rules and of a transparent presentation of financial assets. Energy companies falsified their profits, and at the same time they created artificial power shortages.

CEOs of publicly traded companies are generally assessed, and therefore given larger or smaller bonuses, on two things: the net worth of the company and its quarterly earnings. Lax accounting practices and lack of oversight allowed executives to inflate both during the 1990s. However, the story told to stockholders (who lost a great deal of money because of padded bottom lines) was not that told to the U.S. government (which also lost a great deal of money because of tax avoidance by the companies and the CEOs). For example, publicly available data from 1996 to 1999 shows that Sprint (a single company) reported $5.8 billion more in earnings to its stockholders than to the Internal Revenue Service.

The cultural capital of major corporations and the accounting industry legitimated tax avoidance, overstating earnings, and maximizing personal profit. The former commissioner of the Security and Exchange Commission (SEC), Arthur Levitt, made this point clearly in the *Wall Street Journal* of June 17, 2002 (Pacelle 2002, 7):

> Enron is not an aberration. What troubles me is that what is fueling these corporate implosions are not strategic misjudgments, the rise of new competitors, the sudden appearance of rival technologies, or even basic managerial mistakes. Instead, it is the uncovering of accounting irregularities, inflated balance sheets, and outright corporate deceit and malfeasance.

The SEC tried for ten years to reform the accounting industry, in the face of huge opposition mustered in Congress to block any changes and even pass retaliatory budget cuts for the agency. Political capital was mobilized to allow those who controlled financial capital to obscure what they were doing as they sought short-term personal and corporate economic gain. That cultural capital was again shown as the CEOs of money-losing corporations were given huge salary increases and bonuses at the same time that stockholders lost money, workers were laid off, and pension funds were decimated.

Self-regulation seemed like a good idea. The thinking was that if one firm let another firm get away with something, its own reputation would be tarnished. Yet the opposite happened: If one firm let another get by with something, that firm would repay the favor. In performing "peer reviews" of each other, Big Five accounting firms repeatedly unearthed what the SEC staff considered major flaws in the way audits were conducted. Nevertheless, they gave each other clean bills of health in public reports of the reviews (Weil and Paltrow 2002).

Clearly, a number of institutions have to be in place in order for a modern economy to emerge and prosper. The people in those organizations and the conventions they have for keeping track of assets and evaluating loans play an important role in influencing who has access to financial capital. Do we need new conventions, new ways of keeping track of financial capital in order to support rural economies? The deregulation of banks and the increased mobility of financial capital in a global economy suggest that we need something new.

Forms of Financial Capital

The tangible forms of financial capital are relatively easy to identify. *Capital goods* (built capital) include the physical objects (cars, machines, buildings) that individuals or businesses invest in to generate new resources. A sawmill in Oakridge, Oregon, invests in the equipment needed to saw timber. The meatpacking plants in Garden City, Kansas, invest in the buildings, feedlots, and transportation equipment needed to move cattle in and processed meat out. *Land* becomes an investment because of the resources it has or the development space it offers. Timber companies purchase land, in part for existing stands of timber but also for the land's capacity to sustain new growths of timber. Real estate agents buy land, hoping to realize a profit if the land increases in value. Finally, *financial capital* includes financial instruments—stocks, bonds, derivatives, market futures, and letters of credit—as well as money.

Public Versus Private Capital

Capital can be further classified in terms of who invests it. When individuals or groups invest their own resources, they have used *private capital*. Land, buildings, equipment, and the inventory associated with a small business are part of its private-capital stock. Land owned by farm families, timber companies, or oil companies is private capital. The investment you make in your education is also an example of private capital.

Public capital refers to the resources invested by the community. Tax dollars are used to build roads, install sewer lines, maintain public parks, and finance schools. Governments raise the needed funds and then authorize their investment on behalf of the public good. Capital goods are then owned by the public, typically at the level of government involved in the original purchase. Communities own their street system or industrial park. Counties often own courthouses, county road systems, or landfills. The state owns its state road system and state universities. The federal government owns national parks and federal lands.

Public capital and private capital are often linked through partnerships. For example, some logging companies in the Northwest harvest trees on land owned by the U.S. Forest Service. The logging companies gain access to federal lands in exchange for fees paid to the government. Postsecondary education is funded by both public and private capital. When individuals pay tuition to attend colleges and universities, they are investing private capital in their own development. However, tuition covers only a fraction of the costs of maintaining public institutions. State tax dollars support public colleges and universities; city or county taxes support community colleges.

Mobility of Capital

These various forms of capital differ in how easily they can move. Land and many forms of capital goods, such as buildings and roads, are not mobile. Thus, individuals and communities have to figure out how to make these forms of capital productive. By contrast, financial and human capitals are very mobile. Money can move to wherever it can earn the highest return. People can move to wherever they can earn the best salaries. The mobility of both causes problems for rural communities.

Financial capital has become increasingly mobile. Electronic transfers of capital can take place in seconds not only between communities on either coast but from a rural community to an urban center halfway around the world. Wealth created in New Hampshire can end up as an investment in California or Malaysia as savings deposits in the local bank become financial capital attracted to wherever the money can earn the highest rate of interest.

For example, a farmer in Iowa may sell a truckload of hogs when prices are high and costs of production low. The profit made becomes savings that the farmer can now invest. That farmer phones a broker in Des Moines who buys shares in a New York–based mutual fund by computer. The mutual fund then invests in a garment factory in Malaysia, where the funds receive a higher return than they would have had they been invested in a garment factory in rural Iowa. Capital created in Iowa then turns into wages paid in Malaysia.

Financial Capital
and Community Needs

Nearly all rural communities have depended on financial capital from their very founding. Financial capital not only helps individuals set up homes and businesses but also enables local governments to provide roads, schools, sewers, and other services needed by community residents and businesses. This section examines the public and private needs for financial capital and describes the role played by rural financial institutions.

Public and Private Need for Capital

Seeking to expand and protect its boundaries, the federal government encouraged settlement of the frontier by making capital available in the form of land. During the settlement period, the government had few liquid assets, for the cost of wars kept the federal treasury in debt. Although many families homesteaded, much of the public lands went to large companies such as railroads. The government encouraged the privatization of land by removing it from the public domain and selling it to private holders at reduced prices. This policy encouraged the development in rural communities of private capital held by businesses as well as individuals.

From its inception, the U.S. government recognized the role public financial capital played in community development and growth. First through the Northwest Ordinance of 1787, the federal government gave newly established communities land on which to build public goods (schools and roads) considered necessary for a community to exist and the nation to prosper. Furthermore, the United States and Canada are among the few nations of the world that grant local governments the power to raise public capital through local means, such as property taxes. This ability to tax gave communities a powerful tool by which to become self-reliant, unlike rural communities in other countries that have had to depend on the central government in order to get roads, schools, or a water system.

The increasing cost of public services, combined with a decreasing population and tax base, has made most rural communities more dependent on state and federal sources of financial capital. This dependence has, in turn, made communities less able to control their capital investments. For example, a school district that needs to introduce instruction in Spanish because of an influx of new migrants might instead find itself creating a gifted program because federal funds are available for the gifted program but not for the Spanish-language program. Despite the need to improve a local water system, a county board of supervisors might decide to lengthen a local airport runway, again because of the availability of federal funds. As communities find it increasingly difficult to raise financial capital locally, the locus of control for capital investment shifts to the state or federal level. Communities find themselves acting on state or federal priorities rather than on local ones.

To develop, communities require private capital other than land. Many rural communities were originally dependent in one way or another on farming. Agricultural production, unlike industrial production, is consecutive. Farmers must plow before they plant and plant before they harvest. There are long periods between the major production activities, particularly in crop production. Consequently, selling is done well after initial production decisions are made. That means that many farming communities have erratic income flows; a lot of money comes into the community when the harvest is sold, but little is generated at other times.

During the settlement period, women often sold eggs and cream throughout the year in an effort to even out income flow. When crops failed or a buyer could not be found, however, local residents created other mechanisms for generating financial capital. Individuals and groups formed banks or cooperative financial institutions to provide credit for both consumption and production loans. These institutions were especially important in communities dependent on agriculture, timber, and mining because fluctuations in production—and therefore in income—were often typical.

Rural Financial Institutions

The names of many small-town banks, such as Miners and Merchants Bank (Grundy, Virginia), Farmers and Drovers Bank (Council Grove, Kansas), and Farmers and Miners Bank (Lucas, Iowa), reflect the character of the needs that led to their creation. Capital was also needed for small businesses (Merchants Bank) and for workers seeking credit between paydays (Union Bank). Rural banks generally had local roots and were structured much the same as other local businesses, being either privately held or organized as cooperatively held credit unions. What do the names of the banks in your community tell you about the history of financial capital there?

Because of the amount of capital and risk involved, banks generally formed corporations that separated the owners' assets from those of the bank. Incorporation is a legal strategy often used to limit personal liability. Banks that were incorporated were required to be chartered by the state or federal government. "State" in a bank's name means it is chartered under state law. The terms "national" or "federal" in a bank's name mean it is chartered with the federal government.

Banks make loans to individuals on the basis of risk. The lower the risk, the more inclined the banker is to advance the capital. Common factors used to assess risk include (1) net worth, (2) cash flow, and (3) personal knowledge of the borrower. As banks consolidate, the third factor to assess risk is used less and less.

Although some rural residents are wealthy in terms of land, that wealth has low *liquidity;* that is, it cannot easily be converted into cash. (This feature of land gave rise to the saying that one could be land-rich and money-poor.) When these individuals need money to invest in their businesses, they use their capital assets (land, livestock, or machinery) as collateral to guarantee the repayment of a loan.

For a financial institution, money that is deposited is carried as a debit, or liability, on its books. A *liability* is an obligation to pay back on demand to depositors the amount credited to their accounts. A loan, on the other hand, is an asset, because the bank is owed that money by a third person. A financial *asset* is money or property that can be used to meet liabilities.

Loans made on the basis of net worth compare collateral with indebtedness. Collateral is important to the lender, because if the loan is not repaid, the property can be claimed and sold to repay the loan. Loans based on net worth (the value of collateral minus outstanding indebtedness) are relatively safe loans to make, despite the fact that the lender assumes the assets will retain their value. Consequently, net worth is a traditional criterion for making a loan. This criterion introduces a bias into the flow of financial capital. Those who already have wealth are best able to acquire additional capital.

More adventurous bankers make loans based on a borrower's ability to repay. Determining ability to repay involves a detailed comparison of the costs of expanding production weighed against the increased sales that would result from expansion. Cash flow, not net worth, is the criterion for such loans. Determining cash flow involves gathering more data about a business operation than is necessary when the criterion for loaning money is net worth. It is also somewhat more inexact. Bankers have to estimate not only the future value of assets but also the future costs of needed inputs, future demand for the product, and future prices that will be paid for what is produced.

Basing loans on a borrower's ability to repay avoids the bias created when the net-worth method is used. Because the loan is based on an individual's future prospects for repaying the loan rather than on present assets, those with few assets can obtain a loan. However, loans based on the ability to repay introduce yet another bias. Those who can keep good accounts and work through cash-flow projections are more likely to receive loans. These loans favor the more educated individual. A number of farmers had to become more sophisticated in these methods when land values dropped and their net worth no longer justified the size of the loans they needed to continue operating. For the most part, loans made on the basis of cash flow are more speculative.

Bankers in rural communities traditionally have had a third criterion for making loans: knowledge of the character of the borrower. In a sense, this is a shorthand way of calculating ability to pay. A young person known to be thrifty and hardworking could get a loan based on a handshake, indicative of the faith a banker put in the individual. In small-town settings, such loans were often biased against women and minorities, who were traditionally excluded from those considered worthy of credit. Bankers who know the community well are not likely to make bad loans—but they may fail to make some good loans.

This criterion was especially important in allowing those with little property an opportunity to become small-business owners. For the most part, however, this informal way of assessing risk is disappearing. Although state laws on branch banking and multibank holding companies vary, personal knowledge of the potential borrower by the individual with authority to make the loan is declining. As control of rural banks shifts to metropolitan areas, personal knowledge of the borrower is no longer valued as a method by which to assess risk.

Sources of Capital

In order to create more productive capacity or to get the inputs needed for production, individuals and businesses need capital. One way to get capital is to sell an asset. Another is to spend less money than taken in and thus accumulate savings. But many people, companies, and communities need a large amount of capital at one time in order to purchase a farm, a business, or a major piece of machinery. They do not have enough assets to sell to finance the purchase, and even if they did, selling those assets would mean selling their productive capacity. They also do not save enough to purchase the capital asset in a timely fashion. Therefore they must borrow the money, which banks can provide in a number of ways.

Savings

For most people in the world, income seems insufficient to provide for the necessary expenses of family maintenance and reproduction. Others are able to take in more money than they spend in a given period of time, so they save it. Some savings are voluntary; others are involuntary, such as the contribution to Social Security or other government-mandated pension funds. Regardless of whether they are voluntary or involuntary, savings represent a major source of capital.

In most communities, savers with moderate incomes tend to deposit their money in their local financial institutions. This money is then reinvested by the bank, savings and loan, or credit union to earn interest. Despite the fact that rural financial institutions often offer somewhat lower interest rates, rural banks remain a preferred investment for many citizens. Deposits in most rural banks steadily increased during the 1980s. In the 1990s, deposits in rural banks dropped due to the growing popularity of money-market and mutual funds. These investment alternatives offer services much like those of banks, including automatic teller machines (ATMs) and debit cards. In 1999, Congress passed the Gramm-Leach-Bliley Act, which increased small banks' access to Federal Home Loan Bank funds to finance agricultural, rural, small-business, and low-income community development investments (Dolan 2000). This membership offers many benefits for rural banks, including a steady source of long-term funds. It can provide rural credit markets with another source of liquidity, which may improve a bank's profits, since such funds are less costly than core deposits. This has compensated for the drop in deposits for some rural banks.

Interest

In lending money for a business, the lender generally secures the loan through the collateral of the capital goods acquired with the loan funds or through a lien on the product produced. In short, banks have the right to collect the capital goods purchased or the products produced by the business if it fails to repay the loan. There is also a charge to the borrower for use of the money, called *interest*. A portion of that money goes to the individuals whose savings are used to provide capital. This encourages them to put the excess capital they have into the bank instead of under their mattress or into the purchase of additional consumer goods. A portion of the interest remains with the bank, credit union, or savings and loan. These funds are used to cover the costs associated with managing the loan and to provide the bank with a profit.

The *nominal interest rate* (the interest rate charged to the borrower) varies according to the supply of money available for lending and the demand for money among competing borrowers. However, interest rates are not influenced by local supply and demand for capital. Even in isolated rural communities, interest rates are set daily through monetary and fiscal policies adopted by U.S. and foreign governments. This control decreases the ability of local institutions to redeploy capital to local investments.

In order to compete in the global financial market, projects must have high rates of return and low risk. Investments in rural communities are traditionally the reverse: low return and high risk. As interest rates become bound to global markets, capital leaves rural areas. This phenomenon, known as *capital flight,* describes the extent to which capital originally invested in rural areas eventually is moved elsewhere in search of a higher return.

Interest rates indicate the costs of capital. When interest rates are high, fewer people are able to borrow. When rates are low, more people may be inclined to borrow because it appears easier and cheaper to pay back the loan and interest on it. However, it is important to calculate the *real interest rate,* which is the nominal interest rate minus the rate of inflation. This is the real cost of capital.

In periods of high inflation, nominal interest rates are high, but they are often exceeded by the rate of inflation. In this case, it pays to borrow. The interest charged for the loan is less than the increased value of whatever was purchased. Savers, on the other hand, often lose money on bank deposits, bonds, and other ordinary financial investments. Consequently, they often look for investments whose market price will rise at a rate likely to equal or exceed the inflation rate. Commodities or real estate are frequent choices for such investments. During the 1970s, for example, farmland and urban real estate prices escalated at an extremely rapid rate as investors sought inflation-proof investment opportunities. During the 1990s, farmland prices increased, but at a more gradual rate than during the 1970s. By 2002, prices for farmland had doubled from what they were in the mid-1980s; however, even with the increase, prices when adjusted for inflation were still 15 percent below what they had been in the 1970s. Urban real estate prices declined in the 1990s, whereas prices for real estate in rural areas increased. In many regions, rural areas grew more rapidly because of new housing developments that were built outside of metropolitan areas.

Local banks cannot provide the required financial capital for larger or more risky investments. The risk may be too great, the amount needed may be too large, or the banker may simply lack the expertise to judge the appropriate loan period and rate of return. Rural banks accustomed to making agricultural loans may be unsure when asked to finance a cabinet factory. Agricultural loans are equally difficult for urban banks to evaluate. There are several other sources of private financial capital for such undertakings, such as bonds and equity capital.

Bonds

When a large amount of financial capital is needed for a long-term capital investment, loans can be made in more formal contractual agreements such as bonds. Bonds pay interest and constitute a promise of repayment of a designated amount of money (often more than the amount received as a loan) at the end of an established period of time, usually twenty or thirty years. Businesses can pledge securities or future income to repay the money raised through bonds.

In the 1980s, deregulation of U.S. financial markets allowed the marketing of junk bonds. *Junk bonds* are high-risk, high-interest securities that are often sold at a deep *discount,* an amount well below their face value. The money raised by these bonds was converted into equity capital in new or established businesses. Because the businesses were risky, the bonds paid high rates of interest. Most of these ventures were in urban areas; this drew financial capital out of rural areas. When the businesses failed, many savings and loan institutions, which had invested in venture capital firms and in urban real estate, went under. Rural people contributed to the bailout of urban savings and loans through their taxes.

Governments, including rural towns and counties, can issue *municipal bonds* to raise public financial capital. Usually state law disallows the use of bonds to pay the operating expenses of local governments, schools, and hospitals but permits their use to support buildings or structural improvements. These bonds are guaranteed by the good faith and taxing power of the issuing government. The U.S. government feels so strongly that these local financing mechanisms should be in place that interest earned from personal and corporate investment in these bonds is usually tax-free; this feature provides additional incentive to make financial capital available to local communities.

Bonds are an important mechanism by which rural communities raise financial capital but retain local control. Industrial revenue bonds, for example, can provide investment capital for a local firm. Too often, however, the money raised by such bonds goes to attract a business from another area rather than to create a local firm. Communities run the risk that the business will eventually move, despite local efforts to make it financially attractive for the firm to stay. Privately issued, publicly regulated bonds can provide an important source of seed financial capital for new firms or investment capital for local firms wishing to expand.

Equity Financial Capital

Sometimes a business has neither enough capital assets to provide collateral for a loan nor the proven excess of income over expenses to ensure a steady repayment of further indebtedness. In this case, other sources of financial capital must be found.

One mechanism is to "go public," selling shares in the company to the general public through the stock market. Individuals with savings (or other access to financial capital) invest in shares of the company. In exchange for their financial capital investment, these individuals receive a portion of the company's profits in the form of dividends paid on their shares. Stockholders can also make (or lose) money on their investments by selling their shares on a stock exchange.

Once a business has decided to sell stock, the company no longer belongs solely to the original business owner. However, the assets of the company have increased as a result of the capital investment of the new shareholders. The *equity* of the business is still defined as the total assets less the total liabilities, but the partners or stockholders now hold that equity. In exchange for the financial capital invested in the company, the partners or stockholders share in determining who will manage the company and how it is managed.

Employees can become owners as a way to raise capital through wages invested in the company or through stock earned through bonuses. Such *stock options* were given by many start-up companies in the 1990s as a way to attract talented, highly skilled workers. Partial ownership in a business can be a way to attract reliable labor in areas where there are relatively few available workers (see Box 7.1).

BOX 7.1 Workers as Part Owners

Jose Hernandez is going to be able to retire well someday. At forty-one years old, he has accumulated more than $80,000, and he only works from April to November, for $20,000 a year. As a migrant worker, he has worked hard all his life, but fortunately he has worked for a company that takes care of its workers.

Migrant workers at McKay Nursery in Waterloo, Wisconsin, are reaping the benefits of their difficult work. The nursery has always been known for its generous employee benefits, such as paying migrants overtime, which is very unusual. In 1984, McKay took an extremely bold step and began offering its workers shares in the company through employee stock ownership plans (ESOPs). In 1998, the company employed sixty full-time workers and

Continued on next page

Workers as Part Owners (continued)

nearly a hundred migrant workers at the height of growing season. Migrants are eligible for the plan once they have worked 1,000 hours in a season, which goes from late March through the end of November. Workers are promised that at least 10 percent of their gross wages for the year will be set aside for retirement; the amount is dependent on how much the company earns for the year and how many employees it has. Typically, workers have had 20 percent to 25 percent of their wages set aside, and they can then invest the cash portion in a variety of mutual funds. Money in the workers' retirement plans cannot be withdrawn until they have been with the company for five years. At that time, they can take money out to pay for college bills or to purchase a home. Workers who decide to leave after five years take the cash with them after they sell their shares back to the company.

The nursery's president, Griff Mason, admits honestly that hiring on a seasonal basis is difficult, and it has been challenging to find dependable workers, until now. Since migrant workers are a critical component to the success of the company, he wanted to ensure that many would return every year. As word spread around to friends and family members of the migrant workers employed at McKay, the nursery saw a return rate of 90 percent. McKay has found that building human capital and social capital within the migrant worker community has enhanced the financial capital not only of the workers but also of his business.

SOURCE: Jonathan Kaufman. 1998. "Sharing the Wealth." *Wall Street Journal,* April 9.

The market price of stock is largely dependent on the company's earnings. Stocks are of two types. Preferred stock guarantees a dividend of a specified rate and a specified portion of the assets if the corporation is liquidated. Common stock has a rate of return that fluctuates depending on the corporation's profits. Stockholders have voting rights in choosing the management of the company. Their votes are weighted according to the amount of stock owned. These votes are used to select the board of directors, which then sets policy and names the CEO of the corporation. In seeking financial capital by selling equity, a business owner gives up management control.

Once companies have started up, they often need a high level of initial capital investment in order to upgrade technology and develop markets. Furthermore, they need financial capital that comes from investors who are willing to take risks and be patient as they wait for a return. This kind of equity capital is referred to as *venture capital*. Some have argued that a shortage of venture capital stifles would-be entrepreneurs and hence retards growth and development. Venture capital investment remained at about $3 billion a year during the 1980s. However, the funds were increasingly used for leveraged buyouts of growth companies rather than for investments in new enterprises.

The availability of venture capital boomed in the 1990s due to the rise of technology companies. In 1999, venture capital investment in the United States reached $35.6 billion, a high never seen before. In 2002, venture capital was down—to $20.3 billion for the year—but still far higher than during the 1980s. Venture capital brings with it a say in the management of the company. For start-up businesses, this access to human and social capital is often as helpful as the access to financial capital.

Although selling stock is a useful strategy for raising business financial capital, it is not always viable in rural areas. In order to sell stock on a stock exchange, a business must meet several requirements related to financial disclosure. For small companies in rural areas, putting these statements of financial disclosure together can be expensive relative to the amount of financial capital being raised.

The Changing Rules of Financial Capital

One of the reasons banks were chartered by states or the federal government was to ensure that financial capital would be available locally for local investments. But the control exercised by government and thus the risk involved for the rural community have varied over time. Entering banking was easier when the National Bank of the United States (a forerunner of the Federal Reserve banking system) did not exercise disciplinary and restraining influences; control was loose during the periods 1781–1791, 1811–1816, and 1837–1863. State charters were the exclusive method for creating banking corporations during these periods. During the era of unregulated banking between the 1830s and the 1920s, any entrepreneur who could meet minimal capitalization standards to set up a bank could obtain a state charter. Banks proliferated, particularly in rural communities, peaking at 30,000 banks in the United States in 1921.

The Age of Regulation

More than 10,000 banks failed during the Great Depression of 1929–1933. A large proportion of the failed banks were in rural communities. More demanding criteria for charters were then established by the Banking Act of 1933, including tougher requirements for capitalization and management based on the convenience and needs of the community along with competitive circumstances.

Other limitations were placed on banks in 1933. These regulations set lending limits, limited insider lending, and restricted bank investments. Interest-rate ceilings were established, and interest was prohibited on *demand deposits,* that is, deposits, such as checking accounts, whose account holders could demand their money at any time. In 1933, the *Federal Deposit Insurance Corporation (FDIC)* became a supervisory agency for all national banks and state banks seeking FDIC insurance protection for their depositors. *Federal deposit insurance* offers borrowers insurance on deposits up to $100,000 in banks that agree to be supervised by the FDIC. Few rural banks were established once the regulations were enacted, but few banks failed. In regulating banking activities, the government played a major role in reducing the financial risk to society.

These regulations, which were in effect between the mid-1930s and the early 1980s, specified that different organizations should specialize in different financial functions. For example, banks could not engage in real estate brokerage. Thrift institutions (savings and loans) were forbidden to offer demand-deposit accounts. These prohibitions had two major purposes: (1) to further certain social goals, such as home ownership, and (2) to prevent conflicts of interest within individual firms. As Anthony Downs, an economist concerned about the real estate capital markets and real estate finance, points out,

> Congress apparently believed that the average patron of each financial institution should not have to pass prior judgment on the quality of that institution's management in order to have confidence that the institution's assets would be prudently handled. Such judgments would require knowledge and expertise far beyond the capabilities of the average citizen. (1985: 41–42)

Federal regulatory agencies were therefore established to provide collective supervision of financial institutions, to oversee the safety and socially responsible use of financial capital.

Bank regulation provided a governmental mechanism whereby public trust could be maintained in the major institution that linked financial capital to producers and consumers. In return for the security provided to savers through state and federal deposit insurance, financial capital was made available to borrowers. Public trust in banks and thrifts was gained not only through the insurance of savings but through the oversight provided by the federal and state regulatory agencies.

Deregulation

With the shift in the world economy, which involved devaluation of the dollar in 1971 and the rise in oil prices in 1973, there was a substantial decrease in the real cost of money as a result of inflation. Savers found they could get higher yields from uncontrolled financial institutions by putting their money into newly developed financial instruments, such as *money-market* funds. Banks found that they did not have the financial capital to lend at the rates they were legally able to offer; in other words, they were no longer competitive.

In the 1970s, rural areas found their locally owned and controlled financial institutions competing with nonfinancial institutions not restricted by banking regulations, such as Sears and Merrill Lynch. These institutions, which are multinational in character, channeled financial capital out of rural areas by offering investment opportunities such as money-market funds. A financial capital exodus from traditional banks, including rural community banks, occurred as savers increasingly sought higher interest rates elsewhere.

In addition, the savings and loan institutions, which had traditionally lent money for long-term real estate purchases, found that the short-term interest rates they had to pay to attract depositors far exceeded the long-term rates they were charging borrowers. In the early 1980s, savings and loan institutions were given the right to engage in activities formerly reserved for other institutions in an attempt to shore up their profitability. These changes offered short-term help for savings and loans, but rural banks lost their competitive edge.

Banking deregulation involves a decrease in the degree to which the government limits and oversees (1) the costs of credit and services, (2) the geographic location of financial institutions, and (3) the variety of services offered by financial institutions. The goal has been to increase the *efficiency* of distribution of financial capital. What the lawmakers mean by "efficiency" is the ability of funds to move to where they offer the investor the greatest possible return consistent with the risk involved in their use. With deregulation, return on investment is assessed over an increasingly shorter time frame.

Deregulation has made it relatively easy for financial institutions to capture savings from rural areas and add these funds to a national pool of financial capital that can be directed wherever the highest short-term profit can be made. From the rural perspective, it has become increasingly difficult to keep local financial capital invested locally. Facilitated by a variety of national policies, financial capital now flows easily from one city to another or from one country to another. This international financial capital market has increased the outflow of financial capital from rural areas.

Bankers and other lenders see investments in rural communities as having high risk and low payoffs compared to other options. Deregulation has increased the relative cost of credit for rural areas as compared with urban areas and decreased the availability of credit for rural borrowers. It has further decreased the availability of financial services for the rural poor. The balanced exchange of public trust through regulation and deposit insurance has been moved off center. Gary Green, a rural sociologist who has studied rural banking extensively, advocates reregulation of a type that permits greater flexibility in the form and content of banking practices and organizational structure in return for social responsibility on the part of banks, including reinvestment in rural communities.

Business Financial Capital and Community

For the most part, financial capital has always been less available in rural areas than in urban areas. Changes in the U.S. financial market have recently made it increasingly difficult for rural areas to attract and retain financial capital. This section explores some of the strategies by which financial capital can be attracted to and retained in rural communities.

Keeping Financial Capital Local

In many ways, banks and other lending institutions are like other businesses in rural communities. They also require investment capital, not just savings, to get started. Individuals wanting to start a bank or purchase an existing one take out an individual or business loan from another financial institution.

Starting or acquiring a bank often requires more financial capital than can be obtained through the usual loan procedure. Increasingly, banks require equity capital gained from stockholders. As more and more of those stockholders and owners come from outside the community, concern mounts that decisions on the use of savings deposited in the bank will be used in ways that benefit the shareholders but not necessarily the community. Under the previous ownership pattern, local owners were more likely to perceive benefits that were more consistent with benefiting the community.

Because banks and thrifts enjoy special privileges from the public sector in terms of deposit insurance and oversight, many think that banks should be required to serve the public good as well as stockholders' short-term interests. For banks, however, it is difficult to argue that the interests of the stockholders, who may now live anywhere in the world, are identical with those of the community. Stockholders tend to encourage financial capital use that favors short-term gain, which pays them higher dividends and makes their stocks worth more. This conflicts with the needs of communities, which often need "patient" capital that can be invested locally. This use of financial capital emphasizes long-term gain in recognition of the multiplier effect such financial capital can have in the community. The "income multiplier" is the extent to which money is recirculated in the local economy. In the example shown in Figure 7.1, for example, each dollar turns over six times before leaving the locality and has a cumulative impact on the local currency of $1.66.

Capital and Community

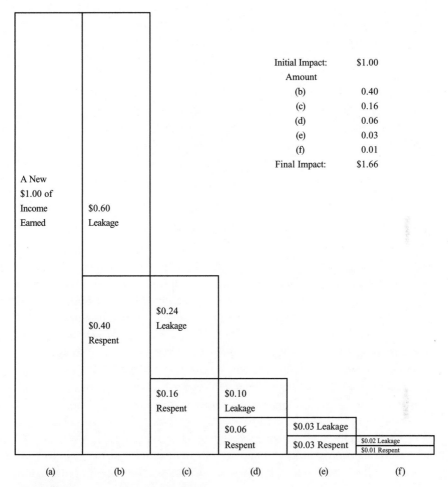

Initial Impact: $1.00
Amount
(b) 0.40
(c) 0.16
(d) 0.06
(e) 0.03
(f) 0.01
Final Impact: $1.66

A New
$1.00 of
Income
Earned

$0.60 Leakage

$0.40 Respent

$0.24 Leakage

$0.16 Respent

$0.10 Leakage

$0.06 Respent

$0.03 Leakage

$0.03 Respent

$0.02 Leakage
$0.01 Respent

(a)　　　(b)　　　(c)　　　(d)　　　(e)　　　(f)

FIGURE 7.1　Income Multiplier

The extent to which financial capital leaves a community can be seen in the declining loan-to-deposit ratios among rural banks. A decreasing ratio means that less of the money deposited by community residents is being reinvested in the community through loans. Instead, the money deposited is exiting the community through urban municipal bonds, certificates of deposits at larger banks, and government securities. The farm crisis significantly reduced traditional loan opportunities in rural communities, and bankers have not found it easy to identify nontraditional loan options.

The Community Reinvestment Act of 1977 encouraged banks to invest their financial capital within the local community. The legislation was aimed primarily at poor urban areas, and few rural banks were forced to reinvest in rural communities under the terms of the act. Until the farm crisis of 1982, lack of rural reinvestment did not appear to be a major problem. Rural banks were eager and able to make agricultural loans locally and often diversified with energy-related loans. The Community Reinvestment Act was revised in 1995, and regulations were put into place to reduce paperwork for evaluation. This new revision, named the Brownfields Act, worked in conjunction with the Environmental Protection Agency to help clean up and restore industrial sites in low-to-moderate-income communities. This action eased fears of financial regulations, liability, and burdens.

Government securities are used to finance the federal debt. They are either short-term or long-term securities sold by the federal government. Rural banks have a much greater percentage of their assets in government securities than do urban banks.

New Sources of Financial Capital

Traditional ways of generating financial capital for rural communities now appear to be inadequate. Indeed, the flow of financial capital from rural areas seems to have exceeded the out-migration of people. Governments as well as private entities and new public-private ventures are attempting to generate investment financial capital in new ways. By 2001, thirty-seven states had implemented targeted investment programs for rural areas. These states subsidize loans or offer loan guarantee programs, grants, tax abatements, or other financial incentives to businesses that process agricultural products (Kilkenny and Schluter 2001).

Rural communities and regions can create Community Foundations to capture some of the intergenerational transfer of wealth that is expected to take place between 2000 and 2020 as elders who acquired wealth in the 1980s and 1990s die. These foundations provide a number of ways for individual citizens to contribute to a fund that, through the interest it earns, then is invested in their communities in both public and private ventures. The Montana Community Foundation has worked hard to build these funds by utilizing political capital to maintain state tax deductions for charitable contributions.

Rural-based venture capital funds are also in place, such as Northeast Ventures in Minnesota. In response to economic restructuring in Minnesota's Iron Range as the mines closed, in 1989, Northeast Ventures was developed to intervene strategically to reduce dependence on a single industry that was in turn dependent on the fickle steel market. Northeast Ventures has the Northeast Entrepreneur Fund, which provides loans and guidance to firms, and the Northeast Ventures Corporation, which makes equity investments in home-grown companies.

The Community Development Financial Institution Fund (CDFI) was created by Congress in 1994 to expand the availability of credit, investment capital, and financial services in distressed urban and rural communities. By stimulating the creation and expansion of diverse locally based community development financial institutions (CDFIs) and by providing incentives to traditional banks and thrifts, the fund's investments strengthen private markets, creating healthy local tax revenues, and empowering residents. CDFIs are specialized financial institutions that work in local market niches that have not been adequately served by traditional financial institutions. CDFIs provide a wide range of financial products and services, including mortgage financing for first-time home buyers, financing for needed community facilities, commercial loans and investments to start or expand small businesses, loans to rehabilitate rental housing, and financial services needed by low-income households and local businesses.

The Lakota Fund was established in 1986 by members of the Ogalala Lakota Nation to develop a private sector in the Pine Ridge Reservation in South Dakota. The fund certified as a CDFI in 1999, giving it access to additional sources of financial capital. The goal was to help tribal entrepreneurs establish jobs, products, and services close to home. New businesses were started by Lakota people on the reservation, and the Lakota Fund diversified to meet other needs for financial capital, including a fund for housing.

Many of these nontraditional lenders and investors are successful because they offer far more than financial capital. They also increase the human and social capital of the entrepreneurs with whom they work. Michelle Sweedman has cared for children in her own home in Bigfork, Minnesota, ever since her first child was born. More and more families came to her seeking high-quality childcare, but she could only take care of four children at a time, given her space. She saw the need in the community for affordable, high-quality childcare and felt that she could hire a few more childcare workers and set up a real business that would increase her income and serve the community. But she had no business experience, and only about $150 in savings. Northeast Entrepreneur Fund showed her how to plan her business and manage income and expenses, and it then lent her the down payment on a suitable house. She now has two employees who, like Michelle, are working on a childcare credential on the weekends at Itasca Community College.

Financial Capital Retention Through Risk Reduction

Another way that risk to commercial banks on any given loan can be reduced is through the use of secondary markets for rural business loans. Secondary markets allow rural banks to package together a number of business loans, which they initiate and service; investors who purchase those securities bear the risk. Such secondary markets have been in place for many years for home mortgages and were initiated for farm loans in 1989. This approach to sharing risk could help rural banks recirculate local financial capital within the community.

Another way to make loans less risky is to provide technical assistance in such areas as personnel management, marketing, accounting, and planning. Both the Small Business Administration of the federal government and the Cooperative Extension Service at the state and local levels have programs that aid small businesses and that can be tied to financial capital investment.

Loan guarantees by the state and federal governments spread the risk of financial capital investment in rural areas between the public and private sectors. Such guarantees function much as does the student loan program, in which private banks make the loan. The individual who borrows the money is obligated to repay the financial capital plus interest, usually at below-market rates. The federal government guarantees that the lender will be repaid at least a certain percentage of the initial loan if the borrower defaults. This strategy is cheaper than if the government makes capital investment directly, and it allows financial capital to be invested in a far greater number of enterprises.

Government's Indirect Role

Another way that governments direct financial capital is through tax concessions. Tax abatements reduce taxes for investments that are made in certain business ventures deemed socially desirable. Alone among developed countries, the United States has viewed home ownership as so socially desirable that its tax code allows a federal tax deduction of all interest paid on home mortgages and local taxes on homes.

Other laws reduce the tax burden of those who invest in specific geographic areas by starting new businesses or expanding existing firms. Governments offer tax abatements in an effort to attract industry. The problem with this strategy is that although it benefits private financial capital investment in a specific area, it may not increase total financial capital investment in the nation. Furthermore, the tax breaks given often increase the need for public financial capital investment in the form of schools, prisons, fire stations, sewers, and roads. The reduced taxation offered to new businesses erodes the tax base needed to support the public financial capital investments.

More and more communities are trying to retain financial capital locally by stopping financial capital leakage and forming local corporations and cooperatives to generate financial capital and invest it locally. When successful, these enterprises build on the strengths of an area and the solidarity of its citizens. Such mechanisms of financial capital generation increase local control. They also tend to have a longer-term time frame than do firms brought in from the outside that have stockholders who provided financial capital in the hopes of reaping short-term gains.

Firms recruited from the outside are often branch plants of large multinational firms that are seeking some advantage such as cheap land or lower wage scales. Transplants often create real difficulties for local financial capital formation in rural communities. Among the problems are low-wage employment, few purchases of local inputs for production, and cutbacks and shutdowns that are more frequent and more likely because of the absentee nature of ownership and management. Still, such an option has great allure for a desperate rural community.

Recent studies have pointed to the weakness such short-term approaches have inserted into community development efforts. Rural communities are being forced to address the problems created by rapid financial capital movement to capture short-term gain. As rural areas organize to create options in providing public and private financial capital needed for their communities to function, they may generate alternative investment models that strengthen the economic base of the country.

Alternative Sources of Financial Capital for Rural Communities

Federal programs have long recognized the need to make capital available for investment in rural America. Rural utilities are given low-interest government loans. Those rural electric cooperatives, in turn, had nearly $11 billion of outside investments in 1997. Yet only $61 million (0.5 percent) went into local business ventures or rural infrastructure. Rural utilities could be an important source of capital for rural America if they were to actually invest in rural America.

Starting in low-income urban communities, nonprofit groups are increasingly providing financial capital for rural businesses.

Most banks make are making it more and more expensive to be an account holder, requiring higher minimum balances and charging higher fees for services. Yet poor people need to cash checks, wire money to relatives, pay bills, and borrow money in a pinch. The number of check-cashing outlets doubled between 1996 and 2001, and they charge 3 percent of a check's face value when they cash it. Many individuals who wire money to their relatives do not realize that a substantial proportion of what they send does not actually reach the recipient, even though they have paid a sending fee, because each financial institution through which the transaction passes takes its cut. These same outlets also offer loans, charging annual rates of 300 percent to 400 percent per year. And when people conduct financial transactions through these outlets, they do not build a credit history and are not offered a way to save some of the money so they will not need a payday lender the next time the car breaks down.

Chapter Summary

Capital is any resource capable of producing other resources. Financial capital consists of instruments that express exchange value and that have a high degree of liquidity compared to other forms of capital. When individuals or groups invest their own resources, they have used private capital. Public capital is the resources invested by the community. The forms of capital differ in how easily they can move. Natural capital, social capital, and some forms of built capital are relatively immobile. Human capital is somewhat mobile. And financial capital is highly mobile. The mobility of political and cultural capital varies; for excluded peoples, it is relatively immobile.

Nearly all communities depend on financial capital, either for private investment in local businesses or for public investment in community services. Communities have often relied on federal and state governments in gaining access to financial capital for local improvements. Individual businesses have turned to local banks. Traditionally, rural banks have made business loans based on an individual's net worth, cash flow, or a banker's knowledge of that individual. As control of rural banks shifts to metropolitan areas, this last criterion becomes less important.

Financial capital is available from a number of sources. Businesses take out loans for which interest is charged. Businesses can also choose to sell stock in order to raise the financial capital needed. In exchange for making financial capital available to the business, stockholders participate in selecting the management of the company and share any profits. Municipal bonds are typically used as a device by which communities borrow the larger amounts of money needed for financial capital improvements.

Deregulation of the banking industry in the early 1980s changed the economic environment in which rural banks functioned. In limiting the interest rates that could be charged for loans or paid out on deposits, banking regulations were more favorable to rural banks. When the regulations were dropped, financial capital began moving to where it could earn the highest short-term return. Financial capital began to flow out of rural areas. Rural communities are working to retain local financial capital, reduce the risk associated with local investments, identify innovative sources of venture capital, and enlist governmental help in making financial capital available to rural businesses.

Key Terms

A financial *asset* is money or properties that can be used to meet liabilities (debts owed). Assets minus liabilities equals net worth.

Capital is defined as resources capable of producing other resources.

Capital flight occurs when funds originally invested or generated in a particular area are moved in order to take advantage of increased earnings elsewhere.

Capital goods consist of objects used to produce other goods or resources.

Collateral, or assets of the borrower that can be sold for cash, is required by many lenders to secure a loan. If the loan is not repaid by the borrower, the lender takes possession of the assets, which it then sells to repay the loan.

Consumption is the use of goods and services for personal enjoyment, which removes them from the stock of goods and services available.

Demand deposits are deposits in commercial banks and savings institutions that may be withdrawn upon demand.

Discount refers to the sale of a security at a price lower than its face value or to a loan on which the lender withholds interest from the principal amount, lending only the net amount (a "discounted" loan).

Efficiency describes the goal of allocating capital in different places so as to maximize the return on the investment, given the level of risk.

Equity is the net worth of a firm or corporation (total assets less total liabilities) belonging to the partners or stockholders.

Federal deposit insurance is a federal program that insures each deposit account to a level of $100,000 and that will provide up to $100,000 to depositors of failed banks and thrift institutions that are insured by the FDIC, the Federal Savings and Loan Insurance Corporation (FSLIC), or other federally sponsored insurance agencies.

Federal Deposit Insurance Corporation (FDIC) is an agency created in 1933 to provide insurance for bank depositors and supervision of insured banks.

Federal Reserve Act of 1913 is the legislation that created the Federal Reserve system to stop recurring money panics through pooling and lending bank reserves and providing a payment mechanism.

Financial capital includes stocks, bonds, market futures, and letters of credit as well as money.

Government securities are either short-term or long-term promises to pay sold by the federal government, such as U.S. savings bonds.

Interest is the charge made for borrowed money.

Junk bonds are high-interest, high-risk securities that are sold at a deep discount, that is, at an amount well below their face value.

Land is a form of capital when it is used to produce other resources.

Liability is the claims of creditors.

Liquidity is the difficulty and cost of converting assets into money. The greater the degree of liquidity, the faster and cheaper the conversion process.

Minority ownership is the status of an investor who owns less than 50 percent of a business. Minority ownership entitles an investor to a voice and part of the profits, but not control of the business.

Municipal bonds are debt obligations of a state, locality, or municipal corporation. Interest on these bonds is exempt from U.S. income taxes.

National Banking Act of 1863 was the first legislative step in the United States toward establishing a stable and uniform currency. It required that all nationally chartered banks meet uniform regulations, back their note issues with government bonds, limit the amount issued to their paid-in capital, and maintain a fund of lawful money in the Treasury for their redemption.

Nominal interest rate is the stated or published percentage cost or return on capital, not corrected for inflation.

Private capital is capital owned and controlled by individuals or groups of individuals.

Public capital is capital owned and controlled by governments or communities, such as schools or bridges.

Real interest rate is the nominal interest rate minus the rate of inflation.

Investors *speculate* when they invest in an asset in the hope it will greatly increase in value. The profit (or loss) is made from the difference in the buying price from the selling price, not from what the asset produces.

Stock options are opportunities given to employees to buy stock at predetermined prices in the company that employs them. Start-up companies that cannot pay competitive salaries often use stock options to attract highly skilled workers and executives.

Venture capital is the capital provided by investors willing to take a higher than average risk for an anticipated higher than average profit in an expanding but capital-short enterprise.

References

Dolan, Julie. 2000. "Rural Banks and the Federal Home Loan Bank System." *Rural America* 15(3):44–49.

Downs, Anthony. 1985. *The Revolution in Real Estate Finance.* Washington, D.C.: Brookings Institute.

Green, Gary. 1991. "Rural Banking." Pp. 36–46 in C. B. Flora and J. A. Christenson (eds.), *Rural Policies for the 1990s.* Boulder, Colo.: Westview.

Kilkenny, Maureen, and Gerald Schluter. 2001. "Value-Added Agriculture Policies across the 50 States." *Rural America* 16, no. 1, 12–18. Also online; available: http://www.ers.usda.gov/publications/ruralamerica/ra161/ra161c.pdf; accessed April 15, 2003.

Northeast Enterprise Fund, Inc. "Success Stories" Online; available: http://www.entrepreneurfund.org/success.htm; accessed April 15, 2003.

Pacelle, Mitchell. 2002. "Former SEC Chairman Levitt Decries Business Ethics in U.S." *Wall Street Journal,* June 17, C7.

Weber, Max. 1978. *Economy and Society.* Vols. 1 and 2. Berkeley and Los Angeles: University of California Press.

Weil, Jonathan, and Scot J. Paltrow. 2002. "Peer Pressure: SEC Saw Accounting Flaws." *Wall Street Journal,* January 29, C1.

8

Built Capital

In Tazwell County, Virginia, a persistently poor rural area, Sara Johnson turns on the faucet. A mucky, grayish solution trickles from the spout. The county water system isn't working again. She'll have to go out and buy water for drinking, washing dishes, and even bathing. Sara will have to take the family's laundry to the Laundromat, a round trip of at least twenty miles. She hasn't the money for gasoline, let alone the time to spare for such a trip. Installed by the coal company, taken over by a private water company, and now owned by someone in another state, the local water system doesn't work half the time.

In Hebron, Nebraska, located in a rural county adjacent to a metropolitan area, Carl Jones no longer takes the most direct route to Center City. In order to deliver his fresh vegetables to the farmers' market, Carl now drives an extra forty miles in his old pickup truck. The bridge over the creek has collapsed. Carl wonders when or if the county plans to replace it. The cost of the extra gasoline sure takes away from what he can make selling vegetables at the market.

Emily Bailey and her husband, Jim Smothers, recently moved to Poplar, Montana, located in a remote rural county. They own a private consulting business that serves clients worldwide. Having grown tired of the hassles of city life, Emily and Jim were looking forward to a rural lifestyle. Much to their surprise, they found that digital switching is not available in the local telephone system. Emily and Jim are unable to hook up facsimile machines or computer modems, both of which are essential for communicating with clients. Their business flounders as they consider moving again.

★   ★   ★

These people face problems—problems with access to clean water, safe bridges, and communications technology—and these problems are not minor. Both Sara and Carl have limited incomes. The extra costs they bear in buying water or traveling an extra forty miles can mean the difference between remaining economically independent or having to turn to others for financial help. Emily and Jim enjoy living in the country, but if they cannot use standard business equipment, they have little choice; they will have to move elsewhere.

These problems are equally serious to the communities. Tazwell County finds it hard to attract business and industry. Basic services, such as clean water, are often unavailable. Hebron continues to decline as more and more of the small vegetable farmers realize that they cannot market their produce. Poplar is unable to take advantage of the new opportunities created by technology. Many businesses no longer need to be located in large cities, but unless Poplar finds a way to install the proper switches and fiber-optic cables, it will be unable to keep people like Emily and Jim.

Water services, bridges, and digital switches are all part of what social scientists call the "built capital" of a community. How we function in everyday life depends on the type, quality, and condition of the infrastructure available to us. How rural communities function in the new economy will depend on the infrastructure available to their residents. This chapter defines the term "built capital" and discusses how it is provided and how rural communities can organize to maintain it.

Defining Built Capital

Built capital provides a supporting foundation that facilitates human activity. Rural development policies are often geared toward enhancing built capital, on the assumption that people's lives will improve, particularly people who are disadvantaged, once new physical structures are in place. Yet concentration on built capital while ignoring social capital has led to the installation of rural water systems that have led to rural sprawl or "gentrification" of rural areas to the point that the original residents can no longer afford to live there. Communities are far more than built capital. Built capital can support the life of the community, but it can also exclude certain people (those on "the wrong side of the tracks") and divert financial capital from other investments.

In the late 1990s, upstate New York communities along the historic Erie Canal made significant investments in tourism facilities and services, with the aid of federal funding from the Department of Housing and Urban Development (HUD). A study by Susan Christopherson of Cornell University and her city and regional planning colleagues (1999) found that investment in built capital by public and private entities to build tourism facilities can have a positive impact on the local and regional economy. However, community capacity (social and human capital) to construct a broad strategy that can take advantage of new and sometimes unexpected opportunities (strategic readiness) is key to long-term, successful economic development.

Small towns (along with state and federal governments) have for decades invested in prison construction as a community economic development strategy. The theory is that prisons will bring jobs, the jobs will bring wages, and those wages will multiply through the local economy. Prisons are certainly a growth industry. The number of people incarcerated is increasing extremely rapidly with mandatory sentencing and heightened concern for national security. But many towns have found that prisons do not buy their supplies from local vendors, nor do they employ local people. Rush City, Minnesota, about sixty miles north of Minneapolis, found that the presence of a prison did not fill empty Main Street shops or employ many Rush City people. The town's future growth depends on it becoming a bedroom community for the Twin Cities rather than a bedroom community for convicts. Built capital has limitations in what it can do for rural communities.

This section defines what we mean by "built capital" and explores current issues that rural communities face in transforming financial, natural, and social capital into built capital.

Built Capital

Built capital is the permanent physical installations and facilities supporting productive activities in a community. It includes roads, streets and bridges, airports and railroads, electric and natural gas utility systems, water supply systems, police and fire-protection facilities, wastewater treatment and waste-disposal facilities, telephone and fiber-optic networks and other communications facilities, schools, hospitals, and other public and commercial buildings. As is obvious from the list, the built capital of a community refers to the equipment needed to support a series of networks that enable people to travel, communicate with one another, and gain access to services and markets.

Built capital can facilitate production in and of itself. Buildings enable a factory to make products that can then be sold. Roads are used to take goods to market or to bring raw materials to a production facility. Power plants provide electricity that is converted into light and energy for a variety of business and domestic functions. These and other elements of a community's built capital enable individuals and businesses to be more productive within the community. Although the built capital of a community is necessary, it cannot ensure the economic health and well-being of that community. People must be able to use the infrastructure in productive ways.

Access and Consumption

Two issues, access and consumption, are involved in people's use of the community's built capital. This section explores each of these dimensions. The following section looks at the types of built capital that emerge from the interaction of these two issues.

Goods and services are considered to be *exclusive access* built capital when particular groups or individuals can be denied access to them. Elements of built capital are *inclusive access* built capital when they are available to all users. Access to many utilities, such as water, electricity, or telephones, is exclusive because people must be hooked up to the utility in order to use it. Most streets and roads are available to anyone who wants to use them and are thus inclusive. Access to public parks or recreational areas is often inclusive, whereas access to Disneyland is exclusive.

The decision as to whether a good or service is inclusive or exclusive depends on a number of factors. One factor is the extent to which access can be controlled. Radio stations, for example, might have a hard time making radio signals exclusive. Television signals are scrambled on pay-per-view television, which makes the signals exclusive, dependent on possession of the right equipment with the right code. A second factor is the decisions made about how a service is organized. Water, for example, can be treated as an inclusive or exclusive service; the category is determined by the way the community chooses to organize delivery of the water.

A second feature of a good or service is the notion of joint consumption versus rival consumption. *Joint consumption* means that even if one person uses a good or service, others are nevertheless able to use it as well. By contrast, *rival consumption* means that if one person uses a good or service, another cannot use it. Roads, television and radio signals, and zoos are all capable of supporting joint consumption. Electricity is subject to rival consumption; clean water is rapidly becoming so also.

The distinction between joint and rival consumption is obviously not clearcut. Goods or services can appear to support joint consumption in some circumstances and rival consumption in others. To some extent, the match between the resources and needs affects how we characterize different forms of built capital. Furthermore, cultural capital determines how built capital is viewed. In some Hopi cultures, a washing machine in a private home is considered open access, whereas most Americans of European descent would be deeply offended—or would call the police—if a distant relative put seven loads of laundry through the washing machine in their basement while they were gone.

Types of Built Capital

The two dimensions of access and consumption can be used to define different types of built capital. As shown in Table 8.1, crossing the two different forms of access with the two different types of consumption leads to four categories of built capital. The extent to which control by the private or public sector seems better suited for each category is briefly explored in this section.

TABLE 8.1 — Types of Goods and Services

Access	Consumption	
	Joint	*Rival*
Inclusive	Collective	Common-pool
Exclusive	Toll	Private

In the lower right corner of the table are goods or services characterized by exclusive access and rival consumption; these are defined to be *private goods*. A landfill for which individuals must pay a fee in order to dispose of garbage is an example of a private form of infrastructure, regardless of whether it is publicly or privately owned.

Until recently, people did not think of waste disposal in terms of rival consumption. When people were free to dispose of garbage wherever they wanted, waste disposal was not even a form of built capital. Once it became clear that dumping garbage in ditches by the road, in ravines, or down old wells contaminated water supplies, bred pests, and was unsightly, disposal of garbage was characterized as rival consumption. Now most people are aware that the amount of garbage one household puts in the landfill limits the amount another household will be able to put in. For example, if rural communities agree to take in out-of-state garbage, that community's capacity to dispose of its own garbage may be limited.

Toll goods or services are those subject to exclusive access and joint consumption. Access is limited, usually by the requirement that a fee be paid, but anyone who can afford the fee can use the facility. Toll roads, long-distance telephone lines, and fiber-optic communication systems are examples of built capital that are toll services. These are goods or services that can be jointly consumed by different people simultaneously. If one person uses a toll service, another person can use the same service without having to replenish it.

Goods or services for which inclusive access is matched with rival consumption are referred to as *common-pool goods*. Public school buildings are normally an example of this type of infrastructure. School buildings are available for use without a fee, but they can accommodate only a limited number of people. Use made of the school by one child might limit the opportunity for another child to use that same facility. Demands for use by a larger number of people require additional buildings or expansion of existing ones.

Finally, goods or services that link inclusive access with joint consumption are referred to as *collective goods*. Streets, roads, and public sidewalks are the most obvious examples of collective goods. Schools can be considered collective goods if the community decides to have the school run two shifts of children each day or increase class size rather than turn children away.

Cultural capital has a great deal to do with the meaning of property to different groups, and thus, different cultures classify built capital in different ways. Some argue that the more goods can be classified as private, the higher the level of innovation. Others argue that the more goods are common-pool goods, the greater the chances for all members of a society have to achieve their potential. How does your community view different kinds of built capital? Has it changed over time?

Issues Facing Rural Communities

Failure of the built capital of rural areas has become a pressing problem. Much of the existing *infrastructure* was built in the 1930s, in conjunction with efforts to rebuild the country economically after the Great Depression. Community planners realized that rural people would prosper only if their communities had a well-developed foundation of streets, roads, public buildings, and utilities. Thus, a variety of public programs and private initiatives were established to assist rural communities in developing stronger infrastructures.

That infrastructure is now deteriorating. In the 1980s, one out of every five rural communities reported that two-thirds of its water pipeline has been in use for more than fifty years. At the end of the 1990s, it was estimated that approximately 45,000 of the nation's 55,000 community water systems serve fewer than 3,300 people; that infrastructure needs extensive upgrading, and the cost of doing so is high. In order to improve water systems in these areas, it will take $31.2 billion dollars over the next twenty years. Many rural communities in the twenty-first century are still waiting for pipeline replacements in order to have fresh, clean water. In rural and remote McKenzie County in North Dakota, the McKenzie Rural Water Association was formed in 1996 in order to work toward improving the water quality. Many people who had well water were not able to drink it because of contamination; some of the people in town would not wash their clothes with it because it left stains. Farm animals were becoming sick from drinking it because of the high levels of sulfates. In 2002, the county worked actively with the State Water Commission and other local coalitions to gain funding for pipeline replacement throughout the rural areas of McKenzie County.

As of 1994, it was estimated that 35.8 percent of the bridges in the United States were local or rural bridges, many of them built prior to 1950. The gap between the cost of replacement and the dollars available to rural governments is huge. Thus, rural areas are faced with difficult choices: to prioritize built capital investments, realizing some built capital will be abandoned; to share what built capital they can, or to change the specifications in order to have affordable built capital. An example of the last would be for rural bridges to be used as one-way-at-a-time bridges, which would decrease the weight load they would have to be built to hold.

Responsibility for maintaining and replacing water and sewer systems, roads and bridges, and public buildings has increasingly shifted from federal and state to local governments. Locally, infrastructure improvements are often financed through tax-exempt municipal bonds. These bonds can be either general-obligation bonds or revenue bonds. General-obligation bonds commit the community as a whole to repayment of the bonds. Consequently, funds are raised through increased taxes or a reallocation of existing tax revenue. The revenue collected as a result of the improvement repays revenue bonds.

Rural communities face a number of problems in financing infrastructure improvements. Rural communities often lack an economic base sufficient to support the large financial outlays required to solve their infrastructure problems. For the many communities that now have a declining tax base, general-obligation bonds are of limited use. *Revenue bonds* depend on a population large enough to make the increased costs manageable. In most cases, the per capita costs of improving or even maintaining built capital in rural communities tend to be rather high.

High per capita costs in rural communities are a function of several factors. Because of the lower population densities there, rural areas must often function under unfavorable economies of scale (low number of users per investment). Serving greater distances makes both the installation and maintenance of many forms of built capital more expensive. That is often the reason given for lack of broadband access in rural and remote and persistently poor areas. In some cases, the higher costs may be offset by simpler technology or individual solutions. Septic tanks and private water systems, for example, may substitute for expensive sewage treatment facilities and water distribution systems needed by more densely populated areas. Fewer streets are needed in rural areas, and they do not need to accommodate the heavy traffic common in urban areas. In general, however, built capital costs considerably more per citizen to build and maintain in rural areas.

Some rural communities are turning to other alternatives, such as special districts or impact extractions. Kentucky, for example, went to a system of creating special districts to fund infrastructure improvements. Special districts allow the costs of improving the infrastructure to be maintained only by those who will benefit directly. Impact extractions involve shifting the costs of development from the public to the developer. Bethel, Maine, a growing amenity-based community, gives developers two alternatives in connecting into the municipal sewer system: The developer can either construct a new replacement for existing lines or pay a sewer-system-development charge. Both options provide the funds needed to upgrade and maintain the community's sewer system (Lynch 1991).

In recent years, the new term "rural sprawl" has appeared. In Missouri, people who are looking to "get away from it all" are causing small towns to grow faster than the big cities surrounding them. In the 1990s, more than 3,500 new housing permits were issued for outlying areas. One of the issues involved in rural sprawl is the handling of municipal waste. In 2002, Oronogo, Missouri (population 976), a rural community outside of Joplin, Missouri, put a stop to new development because of infrastructure constraints (Belsie 2002). Its wastewater treatment plant reached full capacity, and the town faced a $2.6 million bill to expand its water system. Water bills would nearly double if expansion were to begin. Developers in the area argue that they are not promoting sprawl but, rather, trying to meet the needs of people who want to live outside of the city. Alternatives, like those found in Maine, are necessary in areas like Oronogo.

Public Versus Private Provision of Built Capital

Built capital can be provided for and supported in a number of different ways. Public schools and roads, for example, are provided for totally through public investment and control. Private schools and private roads, in contrast, have at least some private financial capital invested. Other forms of built capital, such as telephone systems, are developed through the private sector. Public versus private control is not a simple dichotomy, however. It is a continuum, such that elements of public and private support can be combined in varying degrees. This section examines the four types of infrastructure in terms of how they are provided for and proposes a framework from which to examine the choices a community makes.

Private and Toll Forms

Private and toll goods or services can be supplied by either the private or the public sector. The choice of control, public or private, is typically a function of historical development, economic entrepreneurship, or fiscal prudence. Bridges, housing, water supplies, recreation facilities, and fire protection can all be offered directly to users by private suppliers for a fee that includes cost plus profit. On the other hand, some local governments provide (for a fee) goods usually classified as private, such as electricity or telephone service. Some built capital originally constructed at public expense may be converted to private and toll goods controlled by the private sector. Land in industrial parks or speculative buildings placed on that land are sometimes turned over to private firms as an incentive for them to come to the community. Thus, the three most common alternatives seem to be private development and maintenance, public development and maintenance, and public development but private maintenance.

In many rural communities, natural monopolies maintain segments of the built capital. *Monopolies* are single companies that control the delivery of goods or services without competition. Monopolies can be either public or private. They are typically formed in cases when, even though different providers could offer competitive services, efficiency considerations mean that the services are best provided by a single provider. Water services, electricity, telephone service, and fire protection tend to be offered by single providers through regulation. The company accepts government intervention, usually in the form of price controls and requirements that service be provided to all, in exchange for exclusive rights to do that kind of business in a given area. The 1990s saw increasing deregulation of many of these monopolies, which led to differential impacts for rural and urban areas. The deregulation of telephones has resulted in increasing price competition, whereas in many areas where electricity was deregulated, the companies supposedly in competition instead colluded, creating artificial scarcity, brownouts, and high prices. Although monopolies seem natural when only one delivery system exists, it is possible to provide service on a competitive basis. The recent restructuring of long-distance telephone service is an example. The infrastructure (telephone lines, cables, and switches) is owned and leased to competitors.

Many of the goods and services that now come from monopolies were once provided on a competitive basis. In colonial Maryland, for example, fire protection was initially provided through insurance companies. Private companies sold insurance policies that included fire-fighting services from any number of competing companies. If a fire did break out, only the fire-fighting service identified by the insurance policy responded. One person might purchase such a policy; a neighbor might not carry any insurance at all. Such erratic access to fire protection was inefficient, as well as a danger to the public welfare.

Many communities moved to provide more uniform fire protection through firehouses and fire-fighting equipment purchased and controlled by the community. In some communities, salaried firefighters were hired. Other rural communities organized volunteer fire departments. No longer competitive, fire fighting has become a monopolized part of the built capital in communities.

As local resources become scarcer, some communities use their built capital to generate income. Bethel provides fire protection to several surrounding towns. It charges each town an availability fee—a flat rate for making its fire department available—that is reminiscent of the old insurance policies sold in Maryland. When actually called to a fire, the Bethel Fire Department charges a rental fee for the trucks that show up at the fire scene, labor costs for the firefighters involved, and a fee to cover the overhead for providing the service. The fees have increased nontraditional sources of revenue available to Bethel and, presumably, have made a higher level of fire protection available to the smaller communities (Lynch 1991).

Rural communities still face many issues pertaining to funding these services today. Decisions must be made as to whether fire protection should be supported through public or private means and whether it should be operated as a profit-generating or not-for-profit activity. Are volunteer firefighters sufficient to meet the needs of the local area, or must there be full-time, paid staff? Should states intervene to mandate a certain level of training or commitment to fire fighting, or should communities be allowed to organize the service in response to local resources? If the community opts for public support, what proportion of funds should be derived from public moneys such as assessments of property taxes?

Common-Pool and Collective Goods and Services

Generally, collective goods or services can be provided only by the public sector. Common-pool goods or services are often also provided by the public sector. Because these include types of infrastructures that are accessible without a fee, the private sector has little incentive to provide them.

When collective goods and services are provided to an entire community, they are referred to as *public goods and services.* No one can claim an exclusive share; public goods and services are free to everyone. It is assumed that access to any particular good or service is a right of citizenship or residency.

Semipublic goods and services are those for which only part of the infrastructure cost comes from fees (a variant of private goods) or for which the full cost for a restricted facility comes from public funds (a variant of toll goods). Many municipal swimming pools, libraries, and landfills fall into this category. Generally, the public provides the costs of construction and maintenance, and fees cover the continued operating expenses of the facility.

In contrast to collective goods and services, common-pool goods and services can be made exclusive. Charging an access fee limits who can purchase the good or use the service. If the fee is relatively low, the common-pool good or service begins to resemble a collective good or service. If the fee is relatively high, however, access is effectively limited.

Other methods of exclusion involve limiting access to people of specific ages, ethnic groups, races, or gender. At the beginning of the 1990s, there were two public institutions of higher education in the United States that continued to prohibit the entrance of women: the Virginia Military Institute (VMI) and the Citadel in South Carolina. By the end of the decade, both had begun admitting women to their institutions. The Augusta National Golf Club, home of the Master's Tournament, as of this writing, allows only men to belong to the club. Until recently, only white men could play on the course. Women still are not allowed to buy a membership, and they can only play at the course if they play with a male club member. This exclusive golf club maintains that it has the right to deny access to certain individuals because it is "tradition." Well into the 1960s, blacks were denied access to community services such as schools, swimming pools, motels, rest rooms, and drinking fountains. This exclusion ended when blacks staged large-scale protests and initiated legal challenges, making clear that their rights of citizenship included access to built capital constructed at public expense. Furthermore, citizenship rights also meant that certain goods previously defined as private, such as restaurants and bowling alleys, actually had a semipublic status.

Community Choices

Deciding whether the public or private sector should be involved in organizing for a community's built capital ultimately relates back to the values of the community and its decisionmakers. Max Weber, a nineteenth-century German sociologist, argued that there were really two forms of logic involved in these types of decisions. The first, called *formal rationality*, is used when the provision of needs can be calculated in quantitative terms of profit and loss. *Substantive rationality* applies to situations in which goods or services are provided to people based on values rather than profit. Whether the enterprise is profitable is not important or is of secondary concern. Therefore, profit or loss will often not even be calculated. The values sought might involve a concern for maintaining status distinctions, being fair, or gaining and maintaining power.

Through their local governments, communities make decisions about what infrastructure to develop. These decisions are based on the perceived needs of the local people, often as voiced by organized groups, as well as on the resources available. A community can decide to invest in a new landfill rather than a public swimming pool or in a new school rather than an industrial park. In many cases, investments in built capital generate insufficient profit or are too risky for the private sector to undertake. Thus, local communities must assume construction and maintenance costs if there is a belief that access to the service is a right of citizenship or residence in that community (substantive rationality). If that value is not held so strongly, then the community may choose to do without that particular service.

In the past, the federal government helped local areas with investments viewed as a right of citizenship—for a clean water supply and sewage treatment, for example. These forms of a community's infrastructure were considered valid, regardless of whether a profit could be made. Substantive rationality based on concern for equity placed this form of infrastructure in the public sector. Federal involvement declined in the 1980s and 1990s, however. Access to a clean water supply and sewage treatment is now being approached through mandates. This strategy is less effective, but it is also less costly to the federal government. As discussed in Chapter 11, the costs are shifted to either the state or local level.

All of these decisions involve choices on the part of the community as well as for other levels of government. The examples that follow enable us to explore the choices states and communities face in providing for various types of infrastructure and the problems created by these choices.

Public Choices: Water Systems

When we think about water as part of a community's infrastructure, we normally focus on the system established to deliver water to homes and businesses. Water, like air, is assumed to be available to all.

In parts of the rural West, however, this assumption is no longer valid. Urban growth increases the demand for water, threatening its availability for rural communities. Various governing bodies affect whether water is viewed as inclusive or exclusive and whether its consumption is joint or rival. Furthermore, water services may be viewed as a source of profit, so that access is determined by formal rationality, or a right of every citizen, and thus a matter of substantive rationality. This section explores the larger political context that influences the availability of water as well as the local decisions communities face in providing and maintaining water systems.

Water Services

Assuming that water is available (see Chapter 6), communities can offer access in a number of different ways. People can haul their own water or dig wells, assuming individual responsibility for getting water. Communities can organize a shared water system that can then be publicly or privately owned.

Water as part of a community's infrastructure can theoretically be subject to both exclusive access and rival consumption. Water, especially clean water, is typically distributed throughout the community through pipes. Consequently, potential users can be excluded. Moreover, water resources are finite. Use by one member diminishes the use by another. Until recently, the characteristic of rival consumption of water seemed less noticeable on the local level. The "watering patrols" now used to control the use of public water on lawns or the rationing procedures used during periods of drought illustrate the extent to which water is now seen to involve rival consumption. Wastewater and its storage and treatment has also become a significant problem throughout the rural United States because of outdated or insufficient infrastructure. It is vitally important that the consequences of toxic wastewater are understood (see Box 8.1).

BOX 8.1   What Exactly Is Wastewater? Why Treat It?

Have you ever considered the journey your drinking water made before it came out of your tap? Wastewater is generated by everyone, and each person in the United States uses 75 to 100 gallons of water per day. Seventy-three percent of the population is connected to a centralized (municipal) wastewater collection and treatment system, and the remaining 27 percent uses on-site septic systems. Water does not magically disappear into the earth when it is used on a daily basis; it becomes wastewater, or sewage that is filtered before it can be returned to the environment for reuse. Wastewater contains disease organisms and hazardous substances like cleaning fluids and disinfectants. It is easy to ignore wastewater treatment, until that sort of bacteria appears in the water that comes from your tap at home. If these organisms are in the water, people can become seriously ill. In rural areas, the infrastructure is often outdated and has deteriorated, making it easier for bacteria to form and get into drinking water supplies. Keeping up with the maintenance of wastewater treatment is difficult, and paying for it is sometimes impossible.

SOURCE: Ken Olson, Bridget Chard, Doug Malchow, and Don Hickman. 2002. "Small Community Wastewater Solutions: A Guide to Making Treatment, Management and Financing Decisions." University of Minnesota Extension Service.

Because of these characteristics—exclusion and rivalry—the distribution of water at the local level is potentially suitable for private control. Rural areas are more likely to have private water supplies: wells sunk by individual homes. In urban areas, water is typically managed by the public sector. In general, the belief that all citizens have a right to clean water at a reasonable price has led to public control or regulation. In other words, substantive rationality has dominated over formal rationality.

Water Quality

For people like Sara Johnson, the problem is the quality of water, not its availability. The water that reaches residents of Floyd County is unusable. For years, rivers have been dumping grounds for industry. Sewer systems owned by cities often discharge into rivers or bays that are later used as sources of drinking water. Toxic chemicals from dumps, industry, and agriculture are seeping through soil to taint groundwater. Runoff of the chemicals used in fertilizers and pesticides is contaminating the water of lakes, streams, and reservoirs.

For the most part, rural communities are not prepared to deal with increased concerns about water quality. Coliform bacteria is a source of gastrointestinal diseases and is one of the most common problems found in rural water supplies. If each household provides its own well, testing and water quality is even more difficult to maintain.

In the 1990s, many of the 62 million people living in more than 2,300 rural counties in the United States still lacked access to supplies of clean water and sanitary water disposal facilities (U.S. GAO 1995). The states with the greatest financial need for wastewater treatment facilities are Ohio, Pennsylvania, West Virginia, North Carolina, and New York (see Table 8.2). There is a gap between the amount of funding available and the number of facilities that need to be repaired in small communities (see Figure 8.1) and there are several different types of infrastructure needed in these communities (see Figure 8.2). These communities are eligible for State Revolving Funds, but often those funds do not cover all of the costs (see Figure 8.3). The U.S. Department of Agriculture (USDA) and the Environmental Protection Agency (EPA) offer funding that targets wastewater and sewer projects in rural areas. The 2002 Farm Bill makes provisions for improving rural infrastructure, including water systems. Congress authorized $360 million to fund a backlog of sewer loan and grant applications at the USDA. Provisions were also authorized to help deal with the shortage of resources for small rural communities' water and waste systems by setting aside funds to help communities facing emergency drinking water shortages or system repairs or extensions and grants for improving decentralized water well systems (Gasteyer 2002). Although the provisions are in place and dozens of programs are authorized, that does not necessarily mean that progress will be made; it may take six years to see results, if any.

According to the EPA, small communities that have fewer than 10,000 people need to spend $13.8 billion for wastewater treatment in order to comply with the 1996 Clean Water Act. These communities often rely on state and federal grants and funding to improve their water treatment facilities. However, it is difficult to adequately address every community's problems with contaminated water. A major problem that has affected rural areas of Nebraska is high levels of nitrates in the drinking water, which can cause "blue baby syndrome," an illness in which the level of oxygen carried to a baby's cells and tissues is negatively affected. In 1996, this illness was increasing throughout Nebraska communities, and nitrate levels were found to be at levels that exceeded federal standards. In 2002, the problem was still evident as nitrate levels in irrigation wells increased and research showed that an increase in stomach, throat, and digestive cancer in some areas of Nebraska where nitrate levels were high.

TABLE 8.2 States with Greatest Small-Community Water Treatment Financial Need as a Percentage of Total State Water Treatment Need

	Amount (millions, in 1996 dollars)	% of Total State Need
Ohio	$1,499	21
Pennsylvania	$1,430	24
West Virginia	$950	58
North Carolina	$781	20
New York	$699	4

SOURCE: Adapted from Environmental Protection Agency
http://www.epa.gov/cgi-bin/epaprintonly.cgi

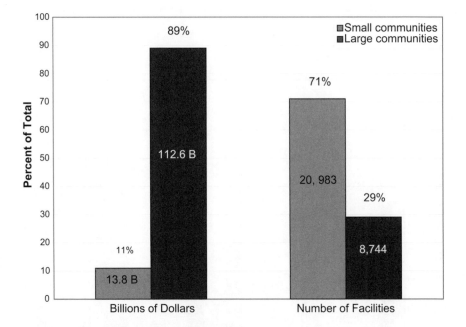

SOURCE: Adapted from Environmental Protection Agency
http://www.epa.gov/cgi-bin/epaprintonly.cgi

FIGURE 8.1 Community Water Treatment Needs (in dollars) and Number of Water Treatment Facilities

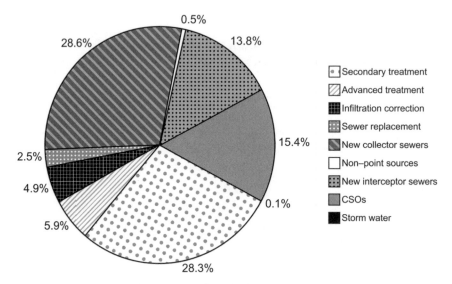

0.5%

28.6%

13.8%

- Secondary treatment
- Advanced treatment
- Infiltration correction
- Sewer replacement
- New collector sewers
- Non–point sources
- New interceptor sewers
- CSOs
- Storm water

15.4%

2.5%

4.9%

0.1%

5.9%

28.3%

Total Small Community Needs = $13.8 Billion

SOURCE: Adapted from Environmental Protection Agency
http://www.epa.gov/cgi-bin/epaprintonly.cgi

FIGURE 8.2   Category of Water Treatment Need (by percentage) of Small Communities

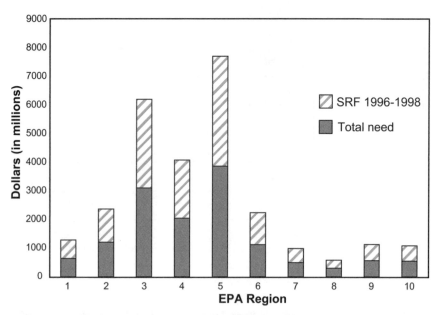

FIGURE 8.3   Total Estimated Small-Community Water Treatment Needs by EPA Region and Proportion of That Need Met by State Revolving Loan Fund Disbursements, 1996–1998

In 2000, the rural community of Jefferson County, Florida, adjacent to the metropolitan area of Tallahassee, Florida, had high levels of coliform bacteria in the water. More than four hundred samples from local wells tested positive for the bacteria, which caused much concern over disease outbreaks. The problem with avoiding water contamination in small, rural communities stems from the difficulty these communities have with obtaining affordable financing for infrastructure improvements (EPA 2000). The EPA's Drinking Water Revolving Fund was put into place to finance wastewater treatment facilities in small areas, but with recent budget cuts, the aid to rural communities is jeopardized. For the fiscal year 2003, $1.25 billion was proposed, which is $100 million less than in 2002 (WIN 2003). Small communities may not receive the funding necessary to remove contaminants from their water supply. Preventing water contamination has become a more significant worry as threats of bioterrorism have begun to pervade the United States in recent years.

In 2002, the concern for wastewater systems became apparent as threats of terrorism became a formidable concern. The issue of water being susceptible to physical, cyber, biological, chemical, and radiological threats was realized after the terrorist attacks on September 11, 2001. Water-related agencies and organizations made security a high priority on their agendas. Emergency plans became necessary for smaller water systems, and close scrutiny of water systems was necessary to pinpoint needed improvements in security and emergency preparedness (Murray 2002). Emergency plans and added security for water systems require more funding. The EPA set aside approximately $23 million to support small and medium drinking water facilities; most Federal funding is for large systems in the United States. Outreach to small communities will be necessary to implement security-related measures. The Rural Community Assistance Program (RCAP Inc.) and its affiliates around the country work with small communities to help them plan and implement solutions for built capital that fit their situation and their goals.

Part of the solution is to treat wastewater and maintain sewage and water lines. Citizens in the small communities throughout Tazwell County are insisting that the small, privately owned water companies make the investments needed to maintain water quality. These citizens rely on local and state governments to ensure that these investments in infrastructure are made.

Another part of the solution is to stop contamination of local water supplies. In some communities, citizen groups work together to see that clean water laws are enforced. These groups trace contamination back to its source and then take public action to block the release of the contaminants. Citizen groups serve as watchdogs to ensure that private individuals and companies do not dispose of their waste at public expense. Private companies are encouraged to increase their investment in built capital for reasons of substantive rationality.

Clearly, public investment is also needed. The fiscal capacity of many rural communities, especially those lacking adequate wastewater treatment facilities and public water systems, is inadequate. State and federal governments have offered little help, although there are some important programs, such as those promoted by the Rural Community Assistance Program Inc. (RCAP Inc.) and its affiliates around the country that mobilize federal funds to create both social and built capital in small rural communities. Changes in the tax structure at all levels and a reassessment of national priorities may be necessary in order to begin to solve these important built problems.

Private Choices: Solid Waste

Built capital includes a means to provide for the collection and disposal of solid wastes generated by households and industries. Urban areas are finding that they no longer have room for the volume of waste they produce and have arranged to transport it to rural areas for disposal. In many rural communities, waste disposal has become a source of revenue. Like water, waste disposal can be placed under either public or private control. As increased demand for disposal sites has been countered with environmental concerns, waste disposal has become an intriguing issue.

Waste as an Economic Venture

Waste disposal involves exclusionary access and rival consumption. It is exclusionary in that most dumps and landfills restrict access, regardless of whether they are publicly or privately owned. Users must pay a fee in order to dump solid waste. Waste disposal involves rival consumption in the sense that land used to store solid wastes is land unavailable for other purposes. Urban areas are well aware of these rival uses; indeed, some have run out of land on which to dispose of their wastes. In rural areas, people sometimes simply leave waste where it is or toss it into the river. Even such casual disposal is ultimately a rival use of land or rivers because these areas fill up and no one else can use them.

In 2000, U.S. residents, businesses, and institutions produced nearly 232 million tons of municipal and solid waste, which is approximately 4.5 pounds of waste per person, per day (EPA 2000). This statistic does not include the hazardous and toxic wastes that are also produced in large quantities and that are even more difficult to dispose of. Because waste disposal is both exclusionary and rival as well as potentially very profitable, private interests have been drawn into providing this type of built capital. Rural communities themselves are looking toward waste disposal as an economic venture.

Jerry Wharton, an independent strip miner, started the Kim-Stan Landfill Company in Virginia. His previous company had specialized in quick profit: clearing ground, mining coal, and leaving the land exposed. Once the coal ran out, Wharton decided that waste disposal was one way to use the holes he had made in the earth. With little investment on the part of Wharton and his Chicago-based partners, the Kim-Stan Landfill Company was launched in a persistently poor area of Virginia. The landfill did a booming out-of-state garbage business as cities and industries desperate for a place to dump their garbage took advantage of the Virginia mountains. This proved extremely profitable, and a great deal of waste was moved into the landfill site.

People paid little, if any, attention to what happened to the waste products once they reached the site. When an unusually high concentration of dangerous contaminants was noticed in the nearby Jackson River, however, an investigation was launched. In May 1990, the Commonwealth of Virginia closed the landfill. After first paying $250,000 to Wharton, the Kim-Stan Landfill Company declared bankruptcy. The public—the Commonwealth of Virginia—was left with the cleanup costs and remaining company debts. The waste at the landfill included 5,000 gallons of waste oils contaminated with mercury, asbestos, and medical waste, which reached depths of eighty feet (EPA 2002). Soon after the site was closed, the EPA put it on their "Superfund" list, meaning that U.S. taxpayers pay 90 percent of the cleanup costs; Virginia taxpayers have to pay the remaining 10 percent. The public is paying for cleaning up toxic substances generated by a now-bankrupt private firm.

Private landfills and waste disposal operations are now common. Certainly, the notion of accepting solid waste from other areas is not especially new. In most rural areas, landfills have been developed regionally, or larger communities have simply charged neighboring towns for the use of their facilities. What is new is the profit that can be made from accepting out-of-state garbage. Strip mines in northern Kentucky have been adapted for use as private landfills. A private firm has proposed a 6,000-acre landfill three miles from Welch, West Virginia, a persistently poor rural community. In return for permits to open the landfill, the developer has promised to build the city a sewer system that would clean up the Tug Fork River (Kilborn 1991). There was much discussion in town both in favor of and against the landfill. Those in favor saw it as providing good jobs (increasing financial capital). Those who opposed it were concerned about pollution and health risks (natural and human capital). The plan was stopped, but as the area's economy continues to decline into the twenty-first century, some still regret the lost jobs. The idea of out-of-state garbage entering the county landfill did not sit well with some of the residents in Welch; others saw it as an opportunity for job growth in the area. There were also concerns about past mining activities that had occurred beneath the proposed landfill site. Protest groups formed to stop the landfill from being built, and by the late 1990s, Capels Resources, Ltd., the company that applied for a permit to build the waste facility, decided not to construct it. There were several restrictions put into place by the county, including on the size of the disposal area, which was ultimately decreased to thirty-five acres from five hundred acres. Capels withdrew their application for a permit, making protesters happy; however, many residents are still upset by what they see as the loss of new jobs with decent wages and benefits in the area. Such conflicts over which capital should be favored often leave long-term divisions in rural communities.

Virginia's experience with the Kim-Stan Landfill illustrates the complex issues involved. Solid waste disposal has implications for the environment shared with others as well as for the profits generated within a private enterprise. Even when the public would profit, as in Welch, decisions made today could compromise the use of land for other purposes in the future.

Governmental Responses

Because of inadequate government oversight, disposal of solid waste, particularly toxic waste, has been more profitable to private waste management firms than valuable to society as a whole. The social costs often become apparent only years after the waste has been improperly disposed of. Consequently, waste management firms have found it easy to pass part of the true cost of waste disposal on to the government. Ultimately, taxpayers pay for the cleanup. Consequently, the public must assume a more active role in solid waste disposal. Governmental involvement may be of two types: regulation of private companies or direct public control of solid waste disposal.

If the first option is chosen, governments must find a way to retrieve the costs of cleanup or insist that those costs be integrated into the operation of the private landfills. As is illustrated by the actions taken by Kim-Stan Landfill Company, retrieving the costs of cleanup can be difficult. Alternatively, governments can develop regulations designed to protect the environment. Firms would be required to take certain precautions designed to protect the groundwater, the air, and the appearance of the landscape. The cost of those precautions would then be integrated into the cost of the business and passed along to the customer through higher disposal fees. These costs would then be closer to the true cost to society and would certainly be cheaper for society as a whole than toxic-waste cleanup after the fact.

If the second option is chosen, both governments and the general public must acknowledge the need to deal with the social costs as well as the physical costs of disposal. This means greater use of recycling, careful selection of landfills, segregation of toxic from nontoxic wastes, and the selection of appropriate means for disposing of toxic wastes. If the local governments do not have the technical capacity to deal with these issues, state or federal governments may need to assume responsibility for developing appropriate procedures and regulations.

Community Responses

Solid waste is now recognized as a collective problem that communities can solve through organization. Solutions are not always arrived at easily, however. As occurs on most issues, opposing forces organize to protect their respective interests. NIMBY ("not in my backyard") groups organized early as wealthy suburban communities sought to protect themselves from private landfills. Other community groups formed coalitions to support recycling or to promote or oppose the choice of a location for new landfills. In Greenup, Kentucky, an organization called Greenup Residents Opposing Waste Landfill (GROWL) was created to block the approval of a private landfill, based on fears that groundwater would be contaminated. Groups may protest the acceptance of waste from out of state or the proposed construction of toxic-waste incinerators. They may also propose delaying a decision until the community can educate itself on both the benefits and risks; the people of Harlan, Iowa, sought a delay when faced with the possibility of a medical-waste incinerator being built.

Recycling is a common response to the growing volume of trash. Participation in recycling programs is voluntary in some locales, mandatory in others. Community-organized programs have been successful in reducing the volume of solid waste needing disposal. Although some recycling enterprises can be profitable or at least break even, most incur costs for the community. Communities offer recycling programs to decrease the amount of solid waste to be processed rather than as a means to generate municipal revenue.

Because recycling programs cost money, the decision to recycle involves substantive rationality. Communities recycle because they are concerned about the environment, not because recycling generates a profit. As the costs of waste disposal increase and as regulations require that the true costs of solid waste disposal be passed on to the consumer, recycling may become more formally rational. Individuals may find it personally profitable to recycle much of their solid waste rather than pay the true costs of having it collected. Communities themselves may find it more profitable to recycle than to open new landfills. As that occurs, private firms may find it possible to earn a profit, and recycling programs may shift to the private sector. Ultimately, recycling works only when the demand for recycled materials offsets the costs of recycling. Governments can increase the demand for recycled products by purchasing them for the military, prisons, and other government institutions.

Federal Role: Making Linkages

By definition, rural residents are more isolated from markets and information than are urban residents. Two forms of built capital, transportation and communication technologies, reduce that isolation. These span larger distances and involve public–private partnerships to ensure rural access, however. Rural communities must provide the local infrastructure, but they then hope to be linked with other networks and hope that private companies will provide the needed services. In the past, the federal government has played an important role in maintaining these forms of built capital.

Transportation

Transportation continues to be crucial to rural areas. At the local level, rural transportation systems suffer from four major problems: inadequate new construction, deferred or otherwise inadequate maintenance of existing structures, inadequate fiscal infrastructure to serve economic needs, and financing problems.

Inadequate maintenance of roads and bridges is particularly acute. Seventy percent of the bridges in the north-central U.S. states, not atypical of other parts of the country, were constructed before 1935 and designed for a fifty-year life (Chicoine 1986). As of 1994, bridges in the northeastern United States were in the worst condition in the nation, with only 40.6 percent of bridges in adequate condition. As a result, many are crumbling. Nationwide, almost one-third of rural bridges are in the rehabilitation or replacement category. There are insufficient or no resources available to reinforce or replace them. The Highway Bridge Replacement and Rehabilitation Program has existed since 1978, and it appropriates funding for states to repair bridges. From 1992 to 1997, funding increased because of the Intermodal Surface Transportation and Efficiency Act of 1991, and $16.1 billion was appropriated over a six-year period. Although this is a lot of money, there are restrictions on its use: Each state is only allowed to spend not less than 15 but not more than 35 percent of the funding on rural roads and bridges (Deller and Walzer 1997). As this infrastructure deteriorates, people such as Carl Jones in Hebron are unable to transport goods to market.

Although some bridges were repaired or rebuilt, many still had outdated constructions, and with increased traffic in rural areas due to farm equipment and heavy trucks, bridges needed attention. County officials said it would take an estimated $1.8 million per year to repair and maintain rural bridges; however, the county officials reported that they only had $696,000 per year set aside for bridges. In towns, officials reported that approximately $42,000 per year would be needed to improve bridges, but they only expected to have $11,000 to spend (Deller and Walzer 1997). There were also financial inadequacies when it came to fixing rural roads. There was an annual gap of $2.8 million in counties and $67,000 in towns. Patterns between 1987 and 1994 were consistent; the costs of maintaining rural roads and bridges is escalating, in part because of inflation but also because of deterioration of the system.

The Transportation Equity Act for the Twenty-First Century that was put into place in June 1998 authorized $171 billion to improve the transportation system in the United States. Although this amount of money is significant, rural funding was not sufficient, in part because of the classification system that was implemented. Local roads and minor collectors, which are defined as low-traffic roads, make up 77 percent of rural roads but received only 15 percent of rural federal highway funds, which equates to $7.7 billion (Brown 1999). Rural areas, under the Surface Transportation Program, are defined as those having populations of less than 5,000, which leaves out many rural communities. There are rural areas that have unmet needs because of this classification, and the condition of roads and bridges in those areas continue to deteriorate because they lack funding.

Public Transportation

The viability of a transportation network is a function not only of well-sited and safe bridges and roads but also of what means of transport are available. The federal government's decision to deregulate transportation has significantly decreased access in rural areas. Railroads abandoned a number of lines, isolating rural communities that produced low-value but high-volume products, such as wheat or timber. Communities such as Garden City, Kansas, invested in their own railroad spur in order to maintain regional linkages to their local infrastructure. Other towns were less able to step in where the private sector had withdrawn. The loss of those linkages meant the loss of a part of the community's economic base.

Public transportation, always deficient in rural areas, has become virtually nonexistent in many communities. Railroads abandoned most passenger service entirely. The interstate bus network has substantially reduced service, eliminating service to communities that do not lie along interstate highways and cutting service even to those that do.

Bus service illustrates the character of the public-private partnership involved in transportation. The public provides the roads, but private companies provide the means of transport. Decisions made to regulate bus service were based on substantive rationality. The goal was equity: ensuring that rural residents had access to public transportation. Regulations linked profit with service. In exchange for the right to serve profitable routes, bus lines were required to serve unprofitable ones. The expectation was that the profit generated along the better routes would exceed the loss generated along the more rural routes.

The Bus Regulatory Reform Act of 1982 reflected a shift from substantive to formal rationality. Communities no longer had the right to bus service. Routes are now selected strictly in terms of their profitability. During the first two years following passage of the act, the number of communities served by intercity buses declined by 20 percent. This equaled the decline that had occurred during the seven years before the legislation was passed. The routes abandoned were those to rural communities with neither air nor rail service.

Rural communities have also been affected by deregulation in the airline industry. Regulation of bus service was designed to ensure access. Regulation of the airline industry was designed to ensure equity in fares. When the airlines were deregulated in 1978, commuter airfares increased sharply. It now costs as much or more to fly the 225 miles from Roanoke, Virginia, to Washington, D.C., as it does to fly five times that distance from Kansas City, Missouri, to Washington, D.C. Although these charges reflect a difference in cost resulting from the lower passenger travel between Roanoke and Washington, they also reflect the lack of competition that exists along such routes. Deregulation initially reduced airfares, but the number of carriers has gradually decreased through economic failure. Fares and services have been left in the hands of fewer companies. Service to some rural communities has been abandoned altogether. Other service continues with the help of funds designated for Essential Air Service (EAS), a federal program meant to bridge the transition from regulation to deregulation.

Telecommunications

As the world economy becomes more integrated, information becomes more central to business operations. Information-age technologies can improve both the economic efficiency and the competitiveness of today's rural commercial enterprises. Rapid information flow is facilitated through modern electronics and telecommunications. These require not only investment by the individual (in computers, modems, and facsimile machines) but also investment by the public (in switching systems, underground cables, and satellite links). E-commerce in small, rural towns, necessary if rural businesses are to compete effectively, has been on the rise (see Box 8.2).

BOX 8.2 Crossing the Digital Divide

Five businesses in and around the small town of Uvalde, Texas, wanted to learn about e-commerce. Cody's Hat Shop was one of these businesses. This three-year-old business provided services to local residents by cleaning and restoring hats. Cody Varnon, owner of Cody's Hat Shop, was ap-

Continued on next page

proached by a professor at the Southwest Texas Junior College about becoming involved in a pilot program offered by the Southwest Texas E-Commerce Business Incubator (STEBI) that began in March 2001. STEBI was a new business incubator that wanted to stimulate business in Southwest Texas. The Rural Community College Initiative team envisioned this new project and received $50,000 in grant money to get it up and running. STEBI's goal was to invest in businesses that showed enthusiasm for learning through e-commerce. Interested small-business owners had to be open to new ideas and had to be willing to spend ample time each week working on their project with other participants. Cody thought it over and decided that he was interested in this chance to learn about e-commerce. Cody's Hat Shop, along with the four other initial participating businesses, began a six-month program that taught them how to put their businesses on the Internet.

Business participants learned how to create Web sites for their businesses, but more importantly, they learned good business practices. Each business was given a budget to use to experiment with advertising. Cody's Hat Shop advertised in an upscale magazine, in a regional newspaper, and on a radio station that played country and western music. The participants learned the importance of effective advertising techniques through a two-hour course they attended each week at the Southwest Texas Junior College. The marketing tactics they learned were invaluable. By the end of the program, not only did Cody have a Web site for his business, but he had also built social capital by networking with people from all over the United States. His research about e-commerce proved to be the most important aspect of the program because he found the best markets to target for his business. The first ten months following the program clearly showed positive results; he had numerous hits on his Web site, and more people inquired about his services. However, the tragedy of September 11, 2001, caused business to decrease. Overall, Cody says the program was entirely beneficial and encourages other small businesses to participate in the project. He has now been in business for five years, and he greatly values his experience with STEBI. He is hoping to add an online store to his Web site in the near future.

The STEBI program proved to be a success, generating an additional $49,000 in sales in the first year of the program for the five businesses. Sales were projected to increase that amount again by the next year. STEBI now asks for applications from businesses that want to take part in

Continued on next page

Crossing the Digital Divide (continued)

the program and hopes to help five more businesses increase their understanding of e-commerce and online marketing.

Adding e-commerce to businesses is a change that is part of a broader
economic restructuring that is occurring worldwide. E-commerce has become an important component of businesses. Business owners have to
learn how to target a wide range of consumers via the Internet. E-commerce, in itself, is a difficult concept to define, categorize, or measure because it is not easily understood. There have been attempts to measure the
impact of e-commerce on the global economy. The first aspect of the measurement is recognizing the "e-readiness" of various countries. Nations that
are "e-ready" are capable of participating in e-commerce; they have the
connectivity, e-leadership, information security, human capital, and e-business climate necessary for e-commerce (Tehan 2002). It has been established that fifty-three countries are e-ready, and these countries together
contain more than two-thirds of the world's population. In the United States,
consumers are extremely capable of making purchases online, and it is
predicted that 130 million Americans will be buying goods online by 2005,
nearly double the number who did so in 2002.

REFERENCES: Rita Tehan. 2002. "E-Commerce Statistics: Explanation
and Sources." CRS Report for Congress. Washington, D.C.: Congressional
Research Service.

Many rural linkages to the world economy are now being made through Internet connections. The Telecommunications Act of 1996 was put into place to
eradicate the monopoly of large telephone companies; it was intended to give
smaller telephone companies a chance to compete. The hope was that phone
service would become more economical and that more rural customers would
have access to more telecommunications services. A Universal Service Fund,
contributed by all telephone customers, usually through their phone bills, was established to ensure investments were made to incorporate hard-to-reach customers (see Box 8.3). However, local service providers need access to technology
that can extend to remote places in the community. Connecting high-speed digital service to all customers' homes is not an easy task; the greater the distance,
the more expensive it is for the rural customer. Many rural and remote areas still
either do not have Internet service or cannot acquire it at a reasonable cost.
Rural areas are now distanced from global business not only by miles of land and
water but also by miles of phone lines, or lack thereof.

BOX 8.3 The Telecommunications Act of 1996: Promoting Rural Inclusion or Exclusion?

The Telecommunications Act of 1996 was enacted to abolish geographic telephone company monopolies and to provide rural and other disadvantaged areas an opportunity for affordable telecommunications services. The federal Universal Service Fund (USF) was established to bridge the digital divide by encouraging investment in high-quality telecommunications service to disadvantaged areas. States have also established such funds.

According to the Federal Communications Commission (FCC), which administers the federal funds,

> The goals of Universal Service, as mandated by the 1996 Act, are to promote the availability of quality services at just, reasonable, and affordable rates; increase access to advanced telecommunications services throughout the Nation; advance the availability of such services to all consumers, including those in low income, rural, insular, and high cost areas at rates that are reasonably comparable to those charged in urban areas. In addition, the 1996 Act states that all providers of telecommunications services should contribute to Federal universal service in some equitable and nondiscriminatory manner; there should be specific, predictable, and sufficient Federal and State mechanisms to preserve and advance universal service; all schools, classrooms, health care providers, and libraries should, generally, have access to advanced telecommunications services. (FCC 2003)

A Federal-State Joint Board was established to work along with the FCC to "determine those other principles that, consistent with the 1996 Act, are necessary to protect the public interest."

For instance, schools and libraries receive discounted telecommunications services based on a sliding scale ranging from 20 to 90 percent. The discount increases according to the percent of students in the particular school district who are eligible for the national school lunch program (those whose families are below 185 percent of the poverty level). An additional discount for rural areas (beyond that of urban areas) declines from 25 percent to 0 percent as the proportion of students eligible for free and reduced lunches increases. Similarly, rural healthcare providers may compete with one another on an annual basis for reduced telecommunications costs (both for equipment purchase and monthly rates paid). Telecommunications companies can apply for

Continued on next page

The Telecommunications Act of 1996: Promoting Rural Inclusion or Exclusion? (continued)

funds to provide discounts to their low-income customers on telephone installation costs and on monthly telephone service. Some 1,500 telephone companies participate in these programs. Although the FCC is in charge of the funding of schools, libraries, and healthcare facilities, it shares responsibility with the states for the low-income and high-cost areas. States must establish their own Universal Service funds and provide up to 75 percent of the total funding for these two programs. By late 1999, only about twenty states had passed legislation that committed their Universal Service Funds to reducing telecommunications rates in rural areas. Local governments, which may already own cable systems or have unused capacity in the telecommunications systems serving city governments, are often the logical provider of new telecommunications services. Although seven states had authorized such efforts, five had prohibited some or all local governments from providing telecommunications services to their citizens (see Strover and Berquist 1999: tables 4.1 and 4.2).

The FCC issued its rules in May 1997 on how universal telecommunications service was to be attained. Under the regulations, although schools, libraries, and rural healthcare facilities were treated equitably, little was done to foster "advanced telecommunications and information services" for the other two categories of consumers covered by the law: low-income households and high-cost areas. Digital services and toll-free Internet were not included under the "supportable" services. Miles Fidelman (1997) argues that the focus on upgrading service on schools, rural healthcare providers, and libraries may actually negatively affect the ability of high-cost regions to gain community-wide telecommunications capability, since three kinds of institutions with the greatest interest in high-quality telecommunications capacity are encouraged to go it alone rather than to contribute to a community-wide effort. While the Universal Service provisions are being implemented to benefit certain otherwise underserved institutions and households, they may actually limit rural and remote communities' ability to recruit or grow their own high-tech firms. Sharon Strover (1999), in a study of rural counties or parishes in four states (Texas, Iowa, West Virginia, and Louisiana), also concluded that federal policies are deterring investment in rural telecommunications systems, which can significantly affect business development in rural areas.

Continued on next page

The Telecommunications Act of 1996: Promoting Rural Inclusion or Exclusion? (continued)

REFERENCES: Federal Communications Commission (FCC). 2003. "Universal Service" (updated January 30). Online; available: http://www.fcc.gov/wcb/universal_service/welcome.html; accessed April 14, 2003.

Miles Fidelman. 1997. "The New Universal-Service Rules: Less Than Meets the Eye" (July 1). Civic.com. Online; available: http://www.fcw.com/civic/articles/1997/CIVIC_070197_53.asp; accessed April 3, 2003.

Sharon Strover. 1999. "Rural Internet Connectivity" (September). Rural Policy Research Institute (RUPRI) report. Online; available: http://www.rupri.org/pubs/archive/reports/1999/P99-13/index.html; accessed December 5, 2002.

Sharon Strover and Lon Berquist, 1999. "Telecommunications Infrastructure Development: The State and Local Role" (November). Rural Policy Research Institute (RUPRI) Rural Telecommunications Panel. p99–12. Columbia, Mo.: Rural Policy Research Institute.

Recent reports have shown that at almost every income level, rural households are less likely to own computers and have Internet access (see Box 8.4). Sharon Strover's studies (1999) vividly illustrate the continued struggle that rural areas have with accessing Internet technology. Internet service providers, or ISPs, may choose not to enter a rural market because they think it is too costly, and rural citizens often do not have the technological skills or knowledge necessary to recognize the importance of digital information and communication in their everyday life. Even when rural infrastructure exists, ISPs are leery of entering the market because the price at which they can offer the service limits the number of customers. Additionally, federal and state policy is not being put into place to invest in rural regions. These obstacles can be overcome if rural citizens become aware of their options for digital communication. Policies can be enacted at the state level to expand the local calling area so that rural areas are not dialing long distance for Internet service; however, many ISPs are unaware of this possibility. Local subscribers must elect to join an extended local calling (ELC) area, but no institution is charged with advertising the existence of this option. Wireless technology is one possible solution to costly Internet service, particularly in sparsely populated areas. In Missoula, Montana, two local Internet providers now offer service from a wireless Internet network. Wireless technology can eradicate the "last mile problem" for remote areas of the country and eliminate the cost of laying cable to reach remote areas; however, the weakness of wireless signals has been one hurdle that providers are still trying to overcome.

BOX 8.4   The Rural-Urban Digital Divide

The U.S. Department of Commerce brought together the following statistics regarding the digital divide:

• At almost every income level, those households in rural areas are less
  likely to own computers than households in urban or central city areas.
• At every income level, households in rural areas are significantly less
  likely—sometimes half as likely—to have home Internet access than
  those in urban or central city areas.
• Black households in rural areas are 1/3 less likely to own a computer
  than the average U.S. Black household, and are 2/5 less likely to access
  the Internet than the average U.S. Black household.
• For rural areas, the Kindergarten–12th grade school is a popular point of
  Internet access: 30.0 percent of rural persons use the school for Internet
  access outside the home, compared to a national average of 21.8 percent.

SOURCE: U.S. Department of Commerce. National Telecommunications
and Information Administration. 1999. "Falling Through the Net: Rural Areas
Magnify the 'Digital Divide'" (July). Factsheet. Washington, D.C.: U.S. Department of Commerce. Online; available: http://www.ntia.doc.gov/ntia-
home/digitaldivide/factsheets/rural.htm, accessed April 14, 2003.

Government involvement is crucial to the development of telecommunications
infrastructure in rural areas. Rural communities often are not attractive to private
companies, which prefer to lay cables in more densely populated areas. Local funds
are often limited. Because information infrastructure links communities to one another and therefore crosses local government boundaries, both state and federal levels of government need to be involved. Such participation may involve direct public
ownership, independent quasi-public or private collectively owned entities (such as
the rural electric cooperatives organized to bring electricity to the nation's farmers),
or subsidies to private firms. Regardless of the form of ownership chosen, the decision to subsidize telecommunications infrastructure in rural areas is a public choice.

Motivation to Act

To what degree and under what conditions do communities and governments
provide the needed infrastructure? When will the communities in Tazwell County
insist on adequate water and sewer facilities? Can Hebron convince the county to

repair its bridge? What will motivate governments to ensure that remote areas receive affordable Internet service?

There are no simple answers to these questions, but research into local support of crime control raises some interesting issues. Sociologists have proposed two explanations for why communities differ in their willingness to support crime control. One explanation, called "public choice," assumes that the demand for police services by the community as a whole determines the extent to which funds are allocated in support of crime control. The second explanation, called the "conflict perspective," acknowledges that perceived need plays a role in the choices communities make. This perspective contends, however, that the felt need of elites has much more weight than those of poor people (see the discussion of political capital in Chapter 5).

Assuming that a community has the capacity to raise funds in support of different forms of built capital, whose needs prevail? Are community choices a reflection of the community as a whole, or do they respond to the elites?

Chapter Summary

Built capital includes the permanent physical installations and facilities supporting productive activities in a community. Examples include roads, bridges, telephone service, and water and sewage treatment and distribution facilities.

Access to various types of infrastructure can be exclusive (limited to some) or inclusive (available to all). Consumption of goods or services provided through the infrastructure can be either joint (simultaneous use) or rival (use by one diminishes the use by another). If we cross the two forms of access with the two forms of consumption, we can identify four types of built capital: private, toll, common-pool, and collective.

The form of built capital is a factor in whether it is provided and supported through private or public organizations. Either the public or the private sector can supply private and toll goods or services. Collective and common-pool forms of infrastructure are typically provided by the public sector. Selection of the provider, public or private, is ultimately a choice made by the community.

Two forms of logic govern such decisions. Formal rationality relies on a quantitative assessment of the choice: The choice must result in profit. Substantive rationality relies upon values other than profit. Federal or state support of local infrastructure is often based on substantive rationality.

Four categories of built capital—facilities for water distribution, solid waste disposal, transportation, and telecommunications—illustrate some of the issues now faced by rural communities. Two issues, water availability and water quality, affect decisions related to the provision of water services. State and federal governments have become involved in issues related to water rights. Communities focus on the distribution and quality of water. For the most part, water is placed under public control.

Because solid waste disposal involves exclusionary access and rival consumption, private control is a possibility. Local, state, and federal governments have found it necessary to intervene, however, in order to protect the environment. Current interest is focused on strategies that ensure consideration of the social as well as the physical costs of disposal.

Finally, transportation and communication technologies all depend on some state and federal involvement. E-commerce has become increasingly important for all businesses; however, rural communities continue to have difficulty getting affordable Internet access. In an unregulated environment, access to services at a reasonable price ceases to exist for many rural communities.

Key Terms

Built capital in a community includes the permanent physical facilities and services needed to support business and community life. Examples include roads, bridges, telephone service, and schools.

Collective goods are forms of infrastructure that involve inclusive access and joint consumption. Roads and public sidewalks are the most common examples.

Common-pool goods are forms of infrastructure that involve inclusive access and rival consumption. An example is a public building with a defined capacity.

Exclusive access is a characteristic of built capital such that individuals can be denied access to the good or service. Utility companies are typically exclusive.

Formal rationality applies to decisions made on the basis of economic calculation of profit or loss.

Inclusive access is a characteristic of built capital such that there is unrestricted access to all who would use it. Public roads are an example of inclusive infrastructure.

Infrastructure is the foundation or supporting framework needed for a structure or organization.

Joint consumption is a characteristic of built capital such that the use of a good or service by one person does not diminish its availability to another.

Monopolies are single enterprises that have sole control over the sale and distribution of a particular class of goods or services in a particular geographic area.

Private goods are forms of infrastructure that involve exclusive access and rival consumption. In most communities, waste disposal in local landfills has become private.

Public goods and services involve forms of built capital that are provided to the entire community at no cost.

Revenue bonds are a type of municipal bond where principal and interest are secured by revenues such as charges or rents paid by users of the facility built with the proceeds of the bond issue. Projects financed by revenue bonds include highways, airports, and not-for-profit health care and other facilities.

Rival consumption is a characteristic of built capital such that the use of a good or service by one person diminishes or even eliminates its availability to another.

Semipublic goods and services include forms of built capital that are supported in part by fees collected from the user.

Substantive rationality applies to decisions made on the basis of values rather than on economic calculation.

Toll goods or services are forms of infrastructure that involve exclusive access and joint consumption. Toll roads are the most common example.

References

Belsie, Laurent. 2002. "Rural America's New Problem: Handling Sprawl" (December 10). *Christian Science Monitor.* Online; available: www.csmonitor.com/2002/1210/p03s01-ussc.htm; accessed January 23, 2003.

Brown, Dennis. 1999. "Will Increased Funding Help Rural Areas?" Economic Research Service, U.S. Department of Agriculture. Agriculture Information Bulletin no. 753. Online: available: http://www.ers.usda.gov/publications/aib753/aib753.pdf; accessed April 14, 2003.

Chicoine, David L. 1986. "Infrastructure and Agriculture: Interdependence with a Focus on Local Roads in the North Central States." In *Interdependence of Agriculture and Rural Communities in the Twenty-First Century,* ed. Peter F. Korsching and Judith Gildner, 141–163. The North Central Regional Center for Rural Development.

Christopherson, Susan, Todd Alexander, Pierre Clavel, Jeffrey Lawhead, Kenneth Reardon, Karen Westmont, and Eric Wilson. 1999. *Reclaiming a Regional Resource: A Progress Report on the U.S. Department of Housing and Urban Development's Canal Corridor Initiative.* Ithaca, N.Y.: Department of City and Regional Planning, Cornell University. Also online; available: http://www.hud.gov/library/bookshelf18/pressrel/canalrpt.pdf; accessed April 16, 2003.

Daniels, Thomas L., and John W. Keller, with Mark B. Lapping. 1995. *The Small Town Planning Handbook.* Chicago: Planners Press, American Planning Association.

Deller, Steven C., and Norman Walzer. 1997. "Rural Roads and Bridges: A Comprehensive Analysis." Washington, D.C.: USDA Transportation and Marketing Division.

Environmental Protection Agency (EPA). 2000. "The Drinking Water State Revolving Fund: Financing America's Drinking Water." Online; available: http://www.epa.gov/safewater/dwsrf.html; accessed January 21, 2003.

_____. 2002. "Region 3: Mid-Atlantic Region Hazardous Site Cleanup Division: Kim-Stan Landfill." Online; available: http://epa.gov/reg3hwmd/super/VA/kim-stan/pad.htm; accessed January 22, 2003.

Federal Communications Commission (FCC). 1996. "Universal Service." Online; available: http://www.fcc.gov/wcb/universal_service/welcome.html; accessed December 6, 2002.

Gasteyer, Stephen. 2002. "Understanding the Debate on International Water Privatization." *Rural Matters,* Summer:13–17.

Lynch, Rodney C. 1991. "Nontraditional Revenues: Keeping the Property Tax Under Control in a Small Town." *Government Finance Review,* June:38–39.

Kilborn, Peter T. 1991. "In Despair, W. Va. County Looks to Trash." *New York Times,* October 16: A1–A2.

Murray, Ann. 2002. "Small Wastewater, Water Systems Deal with Security Concerns, Training Needs." *Environmental Training Newsletter for Small Communities* 11, no. 2:1–2, 4–5, 17.

Strover, Sharon. 1999. "Rural Internet Connectivity." Rural Policy Research Institute (RUPRI) report. Online; available: http://www.rupri.org/pubs/archive/reports/1999/P99-13/index.html; accessed December 5, 2002.

Tehan, Rita. 2002. "E-Commerce Statistics: Explanation and Sources." CRS Report for Congress. Washington, D.C.: Congressional Research Service.

U.S. GAO (General Accounting Office). 1995. "Rural Development: USDA's Approach to Funding Water and Sewer Projects." Report to Honorable William F. Clinger Jr., House of Representatives. GAO/RCED–95–258.

Water Infrastructure Network (WIN). 2003. "EPA Lauds Budget Proposal; Others Unhappy." Online; available: http://www.win-water.org/win_news/020602article.html; accessed January 22, 2003.

Weber, Max. 1968. *Economy and Society: An Outline of Interpretive Sociology.* Ed. Guenther Roth and Claus Wittich. Vol. 1. Berkeley and Los Angeles: University of California Press.

Part 3

How Community Capitals Are Transformed in a Changing World

9

The Global Economy

When John Brooks, at age fifty-five, acquired the old shoe factory in Nelsonville, Ohio, in 1975, he never realized the long journey that his new company and its footwear would take. John felt compelled to buy the company because his uncle had once owned it, but John could not afford to purchase it by himself. He gave the sellers $500 in earnest money, but he needed to come up with the rest, nearly $600,000. John's son Mike contacted a high school friend, who later became the company's chief financial officer, for help. They contacted a congressman in Ohio who did not want the local shoe factory to close. Soon after, they attained assistance from the Farmer's Home Administration, which guaranteed 90 percent of the loan. Five local banks lent them the money, which secured their ownership; however, John sensed that the road ahead would be challenging. If the company failed, John knew he would lose everything.

Mike Brooks, who was selling leather for a Milwaukee tannery, decided to help his father, even though John vehemently opposed his joining this risky venture. Mike had prepared for such an opportunity when, just out of high school, he had attended a shoe-design school in Milan, Italy. It had appeared that he had lost his chance to make his mark in the shoe business when his great-uncle sold the company out from under the family in 1959. He now had a second chance, and he was not going to pass it up.

The people of Nelsonville were thrilled because the shoe company would have closed otherwise; there were no other buyers. It would be locally owned again. However, the business needed more money for operating costs. Soon Brooks Shoes bypassed the local banks for most of its working capital; only banks in Cincinnati and Columbus had the financial capacity to service this growing shoe-manufacturing company. The company first marketed to big retail merchandising firms like Sears and J.C. Penney, who slapped their own brand names on the shoes. These mail order giants continued to place orders with Brooks Shoes because it provided a high-quality shoe at low prices. John Brooks was selling a commodity, not a product. Mike concluded that if they wanted to make a decent profit and generate capital for expansion, they needed a brand name for their footwear. The company began targeting working people who did a lot of walking, including postal workers and law enforcement officials. Soon the company became Rocky Shoes and Boots. The Rocky label received a boost in 1977 when Mike won an award for a square-toed work boot he designed for the company.

Mike believed that they needed to increase the prices of their shoes, but John disagreed, staunchly maintaining "I did not buy the company to get rich." After many arguments, Mike was able to convince his father that they should sever ties with buyers who would not pay them more for their shoes. Mike had success at a trade show, where people lined up and demanded his new footwear for hunting. They had found their market niche: consumers of rugged, outdoor footwear.

John did not agree with some of Mike's ideas about how to run the family business, and he became upset when Mike decided to pursue overseas labor. John believed in using local labor in order to benefit the community. Mike thought the company would have a difficult time sustaining itself without employing cheaper labor. By 1987, Mike, along with their sales manager, the factory manager, their financial adviser, and John (a silent partner), purchased a Dominican Republic plant where the leather uppers were made. The uppers were shipped to Nelsonville, where local workers stitched them into the rest of the boot. A few years later, they opened a Puerto Rican plant.

In 1991, John decided to work only part-time, and he handed his business and its debts equally to his five children. Mike remained president of the company, a position he had occupied since the mid-1980s. Mike was concerned that the heavy debt load stood in the way of obtaining capital for expansion. Mike decided to seek outside investors in Rocky Shoes and Boots through the stock market. In February 1993, Rocky Shoes was listed on the NASDAQ. Good economic times helped double the value of the stock from the initial offering—from ten dollars to twenty dollars—in a few short months. This sudden infusion of capital reduced the debt by $10 million. John Brooks was impressed with his son's achievement. Mike handed him a check for a million dollars for his share of the Dominican plant—his last remaining investment in the company. Mike began planning for a major expansion: "We have a chance to become a Timberland or a Wolverine," he told the *Columbus Dispatch* in 1997.

Mike's decision to expand at the beginning of 1999 was not matched by an increase in demand for Rocky shoes. The company was overloaded with unwanted boots and shoes and had to sell them at cheap prices to elated customers. This meant a net loss of $5 million dollars; Mike had to make some difficult decisions. He did not want to move the factory jobs overseas, but he knew it would be a possibility if profits continued to decrease. Furthermore, he had to share profits with other owners who had bought the company's stock on the NASDAQ. Unlike John, they *were* in the business for the profit; in fact, that was their only interest in the company. Labor in other countries was much cheaper, and Mike knew that it might be a way to recover profits.

Mike would have to make this critical decision on his own; he could not debate the situation with his father, who had passed away in 1996. What Mike and his fellow executives had ignored was that the competitors they had identified (like Wolverine and Timberlake) focused on fashion to grow their firms; the rural and blue-collar workers, such as postal workers, who bought Rocky hunting boots and hiking shoes were not that interested in fashion. The market was dependable but not prone to expand rapidly. He decided to strengthen that market by selling his shoes at Wal-Mart, a company that sells one-third of America's hunting licenses each year. Although the value of Rocky's stock rose again after this marketing move, difficult times were still in sight.

By November 2000, 110 people had been laid off in Nelsonville, as Mike moved these manufacturing positions to the Dominican Republic. The company's stock had plummeted to a fifty-two-week low of $3.69 per share after the layoffs, and many people were angry with Mike because of the way he was handling the business. They scoffed at his new car and even jeered at him at the factory in Nelsonville. The workers felt that he had failed them and the community, and he recognized their pain.

In November 2001, Mike Brooks moved the remaining sixty-seven manufacturing jobs to a factory in Moca, Puerto Rico. An overall mood of sadness was apparent as the last pair of boots produced in Nelsonville came down the assembly line. Manufacturing shoes in Nelsonville meant paying a worker $11 an hour, versus $6 in Puerto Rico or $1.25 in the Dominican Republic. Mike felt that the only way the company could thrive enough to pay dividends to stockholders and revalue its stock was to take full advantage of cheaper overseas labor.

Rocky Shoes was the last shoe company to close its factory doors in Ohio. Although many of the factory workers were unionized, none were offered replacement jobs with the company. The number of white-collar workers in the corporate headquarters in Nelsonville exceeds 260—more than the number of factory workers employed during most of the firm's existence—but working-class jobs for those with a high school education or less are much more scarce in this Appalachian town of 5,000 today than at any time since before coal was mined locally.

The U.S. Department of Labor has reported that fewer than 25,000 shoe jobs remain in the United States, which is down from 235,000 in 1972.

★   ★   ★

Not only are rural and urban areas alike being drawn into a world economy, but the character of the economy has also changed. Financial capital, the money that businesses need to finance their operations, can now be moved easily from one country to another. The Internet has made this even more effortless. Businesses across the globe can be accessed from a consumer's home. Businesses, through online advertising and stores, can target another business's customers; businesses can also sell supplies to one another via the Internet. Thus, the price of money, not the price of raw materials, is driving many business decisions. This chapter explores (1) traditional linkages between rural areas and international markets; (2) changes that have altered the character of the world economy, including e-commerce; (3) the impact these changes are having on rural communities; and (4) the opportunities and problems this new economic environment creates.

Rural Linkages to a World Economy

Newspaper accounts and after-dinner speeches often characterize the world economy as though it were something new, as though the U.S. economy had previously been insulated from world events. Although the character of the U.S. economy has changed, the United States has always been linked to other countries through trade. In the case of rural communities, past linkages occurred through the primary products (lumber, food and fiber, fish, and so on).

Exporting Natural Resources

International trade has always been a part of the U.S. experience. Trading companies, eager to profit from the natural resources the new land offered, financed early European settlements in the New World. New England communities found furs, fish, and lumber to be their most profitable exports. The South depended on cotton and tobacco. For the colonies, these international linkages were so important that the tariff England imposed on American tobacco was among the causes of the Revolutionary War.

Nearly all natural-resource-based economies move through cycles, some influenced by nature but others affected by trends in world markets. Mining towns have gone through boom-and-bust cycles as mineral prices fluctuated on the international market. In the 1870s, the silver streaming out of Nevada nearly ruined Germany, which had a currency based on silver. During World War I, cotton prices soared in response to the demand for uniforms. Once Europe recovered in the 1920s, however, prices dropped to historic lows. Increased grain production in Europe sent American wheat prices plummeting in the 1870s and 1890s and again during the 1920s. Until railroads opened up markets in the Midwest and the East, Oregon lumber interests depended more on foreign than domestic markets. Today, raw logs are exported to Japan from the United States; Japan is the greatest volume buyer of logs, purchasing virtually all sizes and species. The United States, generally, sends more wood fiber, whole logs, and wood chips overseas than any other country.

Oil towns from Texas to Montana prospered when the members of the Organization of Petroleum Exporting Countries (OPEC) limited their oil production in 1973. The OPEC cartel represents the interests of major oil-producing countries, most of which are located in the Middle East. Decreased oil production in the Middle East meant increased prices worldwide, high enough to encourage the development of domestic oil reserves, triggering an economic boom in states such as Texas and Oklahoma unequaled since the days of the gold and silver rushes of the last century. Less than a decade later, however, the same towns that had boomed were struggling. Increased oil production from the OPEC nations had sharply reduced the price of oil worldwide, making U.S. domestic oil no longer competitive.

In 2000, OPEC decided to limit production to 5 million barrels of oil per day, increasing the demand for domestic oil, which caused higher prices. OPEC's decision, along with concern over the war in Iraq, caused oil prices to rise. International events, like the September 11, 2001, terrorist attack or the military conflict in Iraq, create uncertainty about supplies, which led to fluctuation in price. With increasing conflict, members of OPEC have had difficulty reaching a consensus over oil prices and strategies for exporting, increasing price variation (see Box 9.1).

BOX 9.1—The Global Economy and Its Impact on the Environment

OPEC's decision to limit oil production increased the prices for nearly all commodities. Although this stimulated most rural economies, it had a devastating impact on the environment. In the United States, more farmland was put into production. Windbreaks were plowed up, as were terraces that had been put in place in the 1930s in an effort to conserve soil and water. Wheat, raised primarily in the Midwest and Northwest, was added to crop-rotation cycles throughout the country. U.S. Secretary of Agriculture Earl Butz urged farmers to plant fencerow to fencerow. Developing countries also responded. Because of the higher commodity prices, land that had earlier been unprofitable could now be pressed into production. Rain forests were cleared and prairie soils plowed. If roads were needed to provide access to this land, countries simply borrowed money from the oil-rich nations.

The rapid increase in the production of commodities had a number of impacts, some good and others bad. The U.S. economy boomed during the

Continued on next page

The Global Economy and Its Impact on the Environment (continued)

1970s, in part because rural areas were able to export commodities to meet high demand and offset an ever-decreasing dollar value. A number of developing nations, able to improve their road and trade systems, became much more active exporters. Ultimately, however, the environment suffered. Rain forests and fragile prairies were destroyed. Peasants who had come from mountain and coastal areas cleared the land in hopes of escaping poverty by gaining access to land. Developers, whose primary interest was in profit and not settlement of the land, then replaced the peasants. Land conservation principles were cast aside and were reintroduced in the 1980s.

Since the 1980s, conservation has become a much larger issue, one that the 2002 Farm Bill addresses by implementing and reauthorizing conservation programs. Funding will be provided for the conservation of private grazing land, farmland protection, and wetlands, along with other natural resources. The Farm Bill has been called the "single most significant commitment of resources toward conservation on private lands in the Nation's history" (NRCS 2002). On the other hand, the commodity provisions of the 2002 law continue to encourage production of a handful of supported crops and to discourage crop diversification and mixed crop–livestock systems. This monoculture then contributes to the pollution of lakes and streams by nitrates and pesticides. Row-crop production, which is encouraged in the law, also generates soil erosion. Conservation and environmental protection continue to be significant issues in national policy as more and more natural resources are in jeopardy of being disturbed or destroyed.

However, the Farm Bill helps large farms, which receive 60 percent of the payments, whereas small farms will receive little or no support in the new commodity programs. These programs focus more on payments to farmers than on providing supports in the marketplace for income. Supply-control tools, such as acreage limitations, were not restored from the 1990 Farm Bill. Concurrently, 80 percent of farm payments are going to 10 percent of the largest producers in the United States, who turn around and use the added incomes to buy out smaller farmers and continue the trend to even larger farms. Small farmers are going bankrupt while corporate producers are collecting hundreds of thousands of dollars (Rural Coalition 2002).

REFERENCES: National Resources Conservation Service (NRCS). 2002. *Farm Bill 2002: Conservation Provisions Overview.* Washington, D.C.:

Continued on next page

The Global Economy and Its Impact on the Environment (continued)

USDA. Online; available: http://www.nrcs.usda.gov/programs/farmbill/2002/pdf/ConsProv.pdf.
Rural Coalition. 2002. "Campaign for a Just Food and Farm Policy." Online; available: http://www.ruralco.org/html2/farmbillreport.html; accessed December 5, 2002.

Importing Labor

Early linkages with the world economy also included movement of workers, the people needed to harvest the vast natural resources available in the New World. European immigrants seeking to escape religious persecution or simply to get a new start on life harvested New England's furs, fish, and lumber. Slaves were recruited involuntarily from Africa to harvest rice, cotton, and tobacco in the South. The need for low-cost labor to perform domestic work along railroad lines or in mining camps led to heavy recruitment of Chinese laborers. Mine owners in West Virginia recruited experienced miners from eastern Europe. Europeans who were eager to own land settled farms throughout the Midwest.

The need for labor, especially in rural areas, was so great that the United States maintained open borders for nearly a hundred years after independence. Immigration hit an all-time high in the first decade of the twentieth century, leading some to propose that limits be imposed. In 1921, Congress passed the first quota act, limiting the annual number of immigrants from each country to 3 percent of the number of people born in that country and residing in the United States as reported in the 1910 census. The Immigration Act of 1924 was even more restrictive: It used the national origin of each individual in the United States in 1890 as the basis for allocating admission to the flow of immigrants. It was not the numbers of immigrants but their racial and cultural backgrounds that inspired these exclusionary efforts, which were clearly aimed at reducing immigration from Asia and eastern Europe. Over time, some attitudes have changed. National-origin limitations were lifted in 1965, but numerical limits still remain in place, although the limit is referred to as a "flexible worldwide cap." There are no limits on immigrants who are family members of U.S. citizens.

In an effort to safeguard the United States from future terrorist attacks, recent changes in immigration law have been imposed, making it more difficult for immigrants to enter the country. Some of these changes include a program that makes getting and keeping student visas more difficult and an extended waiting period on nonimmigrant visa applications, especially for men from Middle Eastern and Muslim populations. These changes make it far more difficult for well-intentioned immigrants to enter the country, and racial and ethnic discrimination can be an unfortunate by-product. In fact, many Mexican immigrants have received exhaustive questioning and searches when they cross the U.S. border. Julio Sandoval is one such immigrant. Julio is not looking to become a U.S. citizen; he emigrated from Mexico in 1989 and is already a naturalized citizen. However, when he and three other male friends returned to the United States from a recent visit to Mexico, they went through hours of investigation, including a check of police and citizenship records (Adame 2002). Even though Julio understands that strict surveillance of U.S. immigrants is necessary and important, it is clear from this example that men of varied ethnic descent are being targeted at the border because of the events of September 11.

Although our recent history has resulted in immigration restrictions, it is important to remember the extent to which economic activity in rural areas depended on labor imported from other countries. For example, much of the labor in food processing, low-end services, and construction is provided by migrants.

The Growing
Importance of Financial Capital

Rural linkages to world markets are not new, but the character of those linkages has changed dramatically. *Commodities,* bulk natural resources or standardized manufactured products bought and sold on markets, once drove the international economy. The country that could mine copper or weave high-quality cloth at the lowest cost exported the most. Consequently, national industries sought to make their operations more efficient in order to remain competitive.

Today, it is the flow of capital from one currency to another, even more than trade in goods or services, that drives the international economy. Corporations have become multinational, moving their operations to wherever the financial conditions enhance profitability. High-speed electronic communication allows different operations in the value chain to be carried out in different countries in order to enhance the bottom line. As a result, local areas have less control over what happens to them economically. To understand how this came about, we need to examine (1) changes in international monetary policy, (2) changing supply-demand relationships, and (3) the impact of a nation's internal fiscal policy.

International Monetary Policy

As World War II drew to a close, world leaders met in Bretton Woods, New Hampshire, to grapple with the problem of how to reestablish trade. Most felt that the economic chaos of the 1930s had contributed to the Nazi takeover in Europe; thus, they were anxious to develop mechanisms that would ensure stability in the world economy. The Bretton Woods Agreement (1944) created a system of fixed exchange rates among national currencies. *Exchange rates* set the value of countries' currencies relative to one another; consequently, they are important in facilitating trade among nations. Under the agreement, the United States fixed the value of the U.S. dollar to gold at thirty-five dollars per ounce. The exchange rates of other countries were then fixed relative to the U.S. dollar. This system of *fixed exchange rates* did not allow the value of the dollar to fluctuate on world markets.

During the 1950s and 1960s, the United States enjoyed economic predominance throughout the capitals of the world. Its economy grew steadily, filling gaps in trade as the nations of Europe and Japan turned their attention to rebuilding what had been destroyed during World War II. The United States generally favored open trade of its products and enjoyed a trade surplus, exporting more than it imported. The dollar occupied a unique position in the world economy as the standard against which the values of all other currencies were fixed.

As the world economy recovered from World War II and as other nations strengthened their industrial base, U.S. exports faced increased competition. By the early 1970s, the United States was importing more than it was exporting, in part because the dollar was valued much higher than other currencies. There was a net flow of dollars out of the United States and into countries from which it was importing goods.

When the dollars held by other countries exceeded the gold reserves the United States had with which to buy back those dollars, financiers assumed that the United States would increase the price of gold. In other words, increasing the exchange rate for gold from thirty-five dollars to forty dollars per ounce in effect decreases the value of each dollar relative to gold and is an example of currency devaluation against a standard, gold. Financiers began trying to unload their dollars on world currency markets, hoping to sell the U.S. dollars before they were devalued. The flood of dollars on currency markets forced the United States to do just what the financiers feared: devalue the dollar. In August 1971, the United States also suspended the conversion of dollars into gold.

Efforts to establish a new fixed exchange rate failed. In May 1973, President Richard Nixon negotiated the Smithsonian Agreement, which established a *floating exchange rate,* allowing currency values to fluctuate and find their market values. Central banks, including that of the United States, could no longer fix exchange rates except in cases when a nation's currency began fluctuating widely. In general, national controls on currency were reduced and country-to-country banking restrictions were eased.

Financial capital, the money available for investment, now moves more easily from one country to another. This allows private speculators to buy and sell different currencies in an effort to make a profit as exchange rates fluctuate. Capital markets established through this exchange of currency generate a flow of money that is thirty times as great as the money exchanged when countries import or export products. Whether a nation's corn is competitive on the world market, for example, depends as much on the current exchange rate of that country's currency as on the costs of growing that corn. A strong dollar discourages foreign tourists from visiting the United States, but U.S. tourists travel enthusiastically to other countries. When the dollar is weak relative to other currencies, visitors flock to the United States.

The movement of people across borders, whether for pleasure or work, decreased sharply after September 11, 2001, slowing the flow of money across international borders. The concurrent *recession,* defined by the National Bureau of Economic Research as "a period of declining output and employment," has caused some instability in the value of the dollar, and since travel to and from the United States has decreased, the economy has not bounced back quickly. Additionally, scandals involving large corporations like Enron and WorldCom has created skepticism among international investors. The introduction of the euro in twelve countries of the European Union on January 1, 2002, added some competition for the dollar. However, since the dollar's value decreased, it reached a one-to-one parity with the euro in July 2002. Some Europeans were excited and proud of this achievement, but many were not. A weakened dollar hurts European exports, and when European currencies and stock markets rise quickly, it destabilizes the economy (Ford 2002). Some business owners in Europe worried about losing money because of the weakened dollar. The dollar regained strength, which enhanced exports from European countries. However, the strong dollar deterred foreign visitors from traveling to the United States, and such travel was already down because of the threat of terrorism.

The dollar weakened somewhat as a result of the U.S.-led recession that began in early 2001 and as a result of uncertainties spawned by the terrorist attacks in September of that year. As of this writing in 2003, the dollar continues to drop in value.

The concern over the weakened dollar is a valid one for international investors and the United States because it increases costs for importing and investing. A decline in the dollar reduces the value of assets, thereby reducing the wealth of foreign investors. It is possible that a plunging dollar could negatively impact the global economy by deflating consumption and investment internationally. If the dollar weakens substantially, interest rates could increase and throw the U.S. economy into a deep recession. On the other hand, moderate and gradual weakening of the dollar might encourage exports and reduce the massive trade deficits the United States has experienced over the past decade. In the absence of a worldwide recession, such a change would strengthen U.S. agricultural and manufactured exports and would benefit rural areas.

Effect of Increased Production on Competition

The 1970s brought a second milestone in the transition to a global economy. As mentioned earlier, OPEC decided to limit oil production. In making oil scarcer, OPEC effectively increased the price of oil. Urban people in the United States remember long lines at gasoline pumps and occasional fistfights as motorists jockeyed for position to buy the scarce gasoline at unbelievably high prices. Rural people remember five-dollar-per-bushel wheat and twelve-dollar-per-bushel soybeans—prices two to three times higher than usual.

In order to understand how the price of oil is related to the price of wheat, we need to look at capital markets. The sudden increase in oil prices meant that the oil-producing countries developed a trade surplus. The money they received from the oil they exported exceeded the money they spent on imports. Oil-producing nations had "petrodollars" to spare and were suddenly able to import more goods. The Soviet Union, for example, was a major exporter of oil. It also needed food and feed grains with which to support its people. The trade surplus created by higher oil prices enabled the Soviets to purchase larger quantities of basic commodities such as wheat and soybeans. Many oil-producing countries, particularly those with small populations but lots of oil, were anxious to lend poorer, non-oil-exporting countries money to purchase oil, wheat, and other commodities.

As OPEC nations created a higher demand for commodities, the price those commodities brought also increased. Higher prices made it more profitable for others to enter the market. Production increased rapidly, with both good and bad outcomes.

New Linkages of National Economies

The increased price for commodities that followed set off a period of worldwide inflation. *Inflation* occurs when the currency in circulation or the availability of credit increases faster than production grows, leading to a sharp rise in prices. The devaluation of the dollar made U.S. exports extremely competitive in world markets. Percentages and volume of crops exported were higher than they had been during the previous fifty years. By the end of the 1970s, U.S. economic growth depended heavily on the rest of the world, particularly as a market for agricultural products. Just as many developing nations did, the United States moved into a period of "stagflation": high inflation with no real economic growth.

Efforts to curb inflation in the United States focused on internal fiscal and monetary policy. In 1979, the Federal Reserve Board, the governing body that sets monetary policy for the U.S. Central Bank, effectively withdrew dollars from circulation in the economy by increasing the rate that banks charge their best customers, other banks. This strategy reduces inflation. Investment slows or declines because money is more costly, workers are laid off, and people have less money to buy products, all of which reduces demand and stabilizes prices.

To counteract the recessionary impact of the Federal Reserve Board's action, the Reagan administration decreased the federal income tax and, despite making spending cuts in many areas, increased spending for defense, farm programs, and interest rates. Massive tax cuts were made in 1981, with the high-income and corporate sectors of the economy being the primary beneficiaries. The rationale was that tax cuts would free up money for investment in the domestic economy and stimulate economic growth. Increased economic growth did not occur at the projected rate, however. As a result, the federal deficit increased rapidly. The United States became the largest debtor nation in the world, borrowing money from foreign countries rather than raising taxes or cutting spending.

The United States took these actions in an effort to deal with its internal economic problems. As it turned out, however, these actions had an enormous impact on the world economy. Economic theory predicts that if the money supply is reduced, the economy will slow down. A gradual tightening of the money supply may result in a "soft landing"—that is, a mere decrease in economic growth. This was not the case in the early 1980s. If an economy suffers negative economic growth for two consecutive three-month periods, economists say it is in a recession. The trade-off is reduced inflation. The actions taken by the Federal Reserve Board under Presidents Jimmy Carter and Ronald Reagan slowed inflation. Not surprisingly, a recession also occurred. The recession was not limited to the United States, however. It was worldwide. Dollars withdrawn from the national economy were also dollars withdrawn from the world economy.

Why should action taken in the United States to cure its own economic ills affect the world economy? The answer lies, in part, with how easily capital flows from one country to another. Removing dollars from the money supply makes them scarcer and hence more valuable. The growth of the federal deficit meant that the federal government itself was competing for scarce dollars. Real interest rates increased substantially.

High interest rates made U.S. government securities a good investment. Foreign capital flowed into the United States because the U.S. government needed to borrow so much money to service its debt. The U.S. deficit became something of an international black hole, pulling in any and all liquid capital. This made capital scarce for others, and a worldwide recession occurred. The spiral of increasing demand and thus higher prices for commodities came to an abrupt end. Prices of commodities on the world market dropped dramatically.

Although recovery from the recession was evident in urban America by the middle of the 1980s, rural communities that were natural-resource dependent did not experience substantial economic growth until after the rather mild 1991 recession—and then only from a notably smaller population and institutional base than had existed in the 1970s. During the 1990s, rural areas shared to a degree in the prosperity of the nation as a whole. Many communities diversified away from such heavy dependence on resource-based activities into services and routine manufacturing, availing themselves of a gradually shrinking niche in the world system, one that combined willingness to work for low wages (relative to metropolitan U.S. wages but still very high when compared with wage scales in developing countries) with an educated and dedicated workforce (human capital) and adequate built capital along with strong social infrastructure. Persistent poverty areas in the South, Southwest, and Great Plains did not fare so well. The rural routine manufacturing sector, as we saw in the case of Brooks/Rocky Shoes, is very vulnerable to the shifting of production jobs to Latin America, China, or other low-wage parts of Asia.

In early 2003 (as we write this chapter), conditions in the United States are very different from those of the 1970s, 1880s, and indeed the 1990s. The burst of productivity led by the electronic and telecommunications sectors in the 1990s has kept inflation well under control. In 2002, the economy pulled out of a brief recession. Since inflation was not a problem, interest rates were dropped to the lowest point in thirty years. However, people continued to feel leery about spending their money because of the military conflict in Iraq, distrust of large corporations, and the instability of the economy. Americans and foreigners were not investing in the stock market as readily, causing the market, in 2002, to have its worst second-half performance since 1991. Additionally, retailers had difficulty making a profit, since consumers would rather invest in real estate than buy new clothing. Housing prices soared nationwide as the upper middle class moved up the ladder and home ownership increased among the lower middle class. When a recession looms (and there is fear of reentering the recession), consumers, concerned that they may lose their jobs, spend less money on frivolous goods, which ultimately hurts retailers. Locally owned retail stores often feel the effects of the economic downturn the most, since they often do not have the flexibility of large corporate firms in shedding unprofitable activities, slashing their workforce, or selling off built capital. The slow recovery of the economy does cause frustration for many; however, the low interest rates on real estate gives many people the chance to afford to buy a home or to refinance the one they already own—investments that are viewed as much more solid than the alternatives. Low interest rates directly benefit the wealthy, who move up to larger homes, vacating those they left for the middle class.

Like the Reagan administration, the second Bush administration has responded by cutting taxes and greatly increasing military spending. Farm program expenditures, too, have reached all-time highs. Low interest rates decrease the cost of the national debt, but the deficit is increasing at record rates. The United States does not seem to be as good an investment risk as it did in the 1990s.

The New Corporation

What is the impact of these changes? Companies have become multinational and are now online. Competition within natural-resource industries has increased substantially. It is the flow of capital, not commodities, that affects international trade.

The change in corporate structure has been especially dramatic. No longer confined to one country, many of today's corporations have developed branches and subsidiary companies in countries throughout the world. These diversified locations ensure that the company has access to local markets and the flexibility to move resources quickly in response to changes in capital and labor markets (and in order to reduce tax liability). The organizational structure of these companies reflects the multinational character of their operations. Stockholders reside all over the world, as do the board members who make decisions on behalf of the company. Individual countries can do little to control the activities of these new corporations. At this point, no international controls exist.

Impact on Rural Areas

Any discussion of capital flows, fluctuating commodities prices, floating currency exchanges, e-commerce, and foreign investment seems abstract until their collective impact on rural areas is examined. Two examples, one drawn from agriculture and the second from rural manufacturing, illustrate how rural areas have been affected by the changed global economy. Discussed also is the changing character of the rural labor force.

The Farm Crisis of the 1980s

In many respects, the history of U.S. agriculture is one of increased efficiency yet dwindling significance in the economy. In 1790, 95 percent of Americans were farmers. Today, less than 2 percent of the population is engaged in farming. Farm exports accounted for 80 percent of U.S. exports during the decade after the Civil War, but this proportion had shrunk to 32 percent by 1932. In 1996, farm exports made up only 10 percent of the nation's exports, even though 50 percent of farm production is now exported. A recent slump in exports has occurred because of the terrorist attacks and fierce competition from other producer nations. Restaurant sales plummeted because of the slowdown in travel following September 11, so less food value was added to crops and meats grown for domestic use, thereby affecting the agribusiness economy.

Mechanization based on the gasoline engine began in earnest in the 1920s and accelerated after World War II, changing the character of farming operations. Farms became more mechanized for a variety of reasons. The rapid industrialization that developed to serve war needs and later to support European and Japanese reconstruction drew many rural people to urban jobs. Because there were fewer people to work on farms, the cost of labor increased. Massive black migration to the North during and following both world wars diminished the pool of labor in the rural South. Civil rights efforts eventually influenced the wage paid to the African Americans who picked southern cotton. Rather than pay the higher wage for hand picking, owners turned to cotton-picking machines. Throughout the 1960s and 1970s, technology continued to offer increased assistance through bigger tractors, more effective herbicides, or more productive hybrid seed, although farm policy provided the greatest push.

Ultimately, however, mechanization in any industry means that costs shift from labor to capital. Instead of paying wages to farm workers, farmers pay interest on loans for these technological advances or for more land. Consequently, money needed to be available for farmers to borrow at relatively low interest rates. A variety of economic conditions and government programs made this capital available.

The economic environment created by OPEC's decision to limit oil production in 1973 favored both expansion and mechanization. As mentioned earlier, higher oil prices ultimately increased the demand for nearly all natural resources. As the demand increased, prices for these commodities rose to all-time highs. Because the best way to profit from high prices was to acquire more land on which to grow more crops, more and more land was pressed into production. The price of land rose quickly. The real value of land, when controlled for inflation, nearly doubled during the 1970s. When the effects of inflation are added in, the price per acre nearly tripled during this same period (U.S. Department of Commerce 1986).

A number of factors affect a person's ability to borrow money. First, an applicant must have collateral, or equity—something the bank can keep if the applicant is later unable to repay the loan. For most farmers, equipment and land serve as collateral against loans. Second, interest rates must be low enough that the borrower can afford to pay them and still make enough to live on. Because interest rates typically reflect and affect the availability of money, an ample money supply will keep interest rates low. Third, using money to buy more land or equipment must appear to be more profitable than simply putting the money into savings.

Economic conditions during the 1970s encouraged farmers to borrow money. Land was rapidly increasing in value, giving farmers more equity in the land they already held. The shift to floating exchange rates and the devaluation of the dollar made U.S. products very competitive in world markets. Business was booming, and capital was readily available. Moreover, inflation was outstripping interest rates. If inflation averages 10 percent and interest rates are only 8 percent, it makes sense to buy land or equipment rather than to put money into a savings account. Land itself became an excellent investment and a hedge against inflation.

Actions taken in the late 1970s and early 1980s to control inflation and stimulate the domestic economy brought this expansion to an abrupt end. As real interest rates climbed and as the value of the dollar rose, those who had borrowed money found themselves paying more interest with increasingly scarce dollars. When commodities prices fell so dramatically, both crops and land lost much of their former value. Land prices dropped by more than 50 percent, reaching the point where farmers no longer had the equity to justify loans that were still outstanding. In short, a great many farmers faced financial ruin. By 1985, the number of farm foreclosures, forfeitures, or loan defaults reached levels not seen since the Great Depression.

Farmers were not bad managers, nor were banks greedy. Both applied tried-and-true investment principles to the economic environment created by the floating exchange rate and increased oil prices. Monetary and fiscal policies initiated by the federal government (decreasing taxes) and the Federal Reserve Board (cutting the money supply) simply changed that environment.

U.S. farmers now function in a changed economy. The increased worldwide production stimulated by the high commodities prices of the 1970s has flooded the market. The increase in inequalities, in part a result of the structural adjustment policies instituted by the Bretton Woods institutions (the World Bank and the International Monetary Fund [IMF]), has meant that the number of poor people unable to purchase adequate amounts of food has not diminished; rather, the number has grown. In an earlier day, the United States competed with Canada and Argentina in exporting wheat and with Argentina and Australia in exporting beef, for example. Today, U.S. farmers must compete with dozens of nations in nearly every agricultural export. Government willingness to fund programs to tide farmers over is likely to decrease in response to demands from other sectors for government funds. A farmer in Mississippi now competes with a car manufacturer in Japan as capital moves easily from one country to another. Finally, the worth of a farmer's produce has become as much a function of currency markets as it is of the inherent productivity of the farm operation.

Rural Manufacturing

Economic conditions that encouraged farmers to expand also stimulated the growth of rural manufacturing. In about 1960, relatively mature industries began looking to rural areas for cheaper land, an ample labor supply, and lower wage levels. This trend was bolstered by decisions to devalue the dollar and shift to a floating currency. The cheaper dollar made U.S. exports more competitive in world markets. The country's products also became more competitive within domestic markets because it was less costly to manufacture some products at home than to import them from Germany or Japan. The rapid increases in commodity prices that followed OPEC's decision to limit oil production put money in the hands of many developing nations. Their greater purchasing power further increased demand for U.S. products.

Growth in rural manufacturing employment continued during the 1970s, increasing at an annual rate of about 1.4 percent until 1976. By contrast, manufacturing employment in urban areas was declining at a rate of 1.1 percent per year. The availability of low-wage, hardworking, nonunionized rural labor forces attracted many light-manufacturing plants. Rural communities invested heavily in industrial parks and infrastructure developments designed to attract industry. Tax abatements, new-job tax credits, training programs, low-interest loans, and a host of local, state, and federal subsidies added more incentives for industry to move to rural areas. High demand, low wages, and inexpensive capital made it profitable for industries to relocate their more routine production activities to rural counties. By 1979, manufacturing had become the largest employer of the rural workforce.

Actions taken to control inflation and stimulate the domestic economy brought this expansion to a halt. Between 1979 and 1982, employment in rural manufacturing dropped 5.6 percent as nearly every state in the nation lost manufacturing jobs; recession hit the U.S. economy. As the 1980s progressed, the value of the dollar increased, and U.S. goods and services became more expensive on the world market. By the mid-1980s, rural areas found themselves in an entirely different economic environment. The strong U.S. dollar made it more difficult for the United States to compete on world markets. To maintain their profits, some companies felt it necessary to move their plants to the developing nations of Mexico, Thailand, and Bangladesh, where labor could be acquired more cheaply. The sustained economic growth of the 1990s resulted in a renewal of nonmetropolitan manufacturing growth, but the comparative advantage that rural areas had over metropolitan ones remained cheap labor.

As of this writing in 2003, experts believe that the U.S. economy will rebound, but layoffs because the recession worsened the shrinking in the numbers of rural manufacturing jobs. Only areas with defense contracting had stabilized (McKinnon and Sequeo 2003). In the past, rural areas have led the country out of recessions, but the movement that placed rural economies in a leadership role is not in place at the current time (Henderson 2002). Job cuts in the past few years have been much more severe, and the conditions needed for economic growth—stronger service-based activity and less severe manufacturing slowdown—are missing. Natural-resource based recreation areas are not drawing tourists, since people are cautious about spending their money on vacations; therefore, rural communities are losing money and losing jobs. Rural communities will need to find innovative ways to retain local manufacturing companies and to develop or attract flexible, high-end manufacturing firms. Perhaps e-commerce will help in this effort. Although migration to rural areas has been substantial, in the past decade, only 5.1 percent of immigrants are living in nonmetropolitan areas (Immigration Policy Reports 2001).

An International Labor Market

As discussed earlier, rural areas historically depended on immigrant labor. Immigration limits were not imposed until 1921. In the two decades after World War II, only a little more than 60 percent of the legal quota of immigrants entered the country. Labor was needed, however, as the economy expanded.

Permitting temporary immigration offered one solution to the problem, and this was provided through the Bracero Program, a series of bilateral agreements that temporarily admitted agricultural workers to the United States from Mexico, Barbados, Jamaica, and British Honduras. Migrant workers harvested fruits and vegetables, providing low-wage labor at crucial times in the production cycle. Illegal immigrants, those without any formal documentation, also began moving into both urban and rural areas.

As international capital flow increased, so did international immigration to the United States. Foreign-born residents accounted for only 4.7 percent of the U.S. population in 1970, the lowest proportion in the twentieth century. That percentage had more than doubled by 2000, to 10.4 percent. Compare that number with the high mark of 13.6 percent recorded in the 1900 census. Despite a temporary decline in illegal immigrants after the amnesty law of 1986, undocumented migration to this country is again high, with perhaps as many as 7 million undocumented immigrants in the United States on January 1, 2000 (Gamboa 2003). By the 1990s, immigrants, documented and undocumented, represented 13 percent of the U.S. labor force, two and a half times the proportion of the 1960s; more than one in four new workers was an immigrant.

Even with the clampdown after September 11, 2001, immigrant workers are still entering the United States. Many immigrants work in jobs that do not demand a lot of skill, jobs that native-born Americans scorn: as meatpackers, hotel maids, fast-food attendants, fruit and vegetable pickers, nursery and landscape workers, and construction workers. Many rural places in the United States could not survive without immigrant workers.

Agriculture in many parts of the United States has depended on migrant labor at planting, harvesting, and weeding time, but both service and manufacturing communities now increasingly employ immigrants also. Packing plants in the

Midwest, such as a plant in Garden City, Kansas, hire mostly Latinos and Southeast Asians, many of them women. In the small town of DePue, Illinois, manual farm-work is done mostly by Hispanic and Laotian immigrants. Workers can be found in mushroom farming, which includes picking mature mushrooms out of manure. These immigrant laborers show an immense work ethic, and they recognize that native-born Americans generally will not do the manual work, only the mecha-nized labor. A recent report revealed that there were more than 32,000 migrant farm workers in agriculture in Illinois, and local authorities were hoping that laws for immigration might become more liberal (Lydersen 2002). However, with the terrorist attacks and the resulting more-stringent immigration policies, it is un-likely that these migrant workers will receive an amnesty in the near future.

Imported labor will continue to be a feature of rural community life. Rural ar-eas have benefited from the immigration of medical doctors and nurses from de-veloping countries by gaining access to professional skills that have been lacking. The majority of the new arrivals to nonmetropolitan areas, however, have rela-tively few skills and limited education. As in DePue, they are viewed as hardwork-ing employees and thus are often favored over U.S.-born workers of equal skill levels; this keeps wages low among unskilled workers. In good times, immigrant labor helps rural areas deal with a labor deficit. In bad times, immigrants are seen as competing with native workers for jobs, and they present communities with a complex set of social problems. Indeed, the press has noted that the price of more open borders is being paid by those workers least able to afford it.

Long-Term Restructuring

Most experts now agree that the world economy has changed and that the U.S. economy is restructuring in response to these changes. Rural communities have become part of this transformation, and although they exert limited control over the nation's fiscal policies and even less control over what are now worldwide cap-ital markets, they can make intelligent choices. Those choices need to be based on a firm understanding of what drives the global economy. This section examines features of the new global economy and their implications for rural communities.

Features of the Changed Global Economy

The shift to floating exchange rates for currencies and the economic response to OPEC's actions in the early 1970s led to a series of features that now characterize the global economy. According to Peter Drucker (1986), these features are that (1) the industrial economy has become uncoupled from the primary-goods economy;

(2) production has become uncoupled from employment, and (3) the movement of capital has replaced trade as the driving force of the economy. An added feature that Drucker could not have yet realized is the effect of online purchases and e-commerce shipments on manufacturing businesses.

The first feature refers to the fact that manufacturing and other sectors of the economy no longer seem to change in response to prices for natural resources. In the past, the economic health of the industrial sector was linked to the economic health of the raw materials or natural-resources industries. Now U.S. industrial firms get fewer of their raw materials from U.S. sources and sell fewer of their products back to the producers of primary goods. In addition, the materials component of products has diminished as a proportion of the value of those products. This is obvious in the case of the miniaturization of computing that has occurred over the past two decades or so, but it is also true of automobiles, appliances, and other goods not generally considered high-tech. Our industrial economy appears to be functioning independently of our raw-materials economy.

The second feature of the changed world economy is that manufacturing production has become uncoupled from employment. Again, traditional models of the economy predicted that as manufacturing production and employment increased, so did manufacturing employment and wages. For example, when Henry Ford increased wages at the Ford plant, workers were able to buy more cars, thus increasing production. Expanding the industrial base of the economy created more manufacturing jobs.

The worker-to-market-to-manufacturer linkage has now changed. Manufacturing production in the United States increased by nearly 40 percent from 1973 to 1985, but manufacturing employment decreased over that same period. From 1970 to 2000, manufacturing employment dropped by 5 percent, and after the terrorist attacks, more layoffs occurred. Rural manufacturing jobs in 2001 were 5.5 percent below the previous year (Hendersen 2002). Paralleling the economic uncoupling of raw materials from industry, this uncoupling between production and employment results from both a decreased dependence on labor and a shift in the types of manufacturing producers. As an alternative to moving operations overseas to wherever labor costs are lower, industries are looking for ways to mechanize their operations and reduce labor needs. In addition, newer industries are more dependent on knowledge and information and consequently use less labor. The challenge for rural communities is to show that they can become knowledge centers and can provide amenities that will attract knowledgeable workers.

Production itself is growing more international. Capital-intensive parts can be made where capital is the cheapest, and parts can be assembled in countries having low labor costs. Workers also move to areas of potential labor demand, whether the work is in an assembly plant along the border at El Paso, Texas, or a meatpacking plant in rural Kansas.

Third, the movement of capital rather than the movement of goods and services drives the global economy. Traditional economics teaches that the relative value of goods and services is what determines exchange rates. Financial transactions once occurred as a function of trade. The growth of capital markets now means that most financial transactions occur independently of trade. These transactions are what determine exchange rates and hence the extent to which a nation's products are competitive on the world market.

Finally, *e-commerce*—business transactions made over the Internet—is affecting trade and manufacturing businesses. More and more businesses have decided that e-commerce is a successful way to buy and sell goods; in fact, the Internet has become a basic business component for most companies, in terms of selling and purchasing goods and services. Internet businesses that sell goods online employ 17 percent of manufacturing workers, but revenue grows significantly faster than employment. Businesses online either sell to the consumer directly or to other businesses, and both types of transactions are considered to be more efficient. Measuring e-commerce is difficult because of the rapidity of sales and business expansion that can occur on the Internet. For example, Amazon.com used to sell only books, but now they have an expansive range of products, including DVDs, CDs, toys, and other products. Increasingly, businesses have both online and "brick-and-mortar" stores, like Wal-Mart or Target. These stores actually compete against themselves for sales and product availability. E-commerce is a way to market to an immense audience of consumers.

In a physical, brick-and-mortar business, there are several layers of employees; likewise, there are layers of Web-related jobs within e-commerce. Internet businesses for large companies need Web consultants and designers as well as marketing managers for an online audience. Instead of depending on transportation and raw materials, e-commerce depends on high-speed networks and effective software that is easy for the consumer to navigate. Business-to-business e-commerce relationships have the most influence on the economy because the intermediary is eliminated, cutting costs for the consumers. The world economy has become dependent upon these relationships, which will have a large effect on business practices in the long term. E-commerce has and will continue to have an enormous presence in the global economy.

The Impact of Multilateral Trade Agreements on Rural Areas

Tariff reductions and present trade agreements make the effects of globalization on rural communities more immediate, contributing to greater volatility in prices for agricultural products and less certainty about the length of tenure of industries in rural areas. Sometimes it is difficult to separate the effects of trade agreements from those of exchange rates, privatization, removal of subsidies, and other aspects of neoliberal reforms that are sweeping the world.

It is important to examine the impact of the North American Free Trade Agreement (NAFTA) on rural communities, not only because NAFTA is important in its own right but also because it is a model for other such agreements that are being proposed, particularly the Free Trade Area of the Americas (FTAA) agreement. Box 9.2 discusses the effects, both good and bad, foreseen and unforeseen of NAFTA.

BOX 9.2 The North American Free Trade Agreement (NAFTA): Impacts on Rural Areas

Utilizing a carefully designed multisectoral model, the Economic Policy Institute calculated that nearly three-quarters of a million job opportunities—mainly for non–college educated factory workers—were lost from the United States to Mexico and Canada (mostly the former) during the first seven years of NAFTA. It is difficult to sort out what portion of those jobs left the United States because of a lowering of tariff barriers (which actually began several years before NAFTA; a bilateral agreement was signed between the United States and Mexico in 1989) and what portion left because during this period the U.S. dollar was strong. These currency shifts have contributed to a growing U.S. trade deficit with each of the other two North American countries. Because the U.S. dollar was one of the few currencies stronger than Mexico's peso, in 1999 the United States absorbed an astounding 96 percent of Mexico's exports! For the period 1993–2000, all fifty states and the District of Columbia experienced net job losses to our two neighbors.

One might think that at least the U.S. loss is a gain for our neighbors, but that would be an oversimplification. The movement of factories to Mexico did not simply involve firms taking advantage of the lower wage rate in that country. Instead, wages actually fell in Mexico during this period, and, as in the United States, on average workers shifted to economic activities that paid less than did their previous work. Between 1991 and 1998 there was a sharp decline in the proportion of the Mexican workforce that was salaried or received formal-sector wages (from 74 percent to 61 percent of the workforce) and a compensating growth in the self-employed and unpaid (mostly family labor) categories. Wages decreased by 27 percent, and labor income for the self-employed was cut in half in those seven years.

Continued on next page

The North American Free Trade Agreement (NAFTA): Impacts on Rural Areas (continued)

There was a substantial decline in the portion of this shrinking salaried and wage workforce that received benefits of any kind. A *maquiladora* is a factory or assembly point located in a free-trade zone that allows foreign firms to bring raw materials or components in duty free. Once the products are assembled, they can be exported duty free. The Rocky Shoes plant in the Dominican Republic is located in one of these free-trade zones. The "host" country cannot levy value-added or other taxes on them. *Maquiladora* firms, the sector with the greatest job growth, accounted for more than one-third of the new salaried and wage jobs created in Mexico between 1995 and 1999. In spite of the side agreements on labor and the environment that were added onto the NAFTA treaty, *maquiladora*s and other large firms (which are often foreign-owned) are very hostile to independent labor unions. U.S.-based nongovernmental organizations, including the United Electrical Workers Union, the National Labor Committee (see their Web page at http://www.nlcnet.org), and the Campaign for Labor Rights (see their Web page at www.campaignforlaborrights.org; accessed April 10, 2003), have collaborated with labor organizations in Mexico, Central America, and elsewhere to build support for unionization and to bring pressure (including consumer boycotts) against U.S.-based firms that subcontract with *maquiladora*s, particularly for apparel assembly. Mexican environmental laws, although very progressive, are rarely rigorously enforced. Thus, not only do the firms that have crossed the border take advantage of lax enforcement of environmental laws and low wages, but those wages have tended even lower. If the companies are in a free-trade zone, they do not have to worry about paying Mexican taxes.

NAFTA provided for a gradual reduction in tariffs on grains among the three countries. The most important grain grown and eaten by Mexicans is corn. Most peasant farmers grow corn either to feed their families, to sell to feed urban dwellers, or both. Before the 1990s, the Mexican government subsidized the price of corn to farmers. The state agency responsible for provisioning government food stores in low-income areas would buy corn from farmers at above-market prices and sell the cornmeal to working-class urban consumers at lower-than-market prices, absorbing the difference. Pressured by the IMF and the World Bank to eliminate subsidies and

Continued on next page

The North American Free Trade Agreement (NAFTA): Impacts on Rural Areas (continued)

needing government money to pay Mexico's growing international debt, the government disbanded its chain of retail food stores. Rather than waiting until 2009 to completely eliminate the tariffs on U.S. and Canadian grains as provided under NAFTA, the Mexican government telescoped the process into two-and-a-half years (Public Citizen 2001: 23). By 1997, as U.S. and Canadian grain flooded in, the market price of corn had for all practical purposes become the world market price rather than the price previously set by the Mexican government in provisioning its government stores. Although some observers argue that the poorest peasants were spared the shock of plummeting prices, much labor exited the grain sector. Many became workers in the irrigated export vegetable sector, providing fresh vegetables to U.S. consumers in competition with vegetable growers in California, Florida, and south Texas. The decline of labor in the grain-growing sector more or less matched the increase in labor in the vegetable sector. It is unclear what impact this shift had on poverty, but to make this shift, people became agricultural workers rather than their own bosses, and they had to migrate from impoverished labor-surplus areas in southern Mexico to the irrigated areas of Sonora and other northwestern states. This migratory stream was certainly not new, but it did expand. The attraction of much higher wages in the United States meant that growing numbers of workers, once uprooted from their home areas, opted to cross the border. Hence the growing number of Mexican immigrants—many undocu-mented—in the United States. NAFTA is silent on the free exchange of la-bor among its member countries, but it has strengthened economic condi-tions for de facto labor movement between Mexico and the United States.

So what is the overall picture? NAFTA and related *neoliberal policies* (which liberate private enterprise from government rules), have led to cheaper labor in all its member states by encouraging the flow of financial, built, and human capital among its member states.

In the United States, NAFTA has not fulfilled the promises of creating higher-quality jobs, given the trade deficit with our neighboring trading part-ners (and the rest of the world as well). The net effect has been a massive shift of workers with high school or less education from routine manufactur-ing to the service sector, where they invariably earn less and are less likely to have jobs with benefits. The new trade regimes, set by such international

Continued on next page

**The North American Free Trade Agreement (NAFTA):
Impacts on Rural Areas (continued)**

agreements as NAFTA and the World Trade Organization (WTO), have contributed to a steady decline in commodity prices (particularly of food and
feed grains), encouraging greater concentration in the food industry, rapid
increases in farm size, and continued industrialization of agriculture. In
Canada, industrialization of agriculture has similarly increased inequalities
among farmers and stretched the viability of many rural communities. The
same few firms that control marketing, processing, and export of agricultural products in the United States are also dominant in Canada.

The countervailing trends include a greater concern by consumers
about the origin and care of the food they eat. In addition, there are
prospects for using some of the tools of globalization to build multinational
social capital among organizations of environmental groups and trade
unions and for building alternative production, marketing, and processing
firms and organizations that are locally based but that can come together
when necessary to address international issues of mutual concern.

REFERENCES: Economic Policy Institute. 2001. "NAFTA at Seven: Its Impact on Workers in All Three Nations" (April). EPI Briefing Paper. 2001. Online; available: http://www.epinet.org/briefingpapers/nafta01/nafta-at-7.pdf;
accessed April 10, 2003.

Public Citizen 2001. "Down on the Farm: NAFTA's Seven-Years War on
Farmers and Ranchers in the U.S., Canada, and Mexico" (June). Public Citizen's Global Trade Watch. Online; available: http://www.citizen.org/docu-
ments/ACFF2.PDF; accessed April 10, 2003.

The World Trade Organization (WTO) is the only global international organization dealing with the rules of trade between nations. At its heart are the WTO
agreements, negotiated and signed by the bulk of the world's trading nations and
ratified in their parliaments. The goal of the WTO is to help producers of goods
and services, exporters, and importers conduct their business. The organization,
created by the Uruguay Round of trade negotiations, which lasted from 1986 to
1994, was formally established January 1, 1995. It is based in Geneva, Switzerland.
The WTO administers WTO trade agreements, serves as forum for trade negotiations, handles trade disputes, monitors national trade policies, and provides technical assistance and training for developing countries. Many groups take issue with
the WTO's authority to set and enforce universal rules of trade, although there are
special exceptions from the most stringent rules barring state support for exports

for developing countries. The rules are set on the basis of financial capital goals; many criticize the rules of trade because they do not allow countries to impose their own standards regarding human capital (no slave or child labor) or natural capital (green standards are not allowed). The WTO quite rightly says that its goal is to facilitate world trade, and that is what most alarms critics, who feel that world trade harms excluded people by further disadvantaging them through increased competition and lower prices for what they produce.

Rural Communities in the Global Economy

The changed global economy has a number of implications for rural communities, some of which have already become obvious. The collapse of commodities markets and the flight of manufacturing industries during the 1980s suggest that no single economic activity offers stability to rural communities. Urban areas were affected by these same changes; Pittsburgh, Pennsylvania, had the steel slump, and Detroit, Michigan, lost automobile manufacturing jobs. But because they typically have more diversified economies, cities and surrounding suburban areas are often better able to adapt to changes. Clearly, rural communities need to broaden their economic base as protection against the increased uncertainties created by the changing global economy.

Rural communities have to enter the digital economy if they want to interact in the global economy. For many remote areas, the physical barriers for phone lines and telecommunications services are inevitable. However, farmers and agribusinesses are already marketing agricultural products on the Internet. Fertilizer, chemicals, seeds, produce, equipment, and livestock are all advertised and sold online (Staihr 2000). Online transactions allow the consumers to arrange for shipping and the transfer of funds without personal contact, which is a growing business practice across the country. Rural businesses that do not participate in e-commerce run the risk of being thought outdated by consumers and other businesses. Experts see a need for rural businesses to catch up with the global economy if they do not participate in e-commerce now. However, personal communication and building social capital are still necessary components of business practices. Personal contact and e-commerce can work hand in glove.

Low-wage labor and natural resources, the traditional strengths of rural economies, today offer little advantage, unless the natural resources are sustained and enhanced to offer amenities. Most natural-resource-based industries, especially agricultural production, are experiencing increased competition internationally at a time when markets are already flooded. The flight of manufacturing jobs to developing nations and the importation of low-wage workers are phenomena that demonstrate that rural labor has been drawn into competition with labor in other countries. In Puerto Rico, the Economic Revitalization Act of 2001 has been embraced with bipartisan support. This act would work to eliminate any potential exploitation by large corporations and loss of jobs to other countries. In the previous five years, 27,000 jobs had been lost to other countries, such as China, Singapore, and Malaysia. And in any case, the overall decline in blue-collar jobs underscores the futility of capturing low-skill manufacturing industries. Although natural resources and light manufacturing will probably continue to be important contributors to rural economies, the character of these enterprises must change in response to the changed global economy.

The rate at which many natural resources are being depleted has become alarming. Communities relying on natural resources for their economic well-being are beginning to emphasize constructive measures for replenishing those resources. In 1991, the Chesapeake Bay oyster industry, for example, called for a three-year ban on oyster harvesting. The oyster beds, for centuries a source of food and income for Maryland communities around the bay, had been reduced to less than 1 percent of their estimated original stock. Without a complete ban on harvesting to allow the oyster population to reproduce, the entire economic role of the bay would be altered permanently. The preservation of oysters in the Chesapeake Bay area continues as aquatic reefs are being restored and created. This is a long-term project that planners hope will enhance oyster reproduction tenfold by 2010. People are beginning to acknowledge the need for economic practices that maintain rather than deplete finite resources. Choices, both private and public, are being made accordingly.

Natural-resource industries, including food producers, are beginning to expand into value-added activities or to look for market niches. Logging communities, for example, are adding small wood-manufacturing operations to existing milling facilities. This enables the community to capture the economic benefit of value-added activities as well as that realized from the extraction of natural resources. It also diversifies the local economy.

Other communities are beginning to make imaginative use of the resources at hand. After decades of trying to rid their fields of milkweed, some farmers in Ogallala, Nebraska, are now harvesting it. The pods are separated from the stalks, and the fibers within are extracted. This "Ogallala down," as it is called, is then used as filler for pillows, quilts, and other household products. These products are now being marketed and sold online by various bath and linen businesses, and they are high-priced items. Because Ogallala down is considered hypoallergenic, standard Ogallala down pillows are sold for almost $140.00 each online; comforters are sold for as much as $500.00. They have a large target audience because of the many consumers who suffer from allergies.

Local economic planning now takes place within a new context: constant change in a global economy. The world is becoming smaller; people are now global citizens. Cyclical trends in national and global economies affect the stability and growth of even the smallest, remotest rural community. At the same time, improved transportation and communication linkages have increased rural-urban connections, fostering regional and national economic integration. If local planning is to be successful, it must strengthen the international competitive position of local businesses and take advantage of the new opportunities for employment, marketing, tourism, and local cooperation.

Is It Progress?

E-commerce seems to be a necessary progression if rural businesses are to enter the world economy; however, the real concern surrounding Internet business is the availability, access, and resources needed to operate a business online. Additionally, events like those of September 11 that accentuate a recession are uncontrollable. Economic downturns do affect e-commerce, and people are less likely to buy online when money is tight.

E-commerce does have an advantage over Main Street merchants, in that it has been protected from taxation since 1998 by the Internet Tax Freedom Act. The Internet Tax Nondiscrimination Act of 2001 extended this moratorium on taxation, and the more goods are sold over the Internet, the more local communities are adversely affected. Main Street businesspersons argue that it is unfair that most e-tailers do not have to collect taxes while brick-and-mortar businesses do, when they are selling the same product (Glick and Grossfield 2001). Small brick-and-mortar business owners do not think e-tailers are reinvesting in the community as frequently, even though they use community infrastructure to "reap the benefits of doing business in local communities" (Glick and Grossfield 2001). Small brick-and-mortar businesses that do not participate in e-commerce have a difficult time competing with e-tailers, which can ultimately cripple local community businesses.

The larger issue that concerns many social scientists is the relationship between development and equality. Can the shift to a global economy lead to greater equality among people? One perspective, the modernization perspective, assumes that economic development leads to greater equality. Can rural businesses enter the global economy on an equal footing with other businesses because they are online? Is e-commerce necessary for businesses to be considered "modern"? Most experts agree that the Internet is becoming a basic component of all businesses. The digital divide must be closed if rural companies are to compete in a global economy.

A contrasting viewpoint argues that the global economy is reaffirming current inequality. Current economic conditions both increase the extent to which developing nations depend on developed nations and reinforce inequalities internal to each country. In the United States, for example, rural communities continue to have lower income levels and higher incidences of poverty than do urban areas, despite continued efforts in economic development. Other approaches include "clawback" provisions in agreements with newly recruited companies (which forgive taxes as a means of recruiting the companies) or the generation of locally owned businesses rather than the recruiting of outside ones. Locally owned firms, because of social ties, are more likely to take into account the interests of the community along with the bottom line.

Increasingly, sociologists are looking at the impact that investment and trade dependence have on indicators of quality of life: nutrition, health services, mortality, and education. Closing the gap in education and healthcare with digital capabilities is a way to alleviate the negative effects of remoteness, distance, and shifting demographics. Distance learning, which bridges educational gaps for adult learners, is available in rural communities. Telemedicine is an advance that allows rural physicians to teleconference with specialists. These advances in technology suggest that development, if defined as increased linkages to the world system, need not always increase inequality, particularly if that development is embedded in a policy framework that focuses on equal access.

Chapter Summary

Rural communities are being affected by worldwide economic restructuring. Historically, rural areas were linked to international markets by the natural resources they exported and the labor they imported. The character of these linkages has changed dramatically in recent decades. E-commerce has had a huge impact on global links.

Since the close of World War II, national economies have been moving toward integration into a global economy. The shift from a fixed exchange rate (the Bretton Woods Agreement) to a floating exchange rate (the Smithsonian Agreement) reduced controls on international currency. Capital now moves easily from one country to another. OPEC's decision to limit oil production in the early 1970s eventually led to increased production of commodities, drawing more competitors into international markets. Finally, steps taken to control inflation and stimulate the U.S. economy ultimately led to an economic recession worldwide. National economies are now linked to one another, digitally and physically. The events of September 11 have since limited and negatively affected international tourism, which has interrupted some of the cash flow between countries.

The events that signaled the transition to a global economy have had an impact on rural communities. The farm crisis was triggered in part by the same series of events. The expansion in commodities production created by OPEC's decision to limit oil production encouraged farm lending. Steps taken to control inflation and stimulate the local economy later made it impossible for those who had expanded their farm operations to service their debt load. Similar conditions encouraged manufacturing companies to move their operations to rural areas and then, more recently, to foreign countries. Imported labor has become a feature of rural community life.

Most experts now agree that the world economy has changed and that the U.S. economy is restructuring in response to these changes. Features of the new global economy are that (1) the industrial economy is less dependent on the natural-resource economy, (2) manufacturing production is less dependent on labor, (3) the movement of capital is the driving force in the world economy, and (4) the development of instantaneous communication among knowledge centers around the world and the development of e-commerce has allowed for the physical separation of production and marketing components, a separation that was impossible even as recently as the early 1990s. In this changed economic environment, rural communities need to diversify their economies, must be creative in locating market niches or finding new uses for existing resources, and need to develop regional, national, and international linkages that help local businesses remain competitive. Researching e-commerce and finding an online target audience is an important step in this process.

Key Terms

Commodities are natural resources or manufactured products bought or sold on markets.

Devaluation of a currency is a decrease in the value of that currency in relation to other country's currencies. Devaluation used to occur when the exchange rate changed in such a way that more gold was required to equal the same unit of currency; now it occurs when more of a particular currency must be used to buy other currencies.

E-commerce (electronic commerce) is business transactions made over the Internet.

The *exchange rate* is the amount of one currency needed to purchase another currency. Exchange rates vary from source to source for commercial reasons. Banks, credit card companies, and other providers of exchange-rates information will likely differ from the rates provided by the Federal Reserve Bank. When an exchange rate is high, imports are cheap, and a country's exports are less competitive on the world market. When an exchange rate is low, imports become expensive, and it is easier to sell products on the world market. Exchange rates are increasingly determined by market mechanisms—supply and demand—although governments often intervene by either buying or selling their own currency when they see their currency changing in value.

Fixed exchange rates establish a fixed standard against which one currency can be exchanged with another. The Bretton Woods Agreement fixed the price of the U.S. dollar relative to gold.

Floating exchange rates allow the value of one currency to change relative to another in response to the demand for and the availability of currencies.

Inflation occurs when the currency in circulation or the availability of credit increases, leading to a sharp rise in prices.

Neoliberal policies liberate private enterprise from government rules, including favoring international trade and investment through free movement of capital, goods, and services, weakening the power of organized labor, cutting public expenditure for social services like education, health care, and welfare for the poor, deregulation, privatization of services previously provided by the government, such as prisons, social security, and the welfare system, and focus on individual responsibility rather than the public good. Powerful financial institutions, such as the International Monetary Fund (IMF), the World Bank, and the Inter-American Development Bank, as well as the U.S. government, demand the implementation of these policies as a condition for receiving international financial assistance.

A *recession* is typically defined as an overall slowing of economic activity. Since there are many measures of economic activity as well as what constitutes a "slowing," there can be many definitions of what exactly constitutes a recession. The National Bureau of Economic Research, a nonprofit organization that assigns dates to the beginning and end of downturns, defines a recession as "a period of declining output and employment."

References

Adame, Vicki. 2002. "Immigration Anxieties: Changes in Immigration Law Meet with Concern as Well as Understanding" (September 11) *Tri-City Herald:* Columbia, Washington.

Associated Press. 2002. "Cheaper Labor Moves Rocky Shoes Production to Puerto Rico." *Cincinnati Enquirer,* April 29, 2002. Also online; available: http://enquirer.com/editions/2002/04/29/fin_cheaper_labor_moves.html; accessed February 3, 2003.

Bornschier, Volker, and Christopher Chase-Dunn. 1985. *Transnational Corporations and Underdevelopment.* New York: Praeger.

Chase-Dunn, Christopher. 1989. *Global Formation: Structures of the World Economy.* Oxford: Basil Blackwell.

Drucker, Peter. 1986. "The Changed World Economy." *Foreign Affairs* 64:768–791.

Ford, Peter. 2002. "Europe Hit by the Fall of the Dollar" (July 18). *Christian Science Monitor.* Online; available: www.csmonitor.com/2002/0718/p01s03-woeu.html; accessed November 11, 2002.

Gamboa, Suzanne. 2003. "INS counts 7 million immigrants living in the U.S. illegally" (January 31). San Diego Union-Tribune. Online; available: http://www.

signonsandiego.com/news/mexico/20030131-1237-illegalimmigrants.html; accessed May 15, 2003.

Glick, Gary, and Scott Grossfield. 2001. "Who's Plugging the E-Sales Tax Leak?" Online; available: http://www.ccnlaw.com/Articles/sales_tax.html; accessed December 5, 2002.

Henderson, Jason R. 2002. "Will the Rural Economy Rebound with the Rest of the Nation?" *The Main Street Economist.* Kansas City, Mo.: Center for the Study of Rural America.

Immigration Policy Reports. 2001. "U.S. Benefits from Foreign-Born." Online: available: http://www.ailf.org/ipc/policy_reports_2001_benefit.asp; accessed May 15, 2003.

Kowalczyk, Nick. 2001. Part 1: "Rocky Shoes and Boots: A Historical Profile"; part 2: "Shoemaker Fulfills Dream, Revitalizes Company"; part 3: "Rocky Boots Historical Profile"; and part 4: "Rocky Boots Historical Profile." *Post* (Ohio University, Athens, Ohio), January 30, 31, and February 1, 2. Also online; available: http://thepost.baker.ohiou.edu/archives3/jan01/013101/today.html; accessed February 3, 2003.

Lydersen, Kari. 2002. "On the Farm, an Immigrant's Work Is Never Done" (7 October). Alternet.org. Online; available: http://www.alternet.org/story.html? StoryID=14240; accessed November 13, 2002.

National Resources Conservation Service (NRCS). 2002. *Farm Bill 2002: Conservation Provisions Overview.* Washington, D.C.: USDA. Online; available: http://www.nrcs.usda.gov/programs/farmbill/2002/pdf/ConsProv.pdf.

Ohio University Telecommunications Center. 2002. *Rural Communities Legacy and Change: Think Globally.* Part 6 of a 12-part video series, directed by Keith Newman and Gary Mills. Annenberg/CPB Collection, 58 minutes. (Includes an approximately twenty-minute segment on the William Brooks Shoe Company.)

Rural Coalition. 2002. "Campaign for a Just Food and Farm Policy." Online; available: http://www.ruralco.org/html2/farmbillreport.html; accessed December 5, 2002.

Staihr, Brian. 2000. "Rural America's Stake in the Digital Economy." *The Main Street Economist.* Kansas City, MO: Center for the Study of Rural America.

U.S. Department of Commerce. 1986. *Statistical Abstract of the United States.* Washington, D.C.: Bureau of the Census.

Wallerstein, Immanuel. 1983. *Historical Capitalism.* London: Verso.

Wimberley, Dale. 1990. "Investment Dependence and Alternative Explanations of Third World Mortality: A Cross-National Study." *American Sociological Review* 55:75–91.

_____. 1991. "Transnational Corporate Investment and Food Consumption in the Third World: A Cross-National Analysis." *Rural Sociology* 56:406–431.

10

Consumption
in Rural America

It is almost 6:00 P.M. as the Archer family settles into the Tuesday evening meal. They live in a rural community about sixty miles from a metropolitan area. Susan Archer produces small metal parts for automobile air conditioners at the local manufacturing plant. Her shift began at 7:00 A.M. and ended at 4:30 P.M. Her husband, Dan, just came in from his job as an auto mechanic at a local car dealership. They and their three children crowd around the Formica table where Jill, age six, says grace. Susan sets on the table a large bowl of fresh salad greens that she washed and topped with a brand-name dressing that was on sale. The evening meal and the conversation begin in earnest.

Eric, thirteen years old, opens the conversation with a plea for some new sneakers. He is trying out for the middle-school basketball team and asserts that he needs a particular pair, a brand-name shoe endorsed by a professional basketball star. Dan grouses at this request, "Jeez, Eric, those shoes cost a bundle, and they aren't any better than a pair that's half that price. Besides, you'll grow out of them by spring." Eric is visibly upset and begins listing the shoe's features, adding, "And the other guys have already bought theirs!"

Susan finally intervenes on Dan's behalf. She points out that the pair Eric wants is equivalent to about twenty hours of her take-home pay. She then suggests that the family will pay for part of the expensive department-store shoes if Eric pays the rest with his wages from his part-time job with a neighbor, who has a dog-grooming business at home. Eric quickly calculates the difference and estimates that the shoes will cost him about eight weeks' work. A deal is struck.

Dan is curious about where Eric is going to go to buy these sneakers because none of the local merchants carry the expensive brand. Eric smiles and says he can get them on the Internet, which he can access at the public library, if his parents will let him use their credit card. He knows they only have it for emergencies, but he figures this may qualify as one. His parents disagree, saying that they will not use their credit card to buy shoes for growing feet. Eric mentions that they are sold at the Central City Mall, about an hour's drive away. Susan asks him how he will get there and who will take him. After a brief silence, Eric says he'll buy them on the next trip the family makes there. He can wait; they usually go to Central City about every fourth weekend. Susan nods quietly as she glances at Dan.

There is an insistent ding from the microwave oven. The main course is ready. Susan gets up and pulls out a large frozen-food package consisting of turkey and gravy. The peas, also from the freezer, are already on the table. Then she scrapes the instant rice out of a pot on the stove into a bowl that she also sets on the table. She puts the pot in the sink to wash after dinner, which she will do with water from their well.

Eric's plea for new shoes seems to have reached a compromise, so Jake, ten years old, makes his pitch to get his ear pierced when they make their trip to the mall. He says that the guys on MTV sport lots of earrings in each ear, but he is willing to settle for just one. Dan's head jerks up in shock and he chokes on his turkey as he nearly shouts, "No son of mine is going to wear an earring!" Jake sighs, rolling his eyes. He knows fashion. It is clear to him his family will do anything to keep him from demonstrating his sense of style to his friends. His cousin, who is the same age and lives in Los Angeles, tells him that all the guys in Los Angeles have at least one earring. It takes fads forever to reach Jake's town.

After cleaning up the dishes, Jake takes the day's trash out to the garbage can and then takes the can to the road for the Wednesday-morning pickup. The two bags join others full of discarded aluminum foil, newspapers, jars, and plastic containers. None of the garbage is sorted for recycling, for the town of 2,000 has no recycling program. The garbage will end up in a landfill about five miles away.

★   ★   ★

What a difference from a hundred years ago! The majority of rural North American and western European "consumers" in 1900 either grew their own food or purchased it raw and unprocessed. The homemaker cooked over a wood-burning stove in a house with no indoor plumbing, no mechanical refrigeration or freezing, and no electricity. Centuries-old procedures for food preservation were commonly used: drying, salting, smoking, or storage in root cellars. Up to 50 percent of a household's disposable income and an equal proportion of a household's labor were needed simply to eat. Moreover, the common diet was extremely unhealthy, with an excess of salt and fat and a lack of fresh fruits and vegetables (Cotterill 2001).

What we buy and consume has changed as dramatically as the way in which goods and services are produced. Most people are disconnected from the production of what they consume; even most farmers do not directly consume what they produce. We are capable of sustaining healthier diets for a smaller proportion of our disposable income. More items that once were produced at home are now available for purchase: bread, clothing, suntans, and fingernails. We often work in buildings with windows that do not open, process enormous amounts of information on personal computers, and on our computer, access weather information that is based on satellite pictures only minutes old. Most people drive automobiles and rely on in-home, high-tech sound equipment, video recorders, television, compact disk players and recorders, and Web-available music for entertainment. Rural grandparents in the Midwest receive photo images or live video pictures of their grandchildren in Dallas, Texas. Our current consumption habits were not even imaginable just a few years ago.

Consumption has many faces: inputs used for production, needs for day-to-day living, preferences for leisure time, and confirmation of personal identity. As the Archer family illustrates, consumption starts with inputs and ends with landfills, both of which are important to rural communities. This chapter explores various consumption patterns of rural residents and how and why consumption patterns have changed in rural areas.

Why Is Consumption Important?

In 1899, sociologist Thorstein Veblen coined the term "conspicuous consumption." Veblen used this term to characterize the habits of middle- and upper-class individuals who achieved their identity and prestige by what they consumed rather than by what they produced or by the nature of their character. At the time of his writing, such consumption was relatively new. Rich people have always consumed more than poor people, but they tended to limit the visibility of their greater wealth to their own circles. This was partially out of fears of mass uprisings in the face of large inequalities. In some rural areas in the twenty-first century, particularly the Northeast and the Midwest, wealthy people conceal their affluence, driving modest cars and wearing ordinary clothes and jewelry.

Fifty years ago, it was fairly easy to distinguish rural residents from urban ones. Rural residents, particularly those who lived on farms, tended to wear homemade clothes and eat food they produced and processed themselves. Urban residents bought their food and clothing at the store. Urban residents were consumers; rural residents were producers. But by the turn of the twenty-first century, consumption patterns no longer easily distinguished urban from rural residents, although rural residents dress more conservatively and are more cautious in trying new things.

Where we consume, what we consume, and why we consume certain types of commodities and services shape the quality of our lives. Our consumption affects the natural environment as well as our relationships with others.

Societal Trends Related to Increased Consumption

In the United States and Canada, as in other developed nations, most people consume more things than ever before. Economic expansion and the rise in real wages after World War II meant that more and more Americans could afford to buy a wider variety of goods. Increased demand meant increased production, and more companies entered the market, seeking to differentiate themselves from other producers by more than price. Henry Ford's dictum about the Model A—that the consuming public can have cars any color they want as long as it is black—became a thing of the past. By the year 2001, car buyers could choose between internal combustion engines and hybrid cars that linked those engines with electric motors. Color, style, and source of energy became ways of differentiating products and their consumers. The development of commercial television in the 1950s allowed producers to shape but not dictate consumer tastes. Cable television added to this by targeting specific populations and increasing product differentiation, thereby furthering the tendency to base personal or collective identities on what is consumed.

Our consumption patterns have also changed with the transformation of the labor force. As women entered the labor force in greater numbers after World War II, precooked frozen food became more readily available. By the end of the twentieth century, prepackaged salads, precut vegetables and meats for stir fry, and a variety of precooked roasts and ribs were on the shelves of many rural supermarkets. Deli sandwiches, pizza, and hot dogs are available at every convenience store, even in rural areas. Time once spent preparing food has been given over to other work around the house and to leisure. Even in rural areas, carryout meals and fast-food restaurants are growing more popular as working men and women grab a double cheeseburger with large fries rather than pack a lunch. But increasing income inequality means that many in rural areas must choose carefully what they consume, making hard choices between fixing the car to get to work and paying the electricity bill. It may be easier to buy fast food instead of preparing a home-cooked meal, but it is not always the most economical. Money spent on cheeseburgers over the course of a month can add up to a staggering amount, which decreases money needed for paying the household bills.

Janice, age forty-five, lives in a small rural remote town in Kentucky with her husband and sixteen-year-old daughter. Janice is a childcare worker for neighbors' children and receives no compensation. Her husband works for the sanitation department, only making $6.10 an hour. They are not eligible for welfare, and their struggle to survive is immense. Each month, paying the bills causes Janice to have anxiety attacks. She often has to choose between paying part of the electric bill or buying groceries. Consumption in Janice's household is minimal, for basic needs are barely being met (case study from *America's Forgotten Children* 2002).

In the last quarter of the twentieth century, new methods of production and distribution increased the variety of products we could consume. Flexible production, made possible because of the use of computers in operating machine tools, managing inventories, and scheduling transportation, has replaced mass production. The global economy makes it possible to produce clothing in

Malaysia that will be available across the United States at the same time and for the same price.

These and other changes have had a direct impact on consumption patterns in both rural and urban areas. Although a number of economic and social forces have contributed to this change, four phenomena have had extremely significant impacts on rural consumption patterns. All are nationwide trends, but they affect rural communities differently from urban areas:

- Consolidation of retail and service enterprises
- Changes in the structure of the labor force
- Targeted marketing to segmented markets
- Increased income inequality

Consolidation

Why do businesses consolidate? Why do services become regional rather than remain local? One explanation given for centralization is provided by the *central-place theory*, which proposes that population centers, whether small crossroads communities or large cities, are geographically organized into hierarchical retail and public-service markets. Moreover, according to the theory, any particular hierarchy of places reflects a division of labor such that the larger places possess greater economic diversity of products and services for consumption than do smaller places. Correspondingly, the smallest places offer the fewest commodities and services. Thus, there is a system of nested markets.

Perhaps no other aspect of changing consumption patterns is more symbolic of rural social change over the past four decades than the loss of Main Street businesses. The Archer family's trips to Central City Mall are typical of the changing consumption pattern of rural families. This section explores the consolidation of rural businesses, factors that explain why consolidation occurs, and the impact that consolidation is having on rural social services.

Business and Social Service Consolidation

When the railroads pushed across the country, they facilitated mail-order buying, which led consumers to bypass local merchants who could neither provide the wide variety of products nor take advantage of the quantity wholesale discounts available to the mail-order firms. What was true then continues to be true today. Across most retail trade, rural businesses find it difficult to offer the variety available in large central markets, such as urban malls or on the Internet. This has meant a loss in business for local merchants and a decline of revenue for many local governments.

Consolidation has occurred across both the business and social-service communities. Many locally owned stores have disappeared or been bought out by larger retail chains; department stores have either closed or moved into suburban malls, leaving empty buildings on Main Street. Locally owned banks are now members of regional consortiums or have been taken over by large regional banks. Local businesses and services have consolidated at different times and in different ways.

Some small businesses have been replaced by nationally based chain stores. Mom-and-pop stores became franchises that later became national chains, especially in the hardware and automotive businesses. Family-owned and -operated firms were first replaced by franchises such as Western Auto, Gambles, and the like. The franchises are now fighting a losing battle with Wal-Mart and Target, national firms that have incorporated hardware and automotive sections into their diversified merchandising stores. In the grocery business, local groceries and markets were replaced by regional chains, which were then bought out by chains that are national and international in scope. For example, Dillons stores, a regional chain based in Wichita, Kansas, purchased small markets. Kroger, a national chain, eventually purchased Dillons stores.

In contrast, franchise convenience stores/gas stations occupy an important niche. Their comparative advantage is convenience, not price. Consequently, their location is more important than the price they are able to charge. Because economies of scale are not a driving force in their marketing, the parent firm has no advantage in directly managing individual outlets.

This transformation in retail trade is characterized both by a decline in the number of retail merchandising and service enterprises in smaller communities and by the introduction of firms that are national in scope, often in regional trade centers. This pattern is illustrated by comparing Iowa communities influenced by Wal-Mart to similar-sized communities not affected by Wal-Mart. Kenneth Stone (1995) found that the introduction of a Wal-Mart store in ten small trade centers with a population of 3,000 and above resulted in a slightly greater increase in retail trade in those communities compared to the state as a whole. However, smaller towns within a twenty-mile radius of trade centers that had acquired a Wal-Mart within the previous three years showed a greater decline in retail sales than did comparable-sized communities within twenty miles of trade centers without Wal-Marts. Wal-Marts draw business into the regional center, decreasing retail sales in surrounding small towns.

The public sector has also responded to the need to maximize scarce revenue resources. Health, fire, police, public education, and other community services continue to undergo consolidation as rural areas address the increasing quality of service expected and their accompanying expenses. As in the retail sector, rural community health services have found central trade centers siphoning off business that once supported local hospitals. The map in Box 10.1 shows the large number of rural counties served by fewer than three banking firms in 1996, and that number of counties has grown since then. Rural hospitals have closed for a number of reasons. Medicare reimbursement policies pay rural hospitals less than urban hospitals to treat the same medical conditions; the result is lower revenues. Additionally, they are unable to purchase expensive medical technologies or attract trained healthcare specialists. Consolidation in rural areas seems inevitable across all sectors of business and service.

Furthermore, the notion that larger, consolidated schools increase the quality of education in the information age, when advanced courses can be delivered via distance education, has been challenged by research showing that small schools had higher levels of achievement and that more students finished school in smaller schools, although this varies by region. Better student attitudes about themselves and others and higher extracurricular involvement are two aspects of small schools that continue to differentiate rural schools from urban ones. Retaining small schools has a positive impact on rural communities (Lawrence, et al. 2002).

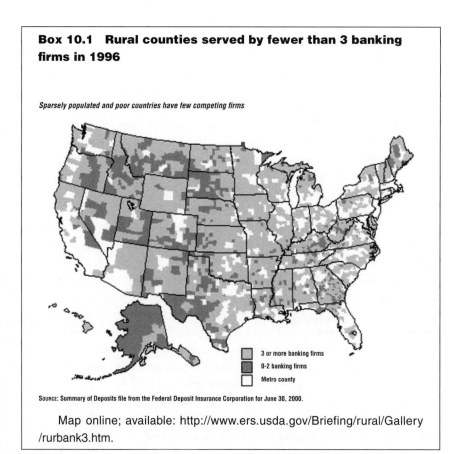

Box 10.1   Rural counties served by fewer than 3 banking firms in 1996

Sparsely populated and poor countries have few competing firms

3 or more banking firms
0-2 banking firms
Metro county

SOURCE: Summary of Deposits file from the Federal Deposit Insurance Corporation for June 30, 2000.

Map online; available: http://www.ers.usda.gov/Briefing/rural/Gallery /rurbank3.htm.

The food industry is increasingly concentrated. Not only do a few transnational firms dominate retail grocery stores, but concentration in the fast-food industry is also increasing at the same rate as fast-food outlets. In 1992, the four
largest firms in the industry (McDonald's; Yum!Brands, Inc., which owns the Taco
Bell, KFC, and Pizza Hut brand names; Burger King; and Wendy's) only controlled
about 11.9 percent of total fast-food sales. By 1997, they accounted for more than
48 percent of the fast-food sales category. The 2002 census of commerce and industry will undoubtedly show that concentration increasing.

Another factor favoring consolidation is *economies of scale*. Such economies occur when a greater volume of business can occur at one particular site, since volume is a way to spread fixed costs (of transportation, land and buildings, equipment, labor) over a larger number of products. Distance and low population in the
market area make it difficult for rural businesses to take advantage of economies of
scale. Thus, central-place theory suggests that there is a constant pressure to cen-
tralize economic activities in larger places.

The theory does not explain when and why consolidation occurs in a particular
sector. Other factors, such as the opportunity to generate profit based on favorable
macroeconomic trends, tax policies, capital availability, and organizational innovation, help explain why centralization occurs at a specific time in a specific industry.
In retail trade, enterprises tend to spill over into rural areas when several elements
are in place. New, more efficient forms of economic organization that are already
fine-tuned in urban areas are introduced in rural areas when they appear to have
promise for profit there. Centralization also occurs when capital is abundant and
the marginal advantage offered by increased urban investment is no greater than
what rural areas provide or when the cost of labor becomes critical and the cheap
labor available in rural areas is central to profitability or the accumulation of wealth.

Retail grocery chains moved into rural areas in the 1960s, after they had already organized the grocery business in urban areas. Grocery chains developed a
transportation system that was sufficiently well organized to enable them to move
perishables from warm-climate areas to regions lacking year-round growing seasons. When rural consumers acquired incomes large enough to demand vegetables
and fruits year-round, that organization could be matched to new markets, and
chains began appearing in rural communities. However, by 2000, grocery stores
were leaving small towns as it became more and more expensive to be supplied by
national distributors, who prefer more densely populated distribution routes. Driving sixty miles for one small store does not fit into their profit plan. The transaction costs of distribution have become critical for retailers. The integrated chains
that most reduce them are poised to make the greatest profit.

Wal-Mart was a pioneer in bringing retail discount general-merchandising
stores to rural areas because it organized itself economically to support volume
sales by attracting rural customers over a wide geographic area through excellent

record keeping and stock management. Furthermore, as their volume grew, they negotiated with suppliers to wait longer periods between delivery and payment, something that disadvantaged small suppliers with limited credit. Wal-Mart was able to offer lower prices and more diverse stock than the mom-and-pop stores, which paid in cash for their stock, and the more specialized franchises that preceded them. Improved transportation, of course, enabled them to draw consumers from a larger region. Strategic site selection coupled with careful inventory control and organization of labor enabled them to be profitable. In general, Wal-Mart stores maintain less inventory and use more part-time workers than do traditional retailers. They also do not allow labor unions, do not pay suppliers until an item is sold, and use part-time workers, who receive fewer benefits (see the discussion of the impact of Wal-Mart in Box 10.2).

This progression from mom-and-pop stores to franchises to the "Wal-Marting" of rural America has multiple impacts. Small, family-owned stores had a limited variety of goods, purchased only occasional display advertisements in the local newspaper announcing a sale, and generally used family labor. When they did hire, these businesses paid low wages to employees who often worked only part-time. In general, their inventory and sales were not organized as efficiently as in the chain stores. Mom-and-pop stores generally had higher prices than either the franchises or the nationally based discount stores that replaced them, mainly because their low volume required substantial markups, and they could not take advantage of volume buying. These locally owned businesses provided a more personal atmosphere for customers, especially those who came from a similar social class as the proprietors. They also offered expertise about the features of competing products, provided repair services, and made it easy to find what one needed.

BOX 10.2 The Wal-Marting of Rural America: Who Wins and Who Loses?

Wal-Mart has affected several small towns since it first opened in the 1960s, and the opening of each new Wal-Mart store has been met with mixed reactions: resistance because of the loss of businesses and excitement for job opportunities. Many groups have retaliated against the opening of a Wal-Mart near their small towns by petitioning and using town zoning rules to make it impossible for Wal-Mart to enter the surrounding area. However, there are definitely numerous sides to the issue of Wal-Mart's force. Because it offers a variety of goods for low prices, many small-town businesses

Continued on next page

The Wal-Marting of Rural America: Who Wins and Who Loses? (continued)

have had to close their doors, but Wal-Mart also provides a large number of jobs for people who need them. For example, in Donaldsonville, Louisiana, a small town on the Mississippi River, arguments over Wal-Mart arose when it proposed moving into town. People who owned small businesses in town felt that a Wal-Mart would wipe out their business, and when they heard that one might be opening outside of town, they panicked. Shop owners closed their businesses without even waiting to see if they would be affected; their theory was that they should "get out while the getting's good" (Ortega 1998). Several other small businesses ended up closing their doors as well. However, the other side of this debate was led by a large population of poorer black residents, who saw Wal-Mart as an opportunity for jobs and cheaper goods. They argued that the rich white business owners feared honest competition. After several debates that ended before the state board commission, Wal-Mart opened a 45,000-square-foot store (Ortega 1998).

Donaldsonville's story is one of the earliest stories of objections to Wal-Mart, and as Ken Stone found, there are countless across the country. In June 2002, Asheville, North Carolina, protested the building of a Super Wal-Mart, which carries groceries in addition to its other retail items. Supercenters have been voted down twice in Asheville because residents think that they will destroy the character of their town. A grassroots organization, Community Supported Development, even handed out fliers and buttons that said "Say No to Super Wal-Mart!" (Williams 2002). Yet there is another side to the debate: Several residents would welcome Wal-Mart because it offers jobs and would clean up a dilapidated area in Asheville. The two sides have significant arguments, but the real debate seems to be over change in consumption patterns. What do you think about the Wal-Mart debate?

REFERENCES: Bob Ortega. 1998. *In Sam We Trust.* New York: Random House.

Melissa Williams. 2002. "Wal-Mart Battle Moves to Asheville City Council" (June 23). *Citizen Times.* Online; available: http://cgi.citizen-times.com/cgi-bin/story/news/15251; accessed April 17, 2003.

Retail franchises had features of both a family firm and a national chain. They offered variety in their inventory and some of the same friendly helpfulness, although they often hired clerks who knew little about the products. They were able to use national advertising and had frequent sales. Their regular prices, how-ever, were not discount prices.

National merchandising firms offer "everyday low prices" but provide little in the way of customer service. For those who define shopping as recreation and for poor people and minorities, who risked unfriendly treatment by the proprietors of family firms, these changes have been acceptable. Others view the reduction in the number of clerks, the use of part-time labor, and the resulting lack of personal service as problematic.

Changes in the Labor Force

Changes in the rural labor force have followed national trends since the end of World War II. Among these, two have had important consequences for consumption patterns of rural people: the entry of women into the nonfarm labor force and the growth of the service sector.

Entry of Women into Nonfarm Labor Force

It now takes more than one income earner in a household to make what one alone could earn in the 1960s. Reduced earning power has led to the entry of more women into the labor force. The increased proportion of women working outside the home has meant that less time is available for the household chores they have traditionally performed, such as food preparation and preservation, the making and maintenance of clothing, housecleaning, and child supervision. That has contributed to an expansion of the service sector and increased the amount of money a household needs to have.

The Archer family is a typical American family for the current time. Both par-ents work. This puts a strain on both spouses in fulfilling traditional role expecta-tions, but it is particularly stressful for women. Women may have entered the workplace, but there is little evidence that they have transferred some of their tra-ditional caretaker roles to other members of the family. Women are still the pri-mary caregivers; they continue to prepare meals, take care of the laundry, and look after the children. For women who are single heads of households, especially women in or near poverty, the burden of being both wage earner and caregiver can be a tremendous source of stress. In order to cope with their increased time in the workplace while continuing to shoulder their traditional caregiving roles, women have changed their consumption patterns. Evidence of this is the growth of convenience foods and the popularity of microwave ovens, as can be attested to by Susan Archer.

In rural areas, lack of childcare has put a special burden on female-headed families, who are an increasing proportion of the rural population and are much more likely to be living in poverty.

Growth of the Service Sector

The service sector has grown because service activities previously performed within firms, farms, and households are now acquired in the market. Consolidation has supported the growth of the service sector because as farms and rural businesses consolidate into large enterprises, the workload is no longer manageable within the family unit. These enterprises now purchase goods and services that they once produced themselves because of their growing specialization. Outsourcing by firms decreases their costs in infrastructure, labor, and benefits and pushes the risk onto the suppliers of both goods and services.

In earlier times, farm women would prepare and take lunch to the field. Now it is much more likely that one spouse or the other will have an off-farm job and that prepared meals will be purchased for whoever operates the farm machinery. In addition, if the family has small children, childcare will become a commodity part of the time; in earlier times, it was handled entirely within the family. Also, since today's farmer is unlikely to obtain the training necessary to apply lethal chemicals, which is now required by law, the application of pesticides to crops may be contracted out to a firm that is licensed to apply them.

At one time, the wife kept the books of the family farm or business, whereas now bills and receipts may be sent to an accounting firm and sent back in the form of a computerized monthly balance sheet. If the family business has grown large enough, a full-time bookkeeper is hired. In either case, a price has been placed on the cost of keeping accounts, making this activity a commodity.

Both adult members of a family hold multiple jobs in rural areas. Teenagers, too, often have jobs, thereby modifying family consumption patterns. Leisure time, an objective of these efforts to maintain or increase family income, ironically becomes scarcer. When young people increasingly work more hours, there is a resulting reduction in their effective consumption of education and extracurricular activities.

In summary, the increases in the number of jobholders per family and the growth of the service sector of the economy have influenced household consumption patterns. Families have substituted prepared foods and fast-cooking technologies, particularly microwave ovens, for the time once spent preserving and preparing food from scratch. Expansion of the service sector has led to the sale of highly processed food rather than the sale of the raw ingredients once taken home for final preparation. The vast expansion of fast-food franchises, salad bars, and delis in grocery stores illustrates how important service has become.

Targeted Advertising
and Segmented Markets

Radio has long targeted its advertising to its desired listener. Rural radio stations in farm country followed daily commodity price information with advertisements for agricultural inputs.

Television and now the Internet have become powerful tools for marketing products. During the early days, advertising was directed at as broad an audience as possible. Advertising became a powerful influence on the consumption patterns of people, rural and urban alike. The introduction of cable television and the rapid proliferation of highly specialized channels now enable advertisers to use this tool to reach very specific audiences. For example, MTV and VH1 video television networks can be considered as continuous advertising that is targeted to very specific groups. The Web pages entered by a computer are tracked through "cookies," and this tracking allows advertising related to one's past behavior to jump onto the screen. When entering the pages of an Internet bookseller, you are immediately informed of purchases made by consumers whose tastes are similar to your own. In this sense, markets have become segmented. Consumption patterns now reflect both mass advertising and the introduction of segmented markets. These two trends have affected those least prepared to deal with increased consumption, the poor.

Targeted Advertising

The Archer family conversation over shoes and body piercing is one repeated among both rural and urban families. Decisions on what is consumed have moved beyond mere functional necessity. Eric Archer's willingness to spend allowance money on a pair of sneakers that he will probably outgrow in a short time is not driven by a rational comparison of competing brands. Rather, his decision is based on the social acceptance he gains by consuming the more expensive pair of sneakers. The disparity in the quality of the merchandise is probably not great enough to account for the significant difference in price. However, the status he acquires from consuming a particular style of shoe has implications at school or when hanging out with peers. Such status is often assigned meaning through mass media advertising and product placement in movies and television shows that are specifically aimed at young males.

Since World War II, the use of multiple media to advertise commodities has expanded. Some observers suggest that the introduction of mass advertising was a calculated response to lagging consumption. Instead of responding to consumer demand, manufacturers now create a demand for a particular product or elaboration of a product. The effort has been so successful that the resultant spending patterns are one reason the United States has one of the lowest savings rates in the industrialized world.

Mass advertising often uses values that are deeply seated in popular culture to create demand. Advertisers employ the rural myth to create positive images of their products. Soft-drink commercials that celebrate the honesty of farm work, family, and the land seek to connect these values to consumption of the manufacturer's product. Other advertisements rely on status attainment. Advertisements for designer tennis shoes and jeans propose that the consumption of a certain piece of clothing or footwear will bestow a particular status on the consumer.

Segmented Markets

Network television and general-interest magazines first enabled advertising to be aimed at as broad an audience as possible. The expansion of cable and satellite dishes has led to the proliferation of channels, many of which are highly specialized. Now advertising can be targeted to the specialized audiences those channels attract. MTV and many other targeted channels include product placement in their noncommercial air time, as well as specific commercials aimed at teenage and preteen consumers.

Similar targeting has occurred in the print media with the proliferation of professional, sports, hobby, and other types of magazines. Rural areas early on were targets of segmented market publication. *Wallaces' Farmer* was founded during the golden ages of farming and journalism, the last era of parity prices for farm commodities and the era when Americans relied on newspapers for all of their news and information. When *Wallaces' Farmer* was founded in 1895, more people lived on farms than in towns, in Iowa as well as the rest of the country. Farmwork was done with oxen, horses, mules, and manual labor. Farm families often had many children to help with the work. Families seldom went to town and had limited opportunities to socialize with other families. Newspapers provided the primary source of information as well as a means of communication with other farm families (Goldman and Dickens 1983).

Farming was a family affair, and *Wallaces' Farmer,* written during this era, was aimed at farm families, not just at farmers. There were sections for every member of the family: plenty of information and advertising about agriculture, "Hearts and Homes" for women, "The Boys' Page," "The 4-H Girls' Club Page," and "Little Recipes for Little Cooks."

More recently, the growth of desktop publishing, made possible by the continued miniaturization of computer technology, has strengthened segmentation, with advertising and news often combined almost seamlessly. One example of such targeting is a beef-industry magazine called *Beef Today*, produced by *Farm Journal*. The magazine is free but is provided only to cattle growers. It is virtually impossible for even a public library to obtain a subscription.

The digital revolution is representative of the revolution currently under way in the quantity and availability of all kinds of information. Although we may or may not be consuming any more information now than our parents did, we are consuming far more specialized information.

Changes in the character and price of communications technologies have made it easier for wealthier rural residents to participate in telecommunications consumption. Indeed, some observers have argued that telecommunications technology represents the greatest leveling force for rural and urban residents. However, the digital divide between rural and urban and rich and poor still exists. There is less demand in rural areas for broadband access partially because it is difficult for rural businesses to know how they would use the new technology. The Cooperative Extension System, which includes national, state, and local extension staff, has been authorized in the 2002 Farm Bill to help rural firms link their business plans to e-business options, much as Extension previously gave away free hybrid seed and conducted artificial insemination. In those cases, once the usefulness of the innovation was established and legitimized, private-sector firms took over the distribution.

Income Inequality

Mass advertising and the mass media in general have become a powerful influence on the consumption patterns of rural people. Mass media can inspire universal demand for certain consumer products. However, economic differences within rural areas make these purchases extremely difficult for some families. Class replaces rural residence as the feature that distinguishes people's consumption patterns.

Inequality of income has been growing in the United States since the early 1970s. The incomes of the working class have stagnated or declined. The purchasing power of the average hourly wage in 2003 is equal to what it was in 1965. Similarly, since the beginning of the 1980s, the lower price of primary goods (agricultural products, timber, and most minerals, except petroleum) has contributed to lower incomes for farmers, miners, and loggers.

The pressures to spend discretionary income are felt by all, although different groups are encouraged to buy different things. Discretionary income is very unequally distributed. Among teenagers, this inequality becomes obvious as many take on part-time work in order to consume such products as the latest in athletic shoes or, in rural areas, to invest in a four-wheel-drive pickup truck. Often they work many hours a week, which has a negative impact on their studies.

What we consume is ultimately limited by income more than by point of sale. Outlet malls, for example, are a current growth area in retail trade. Initially these stores were located near factories to market flawed goods, called "seconds." Because factories were often located in rural areas, outlet malls offered inexpensive merchandise to rural consumers. By the 1990s, major manufacturers had found that outlet malls enabled them to keep production and sales up in the face of continued economic downturn in the U.S. economy. The discount malls have continued to expand in rural areas, in part because of the availability of cheap land in rural areas and in part because upscale department stores that carry the same designer products dislike direct competition located nearby. However, shoppers frequenting these malls are not rural residents; they are predominantly upper-income suburban residents seeking name brands at bargain prices.

Rural people in the immediate area shop the local Dollar Store or Wal-Mart. Furthermore, as economic conditions continue to decline in rural areas, people increasingly shop at used-clothing stores set up by churches and other volunteer groups. Families can indeed get high-quality clothes at these local shops selling "previously owned" attire. Teenagers, however, cannot buy faddish items in the year they are fashionable. Level of income continues to affect consumption patterns.

Are Consumers Really Poor?

The Archer family illustrates the dilemmas encountered in defining inequality. Compared with their parents at the same stage of their life cycle, Susan and Dan consume an enormous number of products. In order to do so, they must both work. The trend toward two incomes is well documented and frequently cited as evidence of growing economic inequality. Ultimately, sociologists wonder to what extent these social patterns actually reflect inequality.

Sociological research shows a dramatic increase in inequality in the U.S. economic structure in the last quarter of the twentieth century. Sociologists differ, however, in their interpretation of how this inequality actually affects individuals. How incomes are adjusted for taxes or food-stamp benefits affects the picture of poverty that emerges. We do know that rural people who are eligible are less likely than the urban poor to request Earned Income Tax Credits or food stamps. Furthermore, the characteristics of poor households have also changed during that same period. Declines in family size and increased educational levels among young people have been offset by increased numbers of female-headed households and a decline in relatively well-paying jobs for those entering the job markets; the number and proportion of children in poverty have remained constant in rural areas since the 1970s.

Children who are being raised in rural, single-mother households are the poorest demographic group in the country (Duncan and Chase-Lansdale 2002). Poor, single mothers in rural areas would need to double their income in order to escape poverty, which means that many single mothers have to double-up and live with other families. In 2000, the poverty rate overall in rural areas was 13.4 percent, versus 10.8 percent in urban areas. Rural areas had 459 of the poorest counties out of 500 in the United States (Miller and Rowley 2002). Included in this poverty are children, who make up 2.5 million of the impoverished people living in rural America. Rural child poverty is widespread from Appalachia to the Deep South to California's Central Valley. These children are unable to consume large amounts of material goods; they are often denied basic needs like adequate healthcare or safe drinking water. Table 10.1 provides a snapshot of one county in Mississippi that has a high percentage of single mothers and a high percentage of child poverty.

To summarize, it is clear that changing consumption patterns are having a significant impact on rural life. The service industry has expanded to meet the increased demand for services once performed by the family. Increased consumption has placed added stress on the environment. Young people define themselves according to the products and services they consume, which ultimately affects the community's culture. Finally, wealth rather than place of residence now determines what and how much families consume. And as the world becomes more connected, the status implications of consumption are clear. No longer can rural residents proclaim, "We didn't know we were poor."

TABLE 10.1 — Snapshot: Quitman County, Mississippi

Population, 2000	10,177: 68.6% black, 30.3% white
High school graduates over 25 years old	approximately 27%
College graduates over 25 years old	approximately 5%
Births to single mothers	75%
Children living in poverty (ages 0–17) in 1999	43.2%

SOURCE: Adapted from *America's Forgotten Children: Child Poverty in Rural America.* 2002. The William and Flora Hewlett Foundation and The David and Lucile Packard Foundation. Online: available: http://www.savethechildren.org/afc/afc_pdf_oz.shtml; accessed May 15, 2003.

Impacts of Increased Consumption

Human Capital

Health. Recent changes in consumption patterns have had a significant impact on human capital in terms of health and education in the United States. The dense calories present in fast foods and their constant presence—from school lunchrooms to shopping malls—have increased serious health problems like obesity. Due to the ease of eating with fast food and microwavable meals, even rural residents spend less time cooking and more time eating than they did thirty years ago. Overproduction of food has been translated into overconsumption. Agribusiness now produces 3,800 calories of food a day for every American, 500 calories more than it produced thirty years ago, and at least 1,000 calories a day more than most people need. Our taboo against gluttony is tempered by the "bargains" we get in super-sized everything and all-you-can-eat buffets.

The National Health Examination Survey found that 30 percent of adults in 1999–2000 were obese by the technical medical definition (having a body-mass index greater than or equal to 30 kg/m^2). That percentage is up from 23 percent in 1988–1994 and 15 percent in 1976–1980. Obesity has more negative health consequences even than smoking, and higher levels of diabetes, high blood pressure, and stroke accompany its increase, which is growing fastest among children. In the United States, obesity is a main focus for research because it is so prevalent in both adults and children. A Healthier U.S. Initiative was launched in June 2002 with a focus on overall health through exercise, proper nutrition, and screenings for disease prevention.

Rural people in the United States are more likely to be obese than are urban people, partly because at one time rural life required enormous physical effort by both men and women. Large meals with lots of meat and potatoes were regularly consumed. The quality of a restaurant in most rural areas is still judged by the size of its portions. The problem is particularly grave among low-income populations because healthy diets are more costly and require more preparation time. Furthermore, socioeconomic status is closely linked to a number of health-related behaviors other than diet, including smoking, the use of seat belts, and physical exercise. On all these measures, rural people's patterns of consumption have a negative impact on their health (see Table 10.2 on comparative obesity by region and by distance from urban centers). Rural people are also more likely to smoke than are urban people, although everyone in the West is less likely to smoke than people in other areas of the country. Smoking by youth is also higher in rural areas (see more on this discussion in Chapter 6, "Human Capital").

Rural-urban distinctions persist in mortality, especially for the rural poor. For example, in North Carolina in the 1990s, infant mortality was much higher in ru-

TABLE 10.2   Obesity Among Persons 18 Years of Age and Over, United States, 1997–1998 (by sex, region, and urbanization level)

Region and Urbanization level	Total(%)	Men(%)	Women(%)
All regions	19.6	19.3	19.7
Metropolitan counties			
Large central	19.1	17.9	20.2
Large fringe	17.7	19.0	16.3
Small	19.8	19.6	19.9
Nonmetropolitan counties	21.6	21.0	22.1
With a city ≥ 10,000 population	20.5	20.1	21.0
Without a city ≥ 10,000 population	22.7	22.0	23.3
Northeast			
Metropolitan counties			
Large central	19.1	18.9	19.2
Large fringe	17.7	19.0	16.3
Small	19.5	19.4	19.3
Nonmetropolitan counties	21.3	19.9	22.6
Midwest			
Metropolitan counties			
Large central	21.9	18.7	24.8
Large fringe	18.5	18.3	18.5
Small	19.8	19.0	20.4
Nonmetropolitan counties	22.8	23.1	22.4
South			
Metropolitan counties			
Large central	19.9	18.9	20.8
Large fringe	18.5	20.5	16.5
Small	20.4	20.3	20.4
Nonmetropolitan counties	21.9	20.4	23.2
West			
Metropolitan counties			
Large central	16.7	15.8	17.5
Large fringe	15.5	17.8	12.7
Small	18.4	18.8	18.0
Nonmetropolitan counties	17.3	17.8	16.9

NOTE: Percents are age-adjusted.

ral areas, a statistic suggesting lack of access to health facilities. The proportion of overcrowded housing was 49 percent higher in the rural areas, and the proportion of housing with inadequate plumbing was 300 percent higher. These figures suggest very different patterns of consumption and well-being at the individual level.

Education.   The second impact of increased consumption is on male educational levels. In the early twentieth century, Eric would have turned his earnings from his part-time job over to his mother to help run the house; now he uses them for his own consumption goals. Normative consumption for young males often includes a car, high-end entertainment equipment, and other expensive items (although these goods are relatively much cheaper than they were even in 1950). Because young men can earn "good" money in jobs like construction (and in earlier times, in mining), they tend to spend more time at work, to devote less time to their studies, and to be less likely to graduate from high school and go to college. Although this will ultimately affect their lifetime earnings, desires for immediate consumption—and the need to make payments on the debt they run up to acquire things—makes the workforce seem a more attractive option. Thus, whereas young women in rural and urban areas are more likely to finish high school and go on to college than they were in 1990, young men are less likely to do so.

Female students are outnumbering males on college campuses, making up 56 percent of the college population (Tyler 2002). It is predicted that in the next decade, 3 million more women than men could be attending college. There are several explanations for the shift in numbers, including the feminist movement, but many young males are entering the workforce directly after high school. Many seek jobs in construction or technology where they can have a steady income without needing a college degree. The gap between Hispanic, Native American, and African American males and females is even larger, with more females attending college than males. One could conclude that male identity, even more than female identity, is based on consumption during the teens and early twenties. By comparison, as late as the 1980s in many rural communities, it was assumed that if anyone went on to higher education after high school, it would be the males. By 2000, more rural females than males were going on to college.

Social Capital

Changed consumption patterns have affected the way people interact. As people work more hours, their interaction with other people decreases. As more goods and services undergo *commodification* (being moved from use value to exchange value), more activities previously done in groups are now done individually. Putnam discusses the problems of "bowling alone," as bowling leagues declined at the same time that the number of lines bowled increased. Prior to the 1950s, entertainment required getting together with friends for community events or going to the local picture show. When first introduced in the 1950s, the person in the neighborhood with a high antenna and a television set had all the neighbors in to watch the favorite network shows. As more homes purchased televisions, viewing became a family activity. But by the 1990s, many homes boasted multiple televisions, and children and adults watched separately. Videos in rural areas substituted for the few rural theaters that remained, and there were fewer opportunities to run into friends in a public gathering to discuss the movie and community issues.

The burgeoning service industry now responds to needs that were previously met within the household or the firm. Goods once produced at home have become commodities, items to be bought and sold. To the extent that they are bought and sold, services have also become commodities, and activities once performed at home, such as laundry or sunbathing, have also become commodities. Leisure once involved reading or visiting neighbors, but now even entertainment is purchased rather than being created at home. A growing sector of the economy now generates new alternatives for the use of leisure time, from extreme sports to "reality" television shows.

Cultural Capital

Distinctions that once differentiated between rural and urban residents have given way to variations based on wealth. Rural communities once valued individuals for what they produced; now, as in urban areas, individuals are valued for what they consume. Different amounts of disposable income limit what any individual and household can consume. Consuming, in terms of purchasing goods, is increasingly looked upon as leisure, with entire families going together to the mall for an afternoon. A family's income, however, limits what family members can buy and how far the parents can drive to buy it. There are different versions of consumption items for different economic groups, and venues range from Saks Fifth Avenue to Dollar Stores; high-end stores cluster in urban areas, whereas Dollar Stores and outlet malls are a rural phenomenon. Yet there are still some rural residents who work hard not to be caught up in a mentality of constant consumption (see Box 10.3).

BOX 10.3   Is It Possible to Stop Wasteful Habits?

Janie Lee, a member of In Praise of Mountain Women in Eubank, Kentucky, regards recycling as a way of life. For her, buying secondhand items is economical and an easy way to decrease the accumulation of waste in landfills.

I have issues with mindset and recycling. As a mountain woman who has not had much, I have learned many ways to recycle that people do not admire

Continued on next page

Is It Possible to Stop Wasteful Habits? (continued)

in our general society. I have used many clothing centers in my life, and over time I have realized that I am recycling someone else's clothing that is good enough for me, but it is stuff that might otherwise go to a landfill.

Janie points out that what people throw away is not always trash; people often discard items simply because they are tired of them. Many Americans, in Janie's eyes, are too concerned with "keeping up with the Jones's," spending money on faddish items in order to keep up with their peers. They buy new things and discard their old, "out of style" goods. Even if these items are donated to a clothing store or secondhand shop, the store may not keep all of the donations because it does not have room for them, as Janie illustrates:

> What happens to the things we have when we get rid of them? They may be given to places that throw them away, case in point: Goodwill Industry. I am a curious person, so one day I looked in their trash bins, and what did I find? Many good things. One year when I first started looking in their trash, I got so many stuffed animals that after I took them home, washed them and let them dry, I had enough to give every child on my son's preschool bus one and still had more for my son. The bus driver told me that one of the children loved their toy so much, it was as if he had never gotten any new toys before. . . . many mountain people are very poor.

Janie contacted the president of Goodwill Industries in Kentucky to let him know that there were items being thrown away at the Goodwill that were not "nasty." He urged her to find a nonprofit organization that would take items discarded by Goodwill. Unfortunately, she could not. Such places, like Goodwill, often cannot keep up with all the donations they receive. The public donated an estimated 975,000 tons of goods in 2002, and charities like Goodwill face big challenges as more and more of their donated items end up in landfills (Goodwill Industries 2003). Electronic waste—old cellular phones, computers, and televisions, for example—is steadily increasing, and there are big costs involved with the handling and disposal of such items because they contain hazardous materials, such as the lead found in computer monitors and television screens.

Continued on next page

Is It Possible to Stop Wasteful Habits? (continued)

Recycling, for Janie, is personal and necessary. However, Janie recognizes that she is often guilty of adding to landfills herself, which frustrates her.

Something else I see myself doing is rather then taking my throwaways and recycling them into crafts or useful objects I throw them away. . . . So many things, like plastic bottles, toilet paper rings or paper towel rings or egg boxes could be painted and reused but I don't have the time, so I just throw them away. I am not a person that likes to waste things like this. Sometimes I do recycle some of my plastic bottles for spray bottles and things, but I know I waste even more. How do we stop all of this? Does any one have any thoughts?

REFERENCES: Selma Juanita (Janie) Lee, a member of In Praise of Mountain Women.

Goodwill Industries. 2003. "Public Policy Priorities for 2003." Online; available: http://www.goodwill.org/index_gii.cfm/1467/; accessed April 5, 2003.

What we consume greatly determines not only our material well-being but also our cultural identity. For example, food preparation has been a significant part of the role women have played as homemakers. However, cooking a frozen dinner in a microwave oven is a profound change in the way we consume food compared with the way we ate just a few decades ago. Our language and culture change as a result of this alteration in consumption patterns; for example, the verb "to microwave" did not exist two decades ago.

More importantly, however, the nature of a homemaker's role has changed from when Susan's grandmother cooked meals for a threshing crew. Her grandmother was concerned with filling the stomachs of hungry workers engaged in hard physical labor, whereas Susan is concerned about nutrition and controlling calories. Susan's grandmother was known throughout the county for pie crusts made flaky by a generous use of lard; Susan, on the other hand, includes low-fat yogurt in her children's lunches. Although their meals may differ, these women were and are viewed by their peers as excellent providers of good food for their families. The definition of "good food" and the amount of time spent in preparing it have changed dramatically: More of Susan's food-preparation time goes into planning meals, and most of her grandmother's time went into cooking meals.

An expensive pair of athletic shoes endorsed by a professional basketball star will not necessarily improve a person's basketball game any more than a much less expensive pair will. Wearing them may bring their user higher status even if not a higher vertical jump. What we consume can become a statement of who we are or want to be, whether in our eyes or in the eyes of others. The group identity provided by consumption makes us painfully conscious of not having or not being able to acquire the symbols that show we are "in style." This is particularly true of young people, who are changing rapidly and whose sense of self is still developing. Both Eric and Jake needed to feel they were part of the "in" group.

For those whose jobs are not inherently satisfying, being able to provide consumer goods and services for their families becomes a reason for working. Increased consumption can give meaning to work. Sociological studies show that an increasing number of people now work because of what their earnings allow them to consume rather than because of what they produce.

Natural Capital

Consumer goods and services require *inputs*, the natural resources or raw materials needed in the production process. Furthermore, once their useful life is over (and that life is becoming shorter and shorter for everything from computers to clothing), they are thrown away. Acquiring a new item, even an automobile, does not mean that it will be kept for several years. People are constantly trading or selling one thing to make a profit or to have something "newer and better."

The consumption that occurs in the process of producing commodities ultimately affects the environment. For instance, fertilizers and seeds are inputs that are consumed in the production of a crop. Electrical power and computers are inputs that are consumed in the process of producing goods or services in an industrial firm or in an educational institution. These inputs are often included in the calculation of costs of production. The costs of other elements consumed in the course of production, such as the quality of water, soil, and air, are often ignored in such calculations. Economists refer to these costs as *externalities*. Sociologists examine consumption in terms of its totality—inputs and externalities. Environmental degradation associated with acid rain, impure water, loss of biodiversity (indigenous plants and animals), toxic-waste dumps, and soil erosion is a by-product of consumption that ultimately affects the quality of life that consumption supposedly enhances.

Per capita energy consumption in the United States has increased greatly since World War II. Presently, the United States consumes approximately a quarter of the world's energy but accounts for less than 5 percent of the world's population. There are few signs that the public will support a decline in level of consumption. Increasing resource efficiency and decreasing the use of resources, particularly nonrenewable resources, could maintain a stable standard of living. Yet as a society, we have not made this a priority. Instead, we depend on relatively cheap foreign sources of energy. The sustainability of this level of resource use seems to be officially questioned only when the sources of cheap energy are jeopardized, as during the oil embargo in the 1970s, the Gulf War in the early 1990s, and the current concern over international terrorism centered in the Middle East. However, the official stance of the U.S. government has been to seek increased production through drilling in environmentally fragile areas rather than to reduce consumption or increase fuel efficiency. Rural areas are particularly dependent on private transportation, and the rural poor drive older, less reliable vehicles that get very low gas mileage. Lack of public transportation in rural areas further hinders the rural poor, whose employment depends on showing up regularly and on time and whose transportation sources are unreliable and costly to operate.

A related uncertainty is the safe and environmentally sound disposal of the waste derived from consumption. The refuse created by production and domestic consumption must go somewhere, and that somewhere is often a rural landfill or incinerator. Rural Americans often have to discard their garbage in their own backyards. When the trash collectors pick up garbage in the cities and the suburbs, few of their residents could tell you its final destination. Rural communities are homes for most waste dumps, including those that contain toxic materials or nuclear waste. Most rural people know exactly where refuse, theirs and that of others, is dumped.

Most environmental degradation is considered to be the externalized by-products of our production and marketing processes. The price of the commodities produced and consumed usually does not include the cost of correcting the environmental degradation caused by use or disposal of those products. For example, the price of the farm commodity produced does not include the costs of cleaning up the waterways or the inestimable health costs of a water table polluted by pesticides that have percolated down from surface applications. These costs are borne by the public sector or the individuals, disproportionately the rural poor, who suffer the health consequences.

The consequences of these trends of production and consumption are of particular importance to rural people. First, their sense of material satisfaction is now dependent upon high levels of consumption, and rural people do not differ greatly from city dwellers in their consumption levels. Second, rural people account for only one quarter of the U.S. population but they live in 98 percent of the land area. That lower population density relative to urban areas makes it politically attractive for decisionmakers (politicians and technicians) to locate dumps for solid, toxic, and nuclear wastes in rural areas.

In general, the less densely populated the rural area, the stronger the inclination to select it as a waste site. From the technician's point of view, the fewer the number of people directly affected, the smaller the social impact. From the politician's point of view, the smaller and more dispersed the population, the less the likelihood of effective political organization in opposition to that particular site. NIMBY ("not in my backyard") opposition may appear anywhere, but all other things being equal, politicians would prefer to have only a few people angry with them.

The increased commodification of leisure activities also creates environmental dilemmas. The number of visitors to the U.S. national parks each year has reached the point that the parks may no longer be able to maintain the pristine environment they were designated to protect (see Box 10.4). The proliferation of off-road vehicles for use in leisure activities threatens environmental damage that may take centuries to repair. Rural residents find themselves affected as consumers, yet they are also affected as residents of the land they enjoy using for recreation. Communities find they must carefully weigh the economic benefits of tourism and recreation against the environmental costs.

BOX 10.4   Yosemite National Park: Wilderness Area or Rural Theme Park?

Yosemite National Park in northern California had 3.4 million visitors in 2002, down from its 1999 peak of 4.2 million. Most came in their own cars. Although 94 percent of the park has been set aside as wilderness, environmentalists charge that Yosemite Valley has been turned into a theme park. Concessions have been contracted out to the Curry Company, a subsidiary of the Music Corporation of America (MCA). There are seventeen acres of asphalt parking lots, 1,700 hotel rooms and cabins, three swimming pools, several tennis courts, numerous restaurants including a pizza parlor and a deli, a video store, twenty-three liquor establishments including a sports bar, and other similar enterprises. This development has occurred in spite of the fact that in 1980, environmentalists succeeded in gaining approval of a master plan under which the park would be de-urbanized and nonessential services would be eliminated. Automobiles were to be banned and replaced by shuttle buses. The Curry Company paid the U.S. Department of Interior an annual franchising fee of $600,000.

The company grossed $85 million on its Yosemite Park operations in 1989. Environmentalists charged that the company blocked implementation of the master plan that would have limited that development, a charge denied by Curry's top management. As a result of ignoring environmental imperatives, Curry lost the concession contract.

Delaware North Parks Services (DNPS), formed in 1993 when Delaware North Companies (DNC)—a family-owned multinational food-service, recre-

Continued on next page

Yosemite National Park: Wilderness Area or Rural Theme Park? (continued)

ational, and hospitality management company with operations throughout the United States, Canada, and the Pacific Rim—won the contract to manage visitor services at Yosemite National Park. Yosemite Concessions Services Corporation is a subsidiary of DNC. The concession contract changed because, according to DNPS, with Yosemite as its model, Delaware North Companies Parks and Resorts offers innovative stewardship programs dedicated to environmental excellence. In its own words, "It was the first concessioner to speak to national park stewards in their own language, understanding that national treasures such as Yosemite and Sequoia national parks are storehouses of American history and repositories of ancient culture" (Delaware North Companies Web site: http://www.delawarenorth.com).

In 2000, a new plan was approved to reduce the number of cars and buildings in the park so that is can accommodate more people than it can now. Although overnight visitors will still be allowed to drive into the park, people visiting just for the day will leave their cars at one of four satellite lots outside the park and take a bus into the valley, where they will be able move around on foot, on a bike, or on a "clean-fuel" shuttle. Park headquarters, employee housing, stores, and many other buildings that do not need to be in the heart of the park will be rebuilt outside Yosemite. The number of overnight accommodations will be reduced by about 20 percent, so that 147 acres of the valley can be restored to its natural condition.

But plan implementation is slow. Both private firms and environmentalists sued. As of February 2003, public hearings were still being held, the plans contested, and work stalled. Although the park had raised admission fees, which could help pay for plan implementation, the litigation meant the park could not spend the money raised. Few parks nationwide collect more in entrance fees than Yosemite, which had thirty-four projects planned to implement the master plan. Park visitors can already see results. Last year, for instance, park officials finished renovating an auditorium behind the Yosemite Valley Visitors Center, where plush, stadium-style seats now invite visitors in for a showing of the introductory movie called *The Spirit of Yosemite.*

Ten of these planned Yosemite projects were postponed, however, because of various lawsuits over planning. For instance, auditors noted that four of the ten stalled projects were put on hold because seventy Yosemite workers were reassigned to work on the legally challenged Yosemite Valley

Continued on next page

Plan. Another project to construct a new wastewater treatment plant and related facilities was delayed to head off potential litigation.

The auditors noted that failure to move ahead with the planned $8.7 million wastewater plant could force the closure of an area used by about 5,000 Yosemite visitors daily. A cumbersome park service review process, which in some cases requires eleven levels of approval, also impeded projects, auditors said.

Although park officials concede the validity of the auditors' concerns, which were spelled out in a report issued in the summer of 2002, they say they have already overcome some of the problems identified. "The nice thing is, knock on wood, all the litigation is finally behind us," Yosemite's spokesperson, Scott Gediman, said (Doyle 2002).

Auditors also want tighter security for the money collected, in several respects. They noted that the "poor physical condition and isolated locations" of some entrance stations at Yosemite and three other parks rendered them vulnerable to theft. They also urged that the seasonal park workers collecting entrance fees undergo background checks; only 42 percent of those surveyed had undergone the checks.

Yosemite officials responded by noting that they had increased the frequency of law enforcement patrols, installed new surveillance cameras, and improved telephone lines to act as a security stopgap until they could build new entrance stations.

"[National Park Service] officials stated that the low number of employee background checks was due in part to the lack of awareness that such checks were required, and the belief that they were too expensive, time consuming and unnecessary for seasonal personnel," auditors noted (Doyle 2002). Park service officials said they would ask for more money to complete the background checks in order to comply with Homeland Security requirements.

REFERENCES: *All Things Considered*. 1990. National Public Radio. Aired October 24.

Mike Doyle. 2002. "National Park Fee Coffers Swelling" (December 24). *Fresno Bee*. Online; available: http://www.yosemite.org/newsroom/clips2002/december/122402.htm; accessed April 5, 2003.

Delaware North Companies, Incorporated, Web site. Online; available: http://www.delawarenorth.com/; accessed May 15, 2003.

Financial Capital

High levels of consumption in the United States have meant a very low rate of savings, which has implications for those who withdraw from the labor force, either voluntarily or involuntarily. They have little cushion when financial needs suddenly arise. Emergency expenses must be taken from current disposable income, leaving many households with few alternatives. Furthermore, the rate of debt in the United States is extremely high. Rural areas do have less debt per capita than urban areas. A large amount of that debt is on credit cards or with relatives, but the relatives of the rural poor are also poor, putting them into the hands of predatory lenders. This has disastrous consequences.

Alma Smith lives in a small, persistently poor rural community with her four children. After a difficult divorce from an abusive husband, she struggled to provide for her family with income from her job in a local textile factory. Active in her church, she participated in Habitat for Humanity and worked hard to help build her new home, which she financed with a low-income loan. The loan was figured based on her income and what she needed for food, utilities, childcare, car expenses, and some spending money for the children. Soon after she moved in, Alma received a phone call offering her the opportunity to refinance her mortgage in order to pay off her debts. At that point, she only had one credit card, paying down the balance due each month, but then the textile factory closed. She began working part-time jobs, waiting tables in several restaurants, but the hours made it difficult to spend time with her children, and tips were undependable. Alma maxed out her credit card and got several more from the many offers that frequently arrived in the mail, using one card to pay off another.

When the same person called again, offering her the opportunity to consolidate her debts with her mortgage if she would refinance the house with them, she gratefully agreed. The new loan paid off the low-interest loan on her house and her credit cards, but then, instead of paying 2 percent interest with $200 monthly house payments, she was paying 10 percent interest and $275 a month for house payments. Gradually Alma fell behind in her house payments, and she eventually lost her house. Alma's debt had again accumulated.

Karen and Ed Adams also had high credit card debt and a substantially higher house payment than Alma. They were baby-boom professionals living in a rural community near a metropolitan area, and their two children were now in college. Ed was an engineer with Enron Corporation, and Karen had just become a partner with the Arthur Anderson accounting firm. The dramatic growth in the stock market during the 1990s greatly increased their paper net worth. They began to anticipate early retirement with an affluent lifestyle once their children graduated from college. They used debt to finance the things they would "need" when they retired: a boat, a remodeled home, and new furniture. In 2002, with the stock market in free fall, both their companies went into bankruptcy. Their "savings" were represented by a partnership in Arthur Anderson and Enron stock. They had no liquid savings (money in the bank) that they could fall back on. Karen was able to get part-time accounting work with several local businesses, and Ed looked for job openings in electrical engineering. They also lost their house and are now renting a small apartment.

Low rates of savings can occur at all income levels, putting both the rich and the poor at risk. As we see in Chapter 7, "Financial Capital," low rates of savings reverberate in the community because there is less available capital to lend to new businesses that might improve economic conditions. Rural residents and rural communities are caught in a vicious circle.

Built Capital

The U.S. National Academy of Sciences has recently addressed the issues of sustainable consumption. They found that the first step toward sustainable consumption is to recognize that consumption patterns will inevitably change in the future, if only by the force of environmental circumstances, such as global warming. A changed approach to built capital can make a huge difference.

If human communities were to deploy all of the ecotechnologies that are already available from innovative businesses (such as energy efficiency, pollution controls, waste management, recycling, cradle-to-grave products, and zero-emissions industry), we could enjoy twice as much material welfare while consuming only half as many natural resources and causing only half as much pollution and waste. Decisions to transform built capital, made by rural entrepreneurs and local governments, could improve both natural and financial capital.

Political Capital

As we are well into the first decade of the twenty-first century, policies are in place to support and expand the current rate and forms of consumption. Bigger is better, and tax breaks to large energy users reinforce that value. Norman Myers (2000) suggests three policy initiatives that could promote the transition to sustainable consumption:

1. Abandon gross national product (GNP) as an indicator of economic well-being. As an indicator, it suggests that we do not need to take account of sustainability. In the United States, per capita GNP rose by 49 percent between 1976

and 1998, whereas per capita "genuine progress" (the economy's output with environmental and social costs subtracted
and added weight given to education, health, and the like)
declined by 30 percent.

2. Ensure that prices reflect all environmental and social costs.
   For example, U.S. society ultimately pays at least six dollars
   to burn a gallon of gasoline (though pollution, road acci-
   dents, traffic congestion, and so on). Pricing gasoline realistically would curtail the excessive car culture and open up
   market demand for improved public transportation. Similar
   considerations would apply to the prices of other products.

3. Stop subsidies that encourage environmental ignorance.
   Such subsidies support fossil fuels ten to fifteen times more
   than clean and renewable sources of energy such as solar
   energy or wind power. There are many other subsidies that
   promote the car culture, overintensive agriculture, wasteful
   use of water, overlogging of forests, and overharvesting of
   marine fisheries. They induce massive distortions in our
   economy and do massive harm to the environment.

These are radical proposals. They have strong implications for rural areas. In
general, rural legislators have resisted much milder policy changes, in part because
the political capital of those who profit from the current forms of consumption is
much greater than those of other citizens.

Chapter Summary

What we consume has changed as dramatically as the way goods and services are
produced. Expanded earnings, increased presence of women in the workforce, and
the technical capacity to produce more varied products have both increased and
changed the character of what we consume. These changes have made a person's
level of income a more distinguishing quality than his or her urban or rural residence, thereby influencing one's self-identity; what matters is not where people
live but how much income they make. Regardless, rural residents are more likely
to be poor than urban ones, particularly in the South and in the Great Plains,
which equates rural residence with low income.

Several economic and social factors have contributed to the change in consumption patterns. Current markets are forcing consolidation of both retail and
service organizations. Changes in the labor force have increased the number of
jobholders per family, stimulating the growth of the service and informal sectors

of the rural economy. The poor in rural areas are more likely to be working than in urban areas. Mass advertising has led to the standardization of products. More recently, advertising has been targeted at market niches. The rural poor have a difficult time ignoring this advertising, especially teenagers who want to keep up with the latest fads.

The way we produce goods and services is linked with the way these commodities are consumed, where they are consumed, and why they are consumed. The life cycle of a commodity or service is much more than the points of production and purchase. The final resting places for many commodities or their remains are the landfills and toxic incinerators located in rural areas. As concern for the environment acquires greater importance, increases in our societal consumption patterns and the consequent concerns about resources, the environment, and waste disposal will become national political issues. These issues, though, are already personal and family issues for rural people and their communities.

Key Terms

Central-place theory proposes that population centers, whether small crossroads communities or large cities, are geographically organized into hierarchical retail and public-service markets.

Commodification is the transformation of a good or service that has previously been available outside the market as a result of community or individual effort into a good or service that is available in the market for a price.

Conspicuous consumption refers to purchases made for social rather than biological needs.

Economies of scale occur when a greater volume of business can occur at one particular site, since volume is a way to spread some costs (of transportation, land and buildings, equipment, and labor) over a larger number of products.

Externalities include the social costs of production not borne by the company producing the goods. These might include the contamination of the soil, air, or water when waste products are released to the environment.

Inputs include the natural resources or raw materials needed in the production process.

References

America's Forgotten Children: Child Poverty in Rural America. 2002. The William and Flora Hewlett Foundation and The David and Lucile Packard Foundation. Online: available: http://www.savethechildren.org/afc/afc_pdf_02.shtml; accessed April 14, 2003.

Cotterill, Ronald W. 2001. "Neoclassical Explanations of Vertical Organization and Performance of Food Industries." *Agribusiness: An International Journal* 17:33–57.

Duncan, Greg J., and P. Lindsey Chase-Lansdale. 2002. *For Better or Worse: Welfare Reform and the Wellbeing of Children and Families.* New York: Russell Sage Foundation.

Goldman, Robert, and David D. Dickens. 1983. "The Selling of Rural America." *Rural Sociology* 48, no. 4:585–606.

Lawrence, Barbara Kent, Steven Bingler, Barbara M. Daimond, Bobbie Hill, Jerry L. Hoffman, Craig B. Howley, Stacy Mitchell, David Rudolph, and Elliot Washor. 2002. *Dollars and Sense: The Cost Effectiveness of Small Schools.* Cincinnati, OH: KnowledgeWorks Foundation.

Meyers, Norman. 2000. "Sustainable Consumption." *Science* 287:2419.

Miller, Kathy, and Tom Rowley. 2002 "Rural Poverty and Rural-Urban Income Gaps: A Troubling Snapshot of the 'Prosperous' 1990s." Rural Policy Research Institute (RUPRI) report. Online; available: http://www.rupri.org/articles/poverty/index.html; accessed April 17, 2003.

Ortega, Bob. 1998. *In Sam We Trust.* New York: Random House.

Stone, Kenneth E. 1995. *Competing with the Retail Giants: How to Survive in the New Retail Landscape.* New York: Wiley.

Tyler, Raven. 2002. "Gender Gap 101" (October 2). PBS Newshour Extra. Online; available: http://www.pbs.org/newshour/extra/features/july-dec02/college.html; accessed November 4, 2002.

Veblen, Thorstein. [1899] 1967. *The Theory of the Leisure Class.* New York: Funk and Wagnalls.

Williams, Melissa. 2002. "Wal-Mart Battle Moves to Asheville City Council" (June 23). *Citizen Times.* Online; available: http://cgi.citizen-times.com/cgi-bin/story/front/15251; accessed August 14, 2002.

11

Governments

Malcolm T. Porter was worried. According to teachers in the consolidated school, children from Coker (pseudonym for a small southern town) had an alarmingly high rate of stomach illnesses. Recently, Malcolm's own elderly aunt had been plagued with ill health. Concerned, he obtained a sample of the local water from the one pipe in town and sent it in to be tested by the state. The report said that there was high *E. coli* content present in the water.

Malcolm had heard of a government program that helped small communities build sewer and water systems. The communities, in turn, run and maintain the water system. But there is a catch: A local government must be directly involved in the process of maintaining the system. Coker had no government.

Coker is a poor, isolated community of fewer than four hundred people. It has been without a mayor or town council for fifty-two years. Back in 1933, the Donovan family "just sat down around a table and decided [they] didn't want it anymore." The Donovans, who were the richest family in town, concluded had that the town did not need a government and closed it down. There was no response from the people in town; nothing happened. People still lived in the homes that had been in the family for generations, although upkeep was difficult. The local church provided the only way for people to congregate, which they did Wednesday nights and twice on Sundays. Over time, things continued to deteriorate in Coker.

In 1995, a handful of the town's black residents, including Malcolm, decided to take action personally. They organized the Coker Community Club, and members sold fried chicken and fish dinners until they had enough money to construct a small house. The house served as a temporary city hall, a recreation center, a library where people could exchange books and magazines, and a community and voter-registration center.

By 1999, they were ready to elect a local government. They held a town meeting, nominated a slate of officers, and elected the first town officials in sixty-six years. Just five hours after the election, however, the Donovan family, who still owned property in Coker but had long left the county, filed suit in the county court. Coker's government would have the right to levy property taxes to support itself, which the Donovans were fighting to avoid. The local government was suspended, pending the outcome of the suit.

Malcolm could not imagine what they were going to do. People had worked long and hard to get the community center up and operating. The homes in the community needed safe drinking water, and children needed to be protected; their performance in school had already been negatively affected because of illness. The *E. coli* had to be eliminated. It was found that the *E. coli* was probably due to the antiquated septic tank, and it needed to be replaced. Without a town council, Coker could not receive the technical assistance and financial support it needed to provide healthy drinking water. Without a government, the people of Coker could not meet even their most basic needs.

★   ★   ★

The residents in Coker understand why they need a government, though most of us do not really consider its necessity. Why do we have town councils, county commissions, water districts, parishes, boroughs, and school boards? State legislatures are also beginning to question whether we might have too many local units of government.

From a sociological perspective, local governments exist for at least three purposes: First, they offer an avenue for citizen participation, inviting those who live in a community to take part in making the decisions that will affect them. Second, local governments also provide the structure by which community needs can be met. Whether it involves distributing food to the poor, constructing roads and bridges, ensuring safe water supplies, or maintaining schools, local governments provide the mechanism by which people can collectively meet common needs. Finally, local governments offer an arena where issues of responsibility are explored. Food, roads, safe water supplies, and schools all cost money, and governments decide how that money will be raised.

Town councils, local school boards, water districts, and county commissions or county boards of supervisors all represent different types of government found in rural areas. Their organization, legal powers, allowance for citizen participation, control of community decisionmaking, and provision of public services all differ markedly. This chapter explores how different local governments are organized in rural areas, what they do, and what problems they face in providing public services. In the last forty years, the balance among local, state, and federal governments has changed, which has had profound effects on the capacity of local governments to respond to rural needs. More and more responsibility has gone to the state and local governments, but the financial capital and human capital to implement those responsibilities has not been increased at the same rate.

Organization and Functions of Local Governments

Ultimately, control over taxation and land use is the central issue for local governments, although this varies by state. The ability to tax enables a government to raise the resources needed to set an agenda and implement policies toward accomplishing that agenda. Planning and zoning, which determine land use, is a power that some local governments can exercise. In this regard, the U.S. system of government differs from that typically found in other nations. This section explores the powers shared with local governments, the different types of local governments found in rural areas, and who does the work of local governments.

Power of Local Governments

Most countries have a unitary form of government, that is, a central government that holds tightly the power to tax. Although there may be local units of government, they are unable to levy taxes on behalf of local needs. There is currently a worldwide move to decentralize authority from central governments to local ones. The resources necessary to exercise authority and responsibility do not always accompany the decentralization of authority and responsibility.

The U.S. system divides power, including the power to tax, between two levels of government. As provided by the Tenth Amendment to the U.S. Constitution: "The powers not delegated to the United States by the Constitution, nor prohibited by it to the States, are reserved to the States, respectively, or to the people." Which powers are reserved only to the states is often in question, and the resulting flexibility enables the balance of power to shift back and forth between the two levels. This form of government is referred to as *federalism*.

Local governments are not mentioned in the U.S. Constitution. They are, in fact, created by each state, thus making for a great deal of variation across the country. Local governments derive their power either from grants of authority in state constitutions, which are known as "home-rule provisions," or by general laws or statutes passed by state legislatures.

In theory, local governments provide the mechanism by which participation, needs, and responsibility are linked. They can allow for direct citizen participation in government, or they can provide representative government, in which local citizens elect officials to act on their behalf. New England town meetings are among the more famous examples of direct citizen participation. Annual town meetings enable all citizens to participate in setting the agenda as well as in making decisions. The number of townships in the United States has decreased from 16,691 in 1989 to 16,629 in 2002; however, many localities still conduct their business through town meetings. Under representative government, local residents elect a group of people (to a town council, city commission, school board, or board of supervisors) who then make decisions. These decisions relate to (1) what services will be provided, (2) who will be hired to provide them, (3) how the revenue will be raised to pay for those services, and (4) how land under township authority can be used.

When communities are small, as they are in rural areas, a higher percentage of residents can play an active role in this process. Wide participation should allow services to be uniquely tailored to the needs of the local population. Having the power to tax enables local governments to ensure that the community accepts responsibility for raising revenue needed for the services that the community values most. Theory often falls short of reality, however. Elite groups in communities like Coker can block the participation of certain categories of residents. Local resources may simply not be available to respond to local needs, at which point other levels of government often become involved.

Types of Rural Governments

Rural governments are as diverse as rural economies. As shown in Table 11.1, the many forms of government can be sorted into two types: general-purpose and special-purpose governments. *General-purpose governments* are, as their name implies, governments created to respond to the general needs of a county, city, or town. They usually have the power to raise revenue and determine its use. State governments may restrict use of certain types of taxes or place ceilings on tax levels, as happened when taxpayers revolted in states like California, limiting property taxes to the levels that were in place prior to 1975–1976. That restriction greatly reduced all local governments' ability to meet the needs of citizens and had serious repercussions on such special-purpose governments as school districts. *Special-purpose governments* are created to respond to specific community needs, such as schools (see Chapter 4, "Human Capital"), water, or medical services. These special districts can usually raise revenue to cover their costs, generally through fees or property taxes. Their freedom to tax is often severely restricted by state governments.

Other special tax concessions in the name of economic development, such as *tax increment financing (TIF)*, can limit their ability to support the services they offer. Tax increment financing is a tool used by municipalities to reduce or eliminate blighting conditions, foster improvement, and to enhance the tax base of every taxing district that extends into the area. TIF provides for redevelopment that would not occur without the support of public investments. This tool allows a city to capture the increase in state and local property and sales taxes that result from a redevelopment, which also contributes to the TIF fund. The city is required to

TABLE 11.1 Number of Local Government Units, 2002, 1987, and 1962

Type of Government	2002	1987	1962
Total local governments	87,849	83,186	91,185
General-purpose governments			
County	3,034	3,041	3,043
Municipal	19,431	19,200	17,997
Township	16,506	16,691	17,144
Special-purpose governments			
School district	13,522	14,721	34,678
Special district	35,356	29,532	18,323

SOURCE: U.S. Census of Governments, 2002. "Government Finance." Online; available; http://www.census.gov/govs/cog/2002COGprelim_report.pdf;   .

prepare a redevelopment plan for each district that identifies uses for the TIF fund. However, the redirection of the taxes means that special-purpose districts, such as school or hospital districts, can lose funding during the period the TIF is in place.

Some local governments also provide services in rural areas, such as municipal power and water companies. Although a number of metropolitan areas have sought to privatize these services in recent years, with mixed success, in most rural communities these services are cost-effective and ensure that community residents have reliable services at reasonable prices. Indeed, these services often contribute to the general revenue of local governments.

The relative importance of any one type of rural government varies by region of the country and from state to state. In some states, small municipalities are the most common type of general-purpose government. In the West and throughout much of the South, counties provide most local governmental services. Villages and towns are often not incorporated. In the West, where counties are much larger than in other regions of the country, county government can be essentially regional in character. In the states across the Great Plains, small municipalities and counties vie for political prominence, often providing complementary services. In New England and across the northern tier of states, townships are the most important general-purpose government. Differences in political traditions and state law are reflected in the diversity found in local governance.

Staffing Rural Governments

Citizen-officials, who receive only symbolic remuneration and thus must have another source of income, often lead small governments. The town mayor (paid for by local taxes) might also be the city postmaster (paid for by the federal government) and local fire chief (not paid at all). In contrast to their urban counterparts, rural governments are highly dependent on citizen volunteers as opposed to paid elected and appointed officials.

Despite the limited time they can devote to their duties, rural officials face many issues similar to those faced by larger governments. Professional networks and associations can be helpful, but officials in rural areas are less likely to participate in such groups than are those from urban areas. Advisory councils and technical assistance available through state agencies often provide information that aids policy decisions. They may also offer training that will improve public management. For example, small municipalities in Pennsylvania receive training and technical assistance in everything from financial investments to rural development. Assistance providers include the State Department of Community Affairs, the Association of Township Supervisors, the Cooperative Extension Service, borough associations, universities and colleges, private consultants, neighboring municipalities, the Pennsylvania Economic League, and others.

Small city councils rely primarily on the advice and expertise of the few people who hold paid management and consulting positions in the local government. They include such people as the town clerk, the city attorney, the county engineer, and the city treasurer. These individuals are extremely valuable to the community, but they can exercise inordinate control over the decisionmaking process.

City or county attorneys and engineers, for example, can act as gatekeepers to the community. Because they often have exclusive control of technical expertise, these officials can limit the information that is shared about an issue or determine which outside resources are sought. These officials can also spend more time on local affairs than elected officials because they have paid positions in the local government. Thus, paid technical staff can exercise a substantial amount of political control over inexperienced or part-time elected officials.

Problems in
Providing Public Services

Rural governments face a common problem: providing adequate levels of public services with limited resources. The problem is common to all rural communities, whether they are experiencing growth or decline. Communities with growing populations must provide services for more people, despite the fact that tax revenue rarely keeps up with the increased demand. Declining rural communities grapple with the problem of providing continued services in the face of an eroding tax base and waning support from the state and federal governments. Poor communities have little tax base with which to provide any services, yet these communities include people whose need for assistance is great.

Local governments in Michigan recently battled to regain funding after the governor vetoed $845 million in revenue sharing to local governments for the 2003 fiscal year. The governor's actions would have forced local governments to make severe cutbacks in police, fire, and emergency services. Additionally, $7.4 million in fire protection grants would have been eliminated, straining fire services in communities that protect state universities and prisons. This was especially troubling for Michigan communities because local governments would have been forced to cut law enforcement during a time of heightened national security concerns. More than 2,000 local officials and members of several associations—including some state-level entities: the Townships Association, the Municipal League, the Association of Counties, the Association of Fire Chiefs, and the Association of Chiefs of Police—rallied on the steps of the Capitol to show their support for overriding the veto (Michigan Townships Association 2002). In August 2002, the override overwhelmingly passed in the Michigan House and Senate. Local officials made their voices heard, winning the fight for their community members.

The problem of losing local funding and services is widespread. A past study of small counties in North Dakota illustrates the difficulty of maintaining services without putting a financial strain on local community members. In 1989, 84 percent of the counties had raised taxes in the previous two years in order to maintain services, and 79 percent reported a decrease in state aid. Because of migration and population change, particularly across the Great Plains, North Dakota lost more than $100 million between 1998 and 1999 (Rathge 2002). More and more young married couples are moving from rural to urban areas; consequently, more and more small counties are losing their footing as viable communities. Richard Rathge suggests that success in saving these counties depends on "cooperative ventures that nurture and promote collaboration among differing levels of governments or organizations" (Rathge 2002:18). However, this cooperation, although important, is often dependent upon federal mandates.

The struggle to provide adequate services in rural areas is complex. Some services are mandated by state or federal governments yet may not be appropriate to rural communities. The mandates require that local resources be spent for those services, however. In other cases, the structure and management of rural communities make it difficult to provide adequate services. Finally, fiscal stress has become a constant companion of many communities. In Michigan, the governor stated that he was trying to provide a "financial cushion in case voters . . . pass[ed] three ballot proposals" (Hockensmith 2002) that he opposed. However, this attempt to balance the state's budget would have slashed budgets in small communities statewide, which caused local officials to take action. The governor's veto would have taken money from municipalities that they had already planned to use in the next fiscal year. Local resources would have been lost to save statewide finances, resulting in local fiscal stress.

Mandated Services

In theory, the services provided by local government are determined by the needs and demands of citizens in the local community. In reality, the types of services provided by a local government are often a function of federal and state mandates. Local communities cannot choose whether to provide clean air, clean water, or schools that incorporate special populations. These mandates have developed from federal and state initiatives. The growth of federal assistance programs, especially during the 1970s, proved to be a double-edged sword. Increased federal assistance was accompanied by increased federal mandates. Table 11.2 lists the mandates, with their new amendments, acts, and standards, that rural governments currently face.

The Safe Drinking Water Act enacted by the federal government in 1974 graphically illustrates the problems that arise from mandated services. Subsequent revisions of that act require all community water systems using surface water as a water supply to filter the water in order to eliminate *Giardia,* regardless of whether they are in a region where the organism is prevalent. Because *Giardia* is an intestinal parasite resistant to chlorine, treating the water chemically cannot eliminate it.

In responding to this mandate, rural water districts have two choices: One possibility is to upgrade their water system to incorporate the filtering process mandated by the act. On a per capita basis, this becomes an especially expensive process for small water systems. Although these federal government mandates did improve filtration systems, federal funds are not widely available for upgrading local water systems. Alternatively, communities can simply close down the public water system, forcing members of the rural water district to obtain their drinking water individually. The 1996 amendments to the act do address improving water protection at the source, including rivers, lakes, reservoirs, springs, and groundwater wells. However, the act does not regulate private wells that serve fewer than twenty-five individuals.

Multiple Structures

The very organization of local government in rural areas presents special problems for the effective delivery of services. The multiple general-purpose and special-purpose governments that serve a single community can lead to conflict. Additionally, the

TABLE 11.2 Federal Mandates and Obligations and Updated Standards, Acts, and Amendments

Type of Mandate	Legislation
Clean water requirements	**Federal Water Pollution Control Act (1972)** **Amendments:** **1977: Renamed the Clean Water Act** **1987:** Construction Grants Program was phased out and replaced by the State Water Pollution Control Revolving Fund, more commonly known as the Clean Water State Revolving Fund. This new funding strategy addressed water quality needs by building on EPA-State partnerships.
Groundwater protection	**Safe Drinking Water Act (1974)** **Amendments:** **1996:** Recognized source water protection, operator training, funding for water system improvements, and public information as important components of safe drinking water.
Solid-waste disposal	**Resource Conservation and Recovery Act (1976)** **New Standards:** **1991:** These regulations establish a protective, practical system for disposing of the nation's trash by specifying design, operating, and closure standards; restrict landfill locations; and require liners and ground-water monitoring. http://www.epa.gov/epaoswer/general/k02027.pdf
Personnel	**Fair Labor Standards Act of 1938** **Small Business Job Protection Act of 1996:** Enacted to provide tax relief for small businesses, protect jobs, creates opportunities, increase take home pay of workers, and amend the Fair Labor Standards Act of 1938 to increase the minimum wage rate and to prevent job loss by providing flexibility to employers in complying with minimum wage and overtime requirements under the Act. http://www.benefitslink.com/small_biz/intro.shtml

Continued on next page

Federal Mandates and Obligations and Updated Standards, Acts, and Amendments (continued)

Type of Mandate	Legislation
Floodplain development restrictions	**National Flood Insurance Act of 1968**
	Amendments:
	National Flood Insurance Reform Act of 1994: Following the multi-billion dollar flood damage in the Midwest during the summer 1993, Congress initiated this Act. The law requires Federal agency lender regulators to develop regulations to direct their federally regulated leaders not to make, increase, extend, or renew any loan on applicable property unless flood insurance is purchased. http://www.fema.gov/fhm/dl_nfira.shtm
Prevailing wages	**Davis-Bacon Act of 1931**
	No amendments:
	Guarantees fair competition on federal and state construction projects.
Medicare	**1986 Deficit Reduction Act**
	Balanced Budget Act of 1997:
	Congress reduced spending on entitlement programs by $122 billion ($115 billion from Medicare) and discretionary appropriations by around $140 billion. Estimates projected a deficit reduction of $127 billion over five years, but a surging national economy sent the budget into surplus for fiscal 1999, earlier than had been expected. http://www.brook.edu/dybdocroot/gs/cps/50ge/endeavors/deficit.htm
Election places	**Voting Accessibility for the Elderly and Handicapped Law of 1986**
	National Voter Registration Act: 1993: "Motor Voter Act":
	The sole purpose of this Act is to make it easier for all Americans to vote. The Act requires all offices of State-funded programs that are provide services to persons with disabilities to ensure that all program applicants have voter registration forms, to assist them in completing the forms, and deliver completed forms to the appropriate State official.
Conditions of aid	**Various Acts of Congress**
Litigation	**Civil Rights Act of 1964**
	Civil Rights Act of 1991: This Act amends the Act of 1964, in an effort to strengthen and improve civil rights laws, to provide for damages in cases of intentional employment discrimination, and to clarify provisions regarding disparate impact actions, and for other purposes. http://www.eeoc.gov/laws/cra91.html
Administrative Activity	**Various Acts of Federal Agencies (FCC, for example)**

types of services needed are also becoming increasingly complex and sometimes highly technical. The capacity of local officials to deal with these issues is limited. Several examples illustrate the character of these problems.

Local governments now deal with issues that have become as complex as the structure of governments themselves. Despite the fact that they are typically volunteers, rural government officials are often responsible for a diverse set of services. They generally lack the expertise needed to deal with such technologically complex issues as hazardous waste, infrastructure financing, or healthcare. The small size of many rural communities also means that these officials are less likely to find a local expert to consult. In an effort to encourage regional cooperation, federal and later state governments created regional government districts. The Area Redevelopment Act of 1965 created a series of regional or multicounty districts through which federally supported area development efforts could be focused. In addition, states have also created multicounty strategies through which to deliver a wide range of services: regional planning; solid waste disposal; health, mental health, and aging services; and so forth. In general, these districts have been created to distribute federal or state aid to local communities and to implement the program and planning activities required to receive the funds. These regional governments, in many states known as "councils of governments" (COGs), when adequately staffed, can provide smaller communities with needed technical expertise and with the knowledge necessary for getting grants, hiring consultants, and generally supplying information about links to outside resources, whether human, financial, social, environmental, or even political.

On the other hand, combined with local governments, these regional agencies create an enormously complex structure to meet the needs of communities. One obvious problem is that conflict is created when local and regional agencies are both addressing the same need. Multiple and overlapping agencies also lead to fragmented efforts that may not necessarily respond to the needs of the entire community. To promote economic growth, for example, a general-purpose government may decide to float TIF bonds on behalf of industries or businesses that that government would like to attract. Any increase in tax collections within the TIF district during the life of the bonds goes toward paying off the bonds for the newly arrived firm(s). The local government that initiates the TIF district essentially commits all other local governments collecting taxes within that district to forego any increase in tax receipts during the same period. The logic is that had the new commercial or industrial firm not been enticed to come, the various general- and special-purpose governments would not have had those taxes to spend because the tax base would not have grown. The rub comes, however, when the new firms generate need for greater public services. School districts are heavily dependent on property-tax revenues for their operation, yet they do not participate in the decisions made by general-purpose governments.

The decision to lower or waive the property taxes charged to local industry helps promote local economic development, but it can be harmful to local schools.

For example, the city commission of Manhattan, Kansas, used tax increment financing to pay for the city's share of costs of building a downtown mall. This method of financing assumes that the development of a mall will result in increased valuation of the property being developed. The increased revenues expected from the higher valuation can then be used to pay off the bonds needed to finance the construction of the mall. Two or three years after the completion of the mall, citizens realized that tax increment financing limited their short-term ability to expand school budgets or upgrade streets in response to new needs because the increased tax revenue had already been committed to the bonds used to construct the mall. One local government, the city commission, had made a decision that affected another local government, the schools.

Dallas County, Iowa, a suburban-rural county that is part of the Des Moines metropolitan area, has been debating a similar issue involving the construction of a large shopping mall. This $200 million project is predicted to cause a "retail boom," and school superintendents have discussed the need for a one-cent sales tax for schools, while the county board of supervisors has discussed a similar tax to be shared by all the taxing bodies in the county (Probasco-Sowers 2002). The counties and the cities can either impose a separate tax or work together and share the money, but only areas that approve the tax can collect and share the funds. This revenue could be used to improve schools and make general improvements within the county, the city, or both. If the estimates are correct, the new mall will generate $5 million a year for taxing bodies that adopt the one-cent sales tax. Local governments will then decide how and where to use the money. Another wrinkle in this complex issue is that the local-option sales tax for schools (which was authorized by the state legislature) has raised the hackles of smaller rural school districts, which argue persuasively that because many of their residents do much of their shopping in regional trade centers and metropolitan areas, people in rural districts are subsidizing schools in larger places. The obvious solution to this latter problem would be to institute a statewide sales tax earmarked for schools (laying aside for the moment the regressive nature of the sales tax). The state could then distribute the school funds in a more equitable fashion. This alternative runs head-on into the bipartisan "no new taxes" mantra of both the governor and the legislature, a mantra being voiced in an increasingly futile effort to drown out the reality of a state fiscal crisis. As an alternative to raising state taxes, state legislatures authorized local governments to raise *their* sales taxes—in a way that is unfair to rural counties whose volume of retail trade does not match the purchases of its residents.

Fiscal Stress

Many rural governments suffer from what is called *fiscal stress.* Fiscal stress occurs when available revenues decrease and the need for services increases. When jobs are lost to plant closure, for example, property tax revenue declines, but demand increases for community services such as job training, welfare, and housing.

Different services also require a certain minimum number of users before it becomes cost-effective to provide them. When a community's population starts to decline, the number of users may drop below that minimum level. Fixed costs must then be shared by a smaller number of remaining residents. At some point, local governments must decide to eliminate a service, allow it to be provided by a higher level of government, or arrange for it to be provided privately. For instance, townships in various midwestern states transferred the upkeep of township roads to county governments when farms were consolidated and the number of farmers declined. Acute fiscal stress frequently triggers decisions in which local governments give up providing services.

Most rural governments are funded by a combination of local, state, and federal funds. In general, rural communities rely upon local sources of revenue for about 70 percent of their budget. Local governments typically rely on property taxes, often supplemented by a local sales tax. Business taxes, user charges, and miscellaneous revenues such as fines and fees bring in lesser amounts. Very few rural counties or towns levy income taxes. The remaining 30 percent of revenues for local rural governments comes from federal and state assistance. State revenues vary highly, sometimes involving sales taxes and other times relying chiefly upon income taxes (Sokolow 1998).

Different types of taxes can be contrasted on the basis of the most-affected taxpayer's ability to pay. *Progressive taxes* place a disproportionate share of the tax burden on those most able to pay: the wealthy. *Regressive taxes* do the reverse, placing a disproportionate fraction of the tax burden on the middle-income and lower-income taxpayers. Local taxes tend not to be progressive. Sales taxes are the most regressive of all. In contrast, real property taxes are more capricious than regressive. They are only loosely related to the ability to pay. For instance, elderly persons who own their own home or small farm and are on a limited fixed income will pay a higher proportion of their income in property taxes than will a prosperous tenant farmer or wealthy banker. Because federal funds are derived primarily from income taxes, they are generally progressive. State funds come from a mixture of progressive and regressive tax sources.

Locally generated taxes depend on local economic activity. The 1980s were a particularly difficult period for rural governments: Farm values declined, the energy economy collapsed, timber and mining activity dwindled, and a nationwide recession occurred, with an attendant decline in retail trade. Thus, the base for property taxes (real property values) and the base for sales taxes (retail trade) decreased sharply. The fiscal capacity of local governments declined at the same time that federal and state governments shifted the burden of particular services to local governments. Local governments suffered acute fiscal stress throughout the 1980s and into the 1990s. Only with the eight-year expansion that coincided with the Clinton administration was fiscal stress lifted. The economic downturn in the third quarter of 2001 and the costs of security measures mandated by Homeland Security have significantly impaired the budgets of state and local governments. Many state governments, in order to have symmetry with federal income tax forms, implemented the tax deductions that were in the Bush administration's federal tax cut package of 2001. They experienced significant loss of revenue through a de facto tax cut (Sawicky 2002). It was estimated that the collective budget gap for all the states would reach $58 billion in fiscal year (FY) 2003, the largest shortfall since 1983, which was in the wake of a major recession (Gold and Gavin 2002). By early 2003, thirteen states had cut Medicaid spending, even though overall Medicaid costs had increased by more than 10 percent between fiscal years 2001 and 2002 because of increasing caseloads and the rising costs of prescription drugs. Twelve states had cut higher education, and nine had reduced spending on elementary and secondary education as well as on corrections. A different group of nine had instituted state employee layoffs. Seven had cut aid to local governments. Although government employment continued to grow at least through September 2002, thereby cushioning the losses in the private sector, the decline in state and local expenditures has become a drag on the economy beginning in 2003 as more states lay off workers (Conference of State Legislatures. NCSL, 2003; Tanner 2003).

In a domino effect, cities also have "institut[ed] hiring freezes, dipp[ed] into reserve funds, and rais[ed] local taxes and fees" to respond to the budget problems (Sawicky 2002). It was estimated that by the end of 2002, cities and states in the United States spent more than $8.6 billion on homeland security (Office of Homeland Security 2002:65). These new costs hit cities and counties at a time when revenue was down due to sharp drops in tourism and to increasingly cautious spending by all consumers. Consumers are uncertain about the direction the economy will take in the near and medium term, given the war in Iraq, insecurity in the Middle East and domestic security threats. Thus, funding homeland security will probably cause deterioration of local services because most local governmental budgets have already been cut to the bone. State budget cuts are affecting local governments. Thus, major cuts in social services at the state level increasing job scarcity will undoubtedly increase the need for greater outlays by counties for General Welfare (the ultimate safety net for poor people, which in most states comes exclusively from county coffers). Small communities have found that establishing the resources necessary for security is an enormous and costly challenge. Cities with only 8,000 people have to comply with many of the same requirements as cities with 78,000 people, but they may not have the resources to do so (Davis 2002).

Although property taxes have been the major source of local government revenue, they became increasingly unpopular in the 1970s and 1980s. Consequently, some rural areas have significantly reduced their reliance on property tax. Very rural areas (counties with fewer than 2,500 urban residents) still collect almost 60 percent of local revenues from property taxes, however.

Efforts at raising additional local non–property tax revenues have proved difficult. Several factors hamper rural governments. These include a lack of staff and leadership to adopt and administer creative financing, the relatively low incomes in some rural areas, shrinking retail sectors in smaller communities, and restrictions by state government on non–property tax sources (Reeder 1990).

In general, current mechanisms for funding local community needs have not proved effective, especially for rural communities faced with a declining economy. The tax burden on rural residents increases as the health of the local economy decreases. The inequity of such a system has become obvious in the financing of schools. Judges in past court decisions in Kentucky and Texas have invalidated state financing strategies, pointing to the tremendous gap between per-pupil expenditures in suburban and rural areas. Courts are insisting that states allocate state educational funds in such a way as to ensure that rural and suburban children alike have access to a high-quality education (see Box 11.1).

**BOX 11.1   Rural Schools and Educational Reform:
The Kentucky Case**

The current educational reform movement is taking shape amid three changes. The first is the social and economic change that is occurring worldwide, putting pressure on schools to begin preparing young people for the more sophisticated jobs needed in the information age. The second is the increased fiscal stress being felt by local governments. The third is the pressure for students to meet educational standards in order for their school to receive federal funding. Kentucky offers an interesting case study regarding the role that each of these changes plays in efforts at educational reform.

The first change relates to the role schools need to play in the new social and economic environment. Post–World War II schools are often described in terms of a "mass production" metaphor: Schools are designed to teach young people existing knowledge bases, punctuality, patience in performing

Continued on next page

Rural Schools and Educational Reform: The Kentucky Case (continued)

rote operations, behaviors appropriate to functioning effectively in a hierarchical environment, and so forth. Business and industry now talk of needing different skills. Increasingly, young people will need to know how to gather, organize, and communicate new information, and they will need to be able to think critically and solve problems readily. The shrinking work-force also means that a much larger proportion of young people need to finish high school and continue on to some form of postsecondary education.

The educational reform movement is also occurring within an economic context. In the 1960s, rural and urban schools alike began challenging the way schools were financed. There was enormous disparity among schools in terms of how much money was spent per student. A series of court cases established that education was not a right under the U.S. Constitution and had to be challenged under state constitutions. Cases brought before state courts met with mixed results. Some state constitutions do define the state's responsibilities for education in such a way that the courts could order the state to develop a more equitable strategy for funding public schools.

In response, states began developing various strategies for ensuring that the amount of money spent on education per child was more equal across different school districts. This reform is complex, however, given that schools have been funded primarily through local property taxes. Two of the more common strategies were (1) to use state funds to supplement local funds raised in support of schools and (2) to put a cap on per-student expenditures in an effort to control what the more wealthy districts could spend. As states began supplementing local funds, however, they also began imposing rules and regulations concerning how schools were run.

Kentucky has found itself caught up in these changes. Kentucky is a poor state; it ranks forty-sixth in the nation for average personal income. High illiteracy rates and low high school completion rates make it questionable whether the state will be able to take part in the new economy. Efforts to improve schools, however, have been hampered by tensions between local and state governments. The state argued that it was contributing more than its share and that local districts were either not collecting property taxes or underassessing properties.

As of 1989, the state was contributing 50 percent of all funds spent on education. Yet the amount spent per student ranged from $1,471 to $3,347

Continued on next page

Rural Schools and Educational Reform: The Kentucky Case (continued)

among individual school districts. A group of sixty-six school districts, most of which were small rural districts in the Appalachian region of eastern Kentucky, filed suit against the state. They charged that the state's methods of financing public schools placed too much emphasis on local resources, with the result being that children in poorer school districts were receiving a less-than-adequate education. Their original suit was successful, but it was appealed to the Kentucky Supreme Court. In a surprising turn of events, that court ruled that Kentucky's entire educational system, not just the finance formula, was unconstitutional. The state was given one year in which to restructure the entire school system.

The Kentucky Educational Reform Act (KERA) was passed by the Kentucky legislature in 1990. It outlined changes in three areas: curriculum, governance, and finance. In exchange for a more equitable funding formula, rural Kentucky schools found themselves faced with increased state involvement in both the curriculum and governance of schools. In 1999, the act was updated, and a study revealed that very little change had occurred. Although some of the disadvantaged schools performed well, most did not. As Phillip W. Roeder pointed out, there are still "large performance gaps" between advantaged and disadvantaged schools. More financial resources are needed, and so are better teachers. However, the need for better teachers and facilities is in the poorer districts, where "the revenue stream has leveled off" from the initial years of KERA (Roeder 1999). In a 2001 update, Roeder demonstrated that there had been some comprehensive change in the early years of KERA but said that in the last few years, "[the] Kentucky public school system has settled into a pattern of relative stability and incremental change" (Roeder 2001).

Over the last decade, many levels of reform have occurred on the national level, and these reforms have an impact on Kentucky's funding. In 1994, the first stage of implementing performance indicators and standards in all of the nation's school districts took effect with the enactment of the Improving America's School Act of 1994. Administrators became aware of the growing need to implement standards-based curricula; however, most were reluctant to link program success in schools with student achievement. Under President George W. Bush's No Child Left Behind Act of 2001, school districts must assess student performance through standardized testing and must hire only teachers who meet the federal definition of "highly qualified."

Continued on next page

Rural Schools and Educational Reform: The Kentucky Case (continued)

Although this act may provide more funding to Kentucky schools, there are several strings attached to this funding. School districts with "low performing" schools must offer students a chance to transfer to a different one, and those that fail to comply could lose federal funding. Although the act implies that control at the state level is enhanced, the district's decisions and performance levels have a direct impact on their federal funds. Judgments of teacher performance and student success are directly linked to standardized test scores, and if performance on both levels is viewed as inadequate, funding is lessened or revoked.

The Support Educational Excellence in Kentucky (SEEK) program was enacted as a part of KERA in 1991 to close the gap between inequitable funding across school districts; this program includes both state and local funding. A ten-year analysis of the SEEK program that was completed by the Kentucky Department of Education established that equity has been improved: "SEEK meets or exceeds the standards much of the time. . . . when an equity measure does not meet one of the standards, it is by a small amount. . . . over time, each measure of equity has improved" (Odden, Fermanich, and Picus 2001). Districts are guaranteed a certain allotment for each student, with the 2001–2002 base at $3,066. The gap in expenditures between low-wealth, property-poor school districts and high-wealth districts has been reduced by more than 36.9 percent, and according to the National Center for Education Statistics, Kentucky ranks thirty-first in the nation in per-pupil expenditures. However, a task force similar to the one formed in the 1980s is challenging the adequacy of the school funding through SEEK. Kentucky is faced with a $300 million dollar revenue shortfall, and school officials are concerned that expenditures for school districts will decline in order to pay off debts. Studies are being done to determine the effectiveness of the SEEK program, and the group that initially forced the state to enact KERA has hired a nationally recognized professor, Deborah Verstegen, to study whether lawmakers are adequately funding Kentucky's public schools (Winston 2002). Local forces may again change state legislation.

Challenges to state funding formulas have been filed in many states. What schools seem to face is a choice between adequate fiscal resources and local control. Rural schools express concern that the state government does not understand the differences across local communities and schools.

Continued on next page

Rural Schools and Educational Reform: The Kentucky Case (continued)

Local differences do exist, but the state argues that schools must be held accountable in their expenditure of state funds. Whose side do you take?

REFERENCES: Odden, Fermanich, and Picus. 2001. "Assessing the Equity of Kentucky's SEEK Formula: A Ten-Year Analysis." Paper prepared for the Kentucky State Board Education.

Phillip W. Roeder. 1999. "Education Reform and Equitable Excellence: The Kentucky Experiment." Online; available: http://www.uky.edu/~proeder/keraweb .htm; accessed April 14, 2003.

_____. 2001. "A Report on KERA Report Cards." Online; available: http://www.uky.edu/~proeder/keraweb.htm; accessed April 14, 2003.

Winston. 2002. "School Group Orders Funding Study." *Cincinnati Enquirer,* June 21. Online; available: http://enquirer.com/editions/2002/06/21/ LOC_school_group_orders.html; accessed May 15, 2003.

Federal Aid to Rural Governments

Historically, rural governments have depended upon federal aid to develop the services needed to create and maintain communities. The federal government played a substantial role in encouraging western expansion and the settlement of rural lands. This section explores the different characters federal aid has adopted in the past, the focus on grants that occupied the period from the 1960s through the mid-1980s, and the "new federalism" that is currently being implemented and that is likely to describe the future (Conlan 1998).

Developing Land and People

Mark Lapping, Thomas Daniels, and John Keller (1989) pointed out that federal involvement in rural issues can be summarized by four broad themes: (1) settling the land, (2) developing the human resources and economic infrastructure needed to support communities, (3) supporting farmers, and (4) alleviating poverty. Each issue has been the dominant one at one time or another, but all are woven through the development of rural communities.

Early federal involvement was directed almost solely toward land settlement. Under a variety of land grants, federally owned land was eventually transferred to private ownership. Mineral laws and subsidies to the timber industry offered further inducement to settle new lands. Grants to railroads and for road, canal, and bridge systems encouraged the development of transportation networks capable of supporting a dispersed population.

This emphasis on land settlement eventually gave way to interest in the development of human resources and the provision of roads, buildings, and services capable of supporting communities. The creation of land-grant universities in 1862 and the introduction of the cooperative extension service in 1914 put the emphasis on the development of human resources. A number of important programs introduced during the Great Depression focused on built capital needs in rural areas. The federal Public Works Administration and the Civilian Conservation Corps built roads, bridges, hospitals, parks, and schools. The Rural Electrical Administration put electrical services in place throughout rural communities and farming areas. A federal highway system added an important dimension to the transportation network and had substantial impact on rural communities. It was a precursor to the interstate highway system, which a generation later was initiated during the Eisenhower administration and was justified under national security.

In the 1960s, federal interest in rural support shifted to the war on poverty. President John F. Kennedy's visit to West Virginia placed the rural poor squarely before the public. President Lyndon Johnson continued this agenda, releasing studies that established the complexity of rural poverty, if not strategies for overcoming it. Farm subsidies introduced during the Great Depression have remained as an instrument for increasing farm-sector income during times of overproduction and low prices. As the number of farmers continued to decline, those subsidies have had a decreasing impact on rural communities. Larger farmers tend to bypass the local community by purchasing inputs in bulk.

Federal Grants-in-Aid

Categorical and block grant programs were created in the 1950s and grew explosively in the 1960s and 1970s. Categorical programs provide funds to local governmental organizations to operate very specific programs, such as vocational-technical training or healthcare centers for migrants. Block grants provide governments with funds to be used for special purposes, such as community development. Although both types of aid can be helpful to rural governments, neither allowed the use of funds to be tailored to more specific local needs. Finally, in 1972, under Richard Nixon's tutelage, the federal government created general-revenue sharing, under which local governments received unrestricted funds for general operations and special programs.

Table 11.3 lists federal programs by development category. According to the Catalog of Federal Domestic Assistance, there are 1,499 programs that provide grants for

TABLE 11.3   Federal Programs by Development Category and Dollars Spent per Person, Fiscal Year 1999

County Type	All Federal Funds	Agriculture and Natural Resources	Community Resources	Defense and Space	Human Resources	Income Security	National Functions
United States	5,542	111	595	671	106	3,277	782
Metro	5,601	35	632	762	102	3,201	870
Nonmetro	5,306	416	445	308	122	3,582	433
By degree of urbanization							
Urbanized	5,232	346	441	339	121	3,553	431
Less urbanized	5,092	250	421	400	116	3,482	424
Totally rural	5,855	931	470	83	130	3,796	444
By economic county type							
Farming dependent	6,688	1,956	544	144	131	3,503	409
Mining dependent	5,268	183	340	137	143	3,887	578
Manufacturing dependent	4,626	197	373	140	104	3,487	325
Government dependent	6,362	165	532	1,429	178	3,431	627
Services dependent	5,192	304	394	212	105	3,665	512
Nonspecialized	5,175	415	515	76	118	3,685	367
By policy county type							
Retirement destination	5,244	51	528	333	91	3,873	369
Federal lands	5,168	93	600	323	129	3,268	755
Commuting	4,600	281	499	195	100	3,295	231
Persistent poverty	5,762	460	441	143	209	4,051	457
Transfer dependent	6,161	258	516	145	195	4,512	535

NOTE: Definitions used in table: Program Functions:
Agriculture and natural resources (agricultural assistance, agricultural research and services, forest and land management, water and recreation resources); Community resources (business assistance, community facilities, community and regional development, environmental protection, housing, Native American programs, and transportation); Defense and space (aeronautics and space, defense contracts, defense payroll and administration); Human resources (elementary and secondary education, food and nutrition, health services, social services, training and employment); Income security (medical and hospital benefits, public assistance and unemployment compensation, retirement and disability includes Social Security); National functions (criminal justice and law enforcement, energy, higher education and research, and all other programs excluding insurance).

SOURCE: Calculated by ERS using Federal Funds data from the Bureau of the Census

community resources, agriculture and natural resources, human resources, and special programs. These programs spent $5,306 per capita in rural areas (defined in this case as places with populations of less than 20,000) in 1999, totaling $731 billion versus $639 billion in 1987, with 17 percent of total funds going to rural areas. As Samuel Calhoun and Rick Reeder (2001) pointed out, rural federal funds mainly come from income security programs, such as Social Security, Medicare, and Medicaid. Federal funding is less in rural areas, but the actual amount of funding also depends on the region and type of county. In 1999, there was a 5.6 percent gap between funding in urban and rural areas. More than 70 percent of federal spending in rural America, however, is actually a redistribution of income to individuals in the form of transfer payments (farm subsidies, social security, and welfare) rather than a grant of funds directly to rural governments or nonprofit organizations.

Federal support of rural areas is substantial, but it remains highly focused on agriculture, which is an increasingly smaller part of the rural economy. The dollar share of federal funding that goes to rural areas is approximately equal to the proportion of rural people in the total U.S. population. However, farm programs account for nearly half of the nonentitlement funds going to rural areas. Although there is an increased emphasis on comprehensive rural development, agricultural support in the form of farm subsidies still dominates federal spending on rural development. In 1987, for example, $29 billion was spent on development programs for all of rural America; an additional $22.4 billion was spent on support for agricultural prices and incomes alone. The Farm Bill signed by President Bush in May 2002 authorizes $95 million in grants for the Rural Strategic Investment Program in order to fund regional plans and infrastructure development. It also authorizes approximately $33 million annually through 2006 for marketing development grants for value-added agricultural products (see Box 11.2). Yet as of 1997, those engaged in farming included only 2 percent of the nation's population and only 7 percent of the nonmetropolitan population (ERS 2002).

BOX 11.2 Rural Development and the Farm Bills

	Highlights
Title VI Rural Development	Provides funding for rural areas to undertake strategic planning, feasibility assessments, and coordination activities with other local, State, and Federal officials. Provides funding for the backlog of pending applications for water and wastewater programs as well as new funding for broadband Internet services, value-added agricultural programs, rural business investments, and training for rural emergency personnel.

Continued on next page

Rural Development and the Farm Bills (continued)

Provisions	1996–2001 Farm Legislation	2002 Farm Bill
Rural Community Advancement Program	The 1996 Farm Act streamlined and consolidated programs to provide a more focused Federal effort and encouraged additional decisionmaking at the State level. The new Rural Community Advancement Program (RCAP) became a vehicle for coordinating and implementing USDA rural development funding in 3 main areas: 1) community facilities, 2) water and waste facilities, and 3) business assistance.	RCAP continues, but the account structure, including the national reserve account, is eliminated.
Comprehensive and strategic regional development planning and implementation	Encouraged on a relatively small scale through the development of State strategic plans, the Empowerment Zone/Enterprise Community Program, the Rural Economic Area Partnership Initiative, and the Rural Community Development Initiative.	A Rural Strategic Investment Program is authorized to fund regional investment boards. The boards plan and implement comprehensive regional rural development strategies. Funding for this program is to come from the Commodity Credit Corporation (CCC). This provision also calls for a national conference on rural America.
		A Multijurisdictional Regional Planning Organizations Program is authorized to fund regional organizations that provide assistance to local governments and organizations involved in local development.
Regional authorities	New regional authorities were established in rural Alaska (the Denali Commission) in 1999 and in the Lower Mississippi Delta (the Delta Regional Authority) in 2000 to plan and fund development strategies in these regions.	The Northern Great Plains Regional Authority is authorized to plan and fund development strategies in that region. The Delta Regional Authority is reauthorized.

Continued on next page

Rural Development and the Farm Bills (continued)

Provisions	1996–2001 Farm Legislation	2002 Farm Bill
Water and wastewater facilities	The authorization for water and waste facility grants was increased to $590 million per year in 1996 Farm Act.	The $590-million upper limit on the annual amount of water and waste facility grants is eliminated. Use of $360 million of CCC funds is authorized for a one-time reduction in the backlog of qualified, pending applications for grants and loans for water and waste disposal and emergency community water assistance. A provision allows for guaranteeing of bond-financed loans for water and waste disposal facilities, if permitted by modifications in the Internal Revenue Service code.
For very small communities	The Emergency Community Water Assistance Grant Program for Small Communities program was also authorized to spend $35 million in fiscal years 1996-2002. At least 50 percent of available funds were to be allocated to very small communities (under 3,000 population).	Changes are made affecting the Emergency Community Water Assistance Program, allowing grants to forestall imminent decline in water quality and quantity. Search grants are authorized for $51 million per year to assist very small communities (under 3,000 population) in preparing feasibility and environmental studies required to meet water and waste environmental standards.
For nonprofit organizations	Nonprofit organizations have been eligible to receive grants to provide technical assistance and training to rural communities.	Newly authorized programs include grants to nonprofits to capitalize revolving loans for water and waste disposal facilities; and grants to nonprofit organizations to finance homeowners' water well systems.
Circuit Rider Program	USDA's Rural Utilities Service has an existing program with the National Rural Water Association to provide Rural Water Circuit Rider Technical Assistance for operations of rural water systems.	Authorizes establishment of a Rural Water Circuit Rider Program, based on the current contract program, to provide technical assistance for daily operations of rural water systems.
For Alaskan and Native American communities	Direct loans and grants for water and waste facilities have been set aside for targeted communities, including rural Alaskan villages and Native American projects.	Grant programs are authorized for water systems for rural and native villages in Alaska, and for water and waste facilities for Native American communities.

Continued on next page

Rural Development and the Farm Bills (continued)

Provisions	1996–2001 Farm Legislation	2002 Farm Bill
Telecommunications programs	The Telemedicine and Distance Learning Program was reauthorized and streamlined in the 1996 Farm Act. Under this program, the Secretary could make grants and loans to assist rural communities with construction of facilities and services to provide distance learning and telemedicine services. Funding was authorized at $100 million annually.	The Telemedicine and Distance Learning Program was reauthorized without changes in substance or funding.
Broadband programs	Amendments to the Telemedicine and Distance Learning Program in 2001 authorized a Broadband Pilot Loan Program to provide funding for construction of facilities and systems providing broadband transmission services to rural consumers. $2 million in funding was provided from the Telemedicine and Distance Learning Program budget.	Grants, loans, & loan guarantees are authorized to improve access to broadband telecommunications services in rural areas. The funds would be for construction, improvement, & purchase of equipment and facilities for rural broadband service in eligible communities. Eligible rural communities have no more than 20,000 inhabitants. A total of $100 million of CCC funds is authorized to provide loans and loan guarantees to cover fiscal years (FY) 2002–07.
Local television access	The Launching Our Communities' Access to Local Television Act provided for a guaranteed loan program intended to facilitate access, on a technologically neutral basis, to signals of local television stations for households located in nonserved areas and underserved areas.	Authorizes $80 million in loan guarantees for the delivery of local broadcast television station signals to satellite television subscribers in unserved and underserved local television markets. The funds are available until December 31, 2006, without fiscal year limitation.
Rural telework	No similar provisions in previous legislation.	A new program would pay the Federal share of the cost of establishing and operating a national rural telework institute. Each grant may be up to $500,000. Authorizes $30 million for each fiscal year.

Continued on next page

Rural Development and the Farm Bills (continued)

Provisions	1996–2001 Farm Legislation	A Rural Electronic Commerce
Rural E-Commerce Extension	No similar provisions in previous legislation.	Extension Program will be established. The program's goal is to expand and enhance e-commerce practices and technology to be used by rural small businesses and enterprises. Funding is authorized at $60 million per year.

SOURCE: Economic Research Service. ERS. 2002. "Farm Policy: Title VI: Rural Development." Online; available: http://www.ers.usda.gov/Features/ farmbill/titles/titleVIruraldevelopment.htm; accessed April 5, 2003.

If farm programs and entitlements are excluded, less than 10 percent of the remainder of federal funding goes to rural areas with populations of less than 20,000. Of particular importance is the fact that only 5 percent of federal spending on human resources goes to rural areas. Human capital is arguably the most important investment that can be made for economic development and certainly for the well-being of individuals who receive it. Currently, rural areas are home to approximately 20 percent of the population. After declining in the 1980s, the rural population showed a rebound in the 1990s; more than 71 percent of all nonmetropolitan counties gained population between 1990 and 1998 (Johnson 1999). Migration seems to be the largest contributing factor, because fewer people are leaving rural areas and more are moving there from urban areas. However, urban residents are not moving into rural areas to farm; in fact, areas dependent on farming and mining have gained the least population. Most of the population growth is in areas that attract retirees or serve as so-called bedroom towns, that is, places from which workers in urban areas commute. Though the population decline in those rural areas that are dependent on farming or mining was less severe than it was in the 1980s, it was still evident in the 1990s. As agriculture continues to decline or disappear as the economic base of rural communities, the need to invest in human resources increases. The combination of the brain drain from rural areas, which was particularly notable in the 1980s, and the failure of the federal government to assist in upgrading rural human capacity does not bode well for the ability of rural areas of the United States to compete economically. Many rural areas were beginning to occupy a position in the world economy similar to that of Third World countries at the end of the 1980s. Even with the population growth in rural areas, the brain drain continues to be a problem in the 2000s, particularly in midwestern states. Several of these states offer incentives such as tax breaks or tuition aid to persuade people to stay in their home state.

After a period of rapid expansion, federal aid to local governments declined during the 1980s, in both absolute and real dollars. This changed relationship is referred to as the "new federalism." Although a rural-federal partnership continues to exist, the character of that partnership has changed considerably.

More Responsibility, Less Money

In 1981, President Reagan and his administration made large-scale reductions in federal assistance to state and local governments a major policy objective. Under this "new federalism," federal support of local communities declined. With passage by Congress of the Omnibus Budget Reconciliation Act in 1981, President Reagan accelerated a trend toward reducing the growth in federal aid to local governments that started during the administration of President Carter. Federal aid as a proportion of total revenues, for example, declined 13 percent between 1981 and 1982 and again between 1986 and 1987. Using 1980 as a benchmark, researchers have shown that federal spending has decreased by 66 percent and loan guarantees by 41 percent (Working Group on Economic Development in Small Communities 1990). The Budget Reconciliation Act also converted seventy-seven categorical grants to nine new block grants. Sixty programs were eliminated.

Cuts in local services were dramatic, and the states were forced to adjust to declining federal support. In 1987, general-revenue sharing was eliminated with equally dramatic results. Some rural governments depended on general-revenue sharing for as much as 15 percent of their general-fund budgets. In response, both state and local governments increased efforts to raise revenues. State aid has not compensated for the decline in federal assistance, however. The situation had become worse by 2003. Tax cuts made at the federal and state levels during a period of economic expansion have left most states facing substantial deficits. Many states are responding by cutting state funds to local governments.

The decline in federal responsibility for rural development has led to increased state efforts to promote economic development (Brace 2002; Eisinger 1988). Today, most states have an economic development program, but unless such programs explicitly include a rural development component, rural communities generally receive much less than their share of state funds. Urban business interests often dominate state economic development programs. In addition, many state economic development programs focus on recruitment of industry, which is more appropriate for metropolitan cities and regional trade centers than for smaller rural communities.

With the cooperation of the National Governors' Conference, the National Conference of State Legislatures, the National Association of Towns and Townships, and other organizations, approximately ten of the fifty states initiated rural development policies between 1985 and 1990. These initiatives are important because of the diversity of rural areas in the United States. States are better able than the federal government to deal with community variations resulting from differences in population growth and decline, in economic base (farms or retirement communities, for example), in rate of entrepreneurial development, and in education levels. Unfortunately, many of these rural development programs are piecemeal.

Yet state policy cannot substitute for an effective national rural policy. In particular, states are an inappropriate level for instituting policies pertaining to industry location, jobs, and income. When viewed from a national perspective, state industrial policies tend to be a zero-sum game. One state can raid other states for industrial firms, but these efforts do not necessarily increase total industrial capacity or expand net employment opportunities in the nation. They simply move jobs from one state to another. Rather than taking the initiative by adopting policies that encourage new job development and discourage industrial raiding across state borders, the federal government is virtually abandoning economic development.

As the federal government withdraws from its rural partnership, rural governments continue to face substantial problems. Resolution of these problems requires political will and power. It is questionable whether rural people have the political clout to obtain a funded comprehensive rural development program. The decline in rural voting power has resulted in large part from demographic shifts in U.S. society.

Moreover, the way we turn population into votes has also changed. Every ten years, states reapportion congressional and state legislative districts based on the decennial census. States may gain or lose congressional seats, and areas within states can have their legislative power eroded. In the 1960s, a series of U.S. Supreme Court decisions on the apportionment of congressional and state legislative assemblies established the "one person–one vote" doctrine, which requires that districts be drawn solely on the basis of population. Rural areas lost electoral (voting) power first to urban and then to suburban areas.

As the relative power of rural areas continues to decline, rural officials may find it beneficial to look for an alliance with those in the inner city. Urban and rural areas alike face decaying roads and buildings, lack of economic growth, low-wage employment, inadequate social services, and poverty.

Government and the Economy

The lawsuit the Donovan family brought to oppose efforts to elect a Coker town council went all the way through the state court system to a federal district court and finally to the U.S. Supreme Court. Ultimately, the Donovans lost.

In 2001, the Coker town government celebrated its two-year anniversary. Malcolm Porter now serves on the town council. The town, with assistance, has set up a new water-filtering and sewer system, which has eliminated the *E. coli* from their water. Children are improving in school because they are no longer having stomach illnesses. The new water and sewer system has also encouraged a few new businesses to move in. Progress is slow, but the people in Coker are encouraged. They now have the tool—a local government—with which to respond to local needs.

Local governments are important. They provide the vehicle for citizen participation and offer local communities access to state and federal funds. The need for these funds is obvious in communities such as Coker. It is the long-term impact of the funds, for the individuals who receive them as well as the communities who apply for them, that remains in question.

For sociologists, the larger issue is how the various levels of government can stimulate healthy local economies. No one questions the need for clean water or adequate food. Ill or malnourished children cannot learn effectively and thus cannot develop the skills they will eventually need to support themselves and their families. It would be preferable, however, if the conditions that underlie the poverty in Coker were eliminated. Do federal programs stimulate local economic development, or do they simply increase rural dependence? Can states carve out a new role as they assume some of the responsibility?

In order to answer these questions, we need to understand just how governments actually shape the economy. No one has a complete picture of how powers are distributed across the three levels of government or of how far this distribution enables governments to stimulate new forms of economic organization (Eisinger 1988). Although the ability of the government to tax is extremely important, its ability to control land use and property may be equally important in sustaining and developing local economies (Campbell and Lindberg 1990). Sociologists and communities such as Coker share an interest in these issues.

Chapter Summary

In the United States, the system of government divides powers between the federal government and the states. States create local governments either through home-rule provisions in their constitutions or through general laws passed in state legislatures. Most local governments are created by legislation.

Local governments are important to rural areas because they (1) offer a structure by which community members participate in local decisions, (2) provide services and community facilities, and (3) link local revenues to local needs. The many forms of local government found in rural areas can be sorted into two categories. General-purpose governments are those created to respond to the general needs of a county, city, or town. Special-purpose governments are those created to respond to specific community needs, such as schooling, water supply, or medical services. Part-time officials and citizen volunteers often staff the governments in rural communities.

Because of their limited resources, most rural governments find it difficult to provide adequate levels of public services. By mandating certain services, state and federal governments can require that local resources be directed to services that may not be needed. Multiple general-purpose and special-purpose governments can lead to conflicted or fragmented responses to local community needs. Finally, most rural governments face fiscal stress that arises from a limited tax base despite increased demand for local services.

The federal role in rural areas has changed substantially. Historically, federal involvement in rural areas focused on settling the land, developing human resources, constructing the roads and buildings needed by communities, supporting farmers, and alleviating poverty. Categorical and block grant programs during the 1960s and 1970s targeted federal funds to specific programs. The "new federalism," initiated by President Reagan in 1981, eliminated general-revenue sharing with local communities. Current federal involvement is characterized more by transfer payments to individuals than by support to community development efforts. States have responded by supporting local development efforts, but this may not be adequate.

Key Terms

Federalism is a system of government in which separate states or provinces are united by a central authority while retaining certain powers, including the power to tax.

Fiscal stress in rural communities arises when a limited tax base is faced an increased need for services.

General-purpose governments are governments created to respond to the general needs of a county, city, or town.

Progressive taxes place a larger share of the tax burden on wealthier citizens and firms. The percent of income paid as income tax, for example, increases as a person's income increases.

Regressive taxes place a disproportionate share of the tax burden on those less able to pay. Consumer sales taxes become a decreasing share of people's income as their income increases. Wealthier people tend to save and invest a higher proportion of their incomes than do poor people.

Special-purpose governments are created to respond to specific community needs, such as schools or water.

Tax increment financing (TIF) is financing based on increased taxes in a particular area. For example, a city may rezone a given area and use the expected increased (or "incremental") real estate taxes to pay for new infrastructure, such as roads and sewers.

References

Brace, Paul. 2002. "Mapping Economic Development Policy Change in the American States." *The Review of Policy Research* 19:161–178.

Calhoun, Samuel, and Rick Reeder. 2001. "Federal Funds in Rural America: Funding Is Less in Rural Than in Urban Areas, but Varies by Region and Type of County." *Rural America* 16, no. 3:51–53.

Campbell, John L., and Leon N. Lindberg. 1990. "Property Rights and the Organization of Economic Activity by the State." *American Sociological Review* 55:634–647.

The Catalog of Federal Domestic Assistance (CFDA). 2002. Online; available: http://www.cfda.gov/public/browse_by_fa.asp; accessed October 25, 2002.

Clark, Michael D. 1999. "Small Towns in Trouble" (March 7). *Cincinnati Enquirer.* Online; available: Enquirer.com/editions/1999/03/07/loc_small_towns_in.html: accessed October 23, 2002.

Conference of State Legislatures (NCSL). 2003. "State Budget Gaps Growing at Alarming Rate According to New NCSL National Fiscal Report" (February 4). *NCSL News,* Washington, D.C. Online; available: http://www.ncsl.org/programs/press/2003/pr030204.htm; accessed February 19, 2003.

Conlan, Timothy. 1998. *From New Federalism to Devolution: Twenty-Five Years of Intergovernmental Reform.* Washington, D.C.: Brookings Institution Press.

Davis, Lance. 2002. "Partnerships Important for Small Cities Facing Big Challenges." *The National League of Cities.* Online; available: http://www.nlc.org/nlc_org/site/newsroom accessed October 30, 2002.

Economic Research Service (ERS). 2002. "Farm Policy: 2002 Farm Bill." Online; available: http://www.ers.usda.gov/Features/FarmBill; accessed August 15, 2002.

Eisinger, Peter K. 1988. *The Rise of the Entrepreneurial State: State and Local Economic Development Policy in the United States.* Madison: University of Wisconsin Press.

Gold, Russell, and Robert Gavin 2002. "Budgetary Crises Present Painful Choices for States" (October 7). *Wall Street Journal Today.* Online classroom edition; available: http://www.wsjclassroomedition.com/wsjtoday/archive/02oct/02oct07_budget.htm; accessed February 19, 2003.

Hockensmith, Dan. 2002. "Revenue Sharing Restored" *Times Herald* (Port Huron, Mich.), August 14.

The Homeland Report. 2002. Online; available: http://www.nlc.org/homeland/homeland1028.htm; accessed October 30, 2002.

Johnson, Kenneth M. 1999. "The Rural Rebound." Population Reference Bureau Reports on America. Online; available: http://www.luc.edu/depts/sociology/johnson/rebound.pdf; accessed October 31, 2002.

Lapping, Mark B., Thomas D. Daniels, and John W. Keller. 1989. *Rural Planning and Development in the United States.* New York: Guilford.

Michigan Townships Association. 2002. "Veto Override—Join MTA at Capital Rally and Call Your Legislators." Online; available: http://www.Michigantownships.org/e_news/august02.htm; accessed May 16, 2003.

National Association of Counties. 2000. "Tax Increment Financing: An Alternative Economic Development Financing Technique." Online; available: http://www.naco.org/Content/ContentGroups/Publications1/issue_Briefs/tax_inc.pdf; accessed April 14, 2003.

North Central Regional Center for Rural Development. 2001. *Vision to Action: Take Charge Too.* Ames: Iowa State University. Also online; available: http://www.ag.iastate.edu/centers/rdev/pubs/contents/182.htm; accessed April 14, 2003.

Probasco-Sowers, Juli. 2002. "Dallas County Entities Look to Mall Windfall" (October 3). *Des Moines Register.* Online; available: http://desmoinesregister.com/news/stories/c4780932/19375475.html; accessed October 30, 2002.

Office of Homeland Security. 2002. *National Strategy for Homeland Security.* Washington, D.C.: U.S. Government Printing Office. Online; available: http://www.whitehouse.gov/homeland/book/nat_strat_hls.pdf; accessed April 17, 2003.

Rathge, Richard. 2002. "The Changing Population Profile of the Great Plains." Unpublished paper.

Reeder, Robert J. 1990. "Introduction." *Local Revenue Diversification, Rural Economies.* Washington, D.C.: Advisory Commission on Intergovernmental Relations, March, 1–6.

Roeder, Phillip W. 1999. "Education Reform and Equitable Excellence: The Kentucky Experiment." Online; available: http://www.uky.edu/~proeder/keraweb.htm; accessed April 14, 2003.

———. 2001. "A Report on KERA Report Cards." Online; available: http://www.uky.edu/~proeder/keraweb.htm.

Sawicky, Max B. 2002. "U.S. Cities Face Fiscal Crunch: Federal and State Policies Exacerbate Local Governments' Budget Shortfalls" (June 13, 6 pp.). EPI Issue Brief, no. 181. Washington, D.C.: Economic Policy Institute. Online; available: www.epinet.org/Issuebriefs/ib181.html; accessed August 15, 2002.

Sokolow, Alvin D. 1998. "The Changing Property Tax and State-Local Relations." *Publius: The Journal of Federalism* 28:165–187.

Tanner, Robert. 2003. "States' Finances Worsening, Report Says" (February 4). Associated Press. AP Online; available: http://enrongate.com/news/index.asp?id=167222; accessed February 4, 2003.

U.S. Census of Governments. 2002. "Government Finance." Online; available: http://www.census.gov/govs/cog/2002COGprelim_report.pdf; accessed April 14, 2003.

Working Group on Economic Development in Small Communities. 1990. *Take Charge: Economic Development in Small Communities.* Ames, Iowa: North Central Regional Center for Rural Development.

Part 4

Mobilizing Community Capitals for Social Change

12

Generating
Community Change

When Sue James and her husband Bart moved with their two teenage children to New Richland, Minnesota, from St. Louis, Missouri, they eagerly anticipated the prospect of the clean air and neighborliness found in rural America. Big-city living had lost its luster, and they were excited to live in the "country." However, a few months after their move, they realized they missed certain elements of living in a larger setting, particularly in terms of recreation. Furthermore, there were few summer jobs for teenagers in a small, rural area.

Bart and Sue often went to a small, locally owned diner for breakfast and coffee on Saturday mornings, and they met many farmers and businesspeople who lived in the town. Bart, being the new school superintendent, was a familiar face already. Bart mentioned his family's love of golf, and several other community members agreed that they wished there was a course in town. Word spread, and soon Bart and Sue decided to open the idea up for town consideration.

First, they placed a notice in the local paper announcing an open meeting to discuss construction of a community golf course; forty people attended. Committees were set up to consider possible sites and organizational structures. At the next meeting, more than a hundred people were present. Interest in the project proliferated, and it helped that all of the meetings were well covered in the local paper.

The site committee presented four potential sites, which in the following weeks were visited by most of the members of the town, even those who did not play golf. At the next community meeting, with several hundred people in attendance, the pros and cons of each site were presented. With all of this information in mind, the assembly voted on the site they wanted. The site that was chosen would be purchased from its owner, a farmer who agreed to sell at the market price for agricultural land. The local community development corporation, established in the early 1970s, was utilized to raise money for the project, and in just two months the purchase price was raised through donations and by selling local shares in the golf course to community members.

The layout of the golf course was designed, and local farmers donated time and equipment to help the city do the necessary construction, including building two wells, one for the clubhouse and one for the fairways and greens. A separate community golf course corporation was established, a manager–golf professional was hired, and the club was off and running! A local couple established a concession stand at the course, and the golf pro set up a pro shop. Students found work in the summers as groundskeepers and caddies, local people were now able to play (and many learned the game), and the course proved to be an attraction for out-of-town players, who found its riverside location attractive and the well-kept nine holes pleasurable to play.

Sue and Bart began to feel like an integral part of the community due to their participation in the creation of the golf course. The community has an additional asset in terms of investing in themselves, and the economic benefits to the community through the creation of new jobs and the attraction of outsiders to the community have proven to be unanticipated benefits of the project.

★   ★   ★

Community development occurred in New Richland because of the community's ability to identify its assets—including levels of bridging and bonding social capital—and to invest them in themselves. They were able to mobilize many sectors of the community to work together to make things happen. In New Richland, with its history of self-investment and community participation, such activities were relatively easy to undertake. Economic development was one of the results, but not the major motivation for the project.

In other communities, community change seems almost hopeless. New people move to town with great dreams for community improvement, but their dreams never materialize. Or local residents concerned about a declining economic base seek to attract industry, with ever-decreasing likelihood of success. What makes the difference between towns that develop and change in response to felt needs and those that seem unable to respond effectively to the current climate of economic deterioration in most rural areas? What are the components of community development, and what makes it happen?

This chapter centers on three models of community development. The assumptions behind them are followed by illustrations of how they can and have been implemented. The three models are then compared in terms of their linkages to the outside and their approaches to the planning process. Then two approaches to economic development are introduced and related to the three models of community development.

Community and
Economic Development

The word "community" comes from the Greek word for "fellowship." Fellowship involves interaction. Hence, *community development* implies that the quality of interaction among the people living in a locality improves over time. Such interaction both depends on and contributes to enhanced quality of life for each member of the community: better housing, better education, enhanced recreational and cultural opportunities, and so on. Central to the concept of community development is the idea of *collective agency*. Collective agency is the ability of a group of people—in this case those living in the same community—to solve common problems together. For community development—and collective agency—to occur, people in a community must believe that working together can make a difference and organize to collectively address their shared needs.

Community development is much broader than economic development. Indeed, one could argue that economic development could be antithetical to community development for two reasons: Economic development does not necessarily involve collective agency, and economic development may not result in an improvement of the quality of life. For instance, the high rates of economic growth in the "boom towns" have a negative impact on community development. The incomes of some members of the community may increase, but as crime rates increase, schools become overcrowded, housing prices soar, and neighborliness declines, the quality of life for the majority of the residents may deteriorate. This is particularly true when economic growth in the community is triggered by an absentee firm, whether it is an oil or coal company, a national meatpacker, a recreational conglomerate, or a transnational manufacturing company.

When we look at community development, we will focus on what local people do to improve the overall quality of life of the community. In the difficult economic times of the 1990s and 2000s, economic development was and is seen as the dominant means for community betterment. But bringing in jobs is not enough. And bringing the wrong type of jobs may decrease the community's quality of life. We will now examine approaches taken by community members and leaders to improve their collective well-being and how these approaches relate to collective agency.

Models of Community Development

Community problem solving does not take place automatically, even in a community like New Richland. Problems have to be identified, potential solutions considered, organizational means put in place, and resources mobilized. There are a number of models of community development that can facilitate this happening.

Let us look at alternative models of community organization to see which might serve in different types of communities.

Three major approaches to community development have been laid out by James Christenson (1989): the self-help, technical assistance, and conflict models. Each of the different approaches identifies a different role for the change agent, a different orientation to task versus process, different clientele, a different image of the individual, a different conception of the basis of change, a different core problem to be addressed, and a different action goal.

Self-Help Model

The *self-help model* emphasizes process: people within the community working together to arrive at group decisions and taking actions to improve their community. The process builds civic capacity for collective action to move toward a shared vision for the future of the community. In this model of community development, the aim is not so much to complete a particular project as to institutionalize a process of change based on building community institutions and strengthening community relationships to work toward desired future conditions. The New Richland golf course contains major elements of self-help community development because putting it into place involved reinforcing patterns of community interaction, cooperation, and decisionmaking. The change agents, the school superintendent and his wife, acted as facilitators for community input rather than sources of infinite knowledge about golf courses. People viewed the development of the golf course as something they had decided together rather than as the result of the best technical advice. The people involved in New Richland were definitely middle class. Both those who play golf and those who have the means to contribute equipment or invest in shares in a community corporation tend to be better off. And the community has developed new ways of working together to bring about an improved, shared future.

It took a while to instigate the golf course project due to the large number of meetings required to obtain everyone's input, form the appropriate committees, and respond to each committee's reports and suggestions. Yet once the golf course was established, it easily became part of the public agenda in terms of local participation in running it and in convincing city government to participate in its maintenance.

However, if the New Richland project had been a purely self-help effort, the initiators would have begun with a more diffuse goal, such as increasing recreational opportunities in the community. The decision to build a golf course—or an alternative recreational facility, such as a lighted softball diamond—would have been part of the process rather than the reason for devising the process. There are a number of assumptions about the nature of rural communities behind the self-help model (discussed by Littrell and Hobbs 1989). When these assumptions about the structure of the community are wrong, self-help as a strategy will be difficult to implement. These assumptions include these: (1) that communities members have a similarity of interest and that community development involves building consensus, (2) that generalized participation and democratic decisionmaking within the community are necessary and possible, and (3) that the community has a degree of autonomy such that community actors can in fact influence the community's destiny.

A central assumption in the self-help model of community development is that communities are homogeneous and based on consensus. In fact, despite the norm of "we're all just folks" endorsed in many rural communities, most communities have increasing disparities in income and access to other resources. Thus, development efforts, which depend on existing local leaders as a basis for community organizing, may systematically bias development efforts away from the problems of the least-advantaged citizens. That bias, in turn, can give rise to increased inequalities and increasing poverty or to conflict-based community development activities. In fact, interests within communities can conflict, as we saw in Chapter 5, "Political Capital."

Participation and democratic decisionmaking are essential to the self-help model of development. The self-help approach assumes that it is indeed possible to motivate a broad-based band of community members to participate in community affairs. However, if community residents are uninterested and unmotivated and do not want to become involved, participation will not take place. Some groups of local residents will not see the community as relevant to their welfare, as happens, for example, with some farmers who feel their well-being depends almost entirely on government programs. Thus, these farmers may simply bypass the community and be actively involved only in their commodity organizations, which focus on the national and not on the community level. If in a particular community no farmers are active participants in efforts to solve community problems, broad-based community participation can be said not to exist for one important segment of the community is uninvolved.

The time commitment mandated by the self-help approach may cause many to drop out, which threatens the processual aspects of this approach. Even if the stated objectives of the community development effort are reached, the effort cannot be said to have been successful if participation in the process was minimal. The approach cannot be used to solve another community problem because no new means of interaction and quality of interaction were enhanced. In a word, the process was not institutionalized, and from the self-help point of view, the effort was not successful. One obstacle to effective use of the self-help approach in small towns is the fact that people know each other in too many roles. Thus, the risk of taking a public stance, which is sometimes necessary for effective discussion, may result in public disagreement with a boss, a customer, or a colleague. This risk is seen as too great in many small towns.

Furthermore, different segments of the community have different levels of participatory skills. Higher education and professional employment give a disproportionate voice to the more privileged segment of any community, in part because they have experience with participation. And as we saw in Chapter 2, "Cultural Capital Legacy," middle-class youth are raised with verbal and discussion skills, whereas obedience—until a situation involving confrontation arises—is part of working-class socialization patterns.

Finally, self-help models of development assume a significant degree of community autonomy. Yet as we have shown in earlier chapters, rural communities are highly involved in regional, national, and even international networks that have enormous impacts on them. Being dependent on the global economy, however, does not mean that it is useless for communities to undertake self-help activities. But it does make it important that the global economic trends are understood. Part of the process of the self-help model therefore includes community education on the community's place in the global economy and the current trends within it.

The case of Ivanhoe, Virginia, illustrates this point. The first effort of the Ivanhoe Civic League following its founding in the mid-1980s was to gain control of a shell building from the county government in the hope that the community would be able to attract an industry to occupy the building. Following major efforts to obtain an industry, the Civic League concluded that adult education and youth programs would be more beneficial to the community. By the year 2003, the Ivanhoe Civic League continues to work to make Ivanhoe a better place for all of its citizens. The education program consists of community-based Adult Basic Education/General Education Development (ABE/GED). The Ivanhoe Civic League's education program offers college classes, youth tutorials that include guidance on college and careers, professional development workshops, and computer and adult literacy classes. In 1993, a vocational component rehabilitated a historic structure in Ivanhoe to provide office and education facilities for the Ivanhoe Civic League.

The citizens of Ivanhoe decided that the assets of their community—their culture and the beautiful setting—should be shared by those who share their vision of a positive future for the community. In the mid-1990s, the Ivanhoe Civic League inaugurated the Volunteers for Communities, now a separate organization, which is currently training seventeen communities throughout the region to host volunteers. Community service and celebration continue to play a major role for the Ivanhoe Civic League. They host an annual all-community Christmas party, a Thanksgiving Prayer Service, and a week-long Jubilee festival, as well as many other community events. They built bonding social capital to help determine the vision and built bridging social capital to mobilize resources to be locally invested for an Ivanhoe where young people and elders prospered together.

Coaching: A New Approach to Self-Help

Although self-help assumes that most of the assets for change will come from the inside and that the energy for change will be generated from within, a number of experiences show how coaches and facilitators can act as brokers to identify assets and passions within the community and link them with appropriate collaborators to achieve entrepreneurial visions (Sirolli 1999) or community visions (Rubin 2001:497). Box 12.1 shows how coaching and a strategic visioning process helped a community college–community team move toward equitable economic development.

BOX 12.1 A Holistic Approach to Positive Community Change: The Rural Community College Initiative (RCCI)

Southeast Community College in Cumberland, Kentucky, illustrates what team building, strategic visioning, and coaching can accomplish. Southeast's RCCI employed a vision-to-action (MDC, Inc. 2000) team to generate and spin off community development and education initiatives. The team includes the college president and selected faculty and staff members, business owners, a banker, a former coal miner, elected officials, grassroots leaders, K–12 teachers and administrators, and human service agency staff members. This diverse, yeasty mix of folks, who before RCCI had not worked together, has looked hard at community issues, come up with innovative ways of recombining community assets, and brought in the resources and partners needed to implement new projects.

Southeast Community College serves three counties in the heart of the Kentucky coalfields: Harlan, Bell, and Letcher. Like much of Appalachia, the region suffers from the loss of mining employment, little business development, and weak public schools with a low college-attendance rate. A small group that has held control for years dominates local politics. The team decided to tackle these problems head-on with projects to (1) make more capital available for new business development, (2) help disadvantaged young people attend college, and (3) broaden the base of community leadership through leadership development programs.

Continued on next page

A Holistic Approach to Positive Community Change: The Rural Community College Initiative (RCCI) (continued)

Southeast's work on business development finance illustrates how the college-community team provided the determination, the innovative ideas, and the right mix of leadership to make things happen. The team began by holding a day-long community workshop where business and civic leaders discussed barriers to small-business development in their counties and learned about development finance models from around the country. After the workshop, team member Ken Thomas, president of Harlan National Bank, and RCCI coordinator Paul Pratt talked with local banks about creating a community development corporation. Five banks signed on to form the Pine Mountain Community Development Corporation (CDC), creating a $105,000 loan fund for small businesses that could not qualify for conventional loans. The college provided a staff person (Paul Pratt) to screen loan applicants and provide technical assistance to borrowers.

The initial fund was lent out within a year, indicating a high unmet demand for microloans in the region. Building on the experience of the Pine Mountain CDC and with encouragement from the RCCI coach and team, Paul Pratt approached the numerous loan funds that serve eastern Kentucky and urged them to pay more attention to the southeastern corner of the state, an area that has been largely ignored. After two years, these conversations led to the creation of the Appalachian Development Alliance, eight development funds that will pool resources and access new sources of public and private capital for business development throughout eastern Kentucky.

Most importantly, that area of Kentucky is able to generate more income for the people who live there, as the college works to provide appropriate skills to individuals who had never thought they could finish high school, much less take college classes. By focusing on the assets of the local people rather than their deficiencies, new investments in the area began to pay off.

SOURCE: Sarah Rubin. 2001. "Rural Colleges as Catalysts for Community Change: The RCCI Experience." *Rural America* 16, no.2:12–19. Also online; available: http://www.ers.usda.gov/publications/ruralamerica/ra162 /ra162d.pdf; accessed April 16, 2003.

Technical Assistance Model

In contrast to the self-help model, the *technical assistance model* stresses the task that is to be performed. A few local leaders might decide that the community needs a golf course. After talking among themselves in private, they call in technical experts to assess the local situation and to find the most efficient way to build and run a golf course. The construction of the course might require receiving government grants or finding a private investor. The consultant and the local leaders would determine the method of funding, and the site would be chosen based on objective criteria determined by experts in golf course construction. The success or failure of the project would be judged on the presence or absence of a golf course at the end of a prescribed period. The combination administrator–golf pro would be chosen on technical criteria. If a capable administrator was found, the project would continue. However, if the club pro proved inefficient or dishonest, it would be up to the town leaders (if publicly owned) or the board of directors (if privately owned), not to users of the golf course or its employees, to correct the situation. Limited oversight could then lead to limited success.

It is assumed in this approach that answers to community problems can be reached scientifically. The problems themselves are phrased in technical terms that require expert advice regarding choices among a variety of technically feasible options. This approach requires that local residents, if they desire to participate in decisions, assimilate and absorb a great deal of information concerning complex legal and scientific issues. This greatly decreases motivation to participate. A common response is to assume that there is only one technically appropriate choice and that the experts should thus be left alone to make it.

Another assumption of the technical assistance approach is that development should be evaluated based on the achievement of predetermined measurable goals. Not only is the achievement of the goal important, but so is the efficiency with which it is achieved. Cost-benefit analysis, a technical tool developed by economists to determine the ratio of costs to benefits to the public of projects, is a particularly appropriate tool for a technical assistance approach. Local citizens are defined as consumers of development, not participants in it.

Government bureaucracies are the most frequent employers of the technical assistance approach. This approach often works to the advantage of the power structure because of its agenda-setting ability (see Chapter 5, "Political Capital"). The power structure is frequently able to prevent a particular problem from reaching the level of public discussion or, in other cases, to prevent certain technically feasible solutions to a publicly defined problem from being considered as a realistic option.

An illustration of how politics and the technical assistance approach relate to one another is in industrial recruitment. Successful growth machines are able to define industrial recruitment as an essential economic development objective, especially in communities experiencing a loss of services or population. This is done by identifying industrial recruitment as the only technically feasible alternative for generating new employment through influential organizations such as the city's chamber of commerce or community development office. It may in fact be true, for example, that in a declining community where the elderly make up a high proportion of the population, transfer payments (including such things as Social Security, Medicare, and Medicaid payments, as well as private pensions and health insurance payments) are a large portion of community income. A program for the development of locally owned services used by retirees would keep that money circulating in the community and could perhaps generate more employment and greater employment stability and income than would a potential new factory. But in most cases, industrial recruitment wins out because the elderly income multiplier does not even get on the agenda. Furthermore, companies considering a move do not want it public until the decision is final. They also prefer to deal with a single person who represents the entire community. Both of these facts militate against broad community participation in efforts to recruit industry.

The Conflict Approach

A *conflict model* is similar to a self-help approach in that it brings people together to articulate their needs and problems, to develop indigenous leadership, and to help organize viable action groups (Christenson 1989: 37). It is different from a self-help approach in that it seeks to redistribute power. A major organizing tool is the confrontation of those seen blocking the agreed-upon solution to the problem. Using a conflict approach, a group of local people outside the local power structure would come together to discuss their problems and needs, which could include recreation and job creation. For example, as a golf course project was put forward by the elite of the town, the group seeking empowerment would mount a counterproposal—a local swimming pool—that would also create jobs and would in addition provide recreation for the young people and poorer members of the community who could not afford golf clubs or lessons. Instead of either calling in outside experts or working in an informal fashion with local elites to mobilize local resources, the conflict-oriented group would identify a potential site and then approach the city council and the local landowner with the demand that the land be donated or purchased. The organizer would focus on building strong groups to make these demands, stressing as an important issue the lack of recreational facilities, particularly for the less-well-to-do members of the community who could not drive to other communities. Emphasis would be on the responsibility of those with power within the community—the city council and local landowners—to act responsibly in response to the needs of the community. In another conflict model scenario, once the golf course was established, the group would demand access to the course for youth, minorities, and the elderly, with subsidized transportation and public equipment, so that the principle of community-wide access to collective resources would be enforced.

The conflict approach to community development has urban origins. The approach was codified by Saul Alinsky, who began as a community organizer in Chicago in the 1930s in a Polish neighborhood known as Back of the Yards. By working with the residents in the working-class community to identify their grievances, the organizers helped them make specific demands of the city government. This methodology has been expanded to black organizing in Chicago, Illinois; Rochester, New York; Boston, Massachusetts; Kansas City, Kansas; and Kansas City Missouri. It has been the basis of organization of the United Farm Workers, since Cesar Chavez had trained with Alinsky's group. The Association of Community Organizations for Reform Now (ACORN), founded by Wade Rathke in 1970 based on Alinsky's organizing principles, has worked hard to implement and refine the conflict methodology. Many community organizers around the country continue to use and modify the approach, including the Land Stewardship Project that organizes farmers in Minnesota and the Industrial Areas Foundation in the colonias along the Mexican border.

Alinsky says that the world and hence any community is "an arena of power politics moved primarily by perceived immediate self-interests" (1971:12). Whereas the technical assistance approach views the existing power structure as having the interests of the community at heart, the conflict approach is deeply suspicious of those who have formal community power.

The conflict approach assumes that power is never given away; it always has to be taken: "Change means movement. Movement means friction" (Alinsky 1971:21). And friction causes heat. The goal of a conflict approach is to build a people's organization to allow those without power to gain it through direct action. Since organizations of the powerless do not have access to significant monetary resources, they must rely on their numbers. Their numerical strength is only realized through organizational strength.

Such organizations must be democratic and participatory. Alinsky believed that downtrodden people (whom he called the Have Nots, as opposed to the wealthy Haves and the Have Some, Want Mores, the middle class) acquire dignity through participation. Experiencing denial of participation is central to their being Have Nots. He saw democracy and participation instrumentally: as means, not ends. The overall ends of community organizing should be such things as equality, justice, or freedom. But in an open society that of the United States, undemocratic organization by the Have Nots can negate those ends. He also placed emphasis on the learning process. Organizing should be accompanied by a conscious effort to broaden horizons. Such education then helps prevent the Have Nots, once they become Have Some, Want Mores, from acting in their immediate narrow self-interest.

Generating Community Change

Now that the basic assumptions and characteristic of each approach have been discussed, we turn to how the three approaches are implemented.

Self-Help Approach

The self-help approach can be implemented in many ways. One of the most common set of steps of implementation, stressed by such existing community development entities as cooperative extension services, is the social action process. The approach involves a number of steps—*visioning*, determining desired future conditions and long-term goals, using broad-based participation, determining the assets in the community, analyzing alternative ways of using those assets to move toward the collective vision, choosing specific projects that move the community toward the desired future, generating community-wide commitment, planning the implementation phase, actually implementing the plan, and finally evaluating. This process focuses on social capital and generally does not address political and cultural capitals. Thus, this approach often places heavy reliance on agenda setting by the existing power structure: The power structure has veto power over any proposal brought to it by the initiators.

Recognizing the cozy relationship with traditional community leaders, which this approach represents, and seeing the need for more rapid change as resource-based communities experience serious problems of out-migration, unemployment, and decline of services, cooperative extension approaches have been modified so as to incorporate broad community participation in the problem-identification phase rather than waiting until the "organizing to sell" phase. Strategic planning methodologies, *futuring* exercises, whereby a representative group from a community is asked to establish priorities based on a strategic plan and the community's mission, and "empowerment" approaches all involve either a careful selection of representatives from a broad spectrum of organizations and occupations or an open town meeting approach to problem selection.

Technical Assistance Approach

In the pure technical assistance approach, a local entity, either a local government or a private entity such as a chamber of commerce, calls upon an outside expert either to develop and assess the effectiveness and efficiency of alternative solutions to a particular problem or to design the most efficient way to perform a certain task, that is, to implement a predetermined solution to a predetermined problem.

In the latter instance, which represents the vast majority of technical assistance consultancies, the expert does not question the task assigned or how it was determined that the particular problem was important. The expert merely develops a plan to implement the solution.

At times, local experts, such as planners, can deliver technical assistance. They generally receive their orders from local or regional governmental officials and are involved in defining how to perform a particular task efficiently. Defining what the task should be is reserved for the politicians. Mark Lapping, Thomas Daniel, and John Keller outline the steps planners should undertake for effective economic development. In the technical assistance approach, an individual with technical competence is called upon to complete each step in the process. Clearly, these steps can also contribute to the self-help approach, depending on who decides what organization or person carries out each step.

1. Gather information and data
2. Identify the problem
3. Analyze the problem
4. Develop goals and objectives
5. Identify alternative solutions
6. Select a solution
7. Implement the solution
8. Enforce the plan
9. Monitor the effort and give feedback
10. Readjust the solution

(from Lapping, Daniel, and Keller 1989)

Conflict Approach

Because of the control exercised by the existing power structure, an outside organizer going into the community generally catalyzes the conflict approach. The following steps are generally followed to build a permanent, multi-issue community organization to achieve its local members' interests and link with other like-minded groups across the state and nation:

1. Community entry by outside organizer, usually at the request of local group wanting change

   1. Appraise the local leadership, looking at both formal and informal institutions in the community.

2. Analyze the community power structure. Who has power and what are their vulnerabilities and strengths?
3. Analyze the situation and the territory. In particular, what seem to the major objective problems, what conflicts would attempts at solution lead to, and which conflicts are winnable?

2. Building a people's organization

1. Stimulate those outside the power structure to voice their grievances. The creation of an organizing committee of community leaders and canvassing residents in their homes are both effective.
2. Synthesize the grievances into a statement of the problem. An effective strategy for this has been neighborhood house meetings. For the conflict approach to be effective, it must concentrate on a single issue at a time, although the organization cannot be a single-issue organization. Crucial in this process is that the issue picked for the organization to focus on be winnable.
3. Link the problem to organizations—working with existing organizations of the disenfranchised, creating new ones, and forming alliances with potential sympathizers. The organizing process must provide opportunities to express anger and overcome fear.

3. Engage in direct action

1. Demonstrate the value of the power of a large number of people working together to makes gains from the traditional power structure through direct action. In particular, to retain legitimacy, people's organizations need to produce a stable supply of what public administration expert Sherry Arnstein terms "deliverables": wins that are quickly achieved and yield visible benefits wrested from political and economic institutions.

4. Formalize the people's organization

1. Develop a permanent organizational structure, with dues and a structure that involves members in policy, financing,

and achievement of group goals and community improvements.

In rural areas, particularly in the Midwest, where conflict with one's neighbors is viewed as disruptive and unmannerly, the most effective use of conflict organizations appears to be in mobilizing against the outside, particularly in efforts to stop nuclear waste dumps, power lines, school consolidation, polluting industries, and the like.

An example of such an organization is Save Our Cumberland Mountains (SOCM, pronounced "sock 'em"). SOCM was established in 1972 as a dues-paying, membership-based group that employs professional organizers. The organization is centered in the Cumberland Plateau region of eastern Tennessee and in 2002 had a membership of 2,000 individuals in chapters that are county or community based.

The SOCM chapter is the primary political unit of the organization. It is a nonprofit Tennessee grassroots citizen's organization working on a local level for environmental, social, and economic justice in areas such as forestry, strip mining, toxic issues, tax reform, and dismantling racism. The various chapter groups send representatives to the larger SOCM Board or to various issue-driven steering committees, such as the legislative committee, which largely lobbies state legislators in Nashville. The SOCM Board and the various committees hold a great deal of power in the SOCM organization and plan many of the group's political activities. In order to qualify for staff assistance, the chapter groups have to show that they have been actively working on an issue that they have identified themselves, in response to some problem originating in their local community. The staff organizer works as a "coach" for the local "teams." SOCM's recent successes include winning a ten-year battle to protect Fall Creek Falls State Park from devastation from acidic mine drainage by designating 61,000 acres as lands unsuitable for mining; they have also hosted their first workshop "in house" to combat racism.

The Kentuckians for the Commonwealth (KFTC), an organization with a similar organizational structure, succeeded after many battles in stopping the strip-mining of land without allowing the surface owner any rights or say in the matter, a practice springing from the *broadform mineral deed,* whereby land purchasers in the early 1900s were able to buy up hundreds of thousands of acres of mineral rights. KFTC was instrumental in getting legislation approved to set up Universal Service Funds as well as in getting the land around the historic Pine Mountain Settlement school declared off-limits to strip mining. In 2001, KFTC had its twentieth anniversary.

All of these instances involved confronting an outside public or private entity in order to stop a project or policy deemed detrimental to the inhabitants of the local community. Organizers from outside the local community and support from the parent organization are important elements in the local chapter's success against such outside forces.

Factors in Effective Change

We will now examine two important factors in all three models in community development—linkages with the outside and the planning process—to see differences and similarities among the models.

Linkages for Community Change

None of the models of community development that we have presented deny the need to obtain outside resources in order for community development to take place. In the technical assistance and the conflict approaches, an outside person or group of people are central to the process. In both cases, an objective of the effort is often to obtain resources from the outside. The self-help approach would appear to be one that emphasizes reliance on local resources. However, as will be seen, the ability to mobilize local resources is often a proof to those who control outside resources that the self-help effort is serious. Thus, there is a complementarity between mobilizing local resources and the ability to obtain resources from outside the community. Creating strategic partnerships is necessary in all cases (Blakely and Bradshaw 2002). This is particularly true under conditions of very limited outside resources because those who control such resources are especially keen to ensure that their funds are well spent. What better place to spend them than on a project that has shown it can obtain resources?

Financial capital from the outside is becoming more and more scarce as both federal and state governments deal with mammoth deficits by cutting funding for social programs, including those that benefit rural communities. As the endowments of most foundations have declined with the stock market, so have possibilities of grants from both private and public sources have declined. There are a variety of state and regional venture capital funds being started by both private- and public-sector groups, which can be an important input into community development (see Chapter 7, "Financial Capital").

However, these linkages to the outside through investment can be risky in terms of the collective agency of a community. There is an old saying: "He who pays the piper calls the tune." This means that the source of funding, whether the federal government or a multinational corporation, can impose a large number of conditions on the delivery of capital resources. Sometimes those conditions actually cost the community more than they gain. For example, a number of studies have shown that the tax abatements, infrastructure construction, and other financial incentives poured into attracting industry in the 1980s did not even pay back the local public investment, much less create wealth in the local community.

Another important type of outside linkage is less hierarchical and therefore less risky in terms of loss of collective agency: More and more communities are forming horizontal linkages with other communities that have faced and dealt with similar problems of their own. This type of lateral learning by community groups tends to foster rather than impede collective agency. Community groups analyze their own situation and consider alternative ways to confront it. Often a community member knows of another community that has faced a similar problem. Citizen-to-citizen exchanges take place as the group that has tried a solution explains both the process and the outcome to the other community.

For example, when Lexington, Nebraska, became the site of a large IBP meatpacking plant, it met with community leaders from Denison, Iowa, where IBP began as Iowa Beef Packers, and from Garden City, Kansas, where IBP's largest processing plant is located, to learn of the problems and discuss potential solutions. As part of the general move to consolidation in the food industry, IBP was purchased by Tyson Foods, Inc., in 2001. Because the communities already had links, they were better able to work together to understand the implications of the change in ownership. The acquisition by communities of information relevant to their needs through lateral learning and technical assistance can strengthen their ability to maintain collective agency when they enter into joint ventures or other means of obtaining capital from the outside in order to improve their own quality of life.

Planning as Part of the Change Process

Increasingly, communities are recognizing that planning is a key part of development. Planning may serve any of the types of community development, but the approach to planning differs significantly according to the model of community development being pursued.

Planning is an integral part of the technical assistance model of community development. Under this model, the primary concern is with the final product, the plan, which can then be used as a map that displays the explicit tasks that must be performed. Professional planners charged with developing community planning documents may consult with the community when necessary either by talking to designated leaders, conducting surveys, or presenting results to community meetings. Community members are involved in the process not as active participants in the decisionmaking process but as passive providers of information on which such decisions are made.

Planners then develop an overall strategy and plan of action. The plan usually consists of a baseline projection, a projection of the desired level of economic activity, and a description of ways of bringing the two projections closer together.

Once written, the plan and its implementing components can then be used to prioritize activities and eliminate options or tasks that are not included in it. In such circumstances, the plan can be used to reinforce the notion of calling on technical rather than political solutions to problems. For example, if the plan calls for a golf course, under the technical assistance model there is little need to get broad community input into the series of decisions that goes into its construction and operation.

The increasing complexity of the decisions communities are forced to make gives a great deal of power to the city engineers or administrators who are closest to the source of technical information. Their clear expertise in understanding the arcane language of, for example, zoning and taxing alternatives aids this process. Just as the city or county attorney in the past was able to dismiss a call for change by saying the proposed change was not legal (and thus forcing the person or group who wanted change to hire their own lawyer to get an alternate opinion, which they then had to take to a higher authority), now the city engineer can dismiss any change in community resource management by saying, "It doesn't fit the plan." At this point, the conflict model of community development becomes appropriate, for groups may mobilize to seek other experts to support an alternative action. But most often, the first "technical" judgment goes unquestioned.

Practitioners of self-help community development favor a different version of the planning process. When conducted in a highly participatory way, planning not only allows for development of a collective vision of community but also provides mutually agreed upon signposts to help achieve it. For example, the commitment and incorporation phases of the social action approach are, respectively, the goal-setting and implementation-design phases of that planning process. But, unlike in the technical assistance model, they are imbedded within a participatory approach. Community members who participate in the social action or similar processes have some role in shaping the goals and means of implementing those goals (although as was discussed earlier, community opinion leaders may have already channeled the social action process toward certain problems and away from others). In most participatory approaches that use the self-help model, there is broad participation in determining the basic questions to be asked. The downside of the self-help approach to planning is that it is clearly more time-consuming than is the technical assistance approach.

The conflict model of community development involves a very different view of planning. Since, by definition, the conflict model is used by those who do not have power, the relationship between goals and means is less obvious than in either of the other two models. The tactical plan for implementation of goals is heavily dependent on the response of the powerful opposition to the prior actions of the group practicing the conflict approach. Tactics may change from day to day. Alinsky emphasized the importance of the element of surprise in responding to those who are in power. This need for flexibility, quick response, and surprise, coupled with the fact that initially the community organizer (who is usually from the outside) must be a catalyst for building an organization, are tendencies that militate toward a narrowing of decisionmaking to a small group of people or sometimes to a single leader. However, the long-term survival and effectiveness of the organization in achieving its goals depend on broad and deep support from within the disadvantaged group. That support is best maintained through broad and active participation. So long as the organization commands few resources, participation, if not democratic decisionmaking, is central to maintaining support for the organization. Numbers are a substitute for financial resources. Thus, there is a permanent tension in the organization or movement between democracy and centralization of control. As the organization becomes more successful in gaining resources, participation and democracy may decline unless democratic decisionmaking processes were explicitly attended to in the organizational phase. Thus, in addition to goal setting, the strategy for organizing is a central part of the planning process for a group using the conflict approach.

Models of Economic Development

Different people have different ideas as to what is entailed by economic development. Some see economic development as identical with an increase in community income. Others view it in terms of an expansion in the number of jobs. Still others would say that economic development involves an increase in population. The relationship between community development and economic development depends on the kind of economic development that is pursued. There are a number of models for how economic development takes place. The model that members of a community adhere to influences the kind of action they undertake to bring about change. In short, there is a relationship between the kind of economic development model pursued and the kind of community development model pursued.

The Firm Recruitment Model

One model of economic development is the *firm recruitment model*. It assumes that private-sector firms have considerable geographic mobility as they seek more-favorable locations. Early tactics aimed at firm recruitment during the growth years of the 1950s through the 1970s were very straightforward, involving such things as the construction of industrial sites and proactive industrial recruiting by more sophisticated cities. It was assumed that any particular locality had a series of advantages to offer and that firms would somehow find them, although by the 1970s it had become clear that despite the favorable climate for domestic industrial growth, a community had to develop a sophisticated approach to firm recruitment if it was to be successful. Planners and social scientists carried out studies to see where firms located and what they looked for when they chose new sites.

By the economic downturn of the 1980s, states and localities had begun to realize that only a few firms moved each year and that those that did usually went overseas for cheaper labor and laxer pollution controls. Competition for the few firms serious about relocating in the United States became intense. States began instituting a wide variety of inducements for firms, including grants, loans, loan guarantees, tax incentives, targeted industrial revenue bond financing, tax increment financing, and state enterprise zones. When one state or locality offered an incentive, others felt obliged to do so.

Less publicized but also prevalent during the 1980s were changes on the state and federal levels that weakened organized labor. Communities used low wages as a bargaining chip in attracting firms. In fact, in a number of high-growth areas where public infrastructural investments and favorable tax structures attracted industries, the jobs that were generated paid so poorly and the working conditions were so bad that immigrant workers had to be recruited to fill them. Meatpacking plants in Kansas and Nebraska are examples of this kind of industrial recruitment. Political scientist Peter Eisenger refers to these attempts to locally reduce the cost of land, labor, capital, infrastructure, and taxes as "supply side development."

The firm recruitment model of economic development is most compatible with the technical assistance approach to community development. Local governments would hire economic development professionals to obtain grants for built capital, to develop local tax incentive packages, and to recruit new firms. These activities required little grassroots participation. In fact, they are antithetical to broad-based community involvement. Getting grants requires technical knowledge of bureaucracies and procedures. Negotiations with firms that might move to the community are best carried out in secret. The firms insist on such secrecy so that communities competing for their branch plants can be played off against each other and so that their present workforce can be kept in the dark about the potential move. Firms considering a move prefer to deal with only one person who can speak for the entire community. Such approaches discourage broad community participation.

The Self-Development Model

In contrast to this model of economic development is what Eisenger refers to as a "demand-oriented" approach to economic development. These include the search for new markets and new products to fit those markets. Instead of simply offering incentives to any firm willing to move, public-private partnerships are formed that help determine what firms will be underwritten by the public as those with the most potential for success—and positive community impact.

One type of demand-side approach that has been effective in rural communities is the *self-development model* of economic development. This involves public-sector groups, usually a city or county government, working with private-sector groups of individuals within a community to establish a locally controlled enterprise. A national inventory of self-development projects by rural sociologists Jan Flora, Gary Green, Frederick Schmidt, and Cornelia Flora identified a number of different types of self-development efforts and mechanisms through which they worked. Key to each of them was local investment of time and capital, coupled with a sound management structure and good links to outside resources of both capital and information. Although the short-term impact on the number of jobs created may not be as great as attracting a branch plant of a major multinational corporation, communities involved in self-development have found that the risk is lower and the gains more consistent than even successful industrial recruitment. Furthermore, self-development communities were more successful in attracting branch plants than were non–self development communities. The choice to emphasize self-development did not preclude firm recruitment, although it did make the communities less likely to offer extreme tax benefits or public investments in infrastructure.

Self-development involves sustained local economic development activities. It encourages broad-based participation, involving newcomers, women, and minorities. It depends on and encourages the development of community organizations. Self-development contributes to community development and it tends to encourage participation. It gives community members a feeling of control over the economic life of their communities. In short, it promotes collective agency. It is most consistent with the self-help form of community development although it can be compatible with the conflict approach.

Successful self-development models reorganize and mobilize local assets (Kretzmann and McKnight 1993; Green and Haines 2002; Feikema, Segalavich, and Jeffries 1997). Local communities and organizations that conduct asset-mapping exercises realize the power of local assets as a mobilizing tool to bring people together, as illustrated in Box 12.2.

BOX 12.2   Holistic Self-Development

In Blue Mound, Illinois, the notion of team effort is well understood. In the early 1980s, leaders in the community realized that they had to make some changes in order to better their economy. This would require extensive planning to implement all of the recommendations made for improving the community, which most towns would find difficult, if not impossible. In Blue Mound, the townspeople believed that revitalizing the town did not have to depend on financial assistance; it could be accomplished through cooperation and hard work.

In many small towns around the country, Main Street has deteriorated and in some cases disappeared. If Blue Mound did not make significant strides to bring new business into town, they would be facing a loss of their downtown. Leaders in Blue Mound soon realized that financial assistance would have to come from local residents; they could not rely on state and federal governments. Local leaders came together and devised a plan of action, sending out more than sixty letters to residents and businesses in the community to invite them to a town meeting to discuss the issues. Representatives from a local community college were also invited to participate in the discussion, which proved to be advantageous because the college had just started working with the University of Illinois–Champaign-Urbana on ways to help small communities improve their local economies.

The town meeting proved successful, and it led to several other meetings with the University of Illinois, which became interested in the project of revitalizing Blue Mound. The university provided a team of graduate students to help the village create a development program that would extend through the year 2000. The village invested $1,500, and the university absorbed the other costs. By 1983, the Blue Mound Development Corporation (BMDC) had been formed as part of the comprehensive plan that the university had designed for the community. A vision statement was formed, and numerous recommendations were laid out for the town to follow, including "designing appropriate land use ordinances, expanding public services, improving local business and economic climate, upgrading the appearance of the downtown, improving housing and social services and strengthening the village financial condition" (Kline 2000: 92). This farming community was able to support retail businesses and new housing, and the residents agreed that they needed to improve these elements of the town in order to attract new people to the community.

Continued on next page

Holistic Self-Development (continued)

The BMDC, made up of seven people, had an annual budget of less than $1,000; however, their vision did not include using money for community development. They wanted to invest people into the project so that all of the residents were part of the town's progress, and it worked. Some of their early attempts to improve businesses in the community backfired; for example, they helped the local metal-making company expand, but after it did, it moved to a bigger city. However, most ventures were a success. The local newspaper relocated to a new, larger building on Main Street after changing ownership in 1986, and after renovating its space, it had room for other businesses to move into the building. A barbershop, an attorney's office, and a golf pro shop moved into the extra space and set up their businesses. Soon after, several other businesses began moving into the downtown area, including entrepreneurs in the area.

Then BMDC began working on filling a void in the community. The residents wanted a dentist; they had had a physician in town for more than thirty years but no dentist. The board already had a connection with the University of Illinois, which made the search for a dentist a bit easier. The board knew they had to make the town look attractive and inviting to a newly graduated dentist. A young doctor who expressed interest in the town was invited to Blue Mound; the BMDC sponsored a potluck dinner, and members of the school district, local business owners, church representatives, and local residents met him and invited him to come to their community. The doctor responded well to the invitation and decided to move to Blue Mound. The community wanted to help him set up his practice, and since the BMDC did not offer financial assistance, people volunteered to help. A local carpenter, plumber, electrician, and other residents donated their time and skill instead of money. The dentist had a new practice in a refurbished building, and Blue Mound had completed another successful project.

Soon after the dentist moved into town, Blue Mound received a devastating blow. The local grocery store burned down, and the grocer decided to retire and not rebuild. The BMDC had to find a replacement, but none of the big grocery chains wanted to move into the small town. It became evident to the board that they would have to build the grocery store themselves, and after selling shares to local residents and leveraging those funds with a loan from a local lender, they opened the Blue Mound Store Corporation

Continued on next page

Holistic Self-Development (continued)

(BMSC) and hired an experienced grocer to run the business. The BMSC did so well that by the late 1990s, it had begun paying dividends to its community stockholders.

The community had several other accomplishments throughout the 1990s, including a plan for constructing senior housing, upgrading the village's water delivery system, and forming a police department, which now employs a full-time police chief, two part-time officers, and five auxiliary policemen. The Blue Mound police department, even though it is in a rural community, has become a state-of-the-art department and was featured in a 1992 issue of *Law and Order* magazine as a model for developing a program entitled Dial-a-Cop. This system allows people to reach a police officer, even when no one is at the station. Most of the improvement and development in the police department came from grants and resident volunteers. Because of the successful new police department, the town is now able to promote their community as being a "safe and secure" environment, which helps attract new residents.

Blue Mound's success by the year 1998 was astounding, and it had come from a holistic effort to improve the community's economy. The key ingredients for success in Blue Mound were leadership, community support and involvement, sound planning, organization, and a sense of accomplishment. Forming connections among many diverse groups of people, working toward common goals, and seeing tangible results from planning efforts were all key components for successful community and economic development in Blue Mound.

REFERENCES: Steven Kline. 2000. "Community Leadership and Vision Pay Off for Blue Mound, Illinois." In *Small Town and Rural Economic Development: A Case Studies Approach,* ed. Peter V. Shaeffer and Scott Loveridge, 88–98. Praeger: Westport, Conn.

Asset mapping is a process of discovery, of learning what is there. If carried out properly, this process will result in new patterns of interaction among community members. Discovery is most effective when it revolves around an issue.

Mapping assets, however, is not enough. There has to be commitment on the part of local people to figure out ways of recombining the assets to address the issue under discussion. The Heartland Center for Leadership Development, the Nebraska Community Foundation, and the Nebraska Cooperative Extension have been engaged in important issue–oriented asset mapping as a basis for community action.

Asset mapping is important because it allows communities to move beyond a victim mentality and recognize that by working together locally, changes can be made. It means putting faith in local people to evolve a people's program (Alinsky 1946: 56). Asset mapping works best when communities begin by addressing pieces of issues that can be quickly alleviated. However, early success should be a learning experience on addressing the more complex aspects of the issue, such as unequal power within the community or long-term disinvestment in the community by public and private sectors.

Focusing on assets does not mean that a community is unaware of the impact of major social forces, including economic concentration, increasing competition, and changes in government programs. Some see an *asset-based approach* as ignoring such issues. Although this can happen, mobilizing local resources in new ways is more likely to create a climate for successfully addressing more difficult structural issues by strengthening local social capital.

Do Communities Act?

Sociologists have long asked, "Do communities act?" (Tilly 1973). How much that happens in a community is determined by the outside and how much by the inside? Sociological research has begun to identify which communities act and under what circumstances (Logan and Molotch 1987). These authors argue that more and more action for social change is occurring not where people work but where they live.

Chapter Summary

Community development is what people do to improve the overall quality of life in the community. Although community development often involves economic development, it implies far more. Central to the concept of community development is the concept of collective agency. Collective agency is the ability of a group of people to solve common problems together.

Contrasting three models of community development illustrates dramatically different approaches to community change. The self-help model focuses on the process by which people work together to arrive at group decisions and take action. It assumes that communities are homogeneous and consensus-based. The technical assistance model focuses on the task to be accomplished and uses outside expertise to help community members accomplish that task. This model assumes that answers can be arrived at objectively, using the scientific method. The conflict model focuses on the redistribution of power among community members. It assumes that power is never given but must be taken away. Each model gives rise to a different community development strategy.

Two factors are important to all three models of community development. The first is linkages. Communities need linkages to outside sources of information. These linkages can be with external agencies or they can be with other communities, enabling lateral learning to occur. The second factor is planning. Planning is a key part of development but will be approached differently depending on the model of community development being followed.

Economic development is one part of community development. Consequently, the type of economic development strategy pursued should match the community development model used. Two of the more common models are the firm recruitment model and the self-development model. For both community development and economic development, new collaborations must be formed inside and outside communities.

Key Terms

An *asset-based approach* to development is used by most community developers now, in contrast to the old *needs assessments*. Whereas a needs assessment focused on what was not in a community and developed a wish list of projects and programs, an asset-based approach links the various capitals existing in a community to see how they can be recombined to achieve a desired future condition.

The *broadform mineral deed* was used by land purchasers in the early 1900s to buy up hundreds of thousands of acres of mineral rights, leaving subsequent surface owners legally helpless to prevent destruction of their homes, yards, and gardens by strip-mining when this technology came into vogue in the middle of the century.

Collective agency is the ability of a group of people to solve common problems together.

Community development is what people do to improve the overall quality of the community.

The *conflict model* of community development focuses on the redistribution of power among community members.

The *firm recruitment model* of economic development assumes that private-sector firms have considerable geographic mobility and seeks to engage community resources to attract those industries to the community.

Futuring is process used by community developers and planners that brings together a small but representative group to assess the current environment, develop a strategic positioning plan, and establish priorities based on the assessment and consistent with the plan and the organization's or community's mission.

The *self-development model* of economic development uses public-sector groups working with private-sector groups to establish locally owned enterprises.

The *self-help model* of community development focuses on the process by which people work together to arrive at group decisions and take action.

The *technical assistance model* of community development focuses on the task to be accomplished and uses outside expertise to help community members accomplish that task.

Visioning is a process used by community developers and planners to work with a broad-based group of citizens to determine desired future conditions and long-term goals for what their community should be.

References

Alinsky, Saul D. 1946. *Reveille for Radicals.* New York: Random House.

_____. 1971. *Rules for Radicals.* New York: Vintage Books.

Arnstein, Sherry. 1972. "Maximum Feasible Manipulation." *Public Administration Review* 32 (September):377–492.

Blakeley, Edward J., and Ted K. Bradshaw. 2002. *Planning Local Economic Development: Theory and Practice.* Thousand Oaks, Calif.: Sage Publications.

Christenson, James A. 1989. "Themes of Community Development." In *Community Development in Perspective,* ed. James A. Christenson and Jerry W. Robinson Jr., 28–48. Ames: Iowa State University Press.

Eisenger, Peter K. 1988. *The Rise of the Entrepreneurial State: State and Local Economic Development Policy in the United States.* Madison: University of Wisconsin Press.

Feikema, Robert J., Joanne H. Segalavich, and Susan H. Jeffries. 1997. "From Child Development to Community Development: One Agency's Journey." *Families in Society: The Journal of Contemporary Human Services* 78, no. 2:185–195.

Green, Gary Paul, and Anna Haines. 2002. *Asset Building and Community Development.* Thousand Oaks, Calif.: Sage Publications.

Kretzmann, John P., and John L. McKnight. 1993. *Building Communities from the Inside Out: A Path toward Finding and Mobilizing Community Assets.* Chicago: ACTA Publications.

Lapping, Mark B., Thomas L. Daniel, and John W. Keller. 1989. *Rural Planning and Development in the United States.* New York: Guilford.

Littrell, Donald W., and Darryl Hobbs. 1989. "The Self-Help Approach." In *Community Development in Perspective,* ed. James A. Christenson and Jerry W. Robinson Jr., 48–68. Ames: Iowa State University Press.

Logan, John R., and H.L. Molotch. 1987. *Urban Fortunes: The Political Economy of Place.* Berkeley and Los Angeles: University of California Press.

MDC, Inc. 2000. *Strategies for Rural Development and Increased Access to Education: A Toolkit for Rural Community Colleges.* Chapel Hill, N.C.: MDC, Inc.

Sirolli, Ernesto. 1999. *Ripples on the Zambezi: Passion, Entrepreneurship, and the Rebirth of Local Economics.* Stony Creek, Conn.: New Society Publishers.

Tilly, Charles. 1973. "Do Communities Act?" *Sociological Inquiry* 43:209–240.

Walzer, N., S.C. Deller, H. Fossum, G. Green, J. Gruidl, S. Johnson, S. Kline, D. Patton, A. Schumaker, and M. Woods. 1995. "Community Visioning/Strategic Planning Programs: State of the Art." (RRD 170). Ames, Iowa: North Central Regional Center for Rural Development. Online; available: http://www.iira.org/pubsnew/publications/RETAC_Other_147.pdf; accessed April 14, 2003.

Index